10 *Rembrandt*
   *Portrait of Hendrickje Stoffels*
   *Mr. and Mrs. Norton Simon, Los Angeles*

# REMBRANDT
# AFTER
# THREE HUNDRED
# YEARS

*An Exhibition of Rembrandt and His Followers*

*Under the high patronage of*
*Her Royal Highness Princess Beatrix of The Netherlands*
*Mrs. Richard M. Nixon*

THE ART INSTITUTE OF CHICAGO · 1969

The Art Institute of Chicago
*October 25, 1969–December 7, 1969*

The Minneapolis Institute of Arts
*December 22, 1969–February 1, 1970*

The Detroit Institute of Arts
*February 24, 1970–April 5, 1970*

*On the cover:*

6  *Rembrandt*
*Self-Portrait*
*Norton Simon Foundation*
*Fullerton, California*

## Committee of Honor

The Hon. William P. Rogers
  *Secretary of State*
The Hon. David M. Kennedy
  *Secretary of the Treasury*
The Hon. Emil Mosbacher, Jr.
  *Chief of Protocol, Department of State*
Mr. Clement E. Conger
  *Deputy Chief of Protocol, Department of State*
Mr. David J. Waters
  *Assistant Chief of Protocol for Public Affairs, Department of State*
Mr. Miles Eugene Briggs
  *Special Agent in Charge, Department of State, Chicago, Illinois*
Mr. John Bacom
  *Assistant Special Agent in Charge, Department of State, Chicago, Illinois*
His Excellency R. B. Baron van Lynden
  *Ambassador of The Netherlands to The United States*
His Excellency C. W. A. Schürmann
  *Former Ambassador of The Netherlands to the United States*
The Hon. Johannes C. van den Berg
  *Consul General of The Netherlands in Chicago*
The Hon. J. William Middendorf
  *Ambassador of The United States to the Netherlands*
The Hon. William R. Tyler
  *Former Ambassador of The United States to The Netherlands*
The Hon. Douglas MacArthur II
  *The Ambassador of The United States to Austria*
His Excellency Dr. Karl Gruber
  *Ambassador of Austria to The United States*
The Hon. Georg Gerstberger
  *Consul of Austria in Chicago*
The Hon. John S. D. Eisenhower
  *The Ambassador of The United States to Belgium*

His Excellency Baron Scheyven
*Ambassador of Belgium to The United States*

The Hon. Henri Perdieus
*Consul General of Belgium in Chicago*

The Hon. Adolph W. Schmidt
*The Ambassador of The United States to Canada*

His Excellency A. E. Ritchie
*Ambassador of Canada to The United States*

The Hon. J. A. Doyle
*Former Acting Consul General of Canada in Chicago*

The Hon. L. H. Ausman
*Consul General of Canada in Chicago*

The Hon. Malcolm Toon
*The Ambassador of The United States to The Czechoslovak Socialist Republic*

His Excellency Dr. Karel Duda
*Ambassador of The Czechoslovak Socialist Republic to The United States*

The Hon. Robert Sargent Shriver
*Ambassador of The United States to France*

His Excellency Charles Lucet
*Ambassador of France to The United States*

The Hon. Jean-Louis Mandereau
*Consul General of France in Chicago*

The Hon. Kenneth Rush
*The Ambassador of The United States to Germany*

His Excellency Dr. Rolf Friedemann Pauls
*Ambassador of Germany to The United States*

The Hon. Eugen C. Betz
*Consul General of Germany in Chicago*

The Hon. Walter H. Annenberg
*The Ambassador of The United States to Great Britain*

His Excellency The Rt. Hon. John Freeman, M.B.E.
*Ambassador of Great Britain to The United States*

The Hon. A. K. Rothnie
*Consul General of Great Britain in Chicago*

His Excellency Jerzy Michalowski
*Ambassador of Poland to The United States*

The Hon. Wajciech Jaskot
*Consul General of Poland in Chicago*

The Hon. Walter J. Stoessel, Jr.
*Ambassador of The United States to Poland*

The Hon. John A. Gronouski
*Former Ambassador of The United States to Poland*

The Hon. Robert C. Hill
*The Ambassador of The United States to Spain*

His Excellency Marques de Merry del Val
*Ambassador of Spain to The United States*

The Hon. Carlos Manzanares
*Consul General of Spain in Chicago*

The Hon. Richard B. Ogilvie
*Governor of the State of Illinois*

The Hon. Richard J. Daley
*Mayor of the City of Chicago*

The Hon. Harold LeVander
*Governor of the State of Minnesota*

The Hon. Arthur Naftalin
*Mayor of the City of Minneapolis*

The Hon. Thomas R. Byrne
*Mayor of the City of St. Paul*

The Hon. William H. Milliken
*Governor of the State of Michigan*

The Hon. Jerome P. Cavanagh
*Mayor of the City of Detroit*

Mr. Frank H. Woods
*President of The Art Institute of Chicago*

Mr. John E. Andrus, III
*Chairman of the Board of Trustees of The Minneapolis Institute of Arts*

Mr. Lee Hills
*President of The Arts Commission of The Detroit Institute of Arts*

## Exhibition Committee

Mr. Charles C. Cunningham, Chairman; *Director, The Art Institute of Chicago*
Mr. Anthony M. Clark, *Director, The Minneapolis Institute of Arts*
Mr. Willis F. Woods, *Director, The Detroit Institute of Arts*
Professor E. Haverkamp-Begemann, *Yale University*
Professor J. Richard Judson, *Smith College*
Professor (emeritus) Jakob Rosenberg, *Harvard University*
Professor Seymour Slive, *Harvard University*
Professor (emeritus) Wolfgang Stechow, *Oberlin College*


The Exhibition is under the auspices of ICOM
(INTERNATIONAL COUNCIL OF MUSEUMS)

The participating museums wish to express their thanks to the following for their assistance in assembling the exhibition:

AUSTRIA

Vienna: Dr. Walter Koschatzky, *Director, Graphische Sammlung Albertina.*

BELGIUM

Brussels: Prof. Dr. Ph. Roberts-Jones, *Conservator in Chief, Musées royaux des Beaux-Arts de Belgique.*

CANADA

Ottawa: Jean S. Boggs, *Director, The National Gallery of Canada.*

CZECHOSLOVAKIA

Prague: Dr. Jiří Kotalík, *Director;* Dr. Ladislav Kesner, *Deputy Director;* Dr. Jaromír Šíp, *Curator of Old Masters, Národní Galerie.*

FRANCE

Grenoble: The Hon. Hubert Dubedout, *Mayor of Grenoble;* Mlle. Hélène Lassalle, *Conservator, F. F. Musée des Beaux-Arts.*

Paris: Michel Laclotte, *Conservator in Chief, Department of Paintings;* Pierre Rosenberg, *Assistant Conservator, Department of Paintings;* Jacques Foucart, *Musée National du Louvre.* Mme. W. Bouleau-Rabaud, *Conservator of Collections, Ecole Nationale Supérieure des Beaux-Arts;* Jean Drucker, *Head, Bureau of Instruction of Sculptural Arts, Ministry of Cultural Affairs.*

Frits Lugt, *Président;* Carlos van Hasselt, *Curator, Institut Néerlandais.*

GERMANY

Berlin: Prof. Dr. Robert Oertel, *Director, Staatliche Museen Preussischer Kulturbesitz, Gemäldegalerie;* Prof. Dr. Hans Möhle, *Director;* Prof. Dr. Matthais Winner, *Curator, Staatliche Museen Preussischer Kulturbesitz, Kupferstichkabinett.*

Braunschweig: Dr. Gert Adriani, *Director;* Dr. Bodo Hedergott, *Curator in Chief, Herzog-Anton-Ulrich Museum.*

Darmstadt: Dr. Gerhard Bott, *Director;* Dr. Götz Adriani, *Curator, Hessisches Landesmuseum.*

Düsseldorf: Dr. Eckhard Schaar, *Curator of Prints and Drawings;* Dr. Dieter Graf, *Assistant Curator of Prints and Drawings;* Dr. Axel von Saldern, *Kunstmuseum der Stadt Düsseldorf.*

Frankfurt: Prof. Dr. Ernst Holzinger, *Director;* Dr. K. Schwarzweller, *Städelsches Kunstinstitut.*

Hamburg: Prof. Dr. Alfred Hentzen, *Director;* Dr. Wolf Stubbe, *Curator of Prints and Drawings, Hamburger Kunsthalle.*

Kassel: Prof. Dr. Erich Herzog, *Director;* Dr. Friedrich Lahusen, *Staatliche Kunstsammlungen Kassel.*

GREAT BRITAIN

Birmingham: Prof. E. K. Waterhouse, *Director, Barber Institute of Fine Arts, The University of Birmingham.*

Brighton: Clifford Musgrave, *Director;* Derek Rogers, *Assistant Curator, Brighton Art Gallery and Museums.*

Cambridge: David Piper, *Director;* Malcolm Cormack, *Assistant Keeper of Print and Drawings, The Fitzwilliam Museum.*

Chatsworth: Thomas S. Wragg, *Librarian and Keeper, Devonshire Collections.*

Edinburgh, David Baxandall, *Director;* Colin E. Thompson, *Keeper of Paintings National Gallery of Scotland.*

Liverpool: Hugh Scrutton, *Director;* Timothy Stevens, *Deputy Director, Walker Art Gallery*

London: Martin Davies, *Director;* George Fox, Michael Levey, *Keeper, The National Gallery.* James Byam Shaw.

Oxford: Dr. Kenneth Garlick, *Keeper;* Hugh Macandrew, *Assistant Keeper, Department of Western Art, The Ashmolean Museum.*

THE NETHERLANDS

Amsterdam: Dr. Arthur van Schendel, *Director General;* Drs. P. J. J. van Thiel, *Curator of the Department of Paintings, Rijksmuseum;* Dr. K. G. Boon, *Director, Rijksprentenkabinet.*

Dr. Simon H. Levie, *Director, Amsterdams Historisch Museum.*

Groningen: Dr. A. Westers, *Director, Groninger Museum voor Stad en Lande.*

Haarlem: Prof. Dr. I. Q. van Regteren Altena, *Conservator, Teylers Museum.*

The Hague: Dr. A. B. de Vries, *Director;* A. J. M. van der Vaart, *Administrator, Koninklijk Kabinet van Schilderijen, "Mauritshuis".*

Nijmegen: Drs. A. V. M. Hubrecht, *Director, Rijksmuseum G. M. Kam.*

Rotterdam: Dr. J. C. Ebbinge Wubben, *Director;* Dr. H. R. Hoetink, *Curator of Drawings, Museum Boymans-van Beuningen.*

POLAND

Warsaw: Prof. Dr. Stanisław Lorentz, *Director;* Prof. Dr. Jan Białostocki, *Curator of European Paintings, Muzeum Narodowe.*

SPAIN

Madrid: G. Gustavino Gallent, *Director, Biblioteca Nacional;* Diego Angulo Iniguez, *Director, Museo del Prado.*

SWITZERLAND

Zürich: Dr. Hans Bänninger; Dr. Fritz Nathan and Dr. Peter Nathan.

UNITED STATES

Baltimore: Charles Parkhurst, *Director, Baltimore Museum of Art.*

Boston: Perry T. Rathbone, *Director, Museum of Fine Arts.*

Brunswick, Maine: Richard V. West, *Curator, Bowdoin College Museum of Art.*

Cambridge, Massachusetts: Miss Agnes Mongan, *Director, Fogg Art Museum, Harvard University.*

Cincinnati: Philip R. Adams, *Director, Cincinnati Art Museum.*

Cleveland: Sherman E. Lee, *Director;* Louise S. Richards, *Curator of Prints and Drawings;* William S. Talbot, *Assistant Curator of Paintings.*

Fullerton, California: James M. Brown III, *Director;* Mrs. Barbara Roberts, *Norton Simon, Inc. Museum of Art.*

Hartford, Connecticut: James Elliot, *Director;* Peter O. Marlow, *Curator of Painting and Sculpture, Wadsworth Atheneum.*

Los Angeles: Kenneth Donahue, *Director, Los Angeles County Museum of Art.*

New York: Thomas P. F. Hoving, *Director;* Theodore Rousseau, *Curator in Chief and Vice Director;* Claus Virch, *Curator, Department of Paintings;* Jacob Bean, *Curator, Department of Drawings, The Metropolitan Museum of Art.* Frederick B. Adams, Jr., *Director;* Miss Felice Stampfle, *Curator, Drawings and Prints, The Pierpont Morgan Library.* Miss Sarah Faunce, *Curator of art properties, Columbia University.* George Szabo, *Curator, The Lehman Collection.* H. Shickman, Norman Leitman, *Director,* H. Shickman Gallery, N.Y.

Pella, Iowa: Lawrence Mills, *Chairman, Division of Fine Arts, Central College.*

Philadelphia: Evan H. Turner, *Director, Philadelphia Museum of Art.* Henri Marceau, *Curator, John G. Johnson Collection.*

Providence, R. I.: Daniel Robbins, *Director;* Stephen E. Ostrow, *Chief Curator, Museum of Art, Rhode Island School of Design.*

Raleigh, North Carolina: Justus Bier, *Director;* Ben F. Williams, *General Curator, North Carolina Museum of Art.*

Rochester, New York: Harris K. Prior, *Director, Memorial Art Gallery of The University of Rochester.*

St. Louis, Missouri: Charles E. Buckley, *Director, City Art Museum.*

San Francisco: Edwin F. Carter, *Curator of Paintings, M. H. DeYoung Memorial Museum.*

Sarasota, Florida: Curtis G. Coley, *Director, John and Mable Ringling Museum of Art.*

Washington, D.C.: J. Carter Brown, *Director;* John Walker, *Former Director;* Perry B. Cott, *Former Chief Curator;* Ernest R. Feidler, *General Counsel;* Kennedy C. Watkins, *Assistant Secretary; National Gallery of Art.* Mr. J. E. Schaap, *Cultural Attaché, Embassy of The Netherlands;* Miss Christine Henny, *First Embassy Secretary, Embassy of The Netherlands.*

Williamstown, Massachusetts: George Heard Hamilton, *Director, Sterling and Francine Clark Art Institute.*

Worcester, Massachusetts: Daniel Catton Rich, *Director, Worcester Art Museum.*

## Acknowledgements

So many people in many parts of the world have assisted in word and deed in the preparation of this exhibition that it is difficult to know where to express our gratitude.

We are particularly honored that Her Royal Highness Princess Beatrix of The Netherlands and Mrs. Richard M. Nixon have graciously consented to give this exhibition their High Patronage.

The Department of State and its Protocol Services Officers and the United States Ambassadors in Europe and their staffs have been particularly helpful in assisting in many details of procuring loans and in arrangements for transport, both of works of art and curatorial personnel accompanying them.

The foreign Ambassadors to the United States and their staffs, as well as the Consuls General and Consuls stationed in Chicago from whose countries we have received loans, have been extremely helpful in many ways, and to them we extend our deepest appreciation. For their sympathetic and generous assistance in many details of the exhibition, we extend our deepest gratitude to Miss Christine Henny, First Secretary of Embassy of The Netherlands, Washington, D.C., and to Wilson P. Dizard, First Secretary of Embassy of The United States, Warsaw.

The Exhibition Committee, of which Charles C. Cunningham acted as Chairman, was composed of five of this country's foremost Rembrandt scholars. We have been privileged to have them serve on this committee and all have been active in the selection of the works included in the exhibition. In six two-day sessions in New York and Chicago, the format of the exhibition was established and the whole content discussed. Each work selected has been seen by one or more members of the committee. To Professor J. Richard Judson of Smith College and Professor E. Haverkamp-Begemann of Yale University, and his assistant Anne-Marie Logan, we are deeply indebted for the catalogue of paintings and the catalogue of drawings respectively. Professor Haverkamp-Begemann has contributed the splendid essay that serves as the introduction to the catalogue.

To Mrs. Henry W. Howell and the staff of the Frick Art Reference Library we extend our deepest appreciation for permitting our committee to use their facilities for meetings in New York and for many other special favors. We are also most grateful to Ruth Schoneman and the staff of the Libraries of The Art Institute of Chicago, and to Dr. Sturla Gudlaugsson and the staff of the Rijksbureau voor Kunsthistorische Documentatie, The Hague, for their generous assistance.

To our colleagues in Holland, Dr. Arthur van Schendel, Director of the Rijksmuseum, Amsterdam, Dr. A. B. de Vries, Director of the Mauritshuis, The Hague, and Dr. J. C. Ebbinge Wubben, Director of the Museum Boymans-van Beuningen, Rotterdam, have been most helpful in suggesting possible loans, in coordinating transport, and in their sympathetic help in many ways. We also thank Dr. A. Westers and Professor Horst Gerson of Groningen for their kind assistance and interest in the exhibition.

In Germany we are deeply grateful to many colleagues whose names are listed elsewhere, but particularly to Dr. Ernst Holzinger and Dr. K. Schwarzweller of the Städelsches Kunstinstitut, Frankfurt, for allowing us to use their museum as a collecting point for loans from Germany. The Louvre and its Chief Curator of Paintings, Michel Laclotte, have graciously consented to coordinate the shipment of loans from France; and in England, Hugh Macandrew of The Ashmolean Museum, Oxford, has consented to do the same for certain loans from Great Britain. In Poland, Professor Jan Białostocki of the National Museum, Warsaw, has been extremely helpful; and Dr. Jiří Kotalík and Dr. Ladislav Kesner of the National Gallery, Prague, have given our requests their wholehearted support. Others to whom we are deeply grateful for favors are David Baxandall, Director of the National Gallery of Scotland, Edinburgh, and Mr. Ernest Feidler and Kennedy C. Watkins of the National Gallery of Art, Washington. John Maxon, the Associate Director, and Harold Joachim, Curator of Prints and Drawings of The Art Institute of Chicago, Samuel Sachs II, Chief Curator, The Minneapolis Institute of Arts, and Frederick J. Cummings, Assistant Director, The Detroit Institute of Arts, have worked closely with the Exhibition Committee.

Many of the staff of The Art Institute of Chicago have been involved in the exhibition in various ways for over two years, but we particularly wish to thank Judith Di Meo, Research Fellow, and her successor, Hanna Henket, for research on the catalogue, and Wallace Bradway, Registrar, for attending to the complex arrangements of transport and insurance. Anselmo Carini, Supervisor of Publications, has patiently and efficiently seen the catalogue through press. The layout has been handsomely designed by Everett McNear. The correspondence, the coordination of loan requests, and many other details have been both cheerfully and efficiently handled by Mary Benisek.

To all these people and to others too many to mention, as well as to the lenders to the exhibition, we extend our heartfelt thanks. We hope that their efforts will lead to a fuller understanding of Holland's greatest artist, Rembrandt van Rijn.

C. C. Cunningham, *Director*
The Art Institute of Chicago

Anthony M. Clark, *Director*
The Minneapolis Institute of Arts

Willis W. Woods, *Director*
The Detroit Institute of Arts

## Lenders to the Exhibition

The Art Institute of Chicago, The Minneapolis Institute of Arts, The Detroit Institute of Arts wish to express their deepest appreciation to the following lenders who have deprived themselves or their visitors of the enjoyment of their paintings and drawings by sharing in our homage to Rembrandt.

Mr. and Mrs. Nathan R. Allen, Greenwich, Conn.
Mr. and Mrs. Winslow Ames, Saunderstown, R.I.
Sidney van den Bergh, Wassenaar
Miss Annette Ruth Brod, London
Miss Monica Hedy Brod, London
Daan Cevat, St. Peter Port
Chr. P. van Eeghen, The Netherlands
The Goldschmidt Collection, New York
G. Henle, Duisburg
Bernard Houthakker, Amsterdam
Dr. Jan B. Hubrecht, Doorn
Mr. and Mrs. Harry G. John, Milwaukee
The Lehman Collection, New York
Dr. Willem M. J. Russell, Amsterdam
H. Shickman Gallery, New York

Mr. and Mrs. Norton Simon, Los Angeles
Mr. and Mrs. Seymour Slive, Cambridge, Mass.
Victor Spark, New York
Earl C. Townsend, Jr., Indianapolis
Mr. and Mrs. Chester D. Tripp, Chicago
Julius H. Weitzner, London
And Several Anonymous Lenders

Amsterdams Historisch Museum (Collection Fodor)
Amsterdam, Rijksmuseum
Amsterdam, Rijksprentenkabinet
The Baltimore Museum of Art
Staatliche Museen Berlin, Gemäldegalerie Dahlem
Berlin, Staatliche Museen Preussischer Kulturbesitz, Kupferstichkabinett
Barber Institute of Fine Arts, University of Birmingham
Boston, Museum of Fine Arts
Braunschweig, Herzog-Anton-Ulrich Museum
Brighton Art Gallery, England
Brunswick, Me., Bowdoin College Museum of Art
Brussels, Musées royaux des Beaux-Arts de Belgique
Cambridge, England, The Fitzwilliam Museum
Cambridge, Mass., Fogg Art Museum, Harvard University

The Art Institute of Chicago
Cincinnati Art Museum
The Cleveland Museum of Art
Darmstadt, Hessisches Landesmuseum
The Detroit Institute of Arts
Düsseldorf, Kunstmuseum der Stadt
Edinburgh, National Gallery of Scotland
University of Edinburgh
Fullerton, Calif.,
    Norton Simon Foundation
    Norton Simon, Inc. Museum of Art
Grenoble, Musée des Beaux Arts
Groningen, Groninger Museum voor Stad
    en Lande
Haarlem, Teylers Museum
The Hague, Royal Gallery of Paintings
    "Mauritshuis"
Hamburg, Kunsthalle
Hartford, Wadsworth Atheneum
Kassel, Staatliche Kunstsammlungen
Leerdam, Hofje van Aerden
Liverpool, Walker Art Gallery
London, The National Gallery
Los Angeles County Museum of Art
Madrid, Biblioteca Nacional
The Minneapolis Institute of Arts
New York, Columbia University
New York, The Metropolitan Museum of Art

New York, The Pierpont Morgan Library
Ottawa, The National Gallery of Canada
Oxford, The Ashmolean Museum
Paris, Coll. F. Lugt, Institut Néerlandais
Paris, Ecole Nationale Supérieure des
    Beaux-Arts
Paris, The Louvre
Pella, Iowa, Central College, The Brower
    Collection
Philadelphia, John G. Johnson Collection
The Philadelphia Museum of Art
Prague, Národní Galerie
Providence, Museum of Art, Rhode Island
    School of Design
Raleigh, North Carolina Museum of Art
George Eastman Collection of the University
    of Rochester
Rotterdam, Museum Boymans-van Beuningen
City Art Museum of Saint Louis
San Francisco,
    M. H. de Young Memorial Museum
Sarasota, Fla.,
    John and Mable Ringling Museum of Art
Vienna, The Albertina
Warsaw, Muzeum Narodowe
Washington, D.C., National Gallery of Art
Williamstown, Mass., Sterling and
    Francine Clark Art Institute
Worcester Art Museum

2  Rembrandt
*Artist in His Studio*
*Museum of Fine Arts, Boston*

# Contents

# Foreword

The year 1969 marks the three hundredth anniversary of the death of Rembrandt Harmensz van Rijn, who died on October 4, 1669. Exhibitions commemorating this anniversary have taken place or are being held in his native Holland, elsewhere in Europe, as well as in Canada and the United States. Only thirteen years ago, on the occasion of the three hundred and fiftieth anniversary of Rembrandt's birth in 1606, exhibitions of the work of Rembrandt, and in certain instances of Rembrandt and his circle, were held in Holland, Poland, Sweden, Russia, and the United States. In 1956, because the valuations of Rembrandt paintings and drawings had not reached the astronomical figures which they fetch today, it was possible, as it is hardly today, to assemble a comprehensive exhibition of Rembrandt's own works. Owners are more reluctant to lend paintings and drawings; and even if they were not, insurance costs are almost prohibitive.

The concept of this exhibition took form early in 1967, and has been discussed with many people, with Rembrandt scholars and officials of many institutions. The decision to hold an exhibition which would contain works by Rembrandt as well as those of his followers was made in order that a comprehensive image be presented of the genius of Rembrandt, and equally of the extraordinary impact which he had on the art of his own times and his own country. Few artists have had a greater influence on their era, the possible exceptions being Leonardo, Raphael, Michelangelo, Dürer, and Caravaggio. Although Rembrandt had many pupils and followers, some fifty in all, it was decided to confine the exhibition to showing, in addition to the various periods of Rembrandt's creative activity, the work of the most accomplished artists of his circle, especially those which come closest to the style of the master. Quality and significance were important elements in the choice of each painting or drawing. Furthermore, it was deemed pertinent by the Exhibition Committee that paintings and drawings, the attribution of which had not found unanimity among experts, should be included so that they could be studied in relation to the works of the master as well as of the pupils. Therefore there are eleven paintings and fourteen or more drawings that were formerly given to Rembrandt but are now assigned to pupils, as well as seven paintings and twelve drawings which still await more positive attribution, but which have been listed as attributed to Rembrandt.

Included in the exhibition are a few paintings and drawings by pupils such as Eeckhout and Maes which show how they departed from the master's style and adopted new modes of expression, such as the increasingly popular Flemish manner, or French, or the genre style of the Delft School.

Whereas past generations have appraised Rembrandt's pupils in terms of disciples following the style of their master, and whereas it was considered that their departures from Rembrandt's style were contrary to his concepts and demeaning to his greatness and theirs, this exhibition attempts to demonstrate that the pupils developed along different lines because their precepts and their integrity were fostered by Rembrandt's own respect for personal freedom.

The exhibitions held in 1956 gave Rembrandt scholars and students, as well as the public, a splendid opportunity to appraise the work of Rembrandt, and the exhibitions held this year should provide further occasions to do this. During the past fifty or more years, there has taken place a general reassessment of Rembrandt's paintings and drawings as a result of a change in attitude of succeeding generations from what Hofstede de Groot called the "somewhat large hearted group" to a group who practiced what he called "hypercriticism." This change on the whole has been a healthy one, for it has eliminated from Rembrandt's *oeuvre*, paintings which do not measure up to his standards.

There are several factors which have made the role of the modern Rembrandt critic far easier today. A half century ago, many paintings and drawings were in private collections, often in inaccessible places, while today the majority of Rembrandt's work has now passed into the public museums of Europe and the United States where they may be easily seen and studied. Another element to be considered is the ease and speed of modern travel, permitting scholars, given time and funds, to study works in the original rather than from photographs. Modern science and new methods of examining works of art through different types of photography, micro-photography, infra-red, ultra-violet, and x-ray photography have added immeasurably to the potential for critical examination of art, as have indeed the scientific analysis of pigments, paint structure, and supports. These are the tools of the art historian which must be added to the vital elements of connoisseurship and critical knowledge. A "Rembrandt Research Project" composed of six eminent Dutch scholars has been established this year to study scientifically, where possible, all paintings attributed to Rembrandt. This exhibition, one of the largest of its kind ever assembled, offers the opportunity to view Rembrandt and his followers in depth, but the last word will undoubtedly still remain to be said.

In the last decade there have been published many books and articles on Rembrandt and his followers, not a few with critical listings of their works. Since 1964, four[1] critical listings of Rembrandt paintings have been published. From Valentiner's total of 743, Bredius in 1935 reduced the number to 620. In 1964, Kurt Bauch in his catalogue further reduced this number to 562. In the past year, Horst Gerson has produced two books, one of which, *Rembrandt's Paintings*, 1968, reduces the number to 421. The same author's 1969 revision of the 1935 Bredius volume brings the number of paintings accepted without question to 376, with another 89 which are questioned but still retain Rembrandt's name. He lists 109 paintings which he rejects as probably by other hands, and 56 paintings are placed in the appendix as totally excluded from Rembrandt's work. Against some of

---

[1] This would include J. Rosenberg's *Rembrandt, Life and Work*, with its reappraisal of Valentiner's two *Klassiker der Kunst* volumes and Bredius' volume of 1935.

these conclusions of Gerson's, there have already been protests, and there will undoubtedly be more. B. Haak's recent book, *Rembrandt, his Life, his Work, his Time*, 1969, reclaims a few works rejected by others. His republication of the inventory of Rembrandt's studio prior to public sale in 1657 shows once again how many paintings are now lost. In the reevaluation process, it is certainly hard for the private owner of a painting or drawing to discover that his prized possession is no longer considered to be by the master. The work remains the same, but its commercial value is reduced to about one-tenth or less of its value were it a genuine Rembrandt. Museums for the most part accept a reattribution of a Rembrandt where the weight of scholarly opinion and their own seems to confirm it. Where else if not in museums can students and the public find the truth? The *Seated Man with a Stick* (cat. no. 23) from the National Gallery, London, was reclassified in 1960 as "Circle of Rembrandt" by the Gallery, and *Christ Washing the Feet of the Disciples* from Chicago (cat. no. 81), was formerly given to Rembrandt but now accepted by the museum as Lievens.

What are the paintings that can be attributed to Rembrandt on contemporary documentary evidence and on which critical evaluation of his art may be based? They are few in number. Unlike Rubens, Rembrandt was not a court painter, and since he never traveled or had only few commissions outside of Holland, there is very little correspondence from his hand. J. Orlers, the burgomaster of Leiden, who wrote a history of his city published in 1641, proudly mentions Rembrandt as one of its distinguished citizens. The five paintings of the "Passion Series" now in Munich are mentioned in Rembrandt's seven letters to Constantijn Huygens who commissioned them for Prince Frederick Henry of Orange. Three paintings, *Rembrandt's Mother* (Windsor), a *Self-Portrait* (Liverpool), and a *Scholar*, now lost, were given to Charles I of England by Lord Ancrum before 1633. The *Huygens* (Hamburg), the *de Gheyn* (Dulwich) and the *Elison* (pair, Boston) are all documented by early inventories. The *Judas* (Marquis of Normandy) is mentioned in Constantijn Huygens autobiography and the *Balaam* (Cognacq-Jay, Paris) is mentioned in a letter of Claude Vignon, the French painter. The two *Anatomy Lessons* (The Hague and Amsterdam) were mentioned being in the Anatomy Theater in Amsterdam during Rembrandt's lifetime. Commissioned works include the *Night Watch*, the *Julius Civilis* and the *Five Syndics*. Then there is the *St. John Preaching* in Berlin which is mentioned by Rembrandt's pupil Samuel van Hoogstraten in writing on his master. Well documented by letters are the three paintings made for the Sicilian Don Antonio Ruffo, *Aristotle* (New York), *Homer* (The Hague) and *Alexander* (probably painting in Glasgow). Finally, there are paintings like *The Blinding of Samson* (Frankfurt) and the late *Self-Portrait* in the Uffizi where the documentary evidence is nearly fool-proof. The paintings that are genuinely signed, and there are a fair number, can be accepted if indeed the signature is genuine. It has been suggested that Rembrandt sometimes signed the work of his pupils, although under guild regulations, this was permissable as long as they were in his studio. Joachim van Sandrart (1675) says that Rembrandt made a profit of 2,000–2,500 florins from the sale of his pupils work. This figure is likely an exaggeration since there is a Rembrandt drawing in the Berlin Print Room on the back of which there is a notation in Rembrandt's hand of a very modest price received for works of two pupils, Bol and Leendert Cornelisz van Beyeren. Signatures can be misleading, particularly as even some genuine Rembrandts have false signatures. It is equally apparent that Rembrandt, although he had pupils throughout his whole life, rarely used assistants, and even in such large paintings as the *Night Watch*, there is no evidence of any other hand but Rembrandt. That Rembrandt frequently added touches to pupils' work is well known and it has been suggested for instance that the figures of the old woman on the steps and the girl in the door of the Chicago painting *Rebecca Welcomed by Abraham* (cat. no. 53) were retouched by Rembrandt. Since they are among the strongest figures in the picture, this could well be so.

The same standards and criteria can be established in the case of the work of the pupils, so that such a painting as *Elisabeth Bas* (cat. no. 30), formerly given to Rembrandt and later by some to Backer, can be established as a work of Bol on the basis of his signed and dated *Portrait of an Old Woman* from Warsaw (cat. no. 31). On the other hand, two signed paintings by Drost included in the exhibition, the Louvre *Bathsheba* (cat. no. 41) and the *Self-Portrait* (cat. no. 40) in the Metropolitan Museum of Art, have only been of moderate help in establishing the work of that artist. Houbraken says that Eeckhout was Rembrandt's most faithful follower and the San Francisco and Hartford pictures (cat. nos. 47 and 46) surely confirm this, but if we did not have evidence in the signature, it would be hard to accept as his the *Party on a Terrace* (cat. no. 50) in Worcester. Not a few of the paintings by pupils in the exhibition have at one time been attributed to other pupils, and who was the artist, if not Rembrandt, who painted the beautiful *Tobias and the Angel* from Berlin (cat. no. 25) or the haunting fragment of the *Virgin Annunciate* (cat. no. 26) from Prague? The striking *Portrait of a Young Man* (cat. no. 80) from Edinburgh has been attributed to Rembrandt, to Ferdinand Bol, and now to Lievens which gives some indication of how close the pupils were to the master and to each other.

A similar situation exists as far as the drawings are concerned, and here again the last word has surely not been said. Why are there no drawings that can be assigned positively to Carel Fabritius, or are some of these lost among those of Rembrandt or other pupils? Hoogstraten's drawings have frequently been mistaken for Rembrandt, but why are there so few Hoogstraten paintings in the Rembrandt manner? Can we be sure that the drawing of the *Tower of the Westerkerk* (cat. no. 176) long given to Rembrandt is not by him but by Furnerius as it has been catalogued? The relationship between Rembrandt's drawings to paintings and drawings by pupils is a fascinating study. Compare for instance the two drawings by Rembrandt of *Joseph Interpreting the Prisoners' Dreams* (cat. no. 103 and 104) with Bol's interpretation of the same subject in Hamburg (cat. no. 152). There are also drawings by Rembrandt and his pupils related to some of his etchings. These drawings with their interrelationship between master and pupil give us a fascinating insight into the workings of Rembrandt's studio and his methods of teaching. There are drawings by Furnerius and Leupenius, but no paintings exist. Were they only draughtsmen?

There are many questions to be asked and some may be answered. Hopefully one day, Rembrandt's pupils may be fully defined as individual artists, as some indeed are, but is it really the purpose of this exhibition? For the art historian, the opportunity to compare artistic styles of master and pupil and pupil with pupil is certainly invaluable. What is even more cogent is to view the exhibition as a product of its times, where the shadow of a great artistic personality is everywhere. Unlike Leonardo or Rubens, Rembrandt brought out the creative genius of his pupils and except perhaps in the case of Carel Fabritius, when they were closest to him, they were closest to greatness.

*C. C. Cunningham*

# Rembrandt as Teacher

Just as Rembrandt was a nonconformist in his life and work, so was he an unorthodox teacher. By age twenty-one he had pupils, and he soon became so successful that from his late twenties until his mid-forties he was the most sought-after master in the Netherlands. Numerous artists came to Amsterdam in order to receive instruction from him, and some of these artists were among the most gifted of the period. Their performance often was at its best as long as they were working with their master; sometimes they even emulated his style so successfully that their works are still confused with those of Rembrandt. But almost invariably these artists sooner or later used mainly other styles as their means of expression. What was it that made these artists perform, and why did they turn away from their master?

To some extent this question is answered by both the written sources and by the works of his pupils, particularly their drawings. By criticizing Rembrandt's instruction and also by giving free rein to his feelings of surprise and envy with regard to Rembrandt's income, Joachim von Sandrart informs us about Rembrandt's teaching. Sandrart undoubtedly knew Rembrandt personally when he was in Amsterdam (1637–1641), and must have known what went on in his studio. "Rembrandt was a very industrious man," he wrote in his *Teutsche Akademie* of 1675, "and he worked relentlessly, and Fortune made him wealthy and filled his house in Amsterdam with almost countless distinguished children for instruction and learning of whom every single one paid him 100 guilders annually, not to speak of the profit which he gained by selling paintings and prints of these pupils which amounted to an additional two to two-and-a-half thousand guilders in cash, and add to that all that he made with his own paintings." It is difficult to know what Sandrart considered "countless," but if any significance can be attached to his being perfectly able to count the "twenty-four or twenty-five students" that annually were instructed in Honthorst's studio, we may suppose he meant that Rembrandt had annually more than twenty-five pupils. This was at the time that Sandrart lived in Amsterdam, when Rembrandt had reached the height of his popularity as a teacher.

As we shall see, some of these pupils probably were formal students for a considerable time, while others studied with Rembrandt temporarily and rather informally. Unfortunately the precise numbers of both groups are not known, but it is nevertheless likely that Rembrandt had more students at that time than any other artist in the Low Countries, except for Rubens.

Some aspects of the simultaneous instruction of a great number of students can be learned from two drawings, one of which is included in this exhibition (cat. no. 147). They show Rembrandt surrounded by pupils drawing from the nude. The drawings conform in their composition to a tradition of representations of such drawing classes, and therefore may not necessarily represent Rembrandt's studio accurately in every respect. We nevertheless do learn that Rembrandt and his pupils were seated and standing in front of a nude model and that they were making studies from this model. A number of studies of nudes in Rembrandt's style but drawn by different artists from slightly different angles prove that this indeed was Rembrandt's practice. Rembrandt even went one step further: at least in one instance, in or about 1646, he etched a nude male model on a prepared copperplate while his pupils were sketching it with pen and ink. We also learn from these views of Rembrandt's studio that the pupils held their paper upright, which accords with the advice given by Samuel van Hoogstraten to the readers of his handbook for artists, advice he may well have learned himself from Rembrandt: "Sit straight up, and hold your paper or sketchbook with your left hand also in an upright position, in order that you don't need to lift up your head or turn up your eye too much when looking up." The plaster casts indicate that Rembrandt let his pupils sketch from these as well as from the nude. The drawings also show that middle-aged and even elderly men were among the students sketching from a model.

Since Rembrandt gave life classes to many students, sometimes perhaps more than twenty-five, this "school" may be called a "private academy" in the seventeenth-century sense of the word: a place where students of art could gather to draw from life and plaster casts, and to copy other works of art, under supervision of a master. The first academy of this type to become renowned and influential, that of the Carracci in Bologna, shows remarkable similarities to that of Rembrandt and probably served directly or indirectly as example. The Carracci tried to reintroduce the study of nature and classical art and attracted with their "Accademia degli Incamminati" or "Accademia del Disegno" many young and lively talents that shared their wish to overcome mannerism. The usual program of such academies, already formulated by Leonardo da Vinci, consisted of instruction in perspective and anatomy, in copying the works of the master and other artists, and in drawing from casts and the nude.

Whether the tradition to organize such academies to draw from the nude and from plaster casts in the Netherlands goes back as far as 1583, when Carel van Mander, Hendrick Goltzius and Cornelis van Haarlem were purported to have founded one in Haarlem, has not been established, but in the early 1630's at least one private academy existed in Amsterdam. It was the "famosa accademia" of Hendrick Uylenburgh, as Filippo Baldinucci called it. Since Hendrick Uylenburgh was an art dealer, publisher and collector, the instruction in his academy may have emphasized the copying of works of art, and it is not known whether any life classes were given. Rembrandt lived with Uylenburgh from 1631 until 1634 or 1635, and may have had a hand in initiating the program or otherwise may have participated in it as a teacher. In 1634 a minor artist from Strasbourg, Jean-Frédéric Brentel, stayed in Amsterdam and made various studies after one male model in different positions. Since the drawings bear no relationship to Rembrandt, he had the opportunity to do this in another studio, but whether this was Uylenburgh's academy or another one is not known. These drawings, however, prove that such classes were given at that time in Amsterdam. It also may be assumed that Honthorst's school, which was highly praised by his pupil Sandrart, who called it an "academy," included life classes.

It is not known when Rembrandt founded his "academy," but it is likely that he did this not long after his move to Amsterdam. It existed by 1646 when Rembrandt etched male models who were also drawn by pupils, and probably by 1641, since Sandrart's statement seems to imply its existence. When Bol, Flinck, De Helst Stoccade, and Strijker founded a "drawing club" in the 1650's, the first two may have followed an example that they experienced themselves in the 1630's when studying with Rembrandt.

Although Rembrandt's academy was not a novelty, it represented a significant departure from traditional teaching methods in Amsterdam inasmuch as it broke with the guild rules of that city. We are less well informed about the specific regulations of Amsterdam's Guild of St. Luke than about those of other cities in the Netherlands, but, in spite of local variations, some general rules applied everywhere. The guilds perpetuated the medieval mode of instruction, which was apprenticeship. Under that system, a restricted number of students went through all stages of the craft under the tutelage of a master, and in his studio, starting with grinding paint and preparing canvases, and ended by becoming a master. The apprenticeship usually took three years. Everything was regulated, with freedom greatly restricted. To some extent the guilds often provided protection for the artist by instituting pensions and insurances.

Rembrandt apparently did not fully believe in the apprenticeship system and in the restrictions the guild imposed upon him as a teacher. His school, as he modeled it upon the example of the Italian academies, was less formal, allowed for a great number of students of different ages and levels of training, and enabled him to select the subjects taught. But Rembrandt's teaching was not all innovation. Let us first discuss some of the traditional aspects that he adopted, and then have a closer look at the novel features.

One traditional element was the emphasis on copying works of the master and of other artists. As early as 1634 an inventory was drawn up of the goods of Lambert Jacobsz, artist and dealer agent in Leeuwarden for Hendrick Uylenburgh, listing a number of copies after Rembrandt, and many others are found in other contemporary inventories, as well as in Rembrandt's own possession in 1656. The public was happy to acquire copies when it could not afford originals, and students had to make them for practice. Students also made drawings after Rembrandt's paintings: a copy of Rembrandt's *Holy Family* is attributed to Maes, and Lambert Doomer copied the companion pieces *Saskia as Flora* and the *Standard Bearer* in two drawings, while Bol copied Rembrandt's *Minerva* of 1635, and numerous other examples exist. As for Rembrandt's drawings, many of the contemporary copies undoubtedly were made by his pupils in an effort to grasp his style.

Rembrandt also continued the traditional practice of selling the works of his students, as we know from a note on the reverse side of one of Rembrandt's drawings. The prices were moderate (five to fifteen guilders), yet they may have added considerably to Rembrandt's income. Sandrart's outrage at Rembrandt's selling his pupils' works for money may partly have been caused by what in Sandrart's eyes was incompatible with an "academy," as he conceived of it.

It always had been the custom that the artist taught his students to work in his style, and Rembrandt laid great weight on his students acquiring the ability to work in his manner. The studies of nude models made by his pupils are so similar to Rembrandt's own that the authorship of some is still debated; and from the students' religious compositions as well as landscapes it is clear how closely the pupils could approximate the style of their master. In the present exhibition, paintings and drawings by or attributed to Bol (cat. nos. 32, and 151–156), Van Borssum (no. 158), Gerard Dou (no. 37), Willem Drost (nos. 41–44), Barent Fabritius (nos. 32 and 170), Govert Flinck (no. 61), Abraham Furnerius (no. 176), Philips Koninck (no. 184), Jan Lievens (no. 197), and Nicolaes Maes (no. 198) show this phenomenon. While they were in Rembrandt's school, the pupils tried to absorb Rembrandt's style and to express themselves in it. This explains the great number of paintings and drawings that remain anonymous because they cannot be considered works of Rembrandt, and at present cannot be attributed to any of his pupils. The authorship of paintings and drawings made by pupils in Rembrandt's style can be established only in those instances where the personality of the artist reveals itself in spite of his efforts to work in Rembrandt's manner, or when paintings are based on drawings by known artists, or when drawings turn out to be studies for paintings that are known to have been painted by one or another pupil. In this respect it should be noted that drawings made by pupils as studies for their paintings often approximate Rembrandt's style more closely than the paintings. Bol's *Joseph Interpreting the Prisoners' Dreams* (cat. no. 152) may serve as example.

Pupils often sketched and painted the same subject as Rembrandt. While they were in Rembrandt's studio, they may have done this in order to carry out the master's wish, but even after they left him, the impact of his choice of subject matter remained strong. The subject matter of the Rembrandt school is thus, to a large extent, defined by one man's preferences.

Rembrandt corrected his pupils' drawings not only verbally, but he sometimes re-drew sections which needed improvement. Invariably, these corrections, as represented in this exhibition by numbers 142–145, were aimed at showing the pupils how to make a stronger point, how to express the essence of a biblical event, or how to represent the meaning of an action or of a figure, rather than to perfect the anatomy of a figure or the perspective of objects. Rembrandt also sometimes corrected his pupils' paintings, as in the case of *Anna and the Blind Tobit* in the National Gallery in London which was mainly painted by Gerard Dou (cf. also cat. no. 36). This phenomenon must be kept in mind in case of a number of student paintings which contain more than one style. In some instances these corrections were acknowledged conscientiously, as in the copy of *Abraham Sacrificing Isaac* in Munich, perhaps painted by Flinck, where is written "Rembrandt verandert En over geschildert 1636" ("Rembrandt changed and overpainted 1636"). Quite a number of drawings corrected by Rembrandt were copied after they had been corrected (see the notes to nos. 142, 143, and 145). Since these copies invariably were made by artists less accomplished than those who had made the drawings that needed correction, we may assume that Rembrandt asked less advanced pupils to copy such corrected drawings in order to gain an understanding of his draughtsmanship.

In spite of the ability of the students to emulate Rembrandt's style, they apparently did not assist him to any substantial degree in his drawings, etchings and paintings. Whether students primed canvases and ground paint for Rembrandt has not been established, but not one painting is known of which the visual surface shows evidence of having been executed by Rembrandt with the assistance of another artist. In this respect Rembrandt differed greatly from Rubens, who used the talents available to assist him in his work, and whose paintings range from those strictly done by himself to such that were almost entirely painted by assistants or pupils after his design, and finally retouched by Rubens himself. Rembrandt was not a man to let things be done by others. Just as he corrected his pupils' drawings to show them how they should do it themselves, he himself preferred to complete his paintings, his drawings, and his etchings without the assistance of others. After initial unsuccessful trials, Rembrandt even went so far as not to accept the widespread practice (so successfully adopted by Rubens) of having other artists make large prints after one's designs, but rather preferred to make the prints entirely himself (*Hundred Guilder Print, Ecce Homo, Three Crosses*). Brush strokes and lines drawn with pen or etching needle were integral parts of his paintings, drawings, and prints, and, to his mind, these could not be left to others.

As for Rembrandt's innovations in teaching, we have noted above that he found in the Italian private academies a pattern for his departure from Dutch tradition. He accepted some of the Italian basic principles: first, the necessity of group study of the nude; and, second, an element of informality unknown under the apprenticeship system. As we have seen, Rembrandt admitted great numbers of students, many of them from outside Amsterdam: Flinck from Cleves, Backer from Friesland, Bol, Maes, Hoogstraten, and Aert de Gelder from Dordrecht, Bernhard Keihl from Denmark, and others from elsewhere.

Rembrandt also taught artists who had learned the basic principles of the craft elsewhere: Backer and Flinck had worked in a pre-Rembrandtesque style as pupils of Lambert Jacobsz before entering Rembrandt's studio (see cat. nos. 150 and 171); Gerbrand van den Eeckhout worked in Lastman's style while at the same time adopting Rembrandt's (cat. nos. 164 and 165); Carel Fabritius probably had already had a basic training before coming to Rembrandt; Van Hoogstraten had first been a pupil of his father, Aert de Gelder one of Van Hoogstraten's. Some of the older figures in the drawing of Rembrandt's "academy" (no. 147) seem somewhat caricatured, and the exaggeration of their age and scholarly looks is the artist's expression of the exceptional nature of the presence of these "characters" that are far beyond the age of an apprentice.

Undoubtedly many visited Rembrandt's academy only for a short time, while others stayed longer than the average number of years. The principle of temporary association apparently applied to the study of painting as well as of drawing. It is not only through chance or lack of documentation that we do not know whether certain artists were actually pupils of Rembrandt (for instance, Barent Fabritius, Jan Victors, Karel van der Pluym, Philips Koninck). Rather, they seem often to have associated freely with him, instead of engaging in a formal master-pupil relationship. Already early in Rembrandt's career, by 1629–30, one artist, who had been painting for many years, associated himself with Rembrandt and absorbed some of the features of his style, which he later relinquished. This was Jan Lievens, and he was no exception, but rather set a pattern for later years.

There is even a more profound difference between Rembrandt's approach to instruction and the traditional apprenticeship system. The guilds were still operating under the assumption that art was a craft, while the aim of Rembrandt and others who opposed the guilds and the apprenticeship system was to consider the artist's profession as a noble art. The academic freedom from drudgery of the basic skills and the concentration on more "artistic" endeavors symbolized this new approach. In this light, Sandrart's statements need to be reinterpreted: when he wrote that Rembrandt instructed "fürnehme Kinder" and that Honthorst's academy was full of "fürnehmer Leute Kinder," he probably did not think mainly of young aristocrats (although some were among them, e.g. Constantijn van Renesse), but rather of young people who were studying the art of painting as a dignified and learned discipline, rather than acquiring the skills to perform a craft.

Although Rembrandt accepted these basic principles of the Italian private academy, he rejected others. This dual opposition against total acceptance of both the traditional apprenticeship system and the new academic insights is a fundamental trait of Rembrandt's approach to teaching. It also explains much of the criticism of later adherents to both systems.

From the studies of nudes made by various pupils at the same session, it is obvious that Rembrandt did not stress the need for anatomical detail and accuracy. What he and his pupils sketched was light and tone rather than structure, as we see it, for instance, also in Rembrandt's female nudes of a later period, here exhibited (nos. 136 and 137). It was precisely this deviation from the academic tradition that aroused Sandrart's ire: "Rembrandt battled against our rules of art, such as anatomy and the proportions of the human body, against perspective and the usefulness of classical statues, against Raphael's art of drawing, against intelligent instruction and also against the academies so necessary for our profession." If an old fashioned artist had omitted the instruction of perspective and anatomy, Sandrart might not have liked it, but probably would have found no reason to criticize it as severely as in Rembrandt's case, who, in his opinion, neglected these essential classical aspects of art instruction while at the same time adopting the academic method of group drawing from the nude. For Sandrart this was tantamount to sacrilege. He wrote his book as the *summa* of what should be taught in the academy in Nuremberg, of which he himself was a director, and which he was enlarging and transforming into a public institution at the time of publication of his book. Rembrandt's lack of interest in anatomy and perspective attacked the classicistic art theory, and therefore the principles of his book, and the foundation of his institution, and thus could not be tolerated. It is understandable that under these circumstances Sandrart praised Rembrandt almost exclusively for his colors and for his industriousness.

In evaluating Rembrandt as a teacher one wants to know whether most pupils sooner or later worked in other styles because of his mode of instruction or in spite of it. Invariably the historians consider their departure from Rembrandt a decline, and generally interpret their change of style as a move against Rembrandt.

This view is questionable for various reasons. Although, as we saw, Rembrandt stressed the necessity for his students to adopt his style, it is very unlikely that he did this in order to submit them to acceptance of his style as their own for the rest of their lives. This is brought out by two contemporary sources. Arnold Houbraken wrote in 1718 about one particular aspect of Rembrandt's instruction. Rembrandt "rented a warehouse on the Bloemgracht where, in order to be able to paint from life without disturbing each other, his pupils made small cubicles, each one for himself, by setting up partitions of paper or oilcloth." By this statement Houbraken implies that Rembrandt rented this warehouse soon after he moved to Amsterdam, and the specific reference to the location of the building lends credibility to his statement. Later in his career Rembrandt also apparently made it a practice to allot individual space to his students, as we learn from one of the conditions set forth at the time of the sale of his belongings in 1658. Then "two stoves and various partitions set up for his pupils in the attick" of his house in the Jodenbreestraat were exempted from the sale because they were considered indispensable for the continuation of his business. Houbraken may have obtained this information from his own teachers, Samuel van Hoogstraten or Jacobus Levecq who had been in Rembrandt's studio in the early 1640's and 1650's respectively.

These cubicles seem to be without precedent in the history of art instruction. It is more likely that Rembrandt wanted his students to concentrate better and develop their own talents, rather than to exercise stiffer control. Small spaces, to quote Leonardo da Vinci, "stimulate the mind" ("ravian lo'ngegno") but the larger ones "distract" ("lo sviano").

Rembrandt knew and told his students that they would find their own way if they learned well what they were taught. This is recorded by Hoogstraten who related that he received the following answer when he had bothered his master with too many questions: "Try to make proper use in your work of what you have learned so far; then you will discover soon enough the hidden things about which you ask." Van Hoogstraten also probably reflected Rembrandt's opinion as well as the traditional concept when he wrote that an artist should copy to learn, but then be original, and that in matters of composition an artist should be free to do what he wants, and choose arrangements that suit best his personality and the subject of his paintings. "As far as we are concerned, we give . . . every one the freedom to follow his pleasure, and don't reject a tulip because it is no rose, neither a rose because it is no lily." To back up his statement he chose as an example the painting that he saw his master paint and that broke the tradition of group portraiture, the *Night Watch*.

Not only the system of cubicles and Hoogstraten's statements, but also the nature of the students' work shows that Rembrandt permitted other styles besides his own. Many of his best students came already formed to his studio, as we have seen, and continued working in another style while with Rembrandt, and also after they had left him. Others employed different styles simultaneously. Govert Flinck's Rembrandtesque drawings (cat. no. 173) are only one phase of his work following and preceding other trends (cat. nos. 171, 172, and 174). A particularly clear example is provided by Gerbrand van den Eeckhout who made drawings in Lastman's style during and after his association with Rembrandt (cat. nos. 164 and 165).

It is difficult to appreciate an artist employing a variety of styles in succession or simultaneoulsy as long as the style of a work of art is considered to express the artist's individuality, and it is equally difficult to associate a disparity of styles with pupils of one artist as long as the term *school* implies the community of styles of a group of disciples of one master. Both the individuality of an artist's style and the homogeneity of the style of a school long have been accepted by art historians as valid concepts. Around the turn of the fifteenth to the sixteenth century, however, a variety of styles was considered a sign of mastery. Carel van Mander wrote about it, and Goltzius and other Mannerists often used different styles for different purposes. This practice was never fully abandoned in the Netherlands, but remained valid in certain circles, particularly in that of Rembrandt and his pupils. In contrast to most Dutch artists who specialized in one subject matter (history, genre, portrait, landscape, etc.) and varied their styles little, Rembrandt's pupils did paint a variety of subjects and used a variety of styles. Whether they preferred this variety because they were less dependent on public demand and less concerned with the consumer, or because they wanted to select the most appropriate style for each subject, is not known, but this application of different styles should be seen in the context of the mannerist tradition rather than as a protest against Rembrandt. Gerbrand van den Eeckhout is, once more, the prime example. His portraits, landscapes, and religious scenes are all sometimes similar to Rembrandt, but in other instances entirely different.

If for this reason alone it is an oversimplification to maintain that Rembrandt's students turned themselves away from him, it becomes a half truth when one considers carefully the *oeuvre* of a number of those artists. In this exhibition Rembrandtesque drawings by Gerbrand van den Eeckhout date from the 1660's (cat. no. 168), and one by Jan Lievens was made in 1665 (cat. no. 203). These are no exceptions: Valentiner convincingly attributed drawings to Ferdinand Bol which are in Rembrandt's style and which were made in the 1650's, more than a decade after he had left Rembrandt's studio. It should be added that this persistence of Rembrandt's style manifests itself particularly in drawings rather than in paintings, and in the case of those artists who treated various subject matter, in religious subjects rather than in landscapes or portraits.

Rembrandt's pupils did go different ways, but this can only be considered a break with Rembrandt if it is assumed that their instruction implied a life long devotion. In that respect they contrast sharply with Rubens's pupils who, with very few exceptions, never escaped his powerful hold. As Edgar Baes formulated it as early as 1882, in spite of the liberalizing effect of the Italian concepts and the ensuing principle of voluntary imitation, they became enslaved by the powerful influence of their master. Rembrandt's instruction as Rubens's opposed the traditional system of apprenticeship which was based on the assumption of continuity of style. In contrast to Rubens, however, Rembrandt was deeply interested in the individual development of each student's talents. That his students went their own way instead of following him meant a success for his instruction rather than a failure.

*E. Haverkamp-Begemann*

BIBLIOGRAPHICAL NOTE

Still basic for our knowledge of Rembrandt's teaching is C. Hofstede de Groot, "Rembrandts onderwijs aan zijne leerlingen," in *Feest-bundel Dr. Abraham Bredius . . .*, Amsterdam 1915, pp. 79–94; since then various essays about the subject have been written of which the following are particularly relevant: the introductions to the catalogue of the exhibitions *Rembrandt's Influence in the 17th Century*, London, the Matthiescn Gallery, 1953, and Raleigh 1956 (see list of abbreviations), respectively by H. Gerson and W. R. Valentiner, and the article by O. Benesch, "Rembrandt's Artistic Heritage," in *Gazette des Beaux-Arts*, VI S., XXXIII, 1948, pp. 281–300. For Academies in general see the fundamental book by Nikolaus Pevsner, *Academies of Art Past and Present*, Cambridge 1940, for that of the Carracci the excellent article by Heinrich Bodmer, "L'Accademia dei Carracci," in *Bologna, Rivista Mensile del Comune*, XXII, no. 8, August 1935, pp. 61–74, and also the more easily accessible recent essay by Milton J. Levine, "The Carracci: A Family Academy," in *Art News Annual*, XXXIII, 1967, pp. 19 ff.; for that of Hendrick Uylenburgh, J. Six, "La Famosa Accademia di Eeulemborg," in *Jaarboek der Kon. Academie van Wetenschappen te Amsterdam 1925/26*, Amsterdam 1926, pp. 229 ff. and H. F. Wijnman, "Rembrandt als huisgenoot van Hendrick Uylenburgh te Amsterdam (1631–1635)," in his *Uit de Kring van Rembrandt en Vondel*, Amsterdam 1959, pp. 1–18. The most recent interpretation of Carel van Mander's "Academy," given by E. K. J. Reznicek, *Die Zeichnungen von Hendrick Goltzius*, Utrecht 1961, pp. 215–220, is also the most cautious one. He also refers to the nude studies of Brentel and to F. G. Pariset, "Les Dessins de Jean-Frédéric Brentel de Strasbourg dans les Pays-Bas, 1634," in *Actes du XVIIme Congrès International de l'Histoire de l'Art 1952*, The Hague 1955, pp. 379–384. A wealth of information on numerous aspects of artistic practice may be found in Ettore Camesasca, *Artisti in Bottega*, Milan 1966.

Since Hofstede de Groot, in his *Die Urkunden über Rembrandt*, The Hague 1906, collected the contemporary sources almost exclusively for the factual information they provide on Rembrandt's life and works, while disregarding their interpretative values, they should be consulted in their contexts in the original editions (or complete reprints of them), and in Seymour Slive's *Rembrandt and his critics*, The Hague 1953. Sandrart's passages of his *Teutsche Academie der Bau- Bild- und Mahlerey-Künste* (1675) quoted or referred to above are to be found in the 1925 edition by A. R. Peltzer on the pp. 173 (Honthorst) and 202–203 (Rembrandt); Hoogstraten's statements in his *Inleyding tot de Hooge Schoole der Schilderkonst*, Rotterdam 1678, pp. 13 (Rembrandt's advice), 26 (position of paper or sketchbook), 176 (freedom of composition and *Night Watch*), 219 (copying); Houbraken's reference to Rembrandt's cubicles in his *De Groote Schouburgh . . .* (1718), in P. T. A. Swillens's edition, vol. I, Maastricht 1943, p. 202.

The first mention of Rembrandt's departure from the guild rules in his teaching and his efforts to ascertain individual instruction was, to my knowledge, G. J. Hoogewerff, *De geschiedenis van de St. Lucasgilden in Nederland*, Amsterdam 1947, pp. 88–90, which provides a useful introduction to the St. Luke's guilds; Benesch (1948, p. 283) mentioned Rembrandt's gifts to develop individual talents and contrasted him in this respect with Rubens. Edgar Baes' astute observation is found in his informative, although disorganized and not entirely reliable article "La Peinture flamande et son enseignement sous le régime des confréries de St-Luc," in the *Mémoires couronnés et Mémoires des savants étrangers, publiés par l'Académie Royale des Sciences, des Lettres et des Beaux-Arts de Belgique*, XLIV, Brussels 1882 (Extrait, p. 153).

I am grateful to J. Richard Judson for his corrections and additions to this essay, particularly with regard to paintings by Rembrandt and his pupils.

# Catalogue of Paintings
## by J. Richard Judson

Rembrandt's Pupils Represented in the Exhibition

### I LEIDEN PERIOD 1625–1631
Jan Lievens
Gerard Dou

### II EARLY AMSTERDAM PERIOD 1632–1642
Jacob Backer
Ferdinand Bol
Govert Flinck
Jan Victors
Philips Koninck
Gerbrand van den Eeckhout
Carel Fabritius

### III MIDDLE AMSTERDAM PERIOD 1642–1653
Abraham Furnerius
Lambert Doomer
Samuel van Hoogstraten
Anthonie van Borssum
Barent Fabritius
Karel van der Pluym
Nicolaes Maes
Constantijn van Renesse
Willem Drost

### IV LATE AMSTERDAM PERIOD 1653–1669
Aert de Gelder
Johannes Leupenius

*All measurements of paintings are in
centimeters; of drawings, in millimeters.
Height always precedes width.
Titles of works shown only in Chicago
are followed by an asterisk.*

# REMBRANDT 1606–1669

J. Orlers, writing in 1641, states that Rembrandt Harmensz van Rijn was born at Leiden on July 15, 1606. His father was the miller Harmen Gerritsz; his mother, Neeltje van Suydtbroeck. The young Rembrandt spent seven years in the Leiden Latin School and at the age of fourteen enrolled in the University where he remained for a short but unknown length of time. Orlers also informs us that Rembrandt first studied in Leiden with Jacob Isaacsz van Swanenburgh for about three years, 1621–23, and then for about six months, in 1624, with Pieter Lastman in Amsterdam. Simon van Leeuwen, writing in 1672, states that Rembrandt studied with Joris van Schooten; and Houbraken, in 1718, wrote that after Rembrandt left Lastman's studio he studied in Amsterdam for some months with Jacob Pynas. During the late 1620's Rembrandt worked very closely with Jan Lievens, and they might even have worked on the same pictures on several occasions. Also, during Rembrandt's late Leiden period, that is, from February 1628 until Rembrandt left for Amsterdam in 1631 or 1632, Gerard Dou studied with him. Rembrandt's earliest dated paintings are from the year 1625 and shortly thereafter he must have started to etch, although the earliest dated etching is from 1628.

We know that Rembrandt was still living in Leiden in June 1631, and it is not until July 1632 that we have the first document telling us that he is in Amsterdam. Because of this, we are not certain when Rembrandt appeared in Amsterdam, but we are sure that he was a success immediately upon his arrival there. Orlers tells us this as does the knowledge of the enthusiastic reception of his 1632 *Anatomy Lesson of Dr. Tulp*. Two years later in 1634 Rembrandt married the daughter of a wealthy and prominent Frisian family, Saskia van Uylenburgh. During the 1630's he was the leading portraitist in Amsterdam, but he also painted a number of important religious pictures, among them the series (6) of Christ's Passion for the Stadtholder, Prince Frederik Hendrik, executed between 1633 and 1639. Beginning in the 1640's his portrait style was not considered fashionable and his commissions declined, but from this time on until his death he created his most brilliant portraits for a select group of connoisseurs like Jan Six. In 1642, he finished the well-received *Night Watch*. His contact with Frederik Hendrik's court in The Hague continued with the completion of two scenes from the life of Christ in 1646. In the 1650's he painted several great portraits, the 1654 *Portrait of Jan Six* and the 1656 *Anatomy Lesson of Dr. Deyman*. In this same year, 1656, he became bankrupt and two years later his personal effects, including his large art collection, were sold at auction. Rembrandt's popularity continued into the 1660's and in 1662 he painted the *Group Portrait of the Cloth Samplers* (Syndics). He also was asked to contribute to the decoration of Amsterdam's new Town Hall and painted the magnificent *Conspiracy of Julius Civilus* which, for reasons still unclear today, was rejected although it was highly praised in a contemporary poem. His final work dates from the year 1669, the unfinished *Simeon in the Temple* which was on his easel at the time of his death on October 4.

I *Self-Portrait*

Rijksmuseum, Amsterdam, loan from Collection Daan Cevat, since 1960

Panel 22.5 × 19 cms. *Ill. p. 88*

PROVENANCE Dr. A. Patterson, Glasgow; J. R. Mackay, Glasgow; Mrs. M. A. Winter, Bearsden, Dunbartonshire; sale London (Sotheby's), 27 May 1959, no. 135 [purchased by D. Cevat].

EXHIBITIONS Delft/Antwerp 1964–65, no. 93 [as Rembrandt]; Leiden, Stedelijk Museum, *Rondom Rembrandt, De verzameling Daan Cevat*, 1968, no. 35, Ill. [as Rembrandt, ca. 1629]; Montreal/Toronto 1969, no. 5 [as Rembrandt, ca. 1628–29].

SELECTED REFERENCES Bauch 1960, p. 174 f., fig. 157 [as a study and used in 1629 Munich *Self-Portrait*, in the 1630 engraved *Self-Portrait* (Münz 1952, I, cat. no. 5, fig. 5) and by J. J. van Vliet in his 1634 engraving]; K. Bauch, "Ein Selbstbildnis des frühen Rembrandt," *Wallraf-Richartz Jahrbuch*, XXIV, 1962, pp. 321, 324 ff. [states that Kassel *Self-Portrait* has no connection with Rembrandt's Leiden style, while Cevat picture is closely bound to master's early period (cf. *Study of an Old Man*, Fogg Art Museum, Cambridge, Mass., on loan from J. P. Warburg, Bauch 1966, no. 114; engraved self-portraits, Munz 1952, I, cat. nos. 5, 9, figs. 5, 9; drawn self-portrait, Benesch I, cat. no. 54, fig. 61); also J. J. van Vliet's 1634 engraving is after Cevat and not Kassel portrait], 328–332, figs. 189–198 [attribution of Kassel portrait to Lievens can be no more than mere assumption]; S. Slive, "The Young Rembrandt," *Allen Memorial Art Museum Bulletin*, Oberlin College, XX, no. 3, 1963, p. 149, note 20 [writes that Cevat version is by a copyist]; Bauch 1966, no. 287 [as ca. 1628]; Rosenberg, Slive, Ter Kuile 1966, p. 267, note 4 [state that Kassel *Self-Portrait* is original and Cevat's is a copy]; F. Erpel, *Die Selbstbildnisse Rembrandt's*, Berlin, 1967, p. 141 f., no. 8, fig. 6 [states that Kassel painting is a copy after Cevat's]; Gerson 1968, p. 489 f., note 30 [writes that Kassel painting is authentic after having seen it and the Cevat picture together in Delft]; Haak 1969, p. 34 f., figs. 42–44 [Cevat's is earliest known self-portrait from ca. 1628; J. J. van Vliet made an etching after this portrait; Kassel painting is a copy of Cevat's which is further strengthened by comparing technique with Munich *Self-Portrait*, signed and dated 1629].

COPIES Formerly Coll. Matvansky, Vienna [see K. Bauch, *Wallraf-Richartz Jahrbuch*, XXIV, 1962, p. 325, fig. 192]; also Sir John Heathcote Amory, Bart., [Bredius. (Gerson), 1969, no. 1, p. 547].

## 2  *Artist in His Studio*

Museum of Fine Arts, Boston, Zoe Oliver Sherman Collection

Panel 25.4 × 31.8 cms. *Ill. p. 89*

PROVENANCE Earl of Morton, Dalmahoy, Kirknewton, Midlothian; Countess of Morton, 1850; Lord Churston; sale Princess Royal & others (Lord Churston), London (Christie's), June 26, 1925, no. 14; with R. Langton Douglas; Zoe Oliver Sherman, Boston; acquired in 1938.

EXHIBITIONS Cambridge, Mass. 1948, no. 2; Rotterdam / Amsterdam 1956, no. 4, ill.; Milwaukee, Art Institute, *An Inaugural Exhibition*, 1957, no. 13, frontispiece; Indianapolis /San Diego 1958, no. 4; Delft /Antwerp 1964–65, no. 94; Tokyo, National Museum of Western Art, Kyoto Municipal Museum, *The Age of Rembrandt*, 1968–69, no. 43, ill.

SELECTED REFERENCES C. Hofstede de Groot, "Rembrandt's Painter in his Studio," *The Burlington Magazine*, XLVII, 1925, p. 265, ill. [cites replica in Coll. W. Chase, N.Y. (ill. in C. Hofstede de Groot 1915, p. 82, fig. 3) states that Douglas version, now Boston, must be an original and figure most likely represents Rembrandt]; C. H. Collins Baker, "Rembrandt's Painter in his Studio," *The Burlington Magazine*, XLVIII, 1926, p. 42 [as by same hand that painted *La Main Chaude*, National Gallery of Ireland, Dublin, here attributed to Gerard Dou; slight falsities of tone are not characteristic of Rembrandt but of Dou; whole plan of painting points to Dou who often places small figures back in his picture, on empty and brightly lit floors; Rembrandt never arranges figures marooned in a flat, evenly lit space but lonely figure is always connected with every part of design by subtle continuity of atmosphere and luminous half-tone]; R. Frey, "Rembrandt's Painter in his Studio," *The Burlington Magazine*, XLVIII, 1926, p. 111 [as Rembrandt forgetting almost entirely the academic ideals of

Lastman]; W. R. Valentiner, "Two Early Self-Portraits by Rembrandt," *Art in America*, XIV, 1926, p. 118 [as self-portrait by Rembrandt]; J. G. van Gelder, "Rembrandt's vroegste ontwikkeling," *Mededelingen der Koninklijke Nederlandse Akademie van Wetenschappen, Afd. Letterkunde*, Amsterdam, XVI, no. 5, 1953, p. 290 f. [as not self-portrait; as 1628 and must be 14 year old Dou]; Bauch 1960, p. 140 f. [as depicting Rembrandt and calls painting *The Easel* of ca. 1628; connects title with emblematic literature *Nulla dies sine linea* ("not a day without its line") published in Justus Reifenberg's *Emblemata Politica*, Amsterdam, 1632, for which illustrations were drawn by 1624]; S. Slive, "Rembrandt's Self-Portrait in a Studio," *The Burlington Magazine*, CVI, 1964, pp. 483 ff. [suggests that strips removed from upper and lower part of panel in 1925 were added by Rembrandt and increased the height by about one-third; states that there is no parallel in Rembrandt's oeuvre for unusual composition with huge dark easel that throws scene out of balance; when upper and lower pieces are added (increases height to about 37 cms.), the relation of artist and furnishings to the size of the interior is compatible with other Rembrandts of the late 1620's; relates Rembrandt's drawing of an *Artist in a Studio*, Coll. F. Springell, Portinscale Keswick, with its high spatial setting to Boston painting before cutting, as did A. M. Hind, "Rembrandt in his Studio," *Old Master Drawings*, I, 1926, p. 9; also cites connections between enlarged Rembrandt and Gerard Dou's studio scenes], 486 [states that it is *Self-Portrait in a Studio* and compares head with drawn *Self-Portrait*, British Museum, London]; Bauch 1966, no. 112 [accepts Slive's interpretation that original was higher and dates it ca. 1628; also restates idea that it has emblematic character]; Gerson 1968, pp. 186, 489, no. 20 [uncertain as to whether it is a self-portrait or a portrait of Dou; not convinced that additions, now cut away, were by Rembrandt]; Haak 1969, p. 36, fig. 46 [some say figure is Dou and others Rembrandt]; Bredius (Gerson) 1969, no. 419, p. 336.

COPY Formerly Coll. W. M. Chase, N.Y. [sale W. M. Chase, New York, (American Art Galleries), May 14–17, 1917, no. 250 (panel 26.7 × 33.6 cms.); A. Ravesteyn, *The Burlington Magazine*, XLVIII, 1926, p. 162 (as a later and inferior copy); S. Slive, *op. cit.* CVI, 1964, 483 f., note 2, for more details].

## 3  *The Tribute Money*

The National Gallery of Canada, Ottawa

Panel 41.4 × 33 cms. signed on cartouche upper right: *RHL 1629 Ill. p. 90*

PROVENANCE with R. Langton Douglas, London; Alfred Beit, London (died in 1906); Sir Otto John Beit (died 1930); Lady Beit, London (died 1946); Sir Alfred Lane Beit, London; with Marlborough Gallery, London, 1966; acquired in 1967.

EXHIBITIONS Cape Town, National Gallery of South Africa, *Old Master Paintings from the Beit Collection, Supplement*, 1950, no. 61; Baltimore, The Baltimore Museum of Art, *From El Greco to Pollock: Early and Late Works by European and American Artists*, 1968, no. 11, ill.

SELECTED REFERENCES Hofstede de Groot, VI, 1916, p. 93, no. 117; W. Weisbach, *Rembrandt*, Berlin, 1926, p. 610 [connects drawing of *Oriental Leaning on a Stick*, Berlin, with Beit picture]; Benesch I, cat. no. 10, fig. 17 [cites drawing of *Oriental Leaning on a Stick*, Print Room, Berlin, as being connected with Ottawa painting]; Sumowski 1957–58, p. 224, fig. 4 [writes that space is important for Rembrandt School, *Presentation in the Temple*, Private Coll., Stuttgart]; Bauch 1966, no. 48; Gerson 1968, pp. 26 [writes that Rembrandt did not exploit dramatic potential of chiaroscuro until 1628–29 in impassioned scenes from life of Christ such as *The Tribute Money* . . .], 182, 489, no. 15 [cites drawing in Berlin as study for one of the figures], ill. on p. 182; Bredius (Gerson), 1969, no. 536, p. 451.

### 4 *Portrait of a Man from the Raman Family, Amsterdam*

Frances and Armand Hammer Purchase Fund, Los Angeles County Museum of Art
Panel, oval 70.2 × 50.5 cms. signed bottom right just above shoulder: *Rembrandt ft 1634* and inscribed just above the left shoulder: *Aet. 47 Ill. p. 91*

PROVENANCE with Kleinberger, Paris; A. de Ridder, Frankfort a./M. [at least by 1910]; sale A. de Ridder, Paris (Galerie Georges Petit), June 2, 1924, no. 55; Ehrich Galleries, New York [at least in 1930–35]; with J. H. Weitzner, N.Y. [at least by 1956]; with P. de Boer, Amsterdam, 1960; H. Kohn, The Hague; acquired in 1969.

EXHIBITIONS Detroit 1930, no. 22, ill. [companion piece, painted in 1636, is in Coll. Lord Kinnaird, Rossie Priory]; The Hague, Mauritshuis, *Tentoonstelling van uit Duitsland teruggekeerde Nederlandsche kunstschatten*, 1946, no. 49; Raleigh 1956, no. 9, ill. [cites Kinnaird picture as a companion piece].

SELECTED REFERENCES Hofstede de Groot, VI, 1916, p. 347, no. 739 [said to be member of Raman family; pendant to Kinnaird portrait]; Br. no. 194 [as pendant to 1634 *Portrait of Young Lady*, Coll. Duke of Sutherland, painting originally comes from Coll. Raman, Amsterdam and sitter very probably was a member of Raman family]; Bauch 1966, no. 374 [as from collection of Raman family, Amsterdam; originally ten-sided; pendant to 1636 Kinnaird portrait]; Gerson 1968, pp. 288, 495, no. 168, ill. on p. 289 [signature is retouched; said to have been in Raman family collections; like supposed Kinnaird pendant, originally ten-sided]. Bredius (Gerson) 1969, no. 194, p. 158 [although the signature is retouched, the attribution to Rembrandt should be sustained].

### 5 *Portrait of a Man*

Earl C. Townsend, Jr., Indianapolis

Panel 77.5 × 64.8 cms. signed to right of lower edge of collar: *Rembrandt fec. 1635 Ill. p. 92*

PROVENANCE Duc de Valentinois, Paris; Count Pourtalès, Paris [at least in 1825]; John Smith, London [sometime between 1825–36]; Lord Ashburton, the Grange [at least by 1836 until 1907]; with A. Sulley & Co., London, 1908–10; with C. Sedelmeyer, Paris, 1911; C. von Hollitscher, Berlin, 1912–22; C. Castiglione, Vienna, 1922–25; sale C. Castiglione (Vienna), Amsterdam, Nov. 17, 1925, no. 71; with Duveen, London, 1925–39; with Duveen Brothers, Inc., N.Y., 1939–59; acquired in 1959.

EXHIBITIONS London, Royal Academy, *Winter Exhibition*, 1890, no. 97; Berlin, *Ausstellung von Werken alter Kunst aus Berliner Privatbesitz*, 1914, no. 129; Philadelphia, *Sesqui-Centennial International Exposition*, 1926; Detroit, Institute of Arts, *Old and Modern Masters*, 1927, no. 46; Detroit 1930, no. 24; Wilmington, Society of Fine Arts, *Masterpieces of Three Centuries*, 1931, no. 30; Amsterdam 1935, no. 6; Grand Rapids, Michigan, Art Gallery, *Masterpieces of Dutch Art*, 1940, no. 64; New York, Duveen Galleries, *Great Dutch Masters*, 1942, no. 43; Chicago 1942, no. 25; Milwaukee, Art Institute, 1943, no. 27; Raleigh 1956, no. 10, ill.; Indianapolis/San Diego 1958, no. 11, ill.; Montreal/Toronto 1969, no. 8, ill.

SELECTED REFERENCES J. Smith, VII, 1836, p. 111, no. 304; Hofstede de Groot, VI, 1916, p. 343 f., no. 730; Bauch, 1966, no. 375 [pendant to 1635 *Portrait of a Young Woman*, Museum of Art, Cleveland (Bauch 1966, no. 485)]; Gerson 1968, pp. 294, 495, no. 180, ill. on p. 295; Bredius (Gerson) 1969, no. 201, p. 164 [as probably pendant to *Portrait of a Lady with Lace-Collar*, Coll. Mrs. F. F. Prentiss, Cleveland, Bredius (Gerson) 1969, no. 350, p. 274.]

6  *Self-Portrait Ill. p. 93*

Norton Simon Foundation, Fullerton, California

Panel 63.3 × 50.6 cms. signed right lower center: *Rembrandt F / 163.* (date has been read as 1633, 1635, or 1638)

PROVENANCE Sale Earl of Portarlington, London (Christie's), 28 June 1879, no. 89 (bought A. Levy); sale Albert Levy, London (Christie's), 3 May 1884, no. 56; with Colnaghi, London; Arthur Pemberton Heywood-Lonsdale, Shavington, Shropshire, before 1890; sale Arthur Heywood-Lonsdale (grandson), London (Christie's), 27 June 1969, no. 70 (bought by Robert Light for Norton Simon, Inc. Museum of Art).

EXHIBITIONS London, Royal Academy, 1878, no. 98; London, Royal Academy, 1890, no. 61; London 1899, no. 64; London, Burlington Fine Arts Club, 1936–37, no. 67; London, Royal Academy, *17th Century Art in Europe*, 1938, no. 121; Edinburgh, National Gallery of Scotland, *Rembrandt*, 1950, no. 9; Amsterdam, Rijksmuseum, *Drie Eeuwen Portret in Nederland*, 1952, no. 141; London 1952–53, no. 177.

SELECTED REFERENCES Hofstede de Groot, VI, 1916, p. 282 f., no. 576; J. G. van Gelder, *The Burlington Magazine*, XCII, 1950, p. 327 f. [dates 1638/9, and mentions engraving by J. B. Le Sueur, supposedly after a portrait by Flinck of 1636]; H. van Hall, *Portretten van Nederlandse Beeldende Kunstenaars*, 1963, p. 268, no. 51 [old replica of 1635 in sale R. Lepke, Berlin, 5 May 1914, no. 62, ill; copy of 1634 in sale H. O. Havemeyer Collection, New York (American Art Association Anderson Galleries), 10.4.1930, no. 102, ill]; Bauch 1966, no. 313 [dates about 1639]; Gerson 1968, no. 229 [probably dates about 1638]; Bredius (Gerson) 1969, no. 32, p. 28.

7  *Visitation*

The Detroit Institute of Arts

Panel 56.5 × 48.1 cms. signed bottom center on lowest step: *Rembrandt 1640 Ill. p. 94*

PROVENANCE King of Sardinia; Prince Eugène of Savoy, Vienna, no. 122; imported into England by Nieuwenhuys about 1807; purchased by Marquis of Westminster, 1812;

Marquis, later Duke, of Westminster, at least until 1899; Alfred de Rothschild, Halton Manor; with M. Knoedler & Co.; acquired in 1927.

EXHIBITIONS London, British Institution, 1834, no. 114; London, Royal Academy, *Winter Exhibition*, 1870, no. 36; London, Royal Academy, *Winter Exhibition*, 1895, no. 88; Amsterdam, Stedelijk Museum, *Rembrandt, Schilderijen bijeengebracht ter gelegenheid van de inhuldiging van Hare Majesteit Koningin Wilhelmina*, 1898, no. 45; London 1899, no. 52; New York 1925, no. 4; Detroit 1930, no. 30, ill.; Los Angeles 1947, no. 16; Cambridge, Mass. 1948, no. 5; New York/Toledo/Toronto 1954–55, no. 62, ill.; Raleigh 1956, no. 13, ill.; Raleigh, North Carolina Museum of Art, *Masterpieces of Art*, 1959, p. 284, no. LII, ill.

SELECTED REFERENCES J. Smith, VII, 1836, p. 22 f., no. 57; Hofstede de Groot, VI, 1916, p. 63, no. 74; J. Bruyn, *Rembrandt's keuze van Bijbelse onderwerpen*, Utrecht, 1959, p. 9 [as unique subject for Rembrandt]; Bauch 1966, no. 70; Gerson 1968, p. 312 f., no. 203, ill. [inspiration is probably Dürer's print while setting is derived from Lastman]; Haak 1969, p. 264 f., ill. [as going back to Dürer woodcut of ca. 1504; here Rembrandt's version follows very closely Luke I: 39–40]; Bredius (Gerson), 1969, no. 562, p. 476.

ENGRAVING J. Burnet, 1813

ETCHING P. J. Arendzen, 1899

8  *Young Girl at an Open Half-Door*

The Art Institute of Chicago, Mr. and Mrs. Martin A. Ryerson Collection

Canvas 102 × 84.2 cms. signed bottom center: *Rembrandt f. 1645 Ill. p. 95*

PROVENANCE sale De Gueffier, Paris (Paillet), 1 March 1791, no. 67; sale Robit, Paris (Paillet and Delaroche), 11 May 1801, no. 120 [purchased by Michael Bryan for George Hibbert]; sale George Hibbert, London (Christie's), 13 June 1829, no. 68; Nathaniel Hibbert, London [as late as 1857]; sale Prince Paul Demidoff, Florence (Palazzo San Donato), 15–17 March 1880, no. 1114 [bought in and transferred to Villa Demidoff, Pratolino]; purchased from Princess Demidoff, Pratolino, by Martin A. Ryerson, 1890; given by latter to Art Institute in 1894.

EXHIBITIONS London, British Institution, 1818, no. 100; London, British Institution, 1844, no. 23; London, British Institution, 1857, no. 87; Chicago, The Art Institute of

Chicago, *Old Dutch Masters and other Pictures*, 1890, no. 5; Chicago, The Art Institute of Chicago, *Paintings, Sculptures and other Objects Exhibited during The World's Congresses*, 1893, no. 5; New York 1909, no. 91, ill.; Detroit 1930, no. 42, ill.; Chicago, The Art Institute of Chicago, *A Century of Progress. Exhibition of Paintings and Sculpture, Lent from American Collections*, 1933, no. 75, ill.; Chicago, The Art Institute of Chicago, *A Century of Progress Exhibition of Paintings and Sculpture*, 1934, no. 107; Amsterdam 1935, no. 12; Chicago 1935–36, no. 4, ill. p. 60; Worcester 1936, no. 4, ill. p. 58; Chicago 1942, no. 27, ill.; Philadelphia, Museum of Art, *Diamond Jubilee Exhibition. Masterpieces of Painting*, 1950–51, no. 37, ill.; New York /Toledo / Toronto 1954–55, no. 63, ill.

SELECTED REFERENCES J. Smith, VII, 1836, p. 170, no. 532; K. Cox, "Art in America. Dutch Paintings in the Hudson-Fullton Exhibition, I," *The Burlington Magazine*, XVI, 1909–10, pp. 178, 184 [finest Rembrandt in exhibition; modelling and facial expression are as subtle as Leonardo]; Hofstede de Groot, VI, 1916, p. 187 f., no. 324 [cites copy in sale W. R. Williams & others, London, 28 Nov. 1903, sold to Dowdeswell]; Van Dyke 1923, p. 160, fig. 145 [as unknown Rembrandt pupil group III; another version with Durand-Ruel, Paris]; D. C. Rich, "The Paintings of Martin A. Ryerson," *Bulletin of The Art Institute of Chicago*, XXVII, no. 1, 1933, p. 12, ill. on cover [as Hendrickje Stoffels]; Chicago 1961, p. 366, ill. p. 185 [as possibly Hendrickje Stoffels; attribution to Nicolaes Maes has been suggested; wears costume of Municipal Orphanage, Amsterdam]; Rosenberg 1964, p. 91, fig. 78 [represents same girl as Dulwich portrait (fig. 77), also dated 1645 and Madonna in Leningrad *Holy Family* (fig. 165) as well as two studies (figs. 79 and 163)]; H. F. Wijnman, "Aantekeningen" in Christopher White, *Biografieën in woord en beeld. Rembrandt*, translated by J. M. Komter, The Hague, 1964, p. 151 [as *Portrait of Geertge Dircks* and wearing costume from her home province, North-Holland]; Bauch 1966, no. 507 [as Geertge Dircks (?)]; Rosenberg, Slive, Ter Kuile 1966, p. 97 [as source for Maes' 1653 *Girl Leaning on a Window Sill*, Rijksmuseum, Amsterdam]; Gerson 1968, p. 342, fig. 248; Bredius (Gerson) 1969, no. 367, p. 288 [possibly by pupil Jan Victors].

ENGRAVING F. C. G. Geyser

COPIES Sale Seger Tierens, The Hague, 23 July no. 224 [ca. 76.2 × 66 cms.]; sale Sir W. R. Williams, Bart., London (Christie's), 28 Nov. 1903, no. 61 [bought by Dowdeswell]; probably 19th–century copy, National Gallery, Prague; with Durand-Ruel, Paris.

## 9 *Winter Landscape*

Staatliche Kunstsammlungen, Kassel

Panel 16.7 × 22.4 cms. signed bottom left: *Rembrandt f. 1646 Ill. p. 96*

PROVENANCE Probably acquired in 1749 for Landgrave Wilhelm VIII of Hesse [inventory of 1749, no. 768]; Musée Napoleon, Paris, 1807–15.

EXHIBITIONS Schaffhausen, Museum zu Allerheiligen, *Rembrandt und seine Zeit*, 1949, no. 132 [as related to pen and wash drawing in Coll. C. Hofstede de Groot]; Paris, Orangerie, *Le paysage hollandais au XVIIe siècle*, 1950, no. 67, pl. 2; Milan 1954, no. 117, ill.

SELECTED REFERENCES J. Smith, VII, 1836, p. 193, no. 609 [as signed and dated 1636 and now in Public Gallery at Hesse, Kassel]; Hofstede de Groot, VI, 1916, p. 430 f., no. 943 [as signed and dated 1646]; R. Hamann, *Rembrandt*, Berlin, 1948, p. 295, figs. 200, 201 [as an exception in 1640's when realistic landscapes were not painted in Holland; compares Kassel painting with drawings that are even more realistic and without sentimentality and pathos of paintings]; Vogel 1958, p. 120 f., no. 241 [cites pen and wash drawing in Print Room, Rijksmuseum, Amsterdam, has similar motif, but not directly related to painting (Henkel 1942, no. 73, pl. 56)]; Rosenberg, Slive, Ter Kuile 1966, p. 60, fig. 38B [contains spontaneity and freshness of etchings and drawings after nature; seems to be direct study of the effects of cold air and winter light; it is exception for Rembrandt as his few known landscape paintings are imaginary with a visionary character]; Stechow 1966, pp. 87 [writes that Esaias van de Velde's *Winter Landscape*, formerly Mansi Coll., Lucca, really feels like winter and that this impression has been vastly enhanced by the free brush as well as the great economy in the coloristic structure; we are very close to Rembrandt's masterpiece of 1646], 90 ff. [Isaak van Ostade's winter landscapes contain reliable dates for years between 1642–47, and there is no reason to assume he painted such scenes at an earlier or later date; some of these Van Ostade scenes are done on a small panel, painted with a quick brush in a sketchy style—one of these is in Berlin (no. 1709) and is very close to Rembrandt's; Rembrandt's is exceptional within history of winter landscapes; one has the impression that the Kassel picture was made on the spot as Rembrandt did with his drawings and an occasional etching; no Rembrandt drawings can be seen as preliminary sketch for Kassel painting]; Bauch 1966, no. 552; Gerson 1968, p. 352, no. 267, ill. p. 352 [as painted fluently and quickly like a sketch; signature is so pressed into wet paint that it can be read in x-rays which is very rare]; Haak 1969, p. 199, fig. 325 [no drawing can be brought into direct relation with Kassel painting, and it could have been painted out-of-doors; winter landscapes were always a popular subject in Dutch painting and Rembrandt's vision is most related to the much earlier works of Esais van de Velde which have same simple directness]; Bredius (Gerson), 1969, no. 452, p. 360.

ETCHING W. Unger

10 *Portrait of Hendrickje Stoffels*

Mr. and Mrs. Norton Simon, Los Angeles

Canvas 66 × 54 cms.                    Frontispiece

PROVENANCE Galerie-Inspektor Pechwell; sale H. W. Campe, Leipzig, 24 Sept. 1827; sale Berlin (Lepke), 18 May 1897, no. 129; Von Gelder, Dresden, 1910; sale O. Huldschinsky, Berlin, 10 May 1928, no. 24; Lord Melchett of Landford, Romney, Hampshire [by 1929]; with Duveen, N.Y. [by 1935].

EXHIBITIONS Berlin, Königlichen Kunst-Akademie, *Ausstellung von Bildnissen des fünfzehnten bis achtzehnten Jahrhunderts*, 1909, no. 108; London 1929, no. 104 [Coll. Lord Melchett]; Amsterdam 1935, no. 18; Toronto, Art Gallery, *Catalogue of Exhibitions, Sixteenth and Seventeenth Century Paintings by European Masters . . . Paintings by Nineteenth-Century French Artists*, 1936, no. 13 [lent by Duveen]; Toledo, Museum of Art, *Artists Unappreciated in their Day*, 1939, no. 1, ill.; Chicago 1942, no. 28; Los Angeles 1947, no. XXII, ill.

SELECTED REFERENCES W. Bode, "Neuentdeckte Bilder von Rembrandt," *Zeitschrift für bildende Kunst*, XXI, 1910, p. 8 [as recalling, in type, costume and execution, the known portraits of Hendrickje Stoffels whom this must represent; it dates from ca. 1654]; Hofstede de Groot, VI, 1916, p. 338, no. 717 [as ca. 1660]; Bauch 1966, no. 513 [as ca. 1654]; Gerson 1968, p. 392, no. 318, ill. p. 318; Bredius (Gerson) 1969, no. 112, p. 100.

11 *Christ and the Woman of Samaria*

The Metropolitan Museum of Art, Bequest of Lillian S. Timken, 1959

Panel 63.5 × 48.9 cms. signed bottom center on stone to right of Christ's foot: *Rembrandt f. 1655 Ill. p. 97*

PROVENANCE sale H. Reydon & others, Amsterdam, 5 April 1827, no. 130 [bought by Brondgeest, 55.9 × 45.7 cms.]; Sheepshanks, Harrogate [at least by 1906]; with R. Langton Douglas, London; with M. Knoedler & Co., London; Marcus Kappel, Berlin [by 1914]; with Van Diemen & Co., Amsterdam; with M. Knoedler & Co., London; Mr. & Mrs. W. R. Timken, N.Y. [by 1930]; acquired in 1959.

EXHIBITIONS Leeds, 1889; Leiden, *Fêtes de Rembrandt, Catalogue de l'Exposition de Tableaux et de Dessins de Rembrandt et d'autres Maîtres de Leyde, du dix-septième siècle*, 1906, no. 47 [as in Coll. Sheepshanks]; Detroit 1930, no. 54, ill.; Amsterdam 1932, no. 30, fig. 30; Los Angeles 1947, no. XXIV, ill.; New York, Wildenstein, *Loan Exhibition of Paintings and Drawings–Masterpieces*, 1961, no. 18.

SELECTED REFERENCES Hofstede de Groot, VI, 1916, p. 80 f., no. 101; E. Redslob, "Ein Kupferstich nach Michelangelo als vorbild für Rembrandt," *Berliner Museen, Berichte aus den ehem. Preussischen Kunstsammlungen*, VI, 1956, p. 18 f., fig. 4 [there is a recognizable connection with Michelangelo's Samaritan woman, known in print by Nicolaus Beatrizet after Michelangelo's drawing]; Sumowski VII, 1957–58, p. 231 [as a pupil's work]; Rosenberg 1964, p. 231, fig. 263 [accepts as Rembrandt and dates painting 1655, remarks on technique characteristic of late style]; Bauch 1966, no. 87 [original was much lower as Rembrandt added the tower later]; Gerson 1968, pp. 108 ff. [as Rembrandt's painting that most clearly embodies the Venetian spirit], 362, no. 273, ill. p. 362; Bredius (Gerson) 1969, no. 589, p. 496.

12 *Portrait of a Young Man*

Wadsworth Atheneum, Hartford, The Ella Gallup Sumner and Mary Catlin Sumner Collection

Canvas 97 × 83.8 cms. signed bottom right: *Rembrandt / 1655* (badly abraded) *Ill. p. 98*

PROVENANCE Frederick Hawker; Trevor Lawther Broderick; sale, London (Sotheby's), 11 June 1947, no. 20, ill.; with Duits, Ltd., London; with Koetser, N.Y.; acquired in 1954.

EXHIBITIONS London, Royal Academy, *Winter Exhibition*, 1910, no. 125; Raleigh 1956, p. 22 [as most outstanding of numerous Titus portraits, where Rembrandt, for the first time, seems to have discovered the poetic charm of youth], no. 27, ill.; New York, M. Knoedler & Co., *Masterpieces from Wadsworth Atheneum, Hartford, Conn.*, 1958.

SELECTED REFERENCES C. C. Cunningham, "A Portrait by Rembrandt," *Wadsworth Atheneum Bulletin*, LVI, April 1955, p. 1 f., ill. [right hand is in similar position to *Portrait of a Young Man*, City Art Museum, St. Louis; Hartford painting suggests comparison, stylistically, to *Man with the Long Stick*, Louvre, and *Man with Pearls in his Cap*, Copenhagen]; W. R. Valentiner, "A Portrait by Rembrandt in the Wadsworth Atheneum," *Art Quarterly*, XVIII, 1955, pp. 215 [should be compared with Mendelsohn *Self-Portrait*, where head is placed in similar manner high up in compositional space, motif of collar is similar and large velvet cap also enframes head; suggests Titus as model although it is difficult to believe sitter is only fifteen, if 1655 date is right], 217 [as wearing same costume often used by Rembrandt in his self-portraits], 219, ill. p. 216 [as placing model into Rembrandt's new sense for classical beauty]; E. H. Turner–B. B. Turner, *Handbook-Wadsworth Atheneum*, Hartford, 1958, ill. opp. p. 77 [unlikely *Portrait of Titus*]; Bauch 1966, no. 413 [*Titus van Rijn* (?), 1655 (?); attribution has been doubted several times].

## 13 *Portrait of a Man with Arms Akimbo*

Columbia University, Gift of Huntington Hartford

Canvas 165.7 × 87.6 cms. signed bottom-left corner: *Rembrandt f. 1658 Ill. p. 100*

PROVENANCE G. Folliott, Vicars Cross, Chester [by 1847] and after his death in 1851 remained in family gallery until 1930; sale Folliott, London (Sotheby's), 14 May 1930, no. 51; with Asscher & Welker, London, 1930; Howard Young Galleries, N.Y.; Huntington Hartford, Los Angeles.

EXHIBITIONS London, British Institution, 1847, no. 43 [as *Dutch Admiral*, Coll. G. Folliott]; New York, World's Fair, *Masterpieces of Art*, 1939, no. 304; Los Angeles 1947, no. XXVIII, ill]; Raleigh 1956, no. 9, ill. [as owned by Columbia University and Huntingford Hartford, N.Y.]; Milwaukee, Art Institute, *Inaugural Exhibition*, 1957, no. 17, ill.

SELECTED REFERENCES Hofstede de Groot, VI, 1916, p. 381, no. 827a [as a *Dutch Admiral* and not known to writer]; T. Borenius, "The New Rembrandt," *The Burlington Magazine*, LVII, 1930, pp. 53–59, ill. [pictorially it has affinities with Rembrandt's *Titus*, Louvre, and portrait, formerly Coll. M. Kann; however, in its simple and effective monumentality, it stands apart from those cited and raises question of Rembrandt's relations to Italy; suggests possible recollection of Raphael's *Portrait of Castiglione* in silhouette and headpiece; way of composing light mass of right hand grasping belt and in transparent shadow presents a parallel to Titian's *Laura de' Dianti*, Coll. Cook, Richmond]; W. R. Valentiner, "Rediscovered Rembrandt Paintings," *The Burlington Magazine* LVII, 1930, p. 260 [composition and pose are similar to Vienna *Self-Portrait*, but technique is broader and form simpler like 1658 Frick *Self-Portrait*]; Bauch 1966, no. 421; Gerson 1968, pp. 406, 501. no. 342, ill. p. 406; Bredius (Gerson) 1969, no. 290, p. 222.

John Maxon points out an even more striking parallel to Titian's work may be noticed in the Venetian master's portrait of Fabrizio Salvaresio in Vienna, which was in Vienna by 1659 and seems to have been known to Teniers before then, in Brussels, for the plates for the *Theatrum pictorium* were circulated in proof form by 1658, the year of this picture.

## 14 *Old Man with Mantle and Beret*

Mr. and Mrs. Nathan R. Allen

Canvas 82.5 × 64.5 cms. *Ill. p. 99*

PROVENANCE with L. Lesser, London; C. A. Waltner, Paris; W. A. Slater, Norwich, Conn.; on loan to Museum of Fine Arts, Boston, 1889 and to Corcoran Gallery, Washington, D.C., at least in 1916; with M. Knoedler & Co., N.Y.; Nathan R. Allen, Sr., Kenosha, Wis.

EXHIBITIONS New York 1909, no. 100, ill. opp. p. 101; Detroit 1930, no. 56, ill.

SELECTED REFERENCES Hofstede de Groot, VI, 1916, p. 234 f., no. 454 [as ca. 1654]; Bauch 1966, no. 220 [as Coll. Whitacker, Kenosha (Chicago) and painted ca. 1657 or somewhat earlier]; Gerson 1968, p. 400, no. 333, ill. p. 401 [as in Coll. R. Whitacker, Kenosha, Wisconsin]; Bredius (Gerson), 1969, no. 282, p. 216.

## 15 *Portrait of Titus*

The Baltimore Museum of Art, The Mary F. Jacobs Collection

Canvas 81.3 × 68.6 cms. signed on back of chair to right of center: *Rembrandt f. 1660 Ill. p. 101*

PROVENANCE Duke of Rutland, Belvoir Castle [at least since 1836]; with Duveen, London; with Krämer, Paris; with Gimpel and Wildenstein, Paris [at least by 1916]; James Stillman, N.Y.; C. C. Stillman, N.Y.; on loan to Metropolitan Museum of Art, N.Y., 1921–26; sale Stillman, N.Y.

(American Art Galleries), 3 Feb. 1927, no. 25; H. B. Jacobs, Baltimore [at least by 1937]; presented to museum by Mary Frick Jacobs.

EXHIBITIONS London 1899, no. 97; New York, Wildenstein, *Rembrandt 1606–1669*, 1950, no. 21, pl. XVIII; Wilmington, Society of Fine Arts, 1951; Baltimore Museum of Art, *Man and his Years*, 1954, no. 82, ill. p. 15; Montreal /Toronto 1969, no. 15, ill.

SELECTED REFERENCES J. Smith, VII, 1836, p. 133, no. 379 [as in Coll. Duke of Rutland, Belvoir]; Hofstede de Groot, VI, 1916, p. 334 f., no. 707 [as signed and dated 1660; with Gimpel and Wildenstein, Paris; cites drawn copy by Mathys van den Berghe in Print Room, Berlin]; Rosenberg 1964, pp. 103–04, 349 (footnote 22), fig. 91 [composition well documented by Mathys van den Berghe pen drawing, signed and dated 1682]; Bauch 1966, no. 430; Bredius (Gerson), 1969, no. 124, p. 112. [notes *pentimenti*, and comments that due to overpainting and restoration, definitive judgment impossible].

The head and hands are very strongly brushed in and typical of Rembrandt's work around 1660. Upon close examination of the painting, *pentimenti* become obvious. Rembrandt changed the position of the thumb several times and corrected the outline of the top of the hat and along the shoulders.

COPY Mathys van den Berghe, Print Room, Berlin, no. 524, drawing: pen brown ink, white highlights, 252 × 199 mm. [Bock and Rosenberg 1930, p. 82, no. 524 (as after Rembrandt's painting in Belvoir Castle)].

## 16 *Titus*

The Detroit Institute of Arts, Bequest of Mr. and Mrs. Lawrence P. Fisher

Panel 40.6 × 34.6 cms. *Ill. p. 102*

PROVENANCE possibly painting in sale, Amsterdam, 15 April 1739, no. 25; possibly painting in sale J. H. Molkenboer, Amsterdam, 6 September 1853, no. 18 [bought by Van Houten]; M. Lermoyez, Paris; M. L . . . , J. L . . . and C. L. . . . Paris; L. P. Fisher, Detroit [at least by 1930]; given by Dollie May Fisher in 1969.

EXHIBITIONS Detroit 1930, no. 57, ill. [as *Titus*, ca. 1655–56]; New York, World's Fair, *Masterpieces of Art*, 1939, no. 303 [as *Titus*, ca. 1655–56].

SELECTED REFERENCES W. R. Valentiner 1921, pp. XXII, 80, ill. [suggests that it could be painting in sales cited above

(1739, 1853); says it could be Titus as Mars or Alexander and dates it ca. 1655–56; perhaps hung together with Alexander that Rembrandt exported to Don Antonio Ruffo, Messina]; Br. no. 125 [as *Titus* and asks if it is identical with Hofstede de Groot, VI, 1916, nos. 787h, 827c]; Bauch 1966, no. 230 [as *An Angel* and painted ca. 1660; cites Sumowski who suggests that perhaps it is study for angel; cf. angel in *St. Matthew and the Angel*, Louvre, Paris, 1661]; Bredius (Gerson) 1969, no. 125, p. 113.

## 17 *Portrait of a Young Man*

George Eastman Collection of the University of Rochester

Canvas 92.7 × 82.5 cms. *Ill. p. 103*

PROVENANCE Lord Carrington, Wycombe Abbey, 1836–95; C. J. Wertheimer, London, 1895; A. Beit, London; O. Beit, London; with M. Knoedler & Co., N.Y.; George Eastman, Rochester, N.Y., 1914; transferred from Eastman House to Memorial Art Gallery in 1969.

EXHIBITIONS London 1899, no. 59.

SELECTED REFERENCES J. Smith, Supplement IX, 1842, no. 28; Hofstede de Groot, VI, 1916, p. 365, no. 782 [as painted about 1660]; Bauch 1966, no. 433 [as signed *Rembrandt f. 1660*]; Gerson 1968, p. 438, no. 394, ill. p. 439 [as signed *Rembrandt f. 1660*]; Bredius (Gerson) 1969, no. 299, p. 229. The painting has recently been cleaned and relined after its recovery from theft in 1967.

## 18 *Christ*

Mr. and Mrs. Harry G. John, Milwaukee

Panel 62 × 49 cms. *Ill. p. 106*

PROVENANCE with E. Plietzsch, Berlin, 1920; Lord Melchett, Melchett Court, Romney, Hampshire; with Duveen Brothers, N.Y. [at least by 1935].

EXHIBITIONS Cambridge, Mass., Fogg Art Museum, *Seventeenth-Century Dutch Art*, 1927; Northampton, Mass., Smith College Museum of Art, *Exhibition of Old Masters*, 1928; Washington, D.C., Phillips Memorial Gallery, *Catalogue of Educational Loan Exhibition*, 1941, no. 50; Montreal, Art Association, *Catalogue of Loan Exhibition of Great Paintings, Five Centuries of Dutch Art*, 1944, p. 33, no. 50; Los Angeles 1947, p. 70, no. XX, ill. [as ca. 1650; another, similar representation of Christ is in Metropolitan Museum of Art, N.Y. (Fletcher bequest); type of Christ should be compared with that of *Lamentation*, Ringling Coll., 1650 (see cat. no. 23) and not model used by Rembrandt ca. 1660].

SELECTED REFERENCES C. Hofstede de Groot, *Die holländische Kritik der jetzigen Rembrandtforschung*, Stuttgart, 1922, p. 41 [gives painting to Rembrandt for first time]; Bauch, 1966, no. 228 [not seen but probably ca. 1660–61]; Gerson 1968, pp. 432, 503, no. 378, ill. p. 433 [as not known to Bauch or me]; Bredius (Gerson) 1969, no. 627, p. 528.

## 19 *Old Man Praying**

The Cleveland Museum of Art, Purchase, Leonard C. Hanna, Jr., Bequest

Canvas 87.6 × 72.4 cms. signed middle-right side: *Rembrandt* [t]. *F166*[?] *Ill. p. 105*

PROVENANCE Castle Rohrau; Count Harrach, Vienna [by 1897]; Harrach Gallery from sometime prior to 1904 until 1939; Mrs. C. Barreiss, Zürich; on loan to Alte Pinakothek, Munich, 1963; sale C. Barreiss, London (Sotheby's), 24 June 1964, no. 5, ill.; acquired in 1967.

EXHIBITIONS Schaffhausen, Museum zu Allerheiligen, *Rembrandt und Seine Zeit*, 1949, no. 141; Schaffhausen, Museum zu Allerheiligen, *Thirty-one Paintings of the 15th–18th Centuries from a Private Collection*, 1952, no. 22, ill.; Rotterdam / Amsterdam 1956, no. 89.

SELECTED REFERENCES Hofstede de Groot, VI, 1916, p. 131, no. 194 [as *The Old Man Praying*]; H. Ritsch, *Katalog der Erlaucht Graeflich Harrachsen Gemälde—Galerie in Wien*, Vienna, 1926, p. 110 f., no. 218, ill.; F. Grossmann, "The Rembrandt Exhibition of Schaffhausen," *The Burlington Magazine*, XCII, 1950, p. 11 [as an Apostle belonging to series painted in 1661]; W. R. Valentiner, "The Rembrandt Exhibitions in Holland, 1956," *The Art Quarterly*, XIX, 1956, p. 400, fig. 1 [as part of Apostle series undoubtedly ordered by some religious organization—perhaps for one of hidden Mennonite churches]; Bauch 1966, no. 234 [as *Praying Apostle*, 1661 and perhaps part of a second apostle group (Bauch 1966, nos. 235, 236, 241, 338)]; S. Lee, "Old Man Praying," *The Bulletin of the Cleveland Museum of Art*, LIV, 1967, pp. 295 ff. [states that originally picture was slightly larger on all four sides; dates clearly from same time as 1661 *St. Matthew with the Angel*, Louvre, because of similarity of technique, appearance, subject and mood], 298 f. [writes that of eight Apostle pictures from or attributable to 1661, four, including Cleveland painting, have roughly comparable dimensions; the Cleveland figure, surely identifiable, though through instinct figure suggests rude fisher-

man, Andrew; cites symbolic relationship between *Old Man Praying* and St. Peter in Raphael's cartoon of *The Miraculous Draught of Fishes*, Victoria and Albert Museum, London], 300 f., ill.; Gerson 1968, pp. 426, 502, no. 365, ill. p. 427 [states that remains of another signature is visible on upper edge of book?; "my reservations about the place of this painting in the late group of Apostles and its attribution to Rembrandt in the first place have not altogether vanished; there is a kind of looseness of surface execution that I have not observed in other Rembrandt works"]; Haak 1969, p. 299, fig. 502 [as *Praying Apostle*, similar in size to several others painted at this time but probably not part of a commissioned series; states that various parts of these pictures are of unequal quality and possibly Rembrandt let a pupil help him (Aert de Gelder ? Titus ?)]; Bredius (Gerson) 1969, no. 616, p. 519 [as *Praying Apostle*].

## 20 *Saint James*

Private Collection

Canvas 94 × 80 cms. signed lower right side: *Rembrandt f. 1661 Ill. p. 104*

PROVENANCE possibly from sale Heirs of Caspar Netscher, A. Schouman and others, The Hague, 15 July 1749, no. 122; MacKenzie, Kintore; Sir Charles J. Robinson, London; E. F. Weber, Hamburg (1891–95); with Sedelmeyer, Paris 1895; Maurice Kann, Paris; with Duveen, New York, Paris; with Henry Reinhardt, New York; John N. Willys, Toledo, Ohio [at least by 1930]; Mrs. I. van Wie Willys, New York (sale Parke-Bernet Gall., New York, 25 October 1945, no. 16, ill.), bought by William Samuel Rosenberg (Billy Rose), New York; Stephen C. Clark, New York, bequeathed to present owners.

EXHIBITIONS Toledo, Museum of Art, *Paintings of the Early English and Dutch Schools, loaned by John North Willys*, 1913, no. 84; Detroit 1930, no. 67, ill.; New York, World's Fair, *Masterpieces of Art*, 1939, no. 309, pl. 69; New York, Wildenstein & Co., *Rembrandt*, 1950, no. 24, pl. XXI; New York, M. Knoedler & Co., *A Collector's Taste* (Stephen C. Clark), 1954, no. 4, pl. 4; New York, The Parke-Bernet Gall., *Art Treasures Exhibition*, 1955, no. 340, ill.

SELECTED REFERENCES C. Woermann, "Meisterwerke Niederländischer Malerei," *Die Graphischen Künste*, XIV, 1891, p. 32 [as *The Praying Pilgrim* or *Saint James*]; *Zeitschrift für Bildende Kunst*, 1892, p. 168 [part of a series of monks painted around 1661] and etching by Albert Kruger facing p. 152; Hofstede de Groot, VI, 1916, p. 121, no. 170; W. R.

Valentiner, "Die Vier Evangelisten Rembrandts," *Kunstchronik und Kunstmarket*, 1920, no. 12, p. 221 [thinks that Saint James may be part of an altarpiece, perhaps commissioned by a church, and representing the Four Evangelists with Jesus and Mary in their middle, surrounded by half-lengths of apostles and monks; points at several pictures dated around 1661, as possible parts of this altarpiece]; Bauch 1966, no. 236 [perhaps it belongs to second series of half-length Apostles (including cat. no. 19)]; Gerson 1968, p. 424, no. 361 ill.; Bredius (Gerson) 1969, no. 617, p. 521.

ETCHING Albert Kruger

## 21 *Lucretia*

The Minneapolis Institute of Arts *Ill. p. 107*

Canvas 105 × 92 cms. signed bottom left *Rembrandt f 1666*

PROVENANCE Radziwill Collection (according to Hofstede de Groot, VI, 1916, no. 220a); sale John Calvert Wombwell, London (Christie's), 4 June 1853, no. 8 (bought by Burdon); sale William W. Burdon, Newcastle-on-Tyne, London (Christie's) 28 June 1862, no. 137 (bought in); J. Purvis Carter, London and Villa Torrigiani, Quinto, Florence (after 1877); with Reinhardt, New York (ca. 1926); sold to Herschel V. Jones, Minneapolis, ca. 1927; acquired in 1934.

EXHIBITIONS Detroit 1930, no. 77, ill; Chicago 1935–36, no. 8, ill; Worcester 1936, no. 10, ill.; Cleveland, Museum of Art, *The Twentieth Anniversary Exhibition*, 1936, no. 178; Chicago 1942, no. 34, ill.; St. Louis, City Art Museum, *Forty Masterpieces*, 1947, p. 98, ill.; Los Angeles 1947, no. XXXI, ill. [cites Shakespeare's poem *The Rape of Lucretia*, published in 1594]; Buffalo, N.Y., Albright Art Gallery, *Painters' Painters*, 1954, no. 9, ill.; Minneapolis, Institute of Arts, *Fortieth Anniversary Exhibition*, 1955, no. 8; Rotterdam/Amsterdam 1956, no. 98; New York, M. Knoedler & Co., *Paintings and Sculpture from the Minneapolis Institute of Arts*, 1957, no. 4, ill.

SELECTED REFERENCES Hofstede de Groot, VI, 1916, p. 144, nos. 220 and 220 A; F. E. Wasburn Freund, "Vom Amerikanischen Kunsthandel," *Der Cicerone*, XIX, 1927, p. 245, fig. 8 [as a truly wonderous work of the late period]; "Institute Acquires Noted Rembrandt," *Bulletin of the Minneapolis Institute of Arts*, XXIV, no. 2, 1935, pp. 71 ff. [as similar to 1664 painting of same subject in Collection Andrew Mellon]; W. Stechow, "Lucretiae statua," *Beiträge für George Swarzenski*, Berlin, 1951, pp. 114–124 [suggests that Rembrandt's *Lucretia* comes from the theater]; O. Benesch,

"Rembrandt and Ancient History," *Art Quarterly*, XXII, 1959, pp. 328, 331 [states that death of Lucretia was one of chief moral subjects of Renaissance art; it was treated either as a dramatic group scene with supporting actors or as a cold display of the mastery of the nude as, for example, by Dürer; Rembrandt stresses the deep human content of the story], 332; Rosenberg 1964, pp. 286–7, fig. 246 [discusses spiritual quality of painting]; Bauch 1966, no. 286; Gerson 1968, pp. 132, 430, no. 372, ill. p. 431 [cord of curtain to right might be a theater prop; however, see M. Hirst's convincing comparison with Caravaggio's *David*]; M. Hirst, "Rembrandt and Italy," *The Burlington Magazine*, CX, 1968, p. 221, fig. 83 [cites connection between Rembrandt's Minneapolis *Lucretia* and Caravaggio's *David*, Borghese Gallery, Rome; suggests that Rembrandt possibly knew the *David* through a painted or drawn copy]; Haak 1969, fig. 540; Bredius (Gerson) 1969, no. 485, p. 395.

As recounted in Livy, *Histories*, I, 57, 58, the story of Lucretia started the revolution against the Tarquinii and the start of the Roman republic.

## ATTRIBUTED TO REMBRANDT

### 22 *Man Reading*

Sterling and Francine Clark Art Institute, Williamstown, Mass.

Canvas 74.1 × 56.2 cms. signed just above book, bottom right: *Rembrandt f. 1648 Ill. p. 108*

PROVENANCE possibly painting cited in Coll. Count of Vence, 1750, 72.4 × 59.1 cms., and dated 1643; possibly in sale Amsterdam, 6 March 1769, no. 8, canvas: 72.4 × 59.7 cms.; possibly in Coll. M. Danoot, Brussels, 1828, 72.4 × 59.1 cms., dated 1643; possibly painting in sale, Paris (Hôtel Drouot), 11 June 1904, no. 23, ill., as School of Rembrandt, canvas; 70.5 × 54 cms.; Count Demandolx-Dedons, Marseilles; with M. Knoedler & Co., N.Y.; purchased by Robert Sterling Clark in 1923.

EXHIBITIONS New York 1925, no. 14; New York, M. Knoedler & Co., *Loan Exhibition of Paintings by Rembrandt*, 1933, no. 6.

SELECTED REFERENCES J. Smith, VII, 1836, p. 67, no. 156 [lists picture dated 1643 and which answers description of Clark painting as do nos. 380, 475 but which are not dated]; Hofstede de Groot, VI, 1916, pp. 11 [writes that one of the greatest puzzles is this very effective subject which occurs often; Smith describes it three or four times and I know of at least six examples—Collections Sir F. Cook, J. G. Johnson, Count de Bésanval, etc.—usually attributed to Carel Fabritius; however, none show style of any known Rembrandt pupil; probably all go back to lost Rembrandt; a copy exists, or did exist, dated 1643, which possibly could be date of lost original], 159, no. 255; A. Bredius, "An Unknown Masterpiece by Rembrandt," *The Burlington Magazine*, XXXVI, 1920, p. 208 f., ill. [connects painting with J. Smith, VII, 1836, no. 255 and perhaps Hofstede de Groot, VI, 1916, no. 246a; states that painting in Coll. Count de Demandolx-Dedons, is original and is signed and dated 1643; stylistically it is unique in Rembrandt's oeuvre]; W. Martin, *AltHolländische Bilder*, Berlin, 1921, pp. 82 ff., figs. 48–50 [illustrates two copies of original which he also believes to be in Coll. Count Demandolx-Dedons, Marseilles, and dated 1645]; A. Bredius, "Trois tableaux de Rembrandt peu connus," *Gazette des Beaux-Arts*, LXIII, no. 3, 1921, p. 215, ill. [cites copies; writes that one does not think of Rembrandt because they differ from his usual way of painting—dark figure against a light background; undoubtedly original with beautiful signature and date of 1645; before cleaning lost cipher looked like a 3]; Valentiner, 1921, no. 56 [as Rembrandt and dated 1648 (?)]; W. Martin, *Kunstwanderer*, III, 1921–22, p. 30 [as Rembrandt]; Br. no. 238 [as Rembrandt and dated 1645]; Williamstown, Mass., Sterling and Francine Clark Art Institute, *Exhibit Twelve—Dutch and Flemish Masters* 1960, no. 422 [as painted in 1645]; Bauch 1966, p. 347 [best version of four known copies after a lost original, which is perhaps by Carel Fabritius; signed and dated 1643]; J. Q. van Regteren Altena, *Oud Holland*, LXXXII, 1967, p. 70 [as Rembrandt]; Bredius (Gerson) 1969, no. 238, p. 190 [as young Barent Fabritius; signature and date of 1645 added later].

COPIES

a. Private Coll., England, 18th century [attributed to Fragonard].

canvas 72.4 × 57.1 cms.

PROVENANCE J. C. Robinson; Sir Francis Cook, 1881–1961; with A. Brod, London, 1961, as Fragonard.

SELECTED REFERENCES C. J. Holmes, *The Burlington Magazine*, VI, 1904–05, p. 330 [as Carel Fabritius].

b. Coll. J. G. Johnson, Phila. [as old copy after Rembrandt].

canvas 73.6 × 59.1 cms.

c. Coll. Count de Bésanval.

d. sale Paul Mersch, Paris, May 1909, no. 27.

[as Carel Fabritius].

e. sale Stockl, Vienna, 5–6 April 1910, no. 32, ill., canvas:

73 × 60 cms. [could this be painting in Coll. Stern, Vienna, cited in J. O. Kronig, *Catalogue of Cook Collection—Dutch and Flemish Schools*, II, 1913, p. 75?].

f. sale Funck-Bretano, Paris (Hôtel Drouot), 29 April 1921, no. 176, 58.5 × 67 cms., [as Carel Fabritius.]

g. Coll. Rath, Budapest.

ENGRAVINGS

a. J. L. Krafft [J. Smith, VII, 1836, p. 155, no. 475].

b. Laffard [*ibid.*, p. 133, no. 380].

c. Anonymous [*ibid.*, p. 67, no. 156, as dated on painting 1643—probably Clark picture].

d. Deboucourt [*ibid.* p. 139, no. 409, as in Coll. Marquis Gerini; Fenaille, *L'œuvre gravé de P. L. Deboucourt*, Paris, 1899, no. 316 [as after painting in Coll. Guérin and signed *Rt. f. 1636*].

e. L. Baskin, 1963 [as *Portrait of Hercules Seghers*].

The painting in the Clark Collection appears to be the best of the many versions cited above. The attribution to Rembrandt still presents problems, but one can say that the signature, which looks genuine, is in the original paint structure. However, the question of the attribution should consider whether or not the background and foreground are by the same hand [as suggested by E. Haverkamp-Begemann] and whether or not the structure of the anatomy is consistent with Rembrandt's output in the 1640's. In any case, whoever may be the artist, Rembrandt himself, a gifted pupil or a copyist working after a lost work by the master, it is certainly one of the most fascinating of all the portraits by Rembrandt, his pupils or his followers. It is, therefore, not surprising that it was once considered to be a *Portrait of Hercules Seghers*, one of the great and original personalities of Dutch art whom Rembrandt collected and admired [W. Fraenger, *Die Radierungen des Hercules Seghers*, Berlin, 1922, p. 88, as *Portrait of Hercules Seghers*].

## 23 *A Seated Man with a Stick**

Trustees of the National Gallery, London

Canvas 137.5 × 104.8 cms. signed very likely falsely, in bottom-left corner: R. (.)mbrandt /(.)6(..) *Ill. p. 109*

PROVENANCE Probably painting by Rembrandt, subject unknown, which, following Joseph Farington, was sold by Sir Thomas Lawrence to Sir George Beaumont, Bart., in July 1794; presented by Sir George Beaumont in 1823 to British Museum until National Gallery was to be established; transferred to National Gallery in 1828.

EXHIBITIONS London, British Institution, 1815, no. 34, lent by Beaumont [very likely painting described as *Head of Rabbi*—see MacLaren 1960, p. 342 f., for discussion of this problem].

SELECTED REFERENCES J. Smith, VII, 1836, p. 141, no. 415 [as a *Jew Merchant* by Rembrandt]; Hofstede de Groot, VI, 1916, p. 214, no. 391 [as about 1650]; MacLaren 1960, pp. 341 ff., no. 51 [states that signature and date are probably false and almost effaced; *pentimento* in top of stick; until now picture has always been accepted as Rembrandt but weaknesses, especially meaningless brush strokes on nose, drawing of right shoulder and rather niggling treatment of right sleeve, suggest this is in part, possibly entirely, by a pupil in Rembrandt's shop; executed ca. 1648–50]; Bauch 1966, p. 48 [quotes W. Sumowski as having attributed this work to Samuel van Hoogstraten]; Bredius (Gerson) 1969, no. 257, p. 539, [not even good enough for Samuel van Hoogstraten].

COPY Painting Gallery, Kassel (Catalogue, 1929, p. 64, no. 253)

MEZZOTINT Samuel William Reynolds, 1816.

MacLaren's reasons for attributing this work, in part or in its entirety, to a Rembrandt pupil working in the shop ca. 1648–50, are extremely well founded. One might also state that for the period the forms are worked out in too much detail, and the paint does not impart a sense of structure to them. Each area of color is clearly separated from the next, which is also unlike Rembrandt.

## 24 *Lamentation*

John and Mable Ringling Museum of Art, Sarasota

Canvas 180.3 × 198.7 cms. signed falsely bottom-right center [signature seems to be above original paint layer]: *Rembrandt f. 1650 Ill. p. 110*

PROVENANCE Marquess of Abercorn [at least by 1836]; Duke of Abercorn, Baron's Court, Ireland, in 1899; on loan to Dublin, National Gallery, around 1880; with Forbes and Paterson, London; Comtesse de Béarn, Paris; Comtesse de Béhague, Paris; sale, London (Christie's), June 28, 1929, no. 76 (later bought by J. Ringling); John Ringling, Sarasota.

EXHIBITIONS London, British Institution, 1835, no. 115; London, Royal Academy, *Exhibition of Works by The Old Masters*, 1876, no. 153; London 1899, no. 94; Detroit 1930, no. 53, ill.; New York 1940, no. 84; New York, Duveen Galleries, *Paintings by the Great Dutch Masters*, 1942, no. 44; Raleigh 1956, no. 19, ill. [states that discrepancy between background figures on right and those in front is due to early restoration and not by different hands as suggested by Bredius]; Milwaukee, Art Institute, *Six Great Painters*, 1957; Montreal/Toronto 1969, no. 44.

SELECTED REFERENCES J. Smith, VII, 1836, p. 41, no. 95 [as painted in the broadest and most accomplished style of the master and may justly be ranked among his finest works, signed and dated 1640]; W. Bode, *Studiën zur Geschichte der holländischen Malerei*, Braunschweig, 1883, pp. 432, note 1, 581, no. 156 [as on loan to National Gallery, Dublin, from Duke of Abercorn and signed and dated 1640]; A. Rosenberg, *Rembrandt des Meisters Gemälde*, Stuttgart & Leipzig, 1908, pp. 533, 566 [as doubtful and possibly by a student]; Hofstede de Groot, VI, 1916, p. 105 f., no. 137 [as signed and dated 1650; states that authenticity is often contested but it is not, as yet, time to decide]; Br. no. 582 [doubt concerning authenticity is unjustified and drawing of this subject in Stockholm is by student and perhaps made after the painting]; A. Bredius, "Rembrandt's Beweening van Christus aan den voet van het Kruis," *Oud-Holland*, LIV, 1937, p. 219, fig. 1 [writes that John is weak and head is from a later time while woman at Christ's feet, Virgin, young girl leaning against Cross, and Joseph of Arimathea are certainly by Rembrandt; points out painted study in Private Collection which includes two thieves on crosses, Christ's empty cross and sky and suggests that Sarasota painting was either cut at top or only half-finished]; W. Suida, *A Catalogue of Paintings in the John and Mable Ringling Museum of Art*, 1949, no. 252, ill. [cites sketch for St. John as being in Stockholm]; Sumowski 1957–58, pp. 231 [following Valentiner, by B. Fabritius], 234 [states that Stockholm drawing of crying boy is not study for Sarasota St. John and is school piece; falseness of attribution of Sarasota painting to Rembrandt can be seen in many borrowings of Rembrandt motifs and their mixture arouses doubt concerning genuineness of signature and date]; 240, fig. 81 [as B. Fabritius (?)]; Bauch 1966, p. 49 [impressive work of an important pupil around 1650, perhaps Nicolaes Maes; the painted study in Swiss private collection recalls the late Jan Lievens]; Bredius (Gerson), no. 582, pp. 492, 610 [very definitely by pupil, B. Fabritius or Hoogstraten, the oil-sketch is a late and superficial work, probably by Jan Lievens].

It is difficult to accept the Sarasota *Lamentation* as a work by Rembrandt. Stylistically it does not compare favorably in handling of the paint which, during the late 1640's and early 1650's, Rembrandt builds up in powerful layers and his light effects are not made up of spotted highlights across the picture surface. The Sarasota painting contains an obvious melancholic quality which is foreign to Rembrandt. There are also too many obvious borrowings from compositions by the master. Sumowski (p. 234) has pointed out a number of motifs taken over from etchings, while the same can be said in connection with Rembrandt's drawings [cf. for example Benesch I, cat. nos. 100 recto, 154, figs. 107, 172; Benesch III, cat. no. 587; Benesch V, cat. no. 926, fig. 1136] and in at least one painting such as the *Lamentation*, National Gallery, London, of ca. 1642 [Bauch 1966, no. 69]. One might also add that the authenticity of the signature is extremely doubtful. The *R* is peculiar when compared with other signatures, and the entire signature does not appear to be in the original layer of paint, but appears to be superimposed.

Recently it has been suggested by Haverkamp-Begemann and David Carter that the picture is more in line with the style of Willem Drost who studied with Rembrandt in the 1650's. This idea could very well be right, especially when one studies the figure leaning on the cross with Drost's *Bathsheba* [cat. no. 40]. Both have a similar melancholy attitude with dark eyes emerging from deep sockets and a highlighted face. The way in which Christ's drapery is rendered with thick white paint and gray-green shadows causing it to stand out against the dark body is also similar to the drapery and the effects it achieves in the *Bathsheba*. The Virgin's bright red headpiece with reflecting white light is painted like the small red highlighted area in the *Portrait of a Man* [cat. no. 38] and *Noli Me Tangere* [cat. no. 42]. There are, to be sure, awkward passages in this composition, especially St. John and his companion in the background, as well as differences in the manner of painting these figures which make one think that it is a student work. Because of the possible affinities with Drost in some of the figures, one might suggest that he painted this work while still experimenting as pupil in Rembrandt's shop.

The composition is, following Rembrandt's predilection, based upon a medieval prototype, and, in this case, it could be Geertgen tot Sint Jans' *Lamentation*, Kunsthistorisches Museum, Vienna. Geertgen's picture was famous in the early seventeenth century as is attested to by the praise it received from Carel van Mander and the print made after it sometime between 1621 and 1630 by Theodore Matham, published by Jacob Matham and dedicated to Jacob van Campen [for documentation see J. E. Snyder, "The Early Haarlem School of Painting," *The Art Bulletin*, XLII, 1960, p. 113].

The painted sketch called a study for the Sarasota painting by Bredius seems to be an expanded copy by a later artist—perhaps made in the eighteenth century.

## 25 *Tobias and the Angel Ill. p. 111*

Staatliche Museen Berlin, Gemäldegalerie Dahlem

Canvas 86 × 74 cms. signed bottom left by later hand: *R*

PROVENANCE with Auerbach, Berlin; sale H. Emden, Berlin (Lepke), 3 May, 1910, no. 80, as Govert Flinck; W. Bode, Berlin, 1910; given by latter to museum, 1910.

SELECTED REFERENCES W. Bode, "Rembrandt's Tobias mit dem Engel am Rande des Wassers in der Berliner Gemäldegalerie," *Jahrbuch der Königlichen Preussischen Kunstsammlungen*, XXXI, 1910, pp. 159–163, ill. [as not by Flinck; with discovery of ca. 1650 preparatory drawing in Coll. Bonnat, Paris, and compositional and landscape similarities with works by Rembrandt executed ca. 1650, Bode attributes painting to Rembrandt and dates it ca. 1650]; Hofstede de Groot, VI, 1916, p. 58, no. 67 [as Rembrandt]; Valentiner 1921, p. xx, note 64, fig. 62 [as Rembrandt ca. 1650]; A. Bredius, "Besprechung von Valentiner's Wiedergefundene Rembrandts," *Zeitschrift für bildende Kunst*, LVI, 1921, p. 160 [as Flinck]; Staatl. Museen zu Berlin, *Beschreibendes Verzeichnis der Gemälde im Kaiser-Friedrich-Museum und Deutschen Museum*, Berlin, 1931, p. 389, no. 828N [as Rembrandt ca. 1650 and signed *R* in later hand]; Lugt 1933, p. 7, no. 1122 [states that painting is not universally accepted, but this does not mean drawing is not Rembrandt; a student during the years 1650–55 could have used the drawing as a model as did Bol in his *Moses Striking the Water*]; Benesch V, p. 266, cat. no. 908, fig. 1119 [writes that a painting by a pupil, based on the drawing of *Tobias and the Angel by the River*, Print Room, Louvre, is in Berlin, Kaiser Friedrich Museum]; Von Moltke 1965, p. 229, cat. no. 24 [as wrongly attributed to Flinck].

In spite of the fact that there are similarities to Rembrandt's composition of ca. 1650 cited by Bode [p. 161], there is a certain softness and decorative quality in the handling of the paint that one does not generally associate with Rembrandt. However, it is possible that the master touched up this picture which seems to have been painted after the Louvre drawing of ca. 1652 by an unknown Rembrandt pupil.

**26** *Fragment of an Annunciation-The Virgin*

Národní Galerie, Prague *Ill. p. 113*

Canvas 88 × 70 cms. signed lower-right corner *Rembrandt F*

PROVENANCE Baron A. von Lanna, Prague; acquired in 1923.

EXHIBITIONS Warsaw 1956, no. 17, ill.

SELECTED REFERENCES V. Krámař, *Mariae Verkundigung von Rembrandt*, Prague, 1926, pp. 46 ff. [states detailed argument for attribution to Rembrandt and dates painting ca. 1650]; J. L. A. A. M. van Rijckevorsel, *Rembrandt en de Traditie*, Rotterdam, 1932, p. 39, fig. 29 [states that the inclusion of the book is traditional since start of Gothic and is commonly present in the Netherlands beginning with Ghent altarpiece, while the bed seen in the background becomes common with Roger van der Weyden], Národní Galerie v Praze, *Sbírka Starého Umení*, 1955, no. 463; O. Benesch, "Die Rembrandt-ausstellung in Warschau," *Kunstchronik*, IX, 1956, p. 199 [as of wondrous beauty and undoubtedly a Rembrandt from the beginning of the 1650's; contains many parallels with Rembrandt's drawings from this time; no one from Rembrandt's School was capable of creating the deep expression of the face]; Sumowski 1956–57, pp. 234 [as not by Rembrandt because the Virgin is an imitation of the Virgin in Rembrandt's 1651 *Noli Me Tangere*, Brunswick; because of connection with the Berlin drawing of the *Annunciation* by Constantijn van Renesse and corrected by Rembrandt (cat. no. 141), one might suggest this to be an early Renesse]; 242 [as Renesse (?)], 246, fig. 64; J. Sip, *Alte holländische Meister*, Prague, 1961, fig. 9 [as ca. 1650 and that many see this as a student work].

**27** *Apostle Thomas (?)*

Staatliche Kunstsammlungen, Kassel

Canvas 120 × 90.5 cms. signed by a later hand on the left along table edge: *1656 Ill. p. 112*

PROVENANCE sale Lambert ten Kate, Amsterdam, 1732, bought for Landgrave of Hessen-Kassel; temporarily in Paris, 1807–15.

SELECTED REFERENCES F. Schlie, *Beschreibendes Verzeichniss der Werke älterer Meister in der Grossherzoglichen Gemälde-Galerie zu Schwerin*, Schwerin, 1882, p. 515, no. 855 [as ascribed to Ribera by Prosch and Waagen but technique is closer to Rembrandt between 1650–1660]; W. Bode, *Studien zur Geschichte der holländischen Malerei*, Braunschweig, 1883, pp. 515, 566, no. 68 [as Rembrandt and signed partly or wholly false *Rembr. 1656*]; O. Eisenmann, *Katalog der Königl. Gemälde-Galerie zu Kassel*, Kassel, 1888, p. 150f., no. 224 [as doubtful Rembrandt]; Hofstede de Groot, VI, 1916, no. 182 [as *St. Thomas* by Rembrandt and probably pendant to *St. Paul at his Writing Table*, Coll. P. A. B. Widener, Philadelphia]; W. Martin, "Zur Rembrandtforschung," *Der Kunstwanderer*, IV, 1923, p. 408f. ill. [as not Rembrandt and lacking plasticity and warm atmosphere when compared with Rembrandts of 1650's like 1656 *Jacob Blessing*; the date was put on later and picture is old copy after a lost original that could have been painted around 1652 at the time of the *Portrait of a Seated Man*, Devonshire Coll., Chatsworth (now National Gallery, London); because Kassel painting was in inventory of 1749, it can hardly be a copy from the eighteenth century]; Van Dyke, 1923, pp. 128, 130 [as possibly by Nicolaes Maes in his middle period and compares it with Maes' *Portrait of Man*, Mauritshuis, The Hague and with *Portrait of an Old Man*, Carstanjen Coll., supposedly by Rembrandt]; Valentiner 1932, 212f., note 8 [as *The Architect* and tentatively given to Drost or Maes by museum authorities; it is by neither of these masters nor by Rembrandt and perhaps an excellent work by Barent Fabritius]; R. Hamann, *Rembrandt*, Berlin, 1948, p. 190 [as an *Architect* and not by Rembrandt himself; is it possible that Titus could have done this in 1655?]; Slive 1953, p. 169f., note 4 [discusses Lambert ten Kate Collection inventory and description of Kassel picture which was called Rembrandt and cites attributions to Drost and Barent Fabritius]; Vogel 1958, p. 122f., no. 246 [attribution is under contention and Nicholaes Maes is chiefly in dispute].

ETCHING N. Mossoloff

COPY W. Troost I, pastel: 352 × 277 mm., Besançon Museum, inv. no. D. 283.

This type of picture must be connected with paintings of similar contemplating Apostles executed by Rembrandt in the late 1650's and early 1660's [cf. Bauch 1966, nos. 217, 221, 234 (cat. no. 19), 236 (cat. no. 20)], but certainly not by the master himself. The light seems to dissolve the forms rather than build them up as in Rembrandt, nor is the paint thickly built up as in the latter. The soft-atmospheric quality of the picture and the way in which the forms blend into each other indicate a closer affinity with Nicolaes Maes. It is difficult to see any connection with Willem Drost who uses strong contours to outline his forms and much brighter light contrasts [cf. cat. nos. 39–44].

The attribution to Barent Fabritius is also hard to maintain [cat. nos. 51–55]. If this picture is from the seventeenth century as it appears to be, it seems closest in style to someone like Maes, and/or the artist who painted *The Woman Paring Her Nails*, The Metropolitan Museum of Art, New York. The attribution must remain open for the time being.

## 28 *Supper at Emmaus*

Musée du Louvre, Paris

Canvas 50.5 × 64 cms. *Ill. p. 111*

PROVENANCE perhaps Coll. d'Angiviller; in the Louvre before 1852; Château of Compiègne, 1874–1901 [as School of Rembrandt]; in Louvre since 1901 [as Rembrandt].

EXHIBITIONS Cologne, Wallraf-Richartz Museum, *Rembrandt durchleuchtet*, 1956, no. 29

SELECTED REFERENCES Louvre, *Catalogue*, 1907, no. 2555A [as by pupil but retouched by master or a sketch started by master and finished by pupil]; Lilienfeld, p. 166 f., no. 98 [the types and color are like those found in a number of De Gelder's works; however, head of Christ is by Rembrandt; suggests that Rembrandt corrected De Gelder's work; it dates ca. 1661 when De Gelder studied with Rembrandt]; Hofstede de Groot, VI, 1916, p. 112, no. 146 [as Rembrandt and painted ca. 1661, cites pen and wash drawing for Louvre picture as being in Coll. C. Hofstede de Groot, The Hague]; L. Demonts, *Catalogue des Peintures exposées dans les Galeries (Musée National du Louvre)*, Paris, III, 1922, p. 22, no. 2555A [as Rembrandt]; Stechow 1934, p. 340 [cites Rembrandt's drawing for *Supper at Emmaus* in Amsterdam as study for ca. 1660 Louvre painting]; Van Regteren Altena 1948–49, p. 23, notes 43 [cites doubts about attribution]; 44 [as much similarity between Louvre panel and larger Van den Eeckhout in Palazzo Corsini, Rome; Louvre picture seems to be earlier than Van den Eeckhout]; Benesch VI, p. 394, cat. no. A66 [as not worthy of Rembrandt nor is the drawing formerly Coll. C. Hofstede de Groot and now Print Room, Amsterdam]; Sumowski 1957–58, pp. 226, 241, 246 [as early De Gelder]; M. Hours, "Rembrandt, observations et présentations de radiographies exécutées d'après les portraits et compositions du musée du Louvre," *Bulletin du Laboratoire du Louvre*, VI, 1961, pp. 4 [the texture of the canvas is more regular and close than in the canvases Rembrandt uses; hands and faces show Rembrandt's manner], 27, ill.; Bauch 1966, p. 49 [as following Sumowski, perhaps an early De Gelder]; Gerson 1968, pp. 416, 502, no. 352,

ill. p. 417 [the picture is in very poor condition but what remains points to an original by Rembrandt]; Bredius (Gerson) no. 597, p. 501.

The attribution of this painting has been questioned by the Louvre authorities. Further study of it in the exhibition may help scholars reach more definite conclusions.

# JACOB BACKER 1608-1651

Jacob Adriaensz Backer was born in Harlingen in 1608. His father was Adriaen Tjerkse; his mother's name is unknown. It is likely that the family originally came from Antwerp to Harlingen, an important Friesian trade center, during the last quarter of the sixteenth century. At an unknown date, perhaps close to 1630, Jacob went to study in Leeuwarden with Lambert Jacobsz who worked in much the same styles as Lastman, Moeyaert, and the Utrecht School. It was also at this time that Backer probably met Govert Flinck, who was also studying with Lambert Jacobsz around 1630. Backer's portrait style was also influenced at this time by another Leeuwarden artist, Wybrand de Geest, who, incidently, was married to Rembrandt's wife's cousin, Hendrickje van Uylenburg. In 1633 Jacob Backer, a fully trained and formed artist, moved to Amsterdam where he immediately fell under the influence of Rembrandt. A year later, in 1634, Backer received his first great commission, *The Portrait of the Lady Regents of the City Orphanage*. Backer died in Amsterdam on August 27, 1651. Backer had a number of pupils, of whom the best known were Adriaen Backer and Jan de Baen.

Jacob Backer was especially successful as a portraitist in the Rembrandt style, but he also maintained something of Lambert Jacobsz's light effects and compositional ideas. His early work is characterized by a sympathetic feeling for the subject and a free brush (see cat. no. 29). Sometime after 1642, he turned away from Rembrandt's style toward the more elegant, courtly manner of Bartholomeus van der Helst. Houbraken, I, p. 265, speaks of his excellent drawing technique and the praise Backer received for his history paintings, especially mythology, in the poems of Jan Vos and Lud. Smids.

## 29 *Portrait of a Boy*

Royal Gallery of Paintings "Mauritshuis," The Hague

Canvas oval, 94 × 71 cms. signed middle right side in light

reddish brown *I: Debacker 1634*, and just beneath a false signature and date *Rembrandt f. 1639 Ill. p. 121*

PROVENANCE Steengracht, The Hague, at least by 1893; sale Steengracht, Paris, 9 June, 1913, no. 2, bought by Mrs. C. A. Rose; presented by Mrs. Rose in 1914.

EXHIBITIONS Amsterdam, Rijksmuseum, *Vereeniging "Rembrandt" Catalogus van de Jubileum-Tentoonstelling*, 1923, no. 42 [as early work from student time with Rembrandt]; Amsterdam, Rijksmuseum, *Veertig Jaren Vereeniging Rembrandt*, 1925, no. 42; London 1929, no. 351 [as Backer]; Rotterdam, Museum Boymans-van Beuningen, *Kerst Tentoonstelling*, 1947, no. 4; Zürich, Kunsthaus, *Holländer des 17. Jahrhunderts*, 1953, no. 9, pl. 26; Milan 1954, no. 7.

COPY Coll. Capt. von Geyer, Wegeholm, Sweden.

SELECTED REFERENCES G. Lafenestre-E. Richtenberger, *La Peinture en Europe. La Hollande*, Paris [ca. 1900], p 62f., no. 543 [as attributed earlier to Bol but as a work characteristic of Backer's second period and similar to his paintings in Dresden and Brunswick]; E. Dacier, "La Galerie Steengracht,"*Revue de l'art ancien et moderne*, XXXIII, 1913, p. 356f.; W. Martin, "Aanwinsten van het Mauritshuis," *Bulletin van den Nederlandschen Oudheidkundigen Bond*, VII, 1914, pp. 244 ff. [discusses validity of signature which was doubted by some and consequently they attributed painting to Thomas de Keyser; Martin secures attribution to Backer by comparing it with works done in similar style such as Backer's ca. 1634 *Regents of the City Orphanage*, City Orphanage, Amsterdam (Bauch 1926, pp. 28, 100, no. 231) and the 1635 *Portrait of Wtenbogaert*, Rijksmuseum, Amsterdam (*ibid.*, pp. 31 f., 91, no. 159, fig. 24]; Bauch 1926, pp. 16 f. [as earliest dated Backer and related to *Regents of City Orphanage* of ca. 1633-34], 92f., pl. 8 [as perhaps pendant to *Portrait of a Girl*, Museum of Fine Arts, Montreal]; Mauritshuis, *Catalogue Raisonné des Tableaux et Sculptures*, The Hague, 1935, p. 6 f., no. 747, ill. [mentions fact that in spite of authentic signature some say it is by Thomas de Keyser]; Martin II, 1936, p. 112 [as very close to Rembrandt in light and composition, but the airy and tender handling of the brush is specifically Backer].

Stylistically the painting is certainly close to the ca. 1634 *Regents of the City Orphanage* and the 1635 *Portrait of Wtenbogaert*. From the reproduction in Von Moltke 1965, p. 253, no. 136, a *Portrait of a Young Boy*, Art Gallery, Johannesburg, also seems to belong to this group of paintings. It has been suggested that the pendant for the Mauritshuis portrait is *The Portrait of a Girl*, Montreal, Museum of Fine Arts, no. 863, formerly van Horne Coll. [Mauritshuis, The Hague, *Beknopte Catalogus der Schilderijen*

*en Beeldhouwwerken*, 1949, p. 5, no. 747]. This cannot be the case as the *Portrait of a Girl* is much smaller (72.3 × 53.1 cms.) than the *Portrait of a Boy* (94 × 71 cms.), and the little girl wears a costume of the early 1640's. Her face and dress are more strongly outlined compared to the atmospheric dissolving of form present in the *Portrait of a Boy*. In the latter picture the soft atmospheric quality of the light, the very rich, painterly brush strokes and the deep folds of the drapery, especially in the right side, are reminiscent of Backer's early years in Leeuwarden with Lambert Jacobsz. (Compare for example the latter's 1629 *St. Paul*, Coll. C. G. Knight, Sacramento, Calif. (ill. in Leeuwarden, Friesch Museum, *Herdenkings-Tentoonstelling Lambert Jacobsz.*, 1936, no. 5.) However, the use of light to stress the face as the main point of interest is typical of Rembrandt in the early 1630's (cf. *Portrait of Nicolaes Ruts*, Frick Coll., N.Y.), but light in the latter is much more forceful and not atmospheric as in Backer.


## FERDINAND BOL 1616-1680

Ferdinandus Bol, son of the surgeon Balthasar Bol, was baptized in Dordrecht on June 24, 1616. Houbraken I, p. 237, tells us that when Ferdinand was two or three years old his family moved to Amsterdam, where he lived until his death. Houbraken also writes that Bol studied with Rembrandt, but does not give the years, although one can suggest sometime about 1633-1635. Rembrandt's drawing of *Susanna and the Elders*, ca. 1637, Print Room, Berlin, contains an inscription on the back written by Rembrandt referring to the sale of paintings by himself of 1635 and of those by his students Bol and Leendert Cornelisz van Beyeren [Benesch II, p. 102, cat. no. 447, fig. 506]. Bol was still on close terms with Rembrandt in 1640, when he was witness to a document drawn up by him. In 1652 Bol became a citizen of Amsterdam. On October 2, 1653, he married Elisabeth Dell; on October 10, 1669, a widower, he married a wealthy widow, Anna van Erckel. His last known painting, the *Portrait of Engel de Ruyter*, Mauritshuis, The Hague, dates from 1669, and in the next year a document describes Bol as a merchant, very likely dealing in cloth. Houbraken II, p. 173, tells us that Cornelis Bisschop was his student, as well as Gottfried Kneller [Houbraken III, p. 183]. He was buried in Amsterdam on July 24, 1680.

Bol was one of Rembrandt's most gifted pupils, and for many years some of their works were confused [cf. for example, cat. no. 30], especially the portraits. After 1650, Bol moved away from Rembrandt's style. In portraiture he was especially attracted by the fashionable mode of Bartholomeus van der Helst. Bol was very much appreciated during his lifetime especially as a portraitist. He also received a number of commissions for history pictures to decorate public buildings in Amsterdam and Leiden. Of greatest interest are his decorations for the Town Hall in Amsterdam [see H. van de Waal, *Drie Eeuwen Vaderlandsche Geschied-Uitbeelding 1500–1800*, The Hague, I, 1952, pp. 216, 218, 221, 230, figs. 47, 78]. Beginning in 1642 he executed etchings under the influence of Rembrandt, while the latter seems to have etched Bol's portrait [Münz 1952, I, cat. no. 58, fig. 65].

30  *Portrait of Elizabeth Jacobsdr Bas* (1571–1649)

Rijksmuseum, Amsterdam

Canvas 118 × 91.5 cms. *Ill. p. 122*

PROVENANCE acquired by the Van de Poll family through inheritance from the families Rey, Meulenaer, and Muilman; presented to the Rijksmuseum in 1880 by S. H. van de Poll, Amsterdam.

EXHIBITIONS Brussels, Paleis voor Schoone Kunsten, *De Hollandsche Schilderkunst van Jeroen Bosch tot Rembrandt*, 1946, p. 16, no. 7; London, 1952–53, no. 223; New York / Toledo /Toronto 1954–55, no. 9, ill.; Leiden 1956, no. 21, fig. 7.

SELECTED REFERENCES A. B. de Vries-N. de Roever, "Rembrandt, Bijdragen tot de Geschiedenis zijner Laatste Levensjaren," *Oud-Holland*, II, 1884, p. 82, note 1 [first identified sitter as Elisabeth Jacobsdr Bas and not Rembrandt's mother]; J. G. Frederiks, "Het Portret der Weduwe van den Admiraal Zwartenhond, door Rembrandt," *Archief van Nederlandsche Kunstgeschiedenis*, VI 1884–87, pp. 265–278, ill. [detailed discussion of genealogy]; C. Vosmaer, "Arendzen's ets naar het Portret van vrouwe Elizabeth Jacobs Bas," *De Nederlandsche Spectator*, 1887, p. 121f.; A. Bredius, "Heeft Rembrandt Elizabeth Bas Wed. van Jochem Hendricksz Swartenhont geschilderd?" *Oud-Holland*, XXIX, 1911, pp. 193–197, ill. [first to attribute painting to Bol ca. 1641–42 and compares meticulous handling to, among others, Bol's signed and dated 1642 *Portrait of a Woman*, Staatliche Museen, Berlin-Dahlem]; idem. "Did Rembrandt Paint the Portrait of Elizabeth Bas?" *The Burlington Magazine*, XX, 1911–12, pp. 330–341, ill. [English version of *Oud-Holland* article]; Jan Six, "Rembrandt's Elizabeth Bas," *Bulletin Nederlandsche Oudheidkundigen Bond*, IV, 1911, pp. 311 ff. [as too good for Bol];

C. Hofstede de Groot, "Meeningsverschillen omtrent Werken van Rembrandt," *Oud-Holland*, XXX, 1912, pp. 74–81 [as Rembrandt from ca. 1636–38 and in style of 1637 *Portrait of Swalmius*, Royal Museum, Antwerp, and *Man Seated in Armchair*, Duke of Sutherland, Mertoun, Scotland; also lists obscure literature on controversy and refutes earlier Bode and Bredius Backer attribution]; A. Bredius, "Kantteekeningen op Dr. Hofstede de Groot's *Meeningsverschil*," *Oud-Holland*, XXX, 1912, pp. 82–86, ill. [sees Rembrandt's 1634 *Portrait of an Old Woman*, National Gallery, London, as prototype for Bol]; C. G. 't Hooft, "Le Portrait d'Elizabeth Bas au Musée de l'Etat à Amsterdam," *La Revue de l'Art Ancien et Moderne*, XXXI, 1912, pp. 459–466 [as Bol and compares it with two Bols, of 1650 and 1651, Amsterdam]; A. Bredius, "The 'Elizabeth Bas' Portrait Again," *The Burlington Magazine*, XXIV, 1913–14, p. 217f. [discovered documents stating Bol was called a painter in Dordrecht in 1635 and consequently went to Rembrandt as early as 1636; Bas could be prior to 1640]; Van Dyke 1923, pp. 7, 46, pl. VI, fig. 22 [as by Backer and same handling as *Portrait of a Woman*, in Antwerp and Berlin]; Bauch 1926, pp. 33ff. [as belonging to group of Backer portraits painted in second half of 1630's and closest stylistically to Berlin *Portrait of a Woman*], 44, 65, note 68 [summarizes attributions], cat. no. 137, pl. 26; C. J. Welcker, "De zoogenaamde 'Moeder van Rembrandt' een Kamper dochter!," *Amstelodamum, Maandblad voor de Kennis van Amsterdam*, XIV, 1927, p. 68f.; A. Bredius, "Rembrandt, Bol oder Backer?," *Festschrift für Max J. Friedländer zum 60. Geburtstage*, Leipzig, 1927, pp. 156 [handkerchief is painted like the one in Bol's *Portrait of a Woman*, Berlin], 158 [the pose, the painting of the drapery silhouetted against the background are like Leningrad Bol of 1651]; 160 [Bol painted only a few strongly Rembrandtesque paintings]; Martin II, 1936, p. 120, fig. 64 [as Bol more than ever in the Rembrandt spirit]; Münz 1952, II, p. 179 [as Bol]; Van Gelder 1953, p. 38 [as from the late 1630's]; O. Benesch, "Die Rembrandtausstellung in Warschau," *Kunstchronik*, IX, 1956, p. 202 [points out strong stylistic affinities between *Elizabeth Bas Portrait* and signed Bol *Portrait of a Woman*, Warsaw, National Museum (cat. no. 31)]; Michalkowa, p. 264f., fig. 7 [compares Elizabeth Bas with signed Bol *Portrait of a Woman*, Warsaw, National Museum (cat. no. 31)]; Valentiner 1957, p. 49; H. Kühn, "Untersuchungen zu den Malgrunden Rembrandts," *Jahrbuch der Staatlichen Kunstsammlungen in Baden-Württemberg*, II, 1965, p. 203 [as ca. 1640]; Haak 1969, p. 165, fig. 258 [as F. Bol (?)].

The meticulous rendering of the face, the strong contours outlining the headpiece combined with the more freely brushed in costume and hands resembles the style of Bol's signed *Portrait of a Woman*, Warsaw (cat. no. 31) and his 1642 *Portrait of a Woman*, Berlin. In these portraits Bol seems to revert to Rembrandt's style of around 1634–36. However, although Rembrandt does paint in a more detailed manner, it is not nearly as precise as one finds in the faces and some of the details in Bol. Rembrandt's brush is much more fluid. Upon first glance it appeared that Rembrandt's signed and dated 1644 *Portrait of a Woman*, Art Gallery of Ontario, Toronto, might be by the same hand as the Elizabeth Bas but this cannot be maintained. The Toronto painting is much freer in application of the paint, especially in the face where there is also a greater variety of colors used to create the forms. The use of light and shadow in the Toronto painting is more atmospheric and the forms blend into the background. In the Elizabeth Bas there is a stronger contrast of light and shadow thereby stressing contours and separation of parts. The same can be said for Bol's 1642 *Portrait of a Lady*, Berlin, which is also similar to the Elizabeth Bas in posture and application of the paint, especially in the handkerchief. Because of this connection with the Berlin *Portrait* and Elizabeth Bas' probable age, certainly a woman in her late sixties or early seventies, it is most likely that the Elizabeth Bas dates shortly after or around 1640.

## 31 *Portrait of an Old Woman*

Museum Narodowe, Warsaw

Canvas 81 × 68 cms. signed lower right just above hands *F. Bol Ill. p. 122*

PROVENANCE Gallery Stanislawa Augusta, 1795 [as Rembrandt]; Gallery Lazienki Palace, Warsaw, 1931, no. 13 [as Bol].

EXHIBITIONS Bordeaux, Galerie des Beaux-Arts, *Trésors d'art Polonais, Chefs-d'oeuvre des Musées de Pologne*, 1961, no. 61; Budapest, Szépmüvészeti Múzeum, *Holland Mestermüvek a XVII. századból*, 1967, no. 4.

REPLICA (?) Coll. Sarasin, Basel, 82 × 66 cms., monogram *AB* [Bauch 1926, p. 95f., no. 194].

SELECTED REFERENCES Bauch 1926, p. 96, no. 194 [as a repetition, better preserved than original in Basel, with signature by Bol and which Hofstede de Groot thinks is closer in style to Backer]; S. Iskierski, *Katalog Galerji Obrazów Palacu w Lazienkach w Warszawie*, 1931, no. 13 [as Bol];

Benesch IX p. 202 [as close stylistically to *Portrait of Elizabeth Bas* and amazed that it is not Backer]; Michalkowa, p. 264f.; Warsaw, Muzeum Narodowe w Warszawie, *Malarstwo Europejskie*, I, 1967, p. 51, no. 119.

Very close stylistically to *Portrait of Elizabeth Bas* (cat. no. 30) and to the *Portrait of a Woman Holding Handkerchief*, Art Gallery of Ontario, Toronto, signed Rembrandt and dated 1644. For further discussion of style see catalogue entry no. 29.

## 32 *Angel Appearing to Hagar*

Walker Art Gallery, Liverpool

Canvas 109.5 × 100.5 cms. *Ill. p. 124*

PROVENANCE possibly picture of this subject cited in Bol's inventory of 1669 and sale Peter Six, Amsterdam, 1704; very likely acquired by Liverpool, Royal Institute in 1842; on loan to Walker Art Gallery, 1893; given in 1948.

EXHIBITIONS Manchester 1857, no. 674; London 1953 M. G., no. 4, ill.; Leiden 1956, no. 19, fig. 6.

SELECTED REFERENCES G. F. Waagen, *Treasures of Art in Great Britain*, III, London, 1854, p. 240; Wurzbach, I, p. 128 [as from sale Peter Six, Amsterdam, 1704]; A. Bredius, "Bol's Kunstchatten," *Oud-Holland*, XXVIII, 1910, p. 233f., no. 36 [possibly Liverpool painting]; H. van de Waal, "Hagar in de Woestijn door Rembrandt en zijn School," *Nederlandsch Kunsthistorisch Jaarboek*, I, 1947, p. 151 [as stressing the human actions to establish psychological conflict and not landscape]; Van Gelder 1958, no. 83 [cites drawing in the Frits Lugt collection, Paris, as the first sketch for the Liverpool painting]; Laren, Singer Museum, *Oude Tekeningen uit De Nederlanden verzameling Prof. E. Perman, Stockholm*, 1962, p. 8, no. 11, fig. 33 [compare with painting in Liverpool]; Liverpool, Walker Art Gallery, *Foreign Schools Catalogue*, Liverpool, 1963, p. 24 f., no. 957 [late 1640's]; idem, *Foreign Schools Catalogue Plates*, Liverpool, 1966, pl. 110.

The subject was very popular with the Rembrandt School and Pieter Lastman. The large angel receiving the full force of the light is reminiscent of Rembrandt during the 1630's [cf. Angel in 1634 etching of *Annunciation to the Shepherds*; 1636 *Tobias Healing His Father*, Staatsgalerie, Stuttgart; 163(9) *Resurrection of Christ*; drawing ca. 1632–34 *Angel Appearing to Manoah and His Wife*, Boymans-van Beuningen Coll., Rotterdam] when Bol studied with him. The dark trees, the light filtering through below and the dramatic sky also recall Rembrandt's style of the 1630's and his interest in Adam Elsheimer which was shared by Lievens in his landscapes [Liverpool, Walker Art Gallery, *op. cit.*, p. 24 f., as observed by H. Gerson].

It is possible that the drawing formerly in the Coll. Rudolf Goldschmidt and sold in Frankfurt, 4–5 Oct. 1917, no. 185, as Eeckhout (Van de Waal, *op. cit.*, fig. 11) was a preparatory sketch for the Liverpool painting, although the handkerchief is omitted in the drawing, and Hagar kneels on one foot. Stylistically the picture seems closest to Bol's signed and dated 1644 *Three Marys at the Tomb of Christ*, Royal Museum, Copenhagen, and the signed and dated 1644 *Angel Appearing to Gideon*, The Hague, Dienst voor's-Rijks Verspreide Kunstvoorwerpen, inv. no. N.K. 2484. Other paintings of this subject by Bol, although differently composed, were with D. A. Hoogendijk, Amsterdam [Van de Waal, *op. cit.*, fig. 12] and on the Berlin art market [Valentiner 1957, p. 56 f., fig. 10].

## 33 *Portrait of Saskia*

M. H. de Young Memorial Museum, San Francisco: Gift of Donald McCloud Lewis *Ill. p. 124*

Panel 67.3 × 52 cms. dated bottom left on balustrade *1642*

PROVENANCE A. J. Sully, London; with Jacques Seligman, N.Y. [at least in 1935–36]; D. McCloud Lewis; given by the latter in 1959.

EXHIBITIONS Chicago 1935–36, no. 10, ill. p. 67 [cites later painting of 1663 which recalls San Francisco *Saskia* and is in the Toledo Museum of Art, Toledo, Ohio; also compare Rembrandt's 1633–34 *Portrait of Saskia*, Kassel]; Worcester 1936, no. 11, ill. p. 67.

SELECTED REFERENCES H. Gerson, "Jan Victors," *Kunsthistorische Mededelingen van het Rijksbureau voor Kunsthistorische Documentatie, 's-Gravenhage*, III, no. 2, 1948, p. 19 f. [proves that signed and dated 1663 Bol *Portrait of Saskia* in Toledo Museum is really a copy of Jan Victor's picture of 1640 in the Louvre; also states that motif of young girl looking out of window was common among Rembrandt's students but the master did not, as far as preserved works are known, use this motif until 1645 in painting in Dulwich; perhaps students used an early Rembrandt that is now lost].

This genre-like portrait type seems to have developed as a popular form around 1640 in the Rembrandt circle. It is possible that it originally stems from the tradition of illusionistic allegorical-genre painting introduced into the

North by Gerrit van Honthorst. The latter's 1623 *Allegory of Merry Violinist*, Rijksmuseum, Amsterdam, shows a figure leaning out over a window balustrade in much the same way as Bol's figure but without the shutter. As far as I know Rembrandt did not isolate this type in his portraiture until later, but such figures do appear in his history pictures as early as the 1630's [cf. Benesch II, cat. nos. 250, 411, figs. 273, 460; Bauch 1966, nos. 14, 55; Münz 1952, I, cat. nos., 174, 196, 204, 207, figs. 193, 219, 229, 230, 233]. Because of this, Gerson's suggestion that this portrait type does go back to a lost Rembrandt is possible. However, as we have seen in other instances concerning the Rembrandt School, the latter's pupils and followers have, more than once, established new compositional formats that were later taken over by the master.

## 34 *Scene from Ancient History*

Worcester Art Museum, Charlotte E. W. Buffington Fund

Canvas 83.2 × 83.5 cms. *Ill. p. 123*

PROVENANCE H. D. Molesworth, London [on loan (?) to Victoria and Albert Museum, London], 1955; with P. de Boer, Amsterdam, 1959; with P. de Boer & F. Mont, Inc., N.Y.; purchased in 1961.

EXHIBITIONS Montreal/Toronto 1969, no. 27, ill. [as *Magnanimity of Scipio*].

SELECTED REFERENCES "La Chronique des Arts," *Supplément à la Gazette des Beaux-Arts*, no. 1117, Feb. 1962, p. 68 [as *Joseph's Cup Found in Benjamin's Sack*].

The identification of the subject is still an open question. Although the Montreal/Toronto exhibition catalogue has interpreted this subject as the *Magnanimity of Scipio*, there is still some doubt as to whether or not this really illustrates Livy, XXVI, 50. This story has often been cited as a supreme demonstration of statesmanship [for short discussion see J. Held, *Rubens Selected Drawings*, London, I, 1959, p. 110].

As far as I know the Dutch and Flemish representations of this theme always include the young couple who do not seem to be present in Bol's painting [for representations of the *Continence of Scipio*, see Rubens' ca. 1615–17 drawings in Berlin and Bayonne (J. Held, *op. cit.*, 1959, cat. nos. 38, 39, pls. 40, 41); Van Dyck's painting in Christ Church, Oxford, and his drawings in the Louvre and Bremen (H. Vey, *Die Zeichnungen Anton van Dycks*, Brussels, I, 1962, cat. nos. 106, 107, figs. 141–43); G. van den Eeckhout's painting of 1658, Toledo Museum of Art and others listed in A. Pigler, *Barockthemen*, Budapest, II, 1956, p. 406 ff.].

Because Bol's sketch is very similar in composition to his representation of *The Intrepidity of Gaius Fabricius in the Army Camp of Pyrrhus*, executed for the Town Hall, Amsterdam, and also preserved in two studies [see H. Schneider, "Ferdinand Bol als Monumentalmaler im Amsterdamer Stadthaus," *Jahrbuch der Preussischen Kunstsammlungen.* XLVII, 1926, pp. 73–78, figs. 3–5], there is little doubt that the Worcester sketch is not an *exemplar virtutis* from Roman history which was to decorate a government building in Holland. However, the subject and the location of the final version are problems still to be answered. Perhaps the key to the meaning of the subject is the woman peering down on the scene from the balcony above.

Stylistically the Worcester sketch must date from the same time as the more Flemish-oriented Bol sketches from the Amsterdam Town Hall—that is 1656. The placement of the scene within a decorative and imaginative architectural setting illustrates the importance of Antwerp for Dutch art around the middle of the century.

**35** *Portrait of a Young Boy in Polish Costume*

Museum Boymans-van Beuningen, Rotterdam

Canvas 158 × 120.5 cms. signed lower right on bottom of drum *F Bol 1656 Ill. p. 125*

PROVENANCE acquired in 1865.

EXHIBITIONS London 1929, no. 354

SELECTED REFERENCES Rotterdam, Museum Boymans-van Beuningen, *Catalogus, Schilderijen tot 1800*, Rotterdam, 1962, p. 25, no. 1071 [coat-of-arms of the family Van der Wayen was added in beginning of nineteenth century; drawing in Museum earlier called a study for portrait is by Leendert van der Cooghen or De Grebber].

This portrait illustrates Bol's movement away from the Rembrandt style beginning around 1650. The stress upon the rendering of the rich material of the costume and attributes, through the use of sharp contours, is typical of the fashionable Amsterdam portrait style inaugurated by Bartholomeus van der Helst in the 1640's and beautifully taken up by Bol in this picture. However, something of Rembrandt is still evident in the dark background. Here Bol combines the best of two styles to produce a warm and sympathetic portrait of his young subject.

# GERARD DOU 1613–1675

Gerard Dou was born on April 7, 1613 in Leiden to the glass-engraver Douwe Jansz. According to Houbraken II, p. 1, Dou first went to study drawing in 1622 with the engraver Bartholomeus Dolendo and after a year and a half changed teachers. He remained with his new master, the gifted glass-engraver Pieter Kouwenhorn, for about two years, when Dou went to work for his father. From 1625–27 Dou was a member of the glazier's guild in Leiden. Houbraken II, p. 2, informs us that at the age of 15, on February 14, 1628, Dou entered Rembrandt's studio where he remained for about three years until Rembrandt moved to Amsterdam sometime in 1631–32.

Dou, a bachelor, lived his entire life in Leiden, and achieved great fame. He was one of the first members of the Leiden Painters' Guild founded in 1648. In 1660 the States of Holland and the East India Company bought several of Dou's paintings as a gift for Charles II of England who invited him for a visit. Dou's paintings were in many royal collections formed in the seventeenth century. Dou had numerous students including Dominicus van Tol, Jacob Toorenvliet, Frans van Mieris the elder, Gabriel Metsu, Pieter van Slingelandt, Godfried Schalcken, Karel de Moor and Matthys Naiveu. Dou died in Leiden on February 9, 1675.

Gerard Dou was a history painter, a portraitist, and, above all, painter of allegorical-genre scenes. His years with Rembrandt were crucial for Dou's future style which based itself upon the former's chiaroscuro and more detailed painting of the late Leiden years. Dou's early training as a glass engraver was also decisive. It was from this background that Dou created his style which started the Leiden School of "fijnschilders" (delicate and precise painters) and which was enormously successful well into the nineteenth century.

**36** *Artist in His Studio*

Collection G. Henle, Duisburg

Panel 66.5 × 50.7 cms. *Ill. p. 120*

PROVENANCE Colonel Legh of Leghall, Knutsford; L. S. Meyers, London; with F. Kleinberger, Paris–New York; Fritz von Gans, Frankfurt a /M.; with Bachstitz, The Hague; Henschel, Kassel; with G. Cramer, The Hague; Private Coll., Amsterdam; sale N. R. Colville and others, London (Christie's), 24 Feb., 1939, no. 37 [as *Self-Portrait* by Rembrandt]; with H. Schaeffer, N.Y., 1948; with F. H. Enneking, Amsterdam, 1958; H. Kisters, Kreuzlingen.

EXHIBITIONS Delft, Prinsenhof, *Xe Oude Kunst- en Antiekbeurs*, 1958, Booth 27, ill., Cologne, Wallraf-Richartz-Museum, *Die Sammlung Henle*, 1964, no. 10.

SELECTED REFERENCES W. Martin, *Gérard Dou*, Paris, 1911, p. 173, no. 63; idem, *Gerard Dou (Klassiker der Kunst)*, Stuttgart-Berlin 1913, pp. 13, 180, ill.; L. Balet, "Die Sammlung Bachstitz," *Der Cicerone*, XIII, 1921, pp. 336 ff., ill; Bauch 1960, pp. 221 ff., ill. [points out that changes were made in the painting, among others the face and back, and attributes them to Rembrandt]; E. Plietzsch, *Holländische und flämische Maler des 17. Jahrhunderts*, Leipzig, 1960, p. 37 f., fig. 36 [as *Self-Portrait* and one of Dou's earliest works, ca. 1628–29, which is very close stylistically to Rembrandt].

There has been a great deal of discussion concerning the subject and attribution. It has been attributed to Rembrandt, to Dou, and also said to have been painted by Dou and retouched by Rembrandt [for details see Cologne, Wallraf-Richartz-Museum, *op. cit.*, 1964, no. 10]. When one compares the Henle painting with paintings of the same subject by Dou, stylistic differences are at once noticeable. For example the *Artist in His Studio*, Cook Coll., Richmond [Martin, *op. cit.*, p. 57] is much flatter, and lacks the plasticity of form and the subtle use of light and shadow to create a sense of space and to unite the various parts of the composition. The same can be said when one compares the Henle painting with the painting formerly with Sedelmeyer, Paris, 1894 [Martin, *op. cit.*, no. 12] and the picture in the New York Historical Society signed *G. Dou* which seems to be a copy [ill. in S. Slive, "Rembrandt's Self-Portrait in a Studio," *The Burlington Magazine*, CVI, 1964, p. 485, fig. 5]. Bauch 1960, pp. 221 ff. (and Cologne, 1964, no. 10) was the first to point out that changes and corrections were made in the painting in the outline of the figure, the easel, the face, the cap, the still-life, etc. Bauch attributes these changes to Rembrandt when Dou was still in his atelier around 1630. Bauch compares the face with Rembrandt's *Laughing Self-Portrait*, Rijksmuseum, Amsterdam [Bauch 1966, fig. 298] and sees a strong similarity. This is difficult to maintain, in that Rembrandt is more painterly and animated by more subtle highlights than the drier hand of the Henle painting. Bauch also sees Rembrandt's hand in the still-life; but when compared with, for example, the the brilliant rendering of the still-life in the *Allegory of the Miser*, 1627, Staatliche Museen, Berlin-Dahlem [Bauch 1966, fig. 110], or the handling of metal objects in Rembrandt's paintings of ca. 1630 [*ibid.*, figs. 117, 120, 295 & *passim*], the still-life in the Henle painting appears to be

more precise and detailed. Bauch suggests that the head [Bauch 1966, p. 29, A7] compares more favorably with self-portraits by Dou from a time later than the 1630's [for Dou possibilities from the 1640's see Bauch 1960, p. 267, note 290]. If this is the case, then it is possible to suggest that Dou himself reworked the painting and that it belongs to his *oeuvre* of the 1640's. For this writer the comparisons with Dou of the 1640's are not convincing. The problem might very well resolve itself in the light of further study during the exhibition.

Visually, the artist conceives this painting in emblematic terms. It is not a description of the artist's studio as in the Cook Coll., but Dou [Martin, *op. cit.*, p. 57] seems to stress the problem of creation. At this time atelier paintings were manifestations of the worthiness and dignity of the artist. It was a continuation of the theme evident in a St. Luke painting the Virgin and Child but now placed in a profane setting. The artist shown in his studio was a manifestation of the self-assurance of the artist as a creative genius and not of a man who worked with his hands. [For a detailed discussion see J. Emmens in Delft/Antwerp 1964–65, pp. 9–13; this emblematic notion is confirmed by the presence of the book and the musical instrument (trumpet) long associated with Clio, the muse of history, while the format of the picture follows earlier examples such as Jacob de Gheyn's 1622 drawing in the Print Room, Munich [J. Q. van Regteren Altena, *The Drawings of Jacques de Gheyn*, I, Amsterdam, 1936 p. 99].

## 37 *Eli Instructing Samuel*
### Anonymous
Canvas 102.9 × 88.2 cms. *Ill. p. 119*

PROVENANCE Verstolk; Cornelia, Countess of Craven, Combe Abbey, no. 12; sale Cornelia, Countess of Craven, London (Sotheby's), 27 Nov., 1968, no. 87; with H. Shickman, N.Y., 1969.

EXHIBITIONS London, British Institution, 1853; Manchester 1857, no. 919 [as Rembrandt]; London 1952–53, no. 200 [as by Jan Lievens].

SELECTED REFERENCES Schneider 1932, p. 32, note. 1 [as not Lievens]; "Dutch Pictures at the Royal Academy," *The Burlington Magazine*, XCV, 1953, p. 33, no. 200, fig. 4 [as not by Lievens but composition is his or Rembrandt's. Dou? or J. G. van Vliet?]; Van Gelder 1953, p. 37.

REPLICA Coll. Schulze, Oldenburg.

As Van Gelder, *loc. cit.*, points out, this cannot be by Lievens, but the composition is close to him or Rembrandt. There are a number of Rembrandt drawings and etchings of old men placed in attitudes similar to Eli's and, of course, the soft light highlighting of the faces, hands, and part of the costumes recalls Lievens and Rembrandt during the late 1620's. However, the brush stroke is more precise and finer than the broader and freer handling found in Lievens and Rembrandt. The care and precision in rendering the details, especially the garments, jewels, and headpiece of Samuel, seem closest to Gerard Dou.

## 38 *Vanitas*

Museum of Fine Arts, Boston, Gift of Mrs. Antonie Lilienfeld in memory of Dr. Leon Lilienfeld

Panel 46.3 × 48.8 cms. *Ill. p. 120*

This painting seems to be typical of the early Gerard Dou when he was still closely associated with Rembrandt. His early and life long care for the rendering of very fine detailed surfaces is evident here. However, the treatment of the upper part of the woman's dress still contains some evidence of Dou's building up of forms in a less detailed and more Rembrandtesque manner than he will do later. For this reason the painting must date ca. 1631, if not earlier. It also contains a clearly lighted and spatially defined interior which one also finds in Dou's work ca. 1628–30 [cf. *Rembrandt in his Studio*, formerly Cook Coll., Richmond] and also Rembrandt's of the same time [*Artist in his Studio*, cat. no. 2].

Dou's picture also was directly influenced by the Leiden school of "Vanitas" painting which became very important in that city beginning in the 1620's. It not only was a subject for still-life paintings but also found its way into seemingly genre representations in the works of Rembrandt [cf. *Two Philosophers*, National Gallery of Victoria, Melbourne, 1628—Bauch 1966, no. 5], Lievens, Metsu and Gerard Dou as in this painting. For detailed discussion of "Vanitas" paintings see I. Bergström, *Dutch Still-Life Painting in the Seventeenth Century*, translated by C. Hedström & G. Taylor, London [1956], pp. 154–62, *passim*.

## WILLEM DROST active ca. 1650–1660's

There is no real documentation of this artist's life. There are, however, six signed paintings, one dated 1653 (*Portrait of a Woman*, Bredius Museum, The Hague); two dated 1654 (*Bathsheba*, Louvre, Paris; *Portrait of a Woman*, Private Collection, Switzerland); and a third said to be dated 1663(?) (*Portrait of Hillegonda van Beuningen*, Private Collection, The Netherlands). There is also an etching dated 1652 (Münz 1952, II, pp. 183 f.). We know Drost's Christian name and the fact that he worked in Amsterdam from the inscription on the *Self Portrait* (?), Metropolitan Museum of Art, N.Y. (cat. no. 40). On the basis of this signature which Valentiner read as Wilhelm Drost, the former has suggested that Drost was born in Germany [*Art Quarterly*, II, 1939, p. 300]. However, this notion becomes highly questionable if we read the first name as "Wilhelmus" which is the Latinized form of the Dutch, Willem [one might also add that "Wilhelmus" is the title of the Dutch national anthem]. Following Hofstede de Groot who in 1913 read the signature as Wilhelmus as did the cataloguers of the 1956 Rembrandt exhibition in Raleigh, this writer would propose a Dutch origin for Drost. Houbraken III, p. 47 f., writes about a Drost who was a Rembrandt pupil and who had been in Rome for a long time where he was a companion of Johann Carl Loth (1632–1698) and Jan van der Meer. A Wilhelm Drost was also a witness to an inventory drawn up in December 1680 in Rotterdam (Bredius V, p. 1626), but we do not know the occupation of this Wilhelm.

Because Drost's dated paintings of 1653–54 and an etching of 1652 contain strong stylistic affinities with Rembrandt's works from ca. 1648–ca. 1654, Houbraken's statement that Drost studied with Rembrandt seems reliable. Using the same reasoning one might also suggest that Drost was in Rembrandt's atelier ca. 1650. Beginning ca. 1655 (MacLaren 1960, p. 107), Drost was beginning to feel the influence of F. Bol and B. van der Helst, while in the 1660's in the *Portrait of Hillegonda van Beuningen*, N. Maes also seems to have attracted Drost.

Drost's oeuvre might very well be expanded after studying the paintings in the exhibition placed under the category of "attributed to Rembrandt" (for example, cat. no. 24).

## 39 *Portrait of a Young Boy*

Private Collection.

Panel 28.5 × 25 cms. signed bottom right *D.f. Ill. p. 148*

PROVENANCE Comte de Dempierre d'Hornoy, Paris [with false Rembrandt signature]; with F. Mont, N.Y., 1968

For similar type of head see the painting ascribed to Drost, formerly in the Coll. Sir William van Horne, Montreal, canvas 99 × 90 cms. [ill. in Valentiner, 1939, p. 317, fig. 19] and the *Portrait of a Young Boy* attributed to Carel Fabritius, Coll. Chiaramonte Bordonaro, Palermo, falsely signed Rembrandt, panel 64 × 48 cms. There is also a strong similarity in the handling of the white drapery around the neck with the thick heavy layers of paint in Drost's *Old Woman Holding a Knife and Leaning out of a Window*, Coll. M. Q. Morris, London, [ill. in Valentiner, 1939, fig. 9]. It is difficult to see the connection with Drost's etched *Self-Portrait* [ill. in Münz 1952, II, pl. 31b] proposed by W. Sumowski in a letter of May 4, 1968 (owner's files). It is on the basis of this comparison that Sumowski suggests that this painting is a self-portrait. The portrait, which could very well be by Drost, must date from the early 1650's—about the same time as the Kassel *Noli Me Tangere* (cat. no. 43).

## 40 *Self-Portrait* (?)

The Metropolitan Museum of Art. Given in memory of Felix Warburg by his wife and children, 1941

Canvas 86.5 × 72.4 cms. signed bottom left on paper *Wilhelm[u]s Drost F./Amsterdam 16. .* (read variously as 1653, 1655, 1656 or 1666) *Ill. p. 148*

PROVENANCE possibly portrait of Jacob Gerritsz van Velsen listed as Drost in Inventory of the estate of Jacob Gerritsz van Velsen, Leiden, 1656 [see Bredius III, pp. 887, 890, no. 2]; sale Amsterdam, 17 Dec. 1850, with pendant; sale A. Levy, London, 3 May 1884, with pendant; sale James MacAndrew, London (Christie's) 4 Feb. 1903, no. 128, with pendant; L. Lesser, London; purchased ca. 1913 by Felix M. Warburg, N.Y.

EXHIBITIONS New York 1940, no. 99 [as signed and dated 1655]; University of Wisconsin, *Old Masters of the Metropolitan*, 1949, ill.; Raleigh 1956, p. 116, no. 21 [as signed *Wilhelmus Drost* and dated 1655]; Montreal/Toronto 1969, no. 39 [as signed *Wilhelm Drost F./Amsterdam*].

SELECTED REFERENCES C. Hofstede de Groot in *Thieme-Becker*, IX, 1913, p. 577 [as signed *Wilhelmus Drost f. 1655*]; Bredius III, pp. 887 [as perhaps the Drost *Portrait of Jacob Gerritsz van Velsen* and signed *Wilhelm Drost f. 1653*], 890; A. Bredius, "Een portret van Willem Drost," *Oud-Holland*, XLVI, 1929, p. 96 f., ill [as signed *Wilhelm Drost f. 1655* on the calling card and being very Rembrandt-esque; he cites head of pendant in Bredius Museum, The Hague, as being model for *Bathsheba*, Luvre (cat. no. 41) and that portraits represent Drost and his wife]; Valentiner 1939, pp. 300 [as clearly signed *Wilhelm* which makes

Drost very likely German in origin]; 303 [the conception is so close to Rembrandt that it seems that painting was made while Drost was in the former's studio], 325, note 4, fig. 4; H. B. Wehle, "A Gift of Paintings and Drawings," *The Bulletin of the Metropolitan Museum of Art*, New York, XXXVII, 1942, p. 160 f., ill. [as signed *Wilhelm Drost F/Amsterdam* and as similar in handling of paint to *Bathsheba*, Louvre (cat. no. 41)]; MacLaren 1960, p. 108 [attributes *Portrait of a Young Woman with her Hands Folded on a Book*, National Gallery, London, to Drost on basis of similarity to *Self-Portrait* (?)]; Haak 1969, p. 223 [signature suggests German origin].

Drost's portrait seems to reflect Rembrandt's portrait style of ca. 1650–55. Valentiner has suggested a strong connection in the facial expression with Rembrandt's *Portrait of Nicolaes Bruyningh*, Kassel, or the *Portrait of Jan Six*, Amsterdam (Valentiner 1939, p. 303). However, Rembrandt's forms are more strongly built up in terms of light and shadow and there is a greater variety of colors while Drost's forms are much weaker, rounder, more decorative and less structurally rendered.

The signature and date on the Metropolitan portrait also present an interesting problem. Following Hofstede de Groot and Raleigh 1956, *Rembrandt and his Pupils*, this writer reads the signature as *Wilhelmus* and not *Wilhelm*. The proposal that Drost was of German origin because the signature has been read as *Wilhelm* (Valentiner 1939, p. 300) is highly questionable. Wihelmus is certainly the Latinized Dutch form of Willem (also the title of the Dutch national anthem) and could refer to some connection with or a reverence for Wilhelmus van Nassau.

The inscription poses a problem in that, according to some, it contains a date and to others just decorative lines. Again following Hofstede de Groot, Bredius and others, it does, indeed, seem to contain a date, but whether it reads 1653, 1655, 1656 or 1666 is difficult to determine. Because the portrait seems to have a long history of association with the *Portrait of a Woman*, Bredius Museum, The Hague, and the sizes are relatively close, we can believe that they are pendants. Bredius' suggestion that they represent Drost and his wife seems plausible when we consider the inscription on the paper held by the man. It contains Drost's name in the same way that Maerten Looten's name appears, as pointed out to me by Stechow, in his portrait in the Los Angeles County Museum of Art. Consequently, it is conceivable that the paper identifies the sitter and the fact that he was in Amsterdam. Because the *Portrait of a Lady* is dated 1653, read by some as 1655, and because the costume of the man is from the early 1650's, one can suggest that this *Self-Portrait* is from 1653.

## 41 *Bathsheba*

Musée du Louvre, Paris

Canvas 101 × 86 cms. signed on paper in lower middle left: *Drost f. 1654* or *Drost fec. 1654 Ill. p. 149*

PROVENANCE sale Dr. Leroy d'Etiolles, Paris, 21–22 Feb. 1861, no. 27; M. de Vandeul, 1866; presented to Museum in 1902 [as Cornelius Drost].

EXHIBITIONS Cambrai, *Exposition circulaire en province*, 1936; Valenciennes-Metz, 1938; Leiden 1956, no. 30, fig. 19; Paris, Louvre, *Exposition de 700 Tableaux tirés des Réserves du département des peintures*, 1960, no. 404; Montreal/Toronto 1969, no. 38

SELECTED REFERENCES L. Demonts, *Catalogue des peintures exposées dans les galeries du Musée National du Louvre, ... Ecoles flamande, hollandaise, ...* 1922, p. 153, no. 2359A [as Jacob or Cornelis van Drost]; C. Hofstede de Groot, "Rembrandt of W. Drost?," *Oud-Holland*, XLVI, 1929, p. 39; A. Bredius, "Een portret van Willem Drost," *Oud-Holland*, XLVI, 1929, p. 98 [as the same model as Drost's *Portrait of his Wife*, Bredius Museum, The Hague]; Martin II, 1936, p. 137 f. [as inspired by Rembrandt's 1654 *Bathsheba*]; Valentiner 1939, pp. 296 [as working with Rembrandt at time of creating *Bathsheba*], 300 ff., fig. I [as recalling Rembrandt's 1654 *Bathsheba*, but Drost's style is more linear], 321 [attributes Dresden *Portrait of a Young Girl* to Drost on basis of similarity of face to Louvre *Bathsheba*]; H. Wehle, "A Gift of Paintings and Drawings," *The Bulletin of the Metropolitan Museum of Art*, XXXVII, 1942, p. 161 [as close in handling of the paint to Drost's *Portrait of a Man*, Metropolitan Museum of Art, N.Y.]; Rosenberg, Slive, Ter Kuile 1966, p. 98, pl. 73A [as inspired by Rembrandt's 1654 *Bathsheba*]; Gerson 1968, p. 188, ill. on p. 120 [as a work of extraordinary charm—at least in terms of finish and technique; element of internal power is another matter]; Haak 1969, p. 223, fig. 373.

Although Drost seems to use Rembrandt's 1654 *Bathsheba*, Louvre, Paris, as his starting point, he changes the composition and content considerably. Drost moves the figure into the foreground and makes it a three-quarter length composition with all our attention focused upon Bathsheba. The figure is bathed in a brilliant white light which stresses the outline of the forms rather than dissolving them as does Rembrandt's light. The rich white, strongly contoured

drapery is typical of Drost (see cat. nos. 42, 45, Oxford, Kassel) and also seems to compare with the shroud upon which Christ rests in the Sarasota *Lamentation* (cat. no. 24). Drost's *Bathsheba* also tends to be more sentimental than Rembrandt's, but this does not detract from the monumental originality of this highly gifted Rembrandt pupil.

## 42 *Ruth and Naomi*

The Visitors of the Ashmolean Museum, Oxford

Canvas 89 × 71 cms. *Ill. p. 150*

PROVENANCE sale C. D. T. Crews, London (Christie's), 1 July 1915, no. 20 [as Carel Fabritius]; with H. A. Butterly, London; F. H. Shiller, London; sale F. H. Shiller, London (Sotheby's), 6 May 1925, no. 16 [as Carel Fabritius]; Mrs. W. F. R. Weldon; presented by latter in 1929.

EXHIBITIONS London, Guild Hall, *Dutch Exhibition*, 1903, no. 139 [as Carel Fabritius]; London 1953 MG, no. 27, ill. [as Barent Fabritius].

SELECTED REFERENCES Sumowski 1957–58, pp. 232, 240 [as Barent Fabritius]; Pont 1958, p. 129 [as unjustly ascribed to Barent Fabritius and attributed to Willem Drost]; *Idem* 1960, pp. 205 f., 208, 210 [points out similarities with Rembrandt in Ruth's gestures, and border decorations of her costume (cf. etching of 1645, *Abraham and Isaac*, Münz 1952, II, fig. 200) and triangular concentration of Naomi's drapery folds (cf. Rembrandt's 1651 *Noli Me Tangere*, Braunschweig)], 218–221 [attributes painting to Drost and dates it ca. 1652–53]; University of Oxford, *Catalogue of Paintings in the Ashmolean Museum*, Oxford, 1962, p. 48, no. 152 [as Drost].

This painting, as first suggested by Pont, seems to belong to the *oeuvre* of Willem Drost. It had formerly been attributed to Carel and Barent Fabritius, but on stylistic grounds the attribution to either of these men cannot be maintained. As Pont writes, [1960, p. 220], the brush stroke is not nearly as free, supple, and broad throughout the entire work as one would find in the work of Barent Fabritius. It also lacks the subtle light effects of Carel and his heavy, thick, multi-colored brush of the 1640's. It certainly cannot be by the Carel Fabritius of the 1650's with the stress on perspective and light backgrounds which started a new style in Delft. The similarities with signed paintings by Drost such as the lighting of Naomi and that of Christ in the Kassel, *Noli Me Tangere* (see cat. no 43) are immediately evident while the similarity in profile between Ruth and the Magdalen [*ibid. p.* 219], the soft and rounded figures created by the use of light and shadow and the strong contrast between light forms placed against a dark background are typical of Drost and compare favorably with his signed and dated 1654 *Bathsheba*, Louvre, Paris (see cat. no. 41). Pont also suggests [*loc. cit.*] that Naomi's drapery is similar to *The Cook*, Coll. Mrs. M. F. Fleischman, London, attributed to Drost by Valentiner [1939, p. 307 f., fig. 9].

It should be interesting to compare the drapery, figure types and light effects of the Oxford, Kassel (see cat. nos. 42, 43) and Paris (see cat. no. 41) pictures with the *Lamentation*, Sarasota (cat. no. 24) generally attributed to the Rembrandt School but possibly by Drost.

The Kunsthalle, Bremen, owns a drawing representing *Ruth and Naomi* which Benesch [VI, p. 392, cat. no. C 100, fig. 1640] calls a good copy by a student working in Rembrandt's studio. Sumowski [1957–58, p. 232] writes that it is not a copy but by a student working in Rembrandt's style, and Pont [1960, pp. 205–221] attributes the drawing to Drost and suggests that it is a study for the Oxford painting. Van den Eeckhout's name has also been suggested [Leiden 1956, no. 112] on the basis of a comparison with his painting in the Museum at Bremen.

## 43 *Noli Me Tangere*

Staatliche Kunstsammlungen, Kassel

Canvas 95.4 × 85.4 cms. signed bottom left on column fragment: *Drost: f. Ill. p. 150*

PROVENANCE sale Jan Agges, Amsterdam, 1702, no. 69; acquired for painting Collection of Landgrave of Hessen-Kassel and cited in Supplement to Inventory of 1749, no. 934.

SELECTED REFERENCES G. Hoet, *Catalogus of Naamlyst van Schilderyen* . . . , The Hague, II, 1752, p. 68 f.; Valentiner 1939, pp. 300 [as containing Caravaggesque elements and dating ca. 1652–53], 304, 308, 311, fig. 5; Van Dyke 1923, p. 61; Vogel 1958, p. 51, no. 261; Pont 1960, pp. 218 f., fig. 3 [relates it to Oxford *Ruth and Naomi* and says Ruth and Magdalen are same model, and play of light and shadow over Christ's body is similar to Naomi's], 221; MacLaren 1960, p. 107.

As pointed out by Valentiner (1939, p. 304), this work by Drost is related to Rembrandt's 1651 painting of the same subject in Braunschweig. However, Drost changes the composition and places the figures close to the foreground. They are no longer small in size but dominate the scene. Drost is Rembrandtesque in his light effects, which stress the facial expressions and gestures, and in his placing of Christ against a lighted background. These features are found in Rembrandt in the late 1640's and early 1650's.

Valentiner attributed to Drost with a question mark a drawing of this subject in the Print Room, Copenhagen (Valentiner 1939, p. 325, note 5, fig. 13). Lugt and Benesch (Benesch VI, p. 400, cat. no. A 84, fig. 1658) reject this attribution while Pont (1960, pp. 212, 218 f., 221) favors the attribution to Drost. Whether the Copenhagen drawing is by Drost is an open question, but it does not seem to be a study for his Kassel picture. Perhaps more closely related to the Drost with regard to large figures placed close to the foreground is Rembrandt's drawing of this subject dated ca. 1655 in the Coll. F. Lugt, Institut Néerlandais, Paris (Benesch V, p. 285, cat. no. 993, fig. 1206).

## 44 *Samuel and Eli*

The Art Institute of Chicago, Wilson L. Mead Fund

Canvas 132 × 110.5 cms. *Ill. p. 151*

PROVENANCE H. L. Terrell, England [formed before 1904]; Mrs. Wilfred Buckley, daughter of Terrell, Moundsmere Manor, Basingstoke, England; sale Mrs. W. Buckley, London (Sotheby's), 23 June 1937, no. 22, purchased by M. Knoedler & Co., London & N.Y.; acquired in 1937.

EXHIBITIONS London 1929, no. 101 [as attributed to Jan Victors and representing *Jacob and Benjamin* ?]; New York 1940, no. 101, ill. [as Barent Fabritius]; Baltimore, Maryland, The Baltimore Museum of Art, *Masterpieces Lent in Honor of the Museum's Golden Jubilee 1914–1964*, 1964 [as Barent Fabritius]; Jerusalem, The Bezalel National Museum, *Works of Faith*, 1965.

SELECTED REFERENCES *Commemorative Catalogue of the Exhibition of Dutch Art held in the Galleries of the Royal Academy, Burlington House London, 1929*, London, 1930, p. 37 [as attributed to Barent Fabritius]; G. W. Longstreet, "A Painting of the Rembrandt School," *Bulletin of the Art Institute of Chicago*, XXXIII, 1939, pp. 1–5, ill. [as being similar in style to 1656 *Apostle Thomas*(?), Kassel, (see cat. no. 27) which has been called Barent Fabritius, Willem Drost, and Nicolaes Maes]; Valentiner 1939, pp. 315 ff., fig. 18 [as probably illustrating *The Departure of Benjamin from Jacob* and painted in a technique closest to Drost]; W. Stechow, "Recent Periodical Literature on 17th Century Painting in The Netherlands And Germany," *The Art Bulletin*, XXIII, 1941, p. 229 [as not by Drost]; Pont 1958, p. 16, note 1 [as attributed to Drost and probably after

1650]; Chicago 1961, p. 159, ill. on p. 189 [as Barent Fabritius and representing *Jacob and Benjamin*].

Not only has there been difficulty in establishing the subject matter of the painting [*Samuel and Eli* or, as Valentiner suggests (1939, p. 315), *The Departure of Benjamin from Jacob*] but also the artist. Valentiner's suggestion that the picture could be by Drost seems possible because none of the pictures generally accepted as being by Barent Fabritius can be compared favorably with the Chicago canvas. Valentiner, in his pro-Drost argument (p. 316 f.) asserts that the subtle and delicate colors are closer to Drost and are very different from those of Barent Fabritius which are strong and direct. Valentiner (p. 315) also suggests that the Chicago painting can be read as a pendant, not in size, but in composition and spirit to the *Hannah and Samuel*, Hermitage, Leningrad, attributed to Drost. One might also add that the general mood, atmosphere and relationship of the figures in the Chicago painting seem to have a close affinity with Rembrandt's *Prodigal Son*, Hermitage, Leningrad, of ca. 1668. This is especially evident in the faces of the elders, half in shadow, looking down upon the young man with such extraordinary warmth and love. Could it be that the idea for the great Rembrandt composition began with the work of a pupil executed in the 1650's, or was the idea already present in a now lost work by Rembrandt?

For a drawing very likely of the same subject but entirely different in composition, see that in the sale Ehlers and others, Leipzig (Boerner), 9 May 1930, no. 136, ill., as Eeckhout, aquarelle in brown, grey, and red: 160 × 205 mm. The two figures are small and set back in space before a building while to the left there is a landscape view. The chief similarity is the placement of darker figures against a light wall.

# GERBRAND VAN DEN EECKHOUT
## 1621–1674

He was born on August 19, 1621 in Amsterdam and was the son of the goldsmith, Jan Pietersz van den Eeckhout. Houbraken, II, p. 79, informs us that Gerbrand was one of the best Rembrandt pupils and that Van den Eeckhout and Roeland Roghman were great friends of Rembrandt during their lifetime (Houbraken, I, p. 137). It is very likely that Van den Eeckhout studied with Rembrandt during the late 1630's, say ca. 1635 to ca. 1640. Van den Eeckhout seems to have worked exclusively in Amsterdam where he died a bachelor and was buried on September 29, 1674. Houbraken, II, p. 80, states that Van den Eeckhout died on September 22, 1674.

Van den Eeckhout was a portrait, history, and genre painter as well as a prolific draughtsman. It was mainly in Van den Eeckhout's religious paintings and drawings that he followed Rembrandt's style—especially the broad manner of the 1640's. After 1660 Van den Eeckhout's style follows Rembrandt's of the 1650's. It was also as early as 1651 (MacLaren 1960, p. 117) that Van den Eeckhout began to paint interiors with gaming soldiers, etc. (see cat. no. 50) which look forward to later works by Pieter de Hoogh. Van den Eeckhout's portraits also follow the more stylish type imported from Flanders rather than Rembrandt's.

## 45 *Isaac Blessing Jacob*

The Metropolitan Museum of Art, New York: Bequest of Collis P. Huntington, 1925 *Ill. p. 129*

Canvas 100.7 × 128.2 cms. signed bottom left of center on step *G. V. eeckhout A° 1642*

PROVENANCE possibly at sale The Hague, 24 April 1737; presented to the museum in 1925 by Collis P. Huntington.

EXHIBITIONS New York, Metropolitan Museum of Art, *The Art of Rembrandt*, 1942; Little Rock, Arkansas Art Center, *Five Centuries of European Painting*, 1963.

SELECTED REFERENCES Sumowski 1957–58, p. 239 f. [as containing Baroque frills typical of his early signed paintings and including shell ornament also often used by Eeckhout and based on original designs in Schwerin Museum]; *idem.*, "Gerbrand van den Eeckhout als Zeichner," *Oud-Holland*, LXXVII, 1962, p. II; Haak 1969, p. 183, fig. 294 [as strongly dependent upon Rembrandt; tankard on table is copy of famous silver piece by Adam van Vianen].

The rich and free application of the paint, the careful highlighting of small details which conveys a sense of the material, and the use of small figures placed in a deep space all bring to mind some of Rembrandt's compositions of the late 1630's and early 1640's [cf. 1640 *Visitation*, cat. no. 7]. Although there is no known painting of this subject by Rembrandt, he did make a number of drawings of this theme in the early 1640's. The ca. 1640–42 sheet, formerly Coll. Van Diemen, Berlin [Benesch III, cat. no. 507, fig. 631] might have been known to Van den Eeckhout. In the drawing one finds a similar decorative treatment of the pillows, the kneeling Jacob with his back to the viewer, Rebecca standing to the left in profile and a stress upon the curtains as an enframing device. However, the space and Isaac's position are entirely different.

This subject was important for the Rembrandt circle around 1640 and Flinck also rendered it in 1638 [Rijksmuseum, Amsterdam, Von Moltke 1965, cat. no. 8, pls. 1–3]. However, the latter places his frontal, three-quarter length figures close to the picture plane. In this way, Flinck's early effort is closer to Rembrandt's preserved drawings from the early 1640's [Benesch III, cat. nos. 508, 510, figs. 632, 633] and the monumental 1656 painting in Kassel of *Jacob Blessing the Sons of Joseph*. This has caused Von Moltke to ask whether or not a lost Rembrandt composition from the 1630's was not behind Flinck's [Von Moltke 1965, p. 17 f.]. One might also ask the same question about the Van den Eeckhout, even though there seems to be some connection between his painting and Rembrandt's drawing formerly with Van Diemen, Berlin. It is also possible that Rembrandt first became aware of the possibilities of this composition through the efforts of his pupils.

## 46  *Daniel Proving the Innocence of Susanna*

Wadsworth Atheneum, Hartford, The Ella Gallup Sumner and Mary Catlin Sumner Collection

Canvas 57.8 × 65.4 cms. *Ill. p. 130*

PROVENANCE perhaps sale Ysselsteyn and others, 26 May 1744, no. 1; perhaps sale Jan Verkolje, the younger, Amsterdam, 24 Oct. 1763, no. 29 [bought by Fouquet]; Earl of Bute, London, 1764–1774; possibly sale de Bèze, Paris, 3 April 1775, no. 48 [bought by Langlier]; sale M. Delplace & others, Paris (Hôtel Drouot), 1958 [bought by J. H. Weitzner]; acquired in 1959.

EXHIBITIONS New York, The Jewish Museum-The Jewish Theological Seminary, *The Hebrew Bible in Christian, Jewish and Muslim Art*, 1963, no. 116.

SELECTED REFERENCES C. C. Cunningham, "Two Paintings by Gerbrandt van den Eeckhout," *Wadsworth Atheneum Bulletin*, V, no. 6, 1960, pp. 14 ff., figs. 7, 8 [as closely following Rembrandt's style of 1640's; weeping Susanna is taken directly from Rembrandt's *Woman Taken in Adultery*, National Gallery, London, 1644; another possible Rembrandt borrowing is Romanesque apse of church seen through opening at left which resembles Temple in Rembrandt's *Reconciliation of David and Absalom*, Leningrad, 1642; Van den Eeckhout probably dates around 1655–1660].

ENGRAVINGS William Baillie, 1764; recut for Earl of Bute in 1774.

This subject was painted and drawn by Rembrandt on a number of occasions and comes from the Vulgate [cf. Cunningham, *op. cit.*, 1960, p. 16]. In this painting Van den Eeckhout clearly returns to his master's style of the 1640's with the strong dependence upon chiaroscuro to draw our attention to the main participants in the story. He also uses Rembrandt's fantastic type of architecture with an opening into the distance on one side [Cunningham, *op. cit.*, 1960, p. 14 f.]. As Cunningham has pointed out, he also borrows a Rembrandt type, the weeping female, in this case Susanna. This crying figure holding a veil to her eyes appears quite often among Rembrandt's pupils and followers and at least twice in Van den Eeckhout [cf. Hartford painting and *Sophonisba*, Duke Anton Ulrich-Museum, Brunswick, 1664]. Van den Eeckhout's technique follows the broad brush of Rembrandt's from the 1640's but in a personal and more crisp manner making his pictures very pleasant to view. They are also somewhat theatrical in character. Because the Hartford picture contains elements similar to those present in works like Van den Eeckhout's *Christ disputing in the Temple*, Munich, 1664; *Sophonisba*, Brunswick, 1664, one might suggest a date from the early 1660's.

## 47  *St. Peter Healing the Lame*

M. H. de Young Memorial Museum, San Francisco, Gift of Mr. and Mrs. George T. Cameron

Canvas 61 × 69.8 cms. signed and dated bottom left on step: *G.v.d. Eeckhout fe A° 1667 Ill. p. 132*

PROVENANCE Gart, Amsterdam, at the latest in 1781; sale G. Hibbert, 13 June 1829, no. 17, bought by J. Neeld; Sir Audley D. Neeld; sale Neeld, London (Christie's), 13 July 1945, no. 60; with F. Mont, N.Y.; W. Heil, San Francisco.

EXHIBITIONS London 1938, no. 144; Leiden 1956, no. 35, fig. 16; Raleigh 1956, no. 22; Montreal/Toronto 1969, no. 47.

SELECTED REFERENCES *The Literary Works of Sir Joshua Reynolds*, edited by H. W. Beechey, London, II, 1835, p. 203 ["some parts of this picture are so exactly like Rembrandt that a connoisseur might without disgrace at first sight mistake it for his"]; J. Byam Shaw, 'Three Drawings of Rembrandt's School,' *Old Master Drawings*, Sept., XIII, 1938, p. 19 f., pl. 17 [as similar to drawing in Coll. Capt. Gathorne-Hardy which also bears slight resemblance to Rembrandt's 1659 etching (Münz 1952, I, cat. no. 239, pl. 276)]; H. Gerson, *Het Tijdperk van Rembrandt en Vermeer*, Amsterdam, 1952, p. 20, fig. 43 [as using Rembrandt's late, broadly painted style found in his history paintings]; Rosenberg, Slive, Ter Kuile 1966, p. 95, pl. 68B [as achieving a truly Rembrandtesque effect with his chiaroscuro and color].

Here Van den Eeckhout uses Rembrandt's free and broad type of brush stroke and chiaroscuro effects of the late 1650's. For a close variant on the composition see painting signed and dated 1666, of this subject in sale Earl of Lonsdale, London (Christie's), 2 July 1937, no. 10, bought by Grant, canvas: 129 × 142 cms., and the drawing for it in the Coll. Capt. G. M. Gathorne-Hardy.

## 48 *Portrait of Jan Pz van den Eeckhout*

Musée des Beaux-Arts, Grenoble

Panel 76 × 58 cms. signed on balustrade bottom left: *G. V. Eeckhout F.A° 1644 Ill. p. 131*

PROVENANCE Very likely portrait described by Houbraken (II, p. 100) as in Coll. Gerbrand van den Eeckhout, son of the wine merchant, Jan; Poullain, Paris; sale Poullain, Paris, 15 March 1780; since 1825 in Musée des Beaux-Arts, Grenoble.

EXHIBITIONS Paris, Petit Palais, *Les chefs-d'oeuvre du Musée de Grenoble*, 1935, no. 60.

SELECTED REFERENCES London 1929, p. 72 [as being similar in composition and style to 1651 *Portrait of Jan Pz van den Eeckhout*, Coll. J. B. Hubrecht, Doorn; also cites 1644 portrait drawing in Print Room, Dresden]; Staring 1948, p. 182 f. [as pendant to *Portrait of Cornelia Dedel* and as more striking than 1651 portrait of same man in Hubrecht Coll.; combines lessons learned from Rembrandt with his own ideas and cites compositional connections with Rembrandt].

Jan Pietersz van den Eeckhout, Gerbrand's father, was a goldsmith who married Cornelia Willemsdr Dedel on February 22, 1633. For further details see next entry.

## 49 *Portrait of Cornelia Dedel*

Dr. Jan B. Hubrecht, Doorn

Panel 75 × 58 cms. signed on balustrade bottom-right corner: *G. V. eeckhout A° 1644 Ill. p. 131*

PROVENANCE In possession of descendants of Cornelia Dedel since her death in 1660.

EXHIBITIONS Leiden, 1850, no. 39; The Hague, Noordeinde Palace, *Tentoonstelling van schilderijen van oude meesters*,

1881, no. 127; Brussels, Palais des Beaux-Arts, *Exposition Néerlandais*, 1882; London 1929, no. 138; Amsterdam, Rijksmuseum, *Drie Eeuwen Portret in Nederland*, 1952, no. 35 [coat of arms is a later addition, and its pendant is *Portrait of Jan Pietersz van den Eeckhout*, Musée des Beaux-Arts, Grenoble].

SELECTED REFERENCES A. Houbraken, *Groote Schouburgh (Quellen-studien zur Holländischen Kunstgeschichte)*, edited by C. Hofstede de Groot, The Hague, 1893, p. 120; E. W. Moes, *Iconographia Batavia*, Amsterdam, I, 1897, no. 1920; Martin II, 1936, p. 129 [as one of the most impressive portraits made in Rembrandt's style]; Staring 1948, pp. 180 f. [as influenced by Rembrandt's chiaroscuro], p. 182 f. [the placement of the sitter at an angle within a window frame and with one hand on the balustrade comes from Rembrandt, for example the 1640 *Self-Portrait*, National Gallery, London, 1641 *Portrait of a Man*, Brussels, 1641 *Portrait of a Woman*, Buckingham Palace], 184 f. [states that *Portrait of Baycken van Bracht (?)*, Coll. Gatacre-De Stuers, is from same time].

The connection between this portrait of Van den Eeckhout's stepmother and portraits by Rembrandt in the 1640's is inescapable. However, the tonality is lighter and there seems to be a great stress on decorative frills. This is especially evident in the painting of the details of the sitter's costume and the curtain to the left. Van den Eeckhout seems to combine Rembrandt's chiaroscuro with the addition of more elegant details found in the fashionable portraiture of the 1640's especially evident in the works of Bartholomeus van der Helst.

## 50 *A Party on a Terrace (Allegory)*

Worcester Art Museum

Canvas 53.6 × 64 cms. signed on terrace bottom left of center: *G. Eeckhout F. Ano. 1652 Ill. p. 132*

PROVENANCE Said to have been in Coll. of King of Holland; possibly Dingwall, London; with R. Langton Douglas, London; with P. & D. Colnaghi and Knoedler & Co., London; with R. Langton Douglas, London; acquired from latter in 1922.

EXHIBITIONS Worcester 1936, no. 24, ill.; Kansas City, William Rockhill Nelson Gallery of Art, *Paintings of Dutch Seventeenth Century Interiors*, 1967-68.

SELECTED REFERENCES E. I. S., "The Garden Party, Gerbrand van den Eeckhout, Dutch, 1621-1674," *Bulletin of the*

*Worcester Art Museum*, XIV, no. 3, 1923, p. 70 ff., ill. [nearness to Rembrandt is shown in richness of costume and color and in treatment of scenes not entirely removed from life of people; influenced by Terborch].

Here Van den Eeckhout continues the long line of elegant garden and terrace parties containing allegorical overtones [for a discussion of this see J. R. Judson, "Dirck Barentsen . . .," *Bulletin der Koninklijke Musea voor Schone Kunsten, Brussel*, 1–2, 1962, pp. 97–108] which began in the sixteenth century. Van den Eeckhout's scene, with the extreme care for the painting of materials and the inclusion of almost living statuary in an atmospheric garden containing elements of classical architecture, must have been known to Pieter de Hoogh who later painted similar scenes during his stay in Amsterdam. This type of painting was also important for Gerard Terborch [see S. J. Gudlaugsson, *Katalog der Gemälde Gerard Ter Borchs*, II, The Hague, 1960, p. 157].

# BARENT FABRITIUS 1624–1673

Barent Fabritius, the younger brother of Carel, was baptized on November 16, 1624 at Midden-Beemster in North Holland. Originally both brothers were known as Barent and Carel Pietersz, but in 1641 this surname was dropped by Carel and replaced by Fabritius (carpenter). By 1650 Barent had also adopted this form. We know that Barent was living in Midden-Beemster in May 1641, in Amsterdam in April 1643, and back in Midden-Beemster in June 1643. He was again in Amsterdam in October 1647 where he signed a document with his brother Carel. A marriage document drawn up in Midden-Beemster in August 1652 informs us that Barent then lived in Amsterdam. It is also likely that Barent visited Delft in the early 1650's, as his wife lived there before their marriage, and Carel was also in residence there from around 1650 until his death in 1654. We know that Barent was living in Midden-Beemster in April 1653 and April 1655, as children of his were baptized there. By 1656, Barent must have been in Leiden where he executed the *Portrait of Willem van der Helm with his Wife and Child*, Rijksmuseum, Amsterdam. Barent was surely in Leiden in January 1657 when he rented a house, and by May 1658 he entered the painters' guild of that city. He is last mentioned in Leiden in October 1658 when he paid his dues to the guild. We find his name in the 1665–1666 register of the Midden-Beemster Church members and three years later he painted a ceiling decoration for a country house near Beemster. After 1669 Barent resided in Amsterdam where he died and was buried on October 20, 1673 in the Leidse Kerkhof (cemetery).

Barent Fabritius was a history, portrait and allegorical-genre painter. His early works, dating from the 1650's, are based on Rembrandt's style of the 1640's although it is not clear from the documents that Fabritius was a Rembrandt pupil. Barent appears to have also been influenced by his brother Carel, Nicolaes Maes, Gerbrand van den Eeckhout, and the Delft School.

## 51  *Self-Portrait* (?)

Museum of Fine Arts, Boston. Lent by the Boston Atheneum

Canvas 64 × 52 cms. *Ill. p. 141*

PROVENANCE Count F. Celestini, Florence, 1883 [as *Self-Portrait* by Rembrandt].

SELECTED REFERENCES C. C. Cunningham, "Four paintings of the Rembrandt School in Boston," *Art in America*, XVII, 1939, pp. 186–188, ill. [dates it about 1647]; Pont 1958, p. 133 [as only known from photograph and therefore unable to judge attribution].

It is possible that this is the same sitter as in Fabritius' ca. 1656–57 *Self-Portrait*, Alte Pinakothek, Munich (Pont 1958, p. 116, no. 33, as *Portrait of a Man*). However, the Boston figure is a bit younger and consequently the portrait would be earlier, perhaps around 1650. The Munich picture is much more three dimensional with a more subtle use of light and shadow to create bolder forms. One might suggest, therefore, that the Boston portrait is either an early work by Barent or, perhaps, even by another hand. Both the Boston and Munich paintings could be the same subject, while the so-called *Self-Portrait of Barent*, Staedelsches Kunstinstitut, Frankfurt, 1650, seems to be another sitter (ill. in Pont 1958, cat. no. 31, fig. 4).

## 52  *The Dismissal of Hagar*

M. H. de Young Memorial Museum, San Francisco, Anonymous Gift

Canvas 108.5 × 108.5 cms. signed falsely to left at bottom: *Rembrandt f. Ill. p. 141*

PROVENANCE possibly sale at Amsterdam, 30 Oct. 1823, no. 233, 103 × 143.5 cms.; Earl of Denbigh, Newnham Paddox [by 1824]; with Colnaghi & Obach, London; anonymous gift to Museum in 1950.

EXHIBITIONS London, British Institution, 1824, no. 100 [as in Coll. Earl of Denbigh]; Manchester 1857, no. 838; London, Guild Hall, *Dutch Exhibition*, 1903, no. 192; Montreal/Toronto 1969, no. 53, ill.

SELECTED REFERENCES J. Smith, VII, 1836, no. 5 [as Rembrandt]; A. Delen in *Thieme-Becker*, Leipzig, X, 1914, p. 355 [as one of many pictures given to Rembrandt but by Van den Eeckhout]; Hofstede de Groot, VI, 1916, p. 26 f., no. 6 [as signed to left of foot: *Rembrandt f.*—a later signature used to be somewhat lower but disappeared in restoration; the authenticity is much disputed and author has not formed any definite conclusion; if genuine, it was painted about 1650; a study in black chalk is in the Albertina (Benesch II, cat. no. 447, fig. 506)]; R. Hamann, "Hagars Abschied bei Rembrandt und im Rembrandt-Kreise," *Marburger Jahrbuch für Kunstwissenschaft*, VIII–IX, p. 15, fig. 14 [points out connection with Lastman in Kunsthalle, Hamburg]; Benesch II, p. 102, cat. no. 447, fig. 506 [says Rembrandt drawing was used by Rembrandt pupil for painting formerly in Coll. Earl of Denbigh]; Pont 1958, pp. 19 f. [as going directly back to Lastman's composition of this subject in the Kunsthalle, Hamburg, of 1612; also points out changes such as greater simplicity in costumes and movements which gives Fabritius' a richer inner life; dates ca. 1650], 103, cat. no. 3, fig. 3 [as a little larger earlier and with false signature: *Rembrandt f.*]; *European Works of Art in the M. H. De Young Memorial Museum*, Berkeley, Calif., 1966, p. 124, ill.

This subject was extremely popular in the Rembrandt circle from about 1640. The general compositional arrangement was not a Rembrandt creation, as pointed out by Hamann, but one established by the master's teacher, Pieter Lastman [for more details concerning the importance of Lastman for Rembrandt's mature years see forthcoming article by Prof. Stechow in *Oud-Holland*]. Rembrandt copied the figures from Lastman's 1612 representation of this subject in a drawing of ca. 1637 now in the Albertina, Vienna [Benesch II, cat. no. 447]. It is this drawing which served as the basic model, but with variations, for Rembrandt's later arrangements, as well as those by his followers [see Benesch III, cat. nos. 499, 525, figs. 499, 654; V, cat. no. 1008, fig. 1222]. Rembrandt makes one important change from Lastman to place Ishmael with his back to the spectator. This occurs in drawings executed in the early 1640's at the time when Fabritius probably knew Rembrandt. A similar arrangement of figures in a landscape, although the central group of three is adult, was used by Gerbrand van den Eeckhout in his representations of *Ruth and Boas*, Museum Boymans-van Beuningen, Rotterdam, 1655; Gallery Léger, Brussels, 1656.

## 53  *Rebecca Welcomed by Abraham*

The Art Institute of Chicago, Wirt D. Walker Fund

Canvas 146 × 180.3 cms.  *Ill. p. 140*

PROVENANCE probably painting described as "Isaac receiving Rebecca, Figures, Camels, etc., Capital . . . Rembrandt," in sale E. Glover, London, 1745, 3rd day, no. 215, purchased by Mrs. Forth; sale Richard Hulse, London (Christie's), 21–22 March, Blackheath 1806, no. 86, bought by Beerens; W. Cole, London, 1836 [as Rembrandt]; E. C. Stuart Cole, London, 1862; sale various properties, London (Christie's), 20 June 1913, no. 85 [as Barent Fabritius], bought by Asher Wertheimer; sale A. Wertheimer, London (Christie's), 18 June 1920 [as Carel Fabritius]; S. del Monte, Brussels, before 1928; on loan to Perth Art Gallery, Australia, 1940–50; on loan to Stedelijk Museum, Gouda, 1952–ca. 1959; sale S. del Monte, London (Sotheby's), 24 June 1959, no. 49, bought by D. Koetser [as School of Rembrandt]; with D. Koetser, Zürich; with Jan Dik, Vevey, 1967; acquired in 1967.

EXHIBITIONS London, British Institution, *Exhibition of the Works of Ancient and Deceased British Artists*, 1862, no. 65; Kunstzaal Kleykamp, The Hague, *De Verzameling Del Monte*, 1932, no. 22, ill.; Sheffield, Art Gallery, *Del Monte Collection*, 1950–51.

SELECTED REFERENCES J. Smith, VII, 1836, p. 258, no. 617; Hofstede de Groot, VI, 1916, p. 24, no. 1 [as Rembrandt's *Abraham Presenting Sarah to Abimelech*]; G. Glück, *La Collection del Monte*, Vienna, 1928, pp. 17 ff., no. 22, pl. 22 [as *Abraham Received by Rebecca* and reflecting spirit of Rembrandt's atelier in 1648–50; describes similarity in style and composition to *Good Samaritan*, Louvre, and suggests N. Maes as artist but retouched by Rembrandt]; A. C. Mayer, "Die Sammlung del Monte in Brussel," *Pantheon*, IV, 1929, p. 442 [as Rembrandt's shop]; P. Bautier, "La Collection del Monte à Bruxelles," *Gazette des Beaux-Arts*, XVIII, 1928, p. 320 f. [as Rembrandt ca. 1650]; Valentiner 1932, pp. 227, [as same hand as *The Robbing of Joseph by his Brethren* (?), Coll. Van Gelder, Brussels, and by Barent Fabritius, ca. 1648], 235, fig. 25 [youth behind camel has same features as *Portrait of Artist* formerly attributed to Rembrandt (Valentiner 1908, no. 346), Wadsworth Atheneum, Hartford, which is possibly Barent's self-portrait]; P. K., "Tentoonstellingen Den Haag, De verzameling Del Monte . . .," *Maandblad voor Beeldende Kunsten*, IX, 1932, p. 283 [as attributed to Barent Fabritius by A. Bredius]; G. W. Longstreet, "A Painting of the Rembrandt School," *Bulletin of the Art Institute of Chicago*, XXXIII, 1939, p. 4

[as Barent Fabritius]; Pont 1958, pp. 126, cat. no. 1* [placed in category of doubtful attributions to Barent Fabritius], 143–146 [as presumably a Rembrandt atelier work because of different styles and very possibly retouched here and there by Rembrandt; relates painting to Rembrandt's ca. 1637 drawing of the *Departure of Rebecca from her Parents' Home* (Benesch I, cat. no. 147, fig. 159); suggests that Drost painted main group which was retouched by Rembrandt and possibly the whole composition is based on an unknown Rembrandt invention; also suggests that Barent Fabritius did the figures on the left and the landscape while Maes those on the right as well as the architecture]; W. Sumowski, "Daniel Pont, Barent Fabritius," [review] *Kunstchronik*, XII, 1959, p. 292 [as more likely Barent under the strong influence of Carel].

There seem to be three different styles present in this painting, but whether or not this was an atelier work by three artists, with Rembrandt's correcting brush, is open to question. It could be one artist experimenting with three different styles. Willem Drost, Barent Fabritius, and Nicolaes Maes worked in Rembrandt's atelier or were closely connected with it in the late 1640's when this picture was probably executed.

C. C. Cunningham has pointed out that according to records [Frank Simpson, "Dutch Paintings in England before 1760," *Burlington Magazine*, XCV, 1953, p. 41f.] this painting fetched the second highest price of any painting attributed to Rembrandt sold publicly in England from 1722–1759. He points out that even though the painting is not by Rembrandt, it did represent the British concept of Rembrandt in the eighteenth century. The landscape in this painting has many similarities to the *Mill* so much admired in England at the time.

## 54  *The Satyr and the Peasant*

Wadsworth Atheneum, Hartford, The Ella Gallup Sumner and Mary Catlin Sumner Collection

Canvas 47.6 × 62.8 cms. *Ill. p. 142*

PROVENANCE David Cartier, N.Y.; Paul M. Warburg, N.Y. [as N. Maes]; sale Nina (Mrs. Paul M.) Warburg, N.Y. (Meredith Galleries), 13 April 1946, no. 823; purchased in 1946 from D. Koefser, N.Y.

EXHIBITIONS Chicago 1935, no. 14; Worcester 1936, no. 15; Hartford, Conn., Wadsworth Atheneum, *In Retrospect— Twenty-one Years of Museum Collecting*, 1949, no. 27; Raleigh 1956, p. 118, no. 31; New London, Conn., Lyman

Allyn Museum, *The Golden Age of Dutch Painting—A Loan Exhibition from New England Collections*, 1962, no. 9; Hartford, Conn., Wadsworth Atheneum, *Harvest of Plenty*, 1963, no. 13.

SELECTED REFERENCES Valentiner 1932, p. 239, fig. 43 [the spatial arrangement and bright lighting of the walls against which the main figures stand out show connection with Carel Fabritius and dates ca. 1652]; C. C. Cunningham, "A Painting by Rembrandt's Pupil Barent Fabritius in the Wadsworth Atheneum," *Art Quarterly*, IX, 1946, pp. 360 ff. [as dating 1652-1656; influenced by Delft School in silhouetting of figures against light background and also influenced in both conception and technique by such works as Rembrandt's Leningrad *Holy Family*]; Wadsworth Atheneum, *Bulletin*, November 1946, p. 1, ill.; Pont 1958, pp. 32 f. [as dating ca. 1653–54 and suggests that Fabritius knew Jordaens' compositions of this subject and that intimate character of painting recalls Rembrandt], 34, 79–82, 113 f., 159, cat. no. 26, fig. 8.

This story, most likely inspired by one of the many representations of this theme painted by Jacob Jordaens and his studio beginning around 1619, illustrates the fable of Aesop. "A certain man made friends with a Satyr and took a meal with him. It was winter and the man feeling cold put his hands to his mouth and blew upon them. When the Satyr asked him why he did this, he answered: 'To warm my hands, which are cold.' When shortly after this the hot dinner was served, the man blew on it, and again being asked why he did so, said: 'To cool my food.' Thereupon the Satyr said, 'I will not have your friendship, for you blow cold and hot from one and the same mouth' " [taken from M. Rooses, *Jacob Jordaens*, translated by E. C. Broers, London-New York, 1908, p. 18].

Barent's stylistic connection with Carel Fabritius and Rembrandt have long been accepted, but one wonders whether Nicolaes Maes may not have influenced the conception of this painting. The silhouetting of forms against a light background on one side of the composition with the other side plunged into darkness can also be documented in Maes' work as early as 1655; for example, the *Allegory of a Maid Scraping a Parsnip*, London, National Gallery. The light, delicate coloring of the mother and child in the center, and the broad handling of the brush creating an intimacy very similar to Maes' works from the 1650's, continue in painting the marvelous family drawings made by Rembrandt in the 1640's. It is possible that Barent met Maes around 1650 in either Amsterdam or Delft, although there is no documentation that Maes ever visited the latter city.

In fact, the interrelationship between Carel Fabritius, Nicolaes Maes, and Pieter de Hoogh is still to be worked out.

For other representations of the subject by Barent, but not related compositionally to the Hartford painting, see Pont 1958, p. 113 f., cat. nos. 26, 27; p. 124 f., cat. nos., 6, 7. Constantijn van Renesse's representation of this subject signed and dated 1653, in the National Museum, Warsaw, shows close stylistic affinities with Fabritius in the handling of the paint and use of chiaroscuro, but there is no connection in the arrangement of the figures—illustrated in H. Gerson, "Rembrandt in Poland," *The Burlington Magazine*, XCVIII, 1956, p. 282 f., fig. 38. One also finds this subject by still another follower of Rembrandt, this time a pupil, Gerbrand van den Eeckhout, in a drawing in the Hamburg, Kunsthalle, no. 21915 [red and black chalk, grey wash: 190 × 258 mm., ill. in Sumowski 1962, p. 11 f., fig. 20]. This is a study for his 1653 painting formerly with Rosenthal, Berlin.

55 *Allegory: Woman Picking Fleas from a Child's Head*
Hessisches Landesmuseum, Darmstadt

Canvas 85 × 72 cms. signed middle-right margin with false signature: *Rembrandt 1652 Ill. p. 142*

PROVENANCE acquired from Artaria, Vienna, in 1810–1811.

SELECTED REFERENCES G. Rathgeber, *Annalen der niederländischen Malerei*, Gotha, 1839, p. 201 [as perhaps painted by Titus van Rijn?]; R. Hofmann, *Die Gemäldesammlung des Grossherzoglichen Museums zu Darmstadt*, Darmstadt, 1872, no. 378 [as perhaps G. Flinck and probably dated 1652]; W. Bode, "Berichte und Mitteilungen . . . zu den Bilderbenennungen der Darmstädter Gemälde-Galerie," *Repertorium für Kunstwissenschaft*, III, 1880, p. 317 [as Barent Fabritius]; Wurzbach, I, p. 525 [as falsely signed *Rembrandt* with an old indistinct signature and a date 1652; reminds one of Jan Vermeer]; F. Back, *Grossherzoglich Hessisches Landesmuseum in Darmstadt, Verzeichnis der Gemälde*, Darmstadt, 1914, p. 141, no. 261, ill. [writes that the attribution to Flinck is as little tenable as that to Maes; at present it seems to be an early work by Barent Fabritius and recalls the color and transparent light of the background found in Fabritius' 1650 portrait, Staedelsches Kunstinstitut, Frankfurt a /M.]; Pont 1958, p. 128, cat. no. 6* [under category of doubtful attributions or unjustly ascribed to Barent Fabritius; however, color scheme recalls Barent, but the linear treatment of the drapery in the lap raises some doubts concerning the attribution to Barent].

Stylistically the picture seems to be closely related to Barent Fabritius in the color tones and the treatment of the wall. Pont (1958, p. 128) likens it to Fabritius' 1662 *Satyr and the Peasant* in Bergamo. It also would be of interest to compare the Darmstadt painting with the Hartford *Satyr and the Peasant* of ca. 1653–54. The Darmstadt painting might be seen as the start of Fabritius' interest in rendering indoor scenes with a real feeling for space and the use of light and shadow to obtain this effect. This could very well be the case, as the *Allegory of the Woman Combing the Child's Hair* bears a date of 1652 which could be original. This interest in creating a readable interior space containing an intimate scene could have been done under the influence of his brother Carel, whom Barent visited in Delft in the early 1650's.

Although there seem to be strong affinities between the Darmstadt painting and Barent Fabritius, this attribution needs further consideration. The soft and rounded drapery with forms bounded by contours and the painting of the white collar and head band also seem to be connected with several paintings attributed to Rembrandt and his Circle. [cf. *Woman Cutting her Nails*, Metropolitan Museum of Art, N.Y.; *Young Woman Sleeping*, Museum of Fine Arts, Springfield, attributed to Samuel van Hoogstraten; *Virgin of the Annunciation*, National Gallery, Prague, cat. no. 26].

The subject appears to have become popular around 1650, and might find its beginnings in the *oeuvre* of Gerard Dou [cf. ca. 1650 paintings in Cook Coll., Richmond and Alte Pinakothek, Munich, ill. in W. Martin, *Gerard Dou; des Meisters Gemälde*, pp. 94–96 and is also present in Gerard Terborch [cf. ca. 1652–53, Maruitshuis, The Hague, ill. in S. J. Gudlaugsson, *Gerard Terborch*, I, The Hague, 1959, p. 254, no. 95], Michael Sweets [Musée des Beaux-Arts, Strasbourg, ill, in Rotterdam, Museum Boymans-van Beuningen, *Michael Sweerts en Tijdgenoten*, 1958, no. 14, ill.] and others.

The subject matter has been explained by Gudlaugsson [*op. cit.*, II, 1959, p. 106 f.] as illustrating the following emblematic text taken from J. Cats, *Spiegel van den Oude ende Nieuwen tydt*, The Hague, 1632: "De kam is wonder nut, de kam is wonder net. De kam is die het hooft in beter orde set" [The comb is wonderfully useful, the comb is wonderfully clean. The comb is that which sets the head in better order].

## CAREL FABRITIUS 1622–1654

Carel Pietersz was baptized on February 27, 1622 at Midden-Beemster. He was the son of Pieter Carelsz, a schoolmaster, but it seems that Carel did not follow his father's profession but in his youth became a carpenter. This probably explains why he added the name Fabritius (*faber* meaning carpenter) to his Christian name sometime before 1641. His brothers Barent and Johannes also adopted this surname. It is possible that Carel began to study painting with his father who, by 1620, painted as a hobby. It is very likely that he moved to Amsterdam, after his wedding in September 1641, as Hoogstraten tells us that they both studied with Rembrandt at the same time. (S. van Hoogstraten, *Inleyding tot de Hooge Schoole der Schilderkonst*, 1678, p. 11). We know that Hoogstraten did not enter Rembrandt's studio before 1641, so it seems likely that Carel entered the atelier in late 1641 and remained through the following year. In June 1643 Carel was back in Midden-Beemster as his name appears on a list of parishioners and a child, very likely his, was buried there in August of the same year. We also know that Carel was in Midden-Beemster in April 1646, but because of the short distance between this town and Amsterdam (MacLaren 1960, p. 126), he could easily have traveled the 15 miles on more than one occasion during the years 1646–48. Perhaps the 1648 *Portrait of Abraham de Potter*, Rijksmuseum, Amsterdam, was painted in Amsterdam, as the latter lived there; but he is also known to have visited Midden-Beemster at least once. Carel married a second time in Midden-Beemster in August 1650, but shortly thereafter the couple is said to have been living in Delft where he resided for the rest of his life. Records from Delft tell us that he was there in May 1651, and in October 1652 he became a member of the Delft painters' guild. Other documents record his presence in Delft in February and August 1653. In July 1654 he received payments for painting two coats of arms, and on October 12, 1654 he died from injuries sustained in the explosion of the Delft ammunition depot.

Fabritius was a portrait, genre, and history painter. There are few documented works from his hand, and the earliest, *The Raising of Lazarus* (see cat. no. 57) clearly shows his connection with Rembrandt's style of the early 1640's and compositions of the early 1630's. His style changes with the 1648 *Portrait of Abraham de Potter*, Rijksmuseum, Amsterdam, toward a much lighter color. He is also said to have executed illusionistic perspective pictures in Delft, especially wall paintings, but only the small perspective picture in London, National Gallery, *The View of Delft*, is still extant (for documentation see MacLaren 1960, p. 126 f.). Pictures like Fabritius' *Sentinel*, Schwerin, and the *Goldfinch*, Mauritshuis, The Hague, demonstrate how influential he was on the new style in Delft which developed shortly

after 1650. He was important for Vermeer, (who may have been Carel's pupil,) Pieter de Hoogh, Emanuel de Witte and others. His only documented student, Mathias Spoors, was killed in the same explosion with Carel.

## 56 *The Beheading of St. John the Baptist*

Rijksmuseum, Amsterdam (as attributed to Carel Fabritius)

Canvas 149 × 121 cms. *Ill. p. 137*

PROVENANCE probably the painting of this subject cited as Fabritius in sale Catharina Deyl, widow of Nic. Roosendael, Amsterdam, 16 May 1687; possibly picture described in sale, Amsterdam, 16 May 1696, no. 76; sale P. Fouquet, Amsterdam, 13 April 1801, as by Rembrandt; National Museum, The Hague, 1808.

EXHIBITIONS Groningen, Museum van Oudheden, *Oude Meesters*, 1946, no. 31; Warsaw 1956, no. 29; Leiden 1956, no. 16 [as Rembrandt School].

SELECTED REFERENCES G. Hoet, *Catalogus of Naamlyst van Schilderyen*, I, The Hague, 1752, p. 37, no. 76; W. Bürger, "Notes sur les Fabritius," *Gazette des Beaux-Arts*, VII, 1865, p. 82; O. Eisenmann, "Die Taufe Johannis des Täufers von Bernhart Fabritius," *Zeitschrift für bildende Kunst*, XVI, 1881, p. 404; H. Havard, *La Peinture Hollandaise*, Paris, IV, 1881, p. 61; C. Hofstede de Groot, *Catalogue of Dutch Painters*, I, 1908, p. 573, no. 2 [as very uncertain attribution and formerly called Rembrandt and for a time Drost]; Hofstede de Groot VI, 1916, pp. 10 [as variously ascribed to Rembrandt, Drost, Carel Fabritius and must be by a contemporary of G. Flinck, F. Bol, and Victors while in Rembrandt's studio ca. 1633–35; old woman recalls Rebecca type in works by Flinck and Victors while executioner and corpse recall Lievens' Leiden period]; 460, note 48; Van Dyke 1923, p. 79 [types hardly suggest Fabritius]; Wijnman 1931, p. 140, fig. 12 [asks if picture by Fabritius of this subject cited in 1687 inventory is the one given to Carel in Rijksmuseum]; Valentiner 1932, pp. 210 ff. [as a rare subject in Dutch art and dating from Carel's apprenticeship with Rembrandt; some features suggest pupils of 1630's like G. Flinck in old woman at left and color scheme and Jan Victors who used similar isocephalic arrangement of background figures; the chiaroscuro and tonal differentiations recall Rembrandt of early 1640's as do certain types— Salome, executioner, old woman at left]; Martin, II, 1936, pp. 504, note 131, 3a, 508, note 242 [as only attributed to Carel; Martin sees even less of the former's hand than did Hofstede de Groot]; K. E. Simon, "Ein neuentdecktes

Werk des Carel Fabritius," *Zeitschrift für Kunstgeschichte*, V, 1936, p. 320 [as ca. 1643 and certainly Carel Fabritius when compared with Warsaw *Raising of Lazarus*]; Starzyński 1935–36, pp. 95–113; G. Knuttel, *De Nederlandsche Schilderkunst*, 1938, p. 276; A. Heppner, "Thoré-Bürger en Holland," *Oud-Holland*, LV, 1938, p. 73 f. [that Thoré-Bürger was first to see this as Carel and not Drost]; A. Bredius, "Een Vroeg Werk van Carel Fabritius," *Oud-Holland*, LVI, 1939, pp. 5, 8, 13, fig. 11; Schuurman 1947, pp. 10–17 [as more than one hand; compares head of old woman on left with Rebecca's in G. Flinck's 1638 *Blessing of Isaac*, Rijksmuseum, Amsterdam; compares executioner with School of Rembrandt, *Study*, Oslo Museum (Br. no. 241); cannot be before 1642 and unable to tell which part Carel painted although he may be the artist]; Starzyński 1956, pp. 402–418 [doubts attribution to Carel and sees G. Flinck as main artist with possibility of several heads being done by Fabritius—possibly those in background]; H. Gerson, "Rembrandt in Poland," *The Burlington Magazine*, XCVIII, 1956, p. 283 [questions attribution to Carel]; Th. H. Lunsingh Scheurleer, "Rembrandt en het Rijksmuseum," *Bulletin van het Rijksmuseum*, IV, 1956, p. 27, fig. 2 [discusses history of picture including fact that it was the first Rembrandt purchased by Rijksmuseum in 1801 and ca. 1850 it was, with sadness, ascribed to Carel Fabritius and G. Flinck]; Rosenberg, Slive, Ter Kuile 1966, p. 93 [as one of earliest paintings attributed to Carel].

MEZZOTINT Signed bottom-left margin *Rembrandt pinx* and bottom-right margin *L. A. Claessens sculp*

To judge from the documented works of Carel Fabritius, it is not possible that this is a mature work by him, nor, as suggested by several writers, an early work by Carel using Rembrandt types. It is evident that more than one painting style is visible in this picture. Perhaps we can see here a student experimenting, or possibly the painting was actually executed by several students or collaborators connected with Rembrandt.

## 57 *The Raising of Lazarus*

Museum Narodowe, Warsaw

Canvas 210 × 140 cms. signed on bottom center of sarcophagus: *Car. Fabr Ill. p. 139*

PROVENANCE perhaps painting cited in sale Amsterdam, 16 Sept. 1739, no. 151 [called *Raising of Lazarus* and by Rembrandt]; Church of St. Alexander, Warsaw by 1855 and attributed to the German imitator of Rembrandt, C. W. E. Dietrich (1712–74).

EXHIBITIONS Warsaw 1956, no. 38, ill.; Leiden 1956, no. 43, fig. 11.

SELECTED REFERENCES Starzyński 1936, pp. 95–113 [first published painting as Carel Fabritius after signature was found during 1935 cleaning. He suggests figures are portraits of Rembrandt and his family and states work is strongly influenced by 1642 *Night Watch*; He dates it between 1643–46 after the *Beheading of St. John the Baptist* (cat. no. 56)]; K. E. Simon, "Ausländische Kunst in Polen—II. Ein neuentdecktes Werk des Carel Fabritius," *Zeitschrift für Kunstgeschichte*, V, 1936, pp. 317–320, figs. 4, 5 [in the 19th century given to Dietrich and also points out connections with Rembrandt such as old man on left behind Mary who recalls Manoah in *Sacrifice of Manoah*, Dresden, 1641; types and gestures recall etching of *Triumph of Mordecai*, ca. 1639–40 (Münz 1952, I, cat. no. 178, fig. 198); composition recalls 1630 and 1642 etchings of *Raising of Lazarus* (ibid., cat. nos. 192, 214, figs. 214, 241); theatrically it belongs to Passion series made in 1639 for Frederik Hendrik]; A. Bredius, "Een vroeg werk van Carel Fabritius," *Oud-Holland*, LVI, 1939, p. 8, figs. 8–10 [as a very early work and under strong influence of Rembrandt's 1632 etching of this subject; woman to left and behind sarcophagus wears pearl head decoration similar to second woman from right in Amsterdam *Beheading of St. John the Baptist* (cat. no. 56).]; Schuurman 1947, pp. 20–27, 28 ff., ill. pp. 21, 27 [as probably painted in 1643, the year Carel probably left Rembrandt's studio, and as recalling works of early thirties such as Rembrandt's *Raising of Lazarus*, Private Coll., California, the ca. 1632 etching (Münz 1952, I, cat. no. 192, fig. 214) and the 1630–32 drawing in the Museum Boymans-van Beuningen, Rotterdam (for proper date of 1640–42 and ill. see Benesch III, cat. no. 518 recto, fig. 644)]; J. Białostocki-M. Walicki, *Europäische Malerei in polnischen Sammlungen*, Warsaw, 1957, p. 529, no. 240, figs. 240–243; Starzyński 1956, pp. 402–418, figs. 1, 6, 7, 9–14 [as first completely independent work probably done just after leaving Rembrandt's atelier; color and light are similar to 1642 *Night Watch*; suggests that Rembrandt's portrait is present in turbaned figure with outstretched arm in center just behind sarcophagus]; MacLaren 1960, p. 125 f. [as showing acquaintance with *Night Watch*]; Gerson 1968, p. 68, ill. [as dated 1642]; Haak 1969, p. 182, fig. 292 [as unmistakably influenced directly by Rembrandt's etchings and painting of this subject].

As suggested in several of the publications cited above, the *Resurrection of Lazarus* must be considered as Fabritius' first known work executed after he left Rembrandt's studio around 1642. This painting can be connected not only with the master's works from about 1630 but also, contrary to Schuurman (p. 28), with those done around 1642. The connections with Rembrandt's painting of this subject done about 1630 in a Private Coll., California, in the posture of Christ, the placement of the tomb, and the terrified gestures of the secondary figures, have all been pointed out by Schuurman. He also discusses the main difference between the master and pupil, the use of chiaroscuro. In the Rembrandt the light comes from an unknown source outside of the composition—a typical Caravaggio idea—while in the Fabritius the light emanates from the rising Lazarus. Schuurman (p. 29) also neatly shows the relationship between the painting and the ca. 1631–32 etching which he finds especially evident in the gestures, positions, and facial expressions (cf. for example Virgin with clasped hands and figure in left background of etching, figure in right foreground of painting and etching). Schuurman also cites a connection with Rembrandt's drawing of this subject in Rotterdam in the placement of the young boy standing next to Christ. However, Schuurman dates the drawing from ca. 1630–32 whereas it certainly belongs to the years around 1640–42 (see Benesch III, cat no. 518r) and differs very much from the earlier painting and etching in the inclusion of a greater number of secondary figures. Fabritius might very well have taken this idea of expanding the number of figures in the scene and combined it with the *Night Watch* idea of placing them in a variety of levels with marvelous highlights striking their hands, parts of their faces, and costumes. Fabritius combined a number of Rembrandt ideas to produce a highly original and monumental rendering of this subject in this, his earliest known independent creation.

## 58  *Head of an Old Man*

Royal Gallery of Paintings "Mauritshuis," The Hague

Panel 26 × 21 cms. *Ill. p. 138*

PROVENANCE Harrach, Vienna; with Hoogendijk, Amsterdam, 1935; H. L. Larsen, Wassenaar; presented to Museum by Susi Larsen, Wassenaar, 1938.

EXHIBITIONS Amsterdam 1936, no. 44; New York/Toledo/Toronto 1954–55, no. 21; Leiden 1956, no. 46.

SELECTED REFERENCES C. Hofstede de Groot, *Jan Vermeer van Delft en Carel Fabritius*, Amsterdam [1907], pp. 7 f., 11, no. 55, ill. [in Vienna first called Spanish School, then Barent Fabritius, and then C. Hofstede de Groot gave it to Carel]; Valentiner 1932, p. 214, fig. 13 [as second half of

the forties]; Mauritshuis, *Catalogue Raisonné des Tableaux et Sculptures, Supplément de 1939, . . .* , The Hague, 1939, p. 7, no. 88, ill.; Schuurman 1947, p. 36, ill. on p. 37 [as done at the same time as the *Study of an Old Man*, Groningen, ca. 1642–43 but more carefully worked out].

COPY Coll. Mrs. Gatacre-de Steurs, De Wiersse, Vorden, canvas: 23 × 19 cms.

The paint is applied in thick, varied patches of color. In the forehead it seems to have been so quickly laid on that it runs to the bridge of the nose. The light brown underpaint plays an important role in this picture and forms the main color from the shoulders down. It is also part of the color scheme of the hat and the beard. The thick multi-colored but fluid paint occurs also in Rembrandt's studies of heads executed in the early 1640's during and after Fabritius worked in the master's shop [see Bauch 1966, nos. 178–181, and *passim*].

Here Fabritius' paint is less structural and the tone is much darker than the *Man with a Helmet* (cat. no. 59). The latter seems to mark a change in Fabritius's style toward the 1648 *Portrait of Abraham de Potter*, Rijksmuseum, Amsterdam, in which a dark form is placed against a light background.

The hat is the type commonly worn by orthodox Jews in Central Europe.

## 59  *Man with a Helmet*

Groninger Museum voor Stad en Lande, Groningen

Panel 38.5 × 31 cms. *Ill. p. 138*

PROVENANCE possibly painting described as "A Soldier's Portrait" (een krijchsmans troonij) in Inventory of Aeltje Velthuysen, 24 April 1643, the wife of Carel Fabritius; possibly *Mars* cited in 1666 Inventory of Adriaan Evertsz van Bleyswijck, Delft which was inherited and listed in Inventory of Anna van Eyck, Delft, 1669; P. Delaroff, St. Petersburg (Leningrad); C. Hofstede de Groot; presented to Groningen in 1931.

EXHIBITIONS Rotterdam, Museum Boymans, *Vermeer*, 1935, no. 20, fig. 20; Brussels, Paleis voor Schoone Kunsten, *De Hollandsche Schilderkunst van Jeroen Bosch tot Rembrandt*, 1946, no. 29, ill.; London 1952–53, no. 155; Zürich, Kunsthaus, *Holländer des 17. jahrhunderts*, 1953, no. 32; Rome, Palazzo delle Esposizioni, *Mostra di Pittura Olandese del Seicento*, 1954, no. 36, fig. 25; Milan 1954, no. 43, ill.; Delft, Het Prinsenhof, *Meesterwerken uit Delft*, 1962, no. 17, fig. 6.

SELECTED REFERENCES C. Hofstede de Groot, *Jan Vermeer van Delft en Carel Fabritius*, Amsterdam [1907], no. 37, ill.; *Idem.*, *Catalogue of Dutch Painters*, I, 1908, p. 576, no. 10 [as placed before a white background like *The Goldfinch*, Mauritshuis, The Hague, and *The Sentinel*, Schwerin]; Van Dyke 1923, p. 80; Wijnman 1931, pp. 112, 128, 140 [cites 1666 and 1669 inventories quoted in Provenance]; Groningsch Museum, *Verzameling Dr. C. Hofstede de Groot. Schilderijen en Teekeningen*, 1931, p. 5 f., no. 4; J. Q. van Regteren Altena, "Groningen's Aanwinsten," *Maandblad voor Beeldende Kunsten*, VIII, 1931, p. 67 f., fig. 1 [as painted from life]; Valentiner 1932, pp. 210 [suggests possibility that this could be *Mars* cited in 1666 and 1669 inventories], 213 f., fig. 7; Martin II, 1936, p. 178 f., fig. 90 [as executed shortly after leaving Rembrandt's shop and in its browns still recalling Rembrandt but placement of dark figure against a light background indicates a new attitude; Schuurman 1947, pp. 36 ff., ill. p. 39 [as dating from 1645–46 and possibly inspired by Rembrandt's work of ca. 1645–46 such as the 1645 *Man Reading*, Williamstown, Mass. (cat. no. 22); also perhaps showing the start of a new palette and technique in rendering wall, while color of jacket relates to Rembrandt of ca. 1645]; Pont 1958, p. 136 f. [reproduces 1643 inventory]; Rosenberg, Slive, Ter Kuile 1966, p. 93.

It is possible that this is the *Mars* cited in the 17th-century inventory above (for a discussion of *Mars* see B. Nicolson, *Hendrick Terbrugghen*, London, 1958, p. 102 f.). That the placement of the dark form against a light background marks a change in Fabritius' use of chiaroscuro is evident when one compares this painting with the *Raising of Lazarus* (cat. no. 57), probably done after Fabritius left Rembrandt in 1643. However, Rembrandt had been using reverse chiaroscuro since the late 1620's (cf. Bauch 1966, nos. 119, 120) and this cannot be seen as a Fabritius innovation. Because the colors and handling of the face and jacket recall those of Rembrandt's in the 1640's, the painting must date from sometime after the Warsaw *Raising of Lazarus* and shortly before the light tonality of the 1648 *Portrait of Abraham de Potter*, Rijksmuseum, Amsterdam. The *Man with the Helmet* also looks forward to *The Sentinel*, Schwerin, of 1654, in the highlighting of the helmet, the use of reverse chiaroscuro and also subject matter.

# GOVERT FLINCK 1615–1660

Govert Teunisz Flinck was born on January 25, 1615 at Cleves, on the German side of the Dutch border. Houbraken II, p. 15, informs us that at an early age Flinck began making drawings of small insects and studies of men, while working as an apprentice for a silk merchant in Cleves. After much objection from his family, Flinck was finally allowed to study painting in Leeuwarden with the Mennonite preacher Lambert Jacobsz who had visited Cleves about 1630. While studying with Lambert Jacobsz, Flinck met Jacob Backer, and the two students went off to Amsterdam to study with Rembrandt around 1631–32. By 1636 he had left Rembrandt's studio. In 1645 he married Inghitta Thoveling, from an old and respected Rotterdam family. She died in 1649, and in 1656 Flinck married Sophia van der Hoeven. Flinck was extremely successful and beginning in the 1640's was commissioned to do a number of group portraits. He also executed the largest portion of the painted decoration for the new Town Hall in Amsterdam beginning in 1656. He died before he was able to complete the decoration on February 2, 1660.

Flinck was a portrait, history, and genre painter. His works until about 1642 were in the style of Rembrandt; after that time he changed to the more elegant, stylish mode of B. van der Helst, which was itself based upon the Flemish portrait style of Rubens and Van Dyck.

## 60 *Hermes and Aglauros*

Museum of Fine Arts, Boston, Martha Ann Edwards Fund

Canvas 72 × 91 cms. signed with a false inscription, bottom left on step *Rembrandt 1652 Ill. p. 126*

PROVENANCE purchased by father of Francis Brooks in Paris 1854 [as Rembrandt]; Francis Brooks, Boston; purchased in 1903 as Rembrandt.

EXHIBITIONS Chicago 1935–36, no. 15; Worcester 1936, no. 16; Michigan, Grand Rapids Art Gallery, *Masterpieces of Dutch Art*, 1940, no. 22; Montreal, Art Association, *Five Centuries of Dutch Art*, 1944; Kleve, Städtisches Museum Haus Koekkoek, *Govaert Flinck*, 1965, no. 13, ill.

SELECTED REFERENCES *Museum of Fine Arts Bulletin, Boston*, I, 1903, no. 4, p. 23 [as *Danaë* by Rembrandt]; C. Hofstede de Groot in Thieme-Becker, *Künstler-Lexikon*, XII, 1916, p. 99 [as Flinck]; Von Moltke, 1965, p. 83, no. 85, pl. 16 [probably painted in 1639 or 1640 and cf. Flinck's *Sacrifice of Monoah*, with C. M. Spink, London, 1969].

The thick, heavy, and rough application of the paint, the placement of the main figures before a building to one side, and a view into a landscape on the other are characteristics taken over from Rembrandt. The awkward figure types are typical of Flinck's oeuvre [cf. Von Moltke, 1965, plates 10, 14, 15].

The story, as first identified by Panofsky, illustrates the moment when Aglauros, a daughter of Cecrops, was punished by Hermes. He turned Aglauros into stone because she tried to keep Hermes from entering her sister Herse's house. Hermes had fallen in love with Herse.

## 61  *The Return of The Prodigal Son*

North Carolina Museum of Art, Raleigh

Canvas 133.4 × 170.2 cms. *Ill. p. 128*

PROVENANCE Justina van Baerle (widow of David Becker), Amsterdam; Sir Francis, Sir Frederick, and Sir Herbert Cook, Richmond, England, no. 257.

EXHIBITIONS London 1899, no. 89 [as Rembrandt]; Raleigh 1956, no. 35; Kleve, Städtisches Museum Haus Koekkoek, *Govært Flinck*, 1965, no. 9, ill; Montreal/Toronto 1969, no. 65, ill. [as ca. 1640].

SELECTED REFERENCES A. Bredius, "Die Rembrandt Ausstellung in London," *Zeitschrift für bildende Kunst*, X, 1899, p. 304 [as Govert Flinck]; C. Hofstede de Groot, "Die Rembrandt Austellungen zu Amsterdam und zu London," *Repertorium für Kunstwissenschaft*, XXII, 1899, p. 164 [as agreeing with Bredius' attribution to Flinck; compares painting with Flincks in Rotterdam, Vienna (*Diana and Endymion*, Liechtenstein Gallery; *Hager in the Wilderness*, Schönborn Gallery)]; W. R. Valentiner, *Catalogue of Paintings, North Carolina Museum of Art*, Raleigh, N.C., 1956, p. 48, no. 48 [as ca. 1640 and influenced by Rembrandt's 1636 etching of this subject]; Von Moltke 1965, pp. 27 [as ca. 1642–43], 76 f., cat. no. 52, pl. 9.

Although a number of authors (Valentiner, p. 48, Von Moltke 1965, p. 76) relate this composition to Rembrandt's 1636 etching of the same subject, the difference between the two works is considerable. Flinck's composition is decidedly different from the Rembrandt etching, but it does combine a number of Rembrandt motifs from the 1630's and early 1640's (Von Moltke 1965, p. 27). The general arrangement of the figures placed upon steps before a fantastic type of architecture with an open view into the distance on one side can be found in several of Rembrandt's biblical scenes from the late 1630's and early 1640's (cf. 1640 Detroit *Visitation*, cat. no. 7). The romantic landscape recedes into the space in terms of parallel planes of alternating dark and light zones; this, as well as the obelisk

in the distance, recalls such Rembrandt landscape paintings of the late 1630's as the *Landscape with Obelisk*, Isabella Stewart Gardner Museum, Boston. This obelisk appears in Rembrandt's etched *Landscape with an Obelisk* (Münz 1952, I, no. 157). It served as a milestone at Halfweg about two miles from Amsterdam.

## 62  *Portrait of a Boy*

Barber Institute of Fine Arts, University of Birmingham, England

Canvas 129.5 × 102.5 cms. signed bottom right *G. Flinck f 1640 Ill. p. 127*

PROVENANCE Sir Francis Seymour Haden, London; sale London (Christie's), 12 April 1940, no. 60, bought by Thomas Agnew & Sons; acquired 1940.

EXHIBITIONS Hull, Ferens Art Gallery, *Dutch Painting*, 1961, no. 26, ill.; Kleve, Städtisches Museum Haus Koekkoek, *Govært Flinck*, 1965, no. 43, ill.

SELECTED PREFERENCES *Catalogue of the Paintings, Drawings and Miniatures in the Barber Institute of Fine Arts University of Birmingham*, Cambridge, 1952, p. 36, ill.; Von Moltke 1965, p. 22 f., cat. no. 407, pl. 47 [fence is Rembrandtesque in brushwork while river and black trees behind it are original in conception]; Haak 1969, p. 130f, fig. 199.

The style of the portrait brings to mind Rembrandt's work from ca. 1630–ca. 1635 (Von Moltke 1965, p. 23) with one side of the face receiving the full intensity of the light and the other side partly in shadow. The free and loose application of the paint in the landscape also is Rembrandtesque. Actually, the more precise style of the figure, especially the face, recalls Flinck, while the landscape is more freely brushed as Rembrandt does in the late 1630's and early 1640's. [cf. 1640 Detroit, *Visitation*, (cat. no. 7) or the *Landscape with Obelisk*, Isabella Stewart Gardner Museum, Boston].

## 63  *Portrait of a Man*

The Minneapolis Institute of Arts

Canvas 85.6 × 70.5 cms. signed in upper-right corner *G. Flinck. f 1654 Ill. p. 127*

PROVENANCE with Julius H. Weitzner, London; acquired 1963

SELECTED REFERENCES Von Moltke 1965, p. 131, no. 306 +, pl. 41.

In spite of the fact that Flinck supposedly moved away from Rembrandt's style in the early 1640's, the painting of the hand, the head and the background retains something of the free brushwork and tonality of the latter's portraiture in the early 1640's. However, the smooth and shiny rendering of the drapery reflects the more elegant Flemish portraiture introduced into Amsterdam in the early 1640's by artists like Van der Helst. The latter style was the popular one with Amsterdam society, but the Minneapolis portrait indicates that Rembrandt's technique was not entirely forgotten by the middle of the seventeenth century.

## AERT DE GELDER 1645–1727

Aert de Gelder was born in Dordrecht on October 26, 1645, into a well established Dordrecht family. According to Houbraken (III, p. 162), De Gelder first studied with Samuel van Hoogstraten but when is not precisely stated. For various reasons, one can suggest the years around 1660. By 1661 he was in the atelier of Rembrandt who also had been the teacher of Van Hoogstraten. De Gelder remained with Rembrandt for a number of years, perhaps until 1667, and even after returning to Dordrecht continued to paint in Rembrandt's style for the rest of his life. De Gelder's earliest dated picture comes from the year 1671 (*Ecce Homo*, Dresden). Upon his return to Dordrecht, De Gelder met A. van Houbraken. De Gelder very likely supplied Van Houbraken with the information about Rembrandt which one finds in the former's publication of 1718. We know from Van Houbraken that De Gelder was still in good health in 1715. During his many years as a productive artist in Dordrecht, De Gelder carried on the style of Rembrandt in his many history, portrait and landscape paintings. He died unmarried on August 27, 1727.

**64** *Forecourt of a Temple, Figures Before an Imaginary Structure*

Royal Gallery of Paintings, "Mauritshuis," The Hague

Canvas 70.7 × 91 cms. signed upper left on block of stone *A De Gelder. f. 1679 Ill. p. 152*

PROVENANCE Possibly painting described as *Sacrifice* in Inventory of Aert de Gelder, 29 August 1727 [Lilienfeld, pp. 172, **276**]; very likely painting at sale Seger Tierens, The Hague, 23 July 1743; M. van Bremen, The Hague, 1752; sale Duke of Buckingham, Stowe, 15 August 1848, no. 408, bought by Anthony; Whatman, 1857; with Lesser, London, 1887; with M. Colnaghi, London; J. Porgès, Paris, until 1911; with Kleinberger, Paris; presented to Mauritshuis in 1911.

EXHIBITIONS Manchester, *Catalogue of the Art Treasures of the United Kingdom. Collected at Manchester in 1857* [London], 1857, no. 672 [as in Coll. Whatman]; Paris, Jeu de Paume, *Expositions des Grands et Petits Maîtres Hollandais du XVIIᵉ Siècle*, 1911, no. 3 [as *The Sacrifice*]; Paris, *Exposition Hollandais. Tableaux, Aquarelles et Dessins anciens et modernes*, 1921, no. 12; London 1929, no. 275; Brussels, Paleis voor Schoone Kunsten, *De Hollandsche Schilderkunst van Jeroen Bosch tot Rembrandt*, 1946, no. 33; Manchester, Art Gallery, *Art Treasures Centenary European Old Masters*, 1957, no. 121; Montreal/Toronto 1969, no. 66, ill.

SELECTED REFERENCES W. Bürger, *Trésors d'Art en Angleterre*, Paris, 1856, p. 256 f. [as the *Synagogue* and at first glance can be taken for a sketch by Rembrandt]; G. H. Veth, "Aanteekeningen omtrent eenige Dordrechtsche Schilders," *Oud-Holland*, VI, 1888, p. 186; W. Martin, "Ausstellung althollandischer Bilder in Pariser Privatbesitz," *Monatshefte für Kunstwissenschaft*, IV, 1911, p. 436 [as *The Sacrifice*, Coll. Porgès and close to Dresden *Ecce Homo* and fully signed and dated 1677]; K. Lilienfeld, "Rundschau-Sammlungen-Haag," *Cicerone*, IV, 1912, pp. 140 ff., ill. [gives provenance, calls it *Holy Family Entering Temple*, says it is close stylistically to 1671 Dresden *Ecce Homo* by De Gelder and recalls Rembrandt's etchings of the *Presentation in the Temple* (Münz 1952, I, cat. no. 210, fig. 237) and the *Synagogue* (ibid. cat. no. 273, fig. 318) while the color is close to Rembrandt's after 1660]; W. Martin, "Mauritshuis," *Bulletin van den Nederlandschen Oudheidkundigen Bond*, V, 1912, pp. 20–23 [as Rembrandtesque in painting and composition (cf. Rembrandt's etching of *Presentation in Temple* Münz 1952, I, cat. no. 210, fig. 237) for similar breadth. States that subject could be, as also suggested by Lilienfeld, the *Visit of Holy Family to the Temple* who is seen to the right of center in the middleground behind old woman with basket; positioning and stance of two figures in left foreground recall the Captain and Lieutenant in Rembrandt's *Night Watch*]; Lilienfeld, p. 171 f., no. 111 [as more likely representing *Peter and John at the Gates of the Temple*; the group in the far right with two figures standing before the sick man recalls Rembrandt's etching of *Peter and John healing the Cripple before the Temple* (Münz 1952, I, cat. no. 239, fig. 276); stylistically the picture is close to De Gelder's

1671 Dresden *Ecce Homo* while the grouping of the figures brings to mind Rembrandt's etchings like the *Presentation in the Temple* and the *Synagogue* (Münz 1952, I, cat. nos. 210, 273, figs. 237, 318)]; Mauritshuis, *Catalogue Raisonné des Tableaux et Sculptures*, The Hague, 1935, p. 99 f., no. 37.

As Lilienfeld (p. 172) has pointed out, the composition with the figures arranged in a relief-like setting parallel to the picture plane, in a readable shallow space, is typical of the early works of Aert de Gelder. The deep, warm, beautiful color tonality recalls Rembrandt of the 1660's when De Gelder studied with the master. The figure groupings, on the other hand, illustrate De Gelder's knowledge and ingenious use of earlier Rembrandt compositions beginning in the 1640's.

The subject represented presents a problem, but it can be safely assumed that the scene does not illustrate *Peter and John healing the Cripple before the Temple*, because the two figures are dressed in exotic Jewish costumes. However, Lilienfeld's original idea that it might represent the *Holy Family* should be investigated further. Prof. Stechow also suggests that Anna, who plays such an important role in Rembrandt's oeuvre, might be the old woman placed in the center just in front of the *Holy Family* (?). The secondary figures and the architecture seem to set off this group—especially the rising staircase which reinforces their central position—while the other participants are dispersed in unrelated groups before and within the building. These figures, carrying on their worldly activities, might be an allusion to the state of the Temple before Christ cleansed it. The architecture, including the large curtain acting as a *repoussoir*, and the deployment of the figures could very well have been inspired by the theater to which Rembrandt also turned in his 1648 etching of Medea, for example (Münz 1952, I, cat. no. 270, figs. 314–315). However, if this is the case and the subject illustrates a scene from a play, it is unlikely that it could represent a scene from the life of Christ, which was not allowed to be presented in the theater. Whatever the subject may be, the key to its explanation seems to be the four central figures whose presence is stressed by the architecture.

For the preliminary drawing of the main and subordinate figures on the left see cat. no. 181. When comparing the study and the painting, slight changes are evident. For example, the fourth head from the left in the preparatory study is seen in clear profile, while in the painting it is frontal and partially overlapped. The drawing also contains a sixth head not in the painting.

## 65 *Esther and Mordecai Writing Letters to the Jews*

Museum of Art, Rhode Island School of Design, Providence, R.I.

Canvas 59.7 × 143.5 cms. *Ill. p. 152*

PROVENANCE Sanford [as Bol and called *The Misers*]; with Meyer Reifstahl; purchased from latter in 1917.

EXHIBITIONS Chicago 1935–36, no. 18; Worcester 1936, no. 19; Raleigh 1956, p. 119, no. 46; New York, The Jewish Museum, *The Hebrew Bible in Christian, Jewish and Muslim Art*, 1963, no. 114; Montreal/Toronto 1969, no. 70, ill.

SELECTED REFERENCES L. E. Rowe, "A Painting by Aert de Gelder," *Bulletin of the Rhode Island School of Design*, IX, 1921, pp. 39 ff., ill. [as painted before 1685].

The delicate color and touch of the brush, especially in Esther's costume, are different from the heavily built up forms generally associated with De Gelder's work from the 1680's. [cf. *Portrait of a Girl*, Chicago, cat. no. 68]. Because of this more decorative, sensitive, and detailed application of the color, the picture seems to have more in common with De Gelder's works executed in the eighteenth century than with the paintings of this same subject now in Budapest and Dresden. The Budapest picture is dated 1685, while the Dresden painting may be a bit earlier. It has also been suggested that the models for these pictures were De Gelder's lawyer-brother and his wife [Lilienfeld, p. 143 f., fig. 6 and, for illustration of Dresden painting, see H. Posse, *Meisterwerke der Staatliche Gemäldegalerie in Dresden*, Munich, 1924, p. 242]. From the reproductions this idea seems to be difficult to maintain.

It is also of interest to note that this same book from the Old Testament seems to have been an important one for Rembrandt's choice of subject matter. One can only speculate as to why the *Book of Esther* fascinated both men. In the case of De Gelder, he is known to have painted at least four pictures of *Esther and Mordecai Writing Letters to the Jews* [*Book of Esther* ix:20–22; for list of pictures see Lilienfeld, p. 143 f., nos. 38–40]. Professor Kahr rightly suggests that the large number of pictures by Rembrandt and his circle taken from the *Book of Esther* must have had patriotic as well as religious significance for the period. [See M. Kahr, "Haman or Uriah?," *Journal of the Warburg and Courtauld Institutes*, XXVIII, 1965, p. 271 f. For an argument against this thought see J. Nieuwstraten, "Haman, Rembrandt and Michelangelo," *Oud-Holland*, LXXXII, 1967, pp. 61 ff.]. Prof. Kahr cites Calvinistic belief that the Dutch, like the Jews of the Old Testament, were God's chosen people which led to a greater interest in the Old Testament, and that parallels were drawn between the two peoples in seventeenth-century Dutch sectarian religious writings.

It is also possible that the Providence painting has been cut on all four sides.

## 66 *Rest on the Flight into Egypt*

Museum of Fine Arts, Boston, Maria T. B. Hopkins Fund
Canvas 109 × 118 cms. *Ill. p. 153*

PROVENANCE Esterhazy, Nordkirchen, no. 64, sometime between 1859–1904; Arenberg, Brussels, 1904–1956; with E. Speelman, London; acquired in 1957.

EXHIBITIONS Düsseldorf, *Kunsthistorische Ausstellung*, 1904, no. 303; San Francisco/Toledo/Boston 1966–67, no. 97, ill. [as about 1690]; Montreal/Toronto 1969, no. 72, ill.

SELECTED REFERENCE Lilienfeld, pp. 148 ff., no. 53.

The smooth, rich, painterly surface containing an occasional decorative highlight added to the costumes in thick and heavy bits of paint is similar to the type of surface found in the Leningrad *Self-Portrait* of ca. 1685–90. Although De Gelder's earlier works do contain such painted surfaces, they usually are combined with a style that is more broken up, rougher and detailed [cf. figures in left and right foreground of 1679 *Forecourt of a Temple* (cat. no. 64)]. Because of the affinity in style with the Leningrad *Self-Portrait*, it is possible to suggest a date of ca. 1685–90 for the Boston *Holy Family*.

The Virgin's deep brownish-red drapery combines with Joseph's dark grey-brown clothes to create a very quiet and intimate scene bringing to mind Rembrandt's renderings of this subject. De Gelder, following Annibale Carracci [Münz 1952, I, p. 19, fig. 50] as introduced to the North by Rembrandt, includes the unusual motif of Joseph reading from a large book (*Scriptures?*). Rembrandt does this in his ca. 1651 drawing of the *Holy Family*, Print Room, Berlin, [Benesch V, cat. no. 873, fig. 1085] and the etchings of 1631–32 and ca. 1656–57 [Münz 1952, I, cat. nos. 193, 237, figs. 216, 270, 271], while Ferdinand Bol also includes the book in his etching of 1645 [Münz 1952, II, pl. 23b]. However, contrary to Rembrandt's etchings, both Bol and De Gelder dress their Virgins as gypsies. [For the costume, especially the hat, see F. de Vaux de Foletier, "Iconographie des 'Egyptiens,' précisions sur le costume ancien des Tsiganes," *Gazette des Beaux-Arts*, LXVIII, 1966, pp. 165–171]. Whether or not Bol and De Gelder used the gypsy

headpiece simply because it may have been an exotic studio prop presents an interesting question. Because Rembrandt used a simple headdress from daily life and because the Holy Family has been connected with gypsies, one wonders whether or not the Boston painting might not reflect an unknown seventeenth-century legend of this type. Could it even be a gypsy family reading the story of *The Flight*?

## 67 *Vertumnus and Pomona*

Národní Galerie, Prague

Canvas 93.5 × 122 cms. signed and dated falsely lower left quarter *Rembrandt fe 1649 Ill. p. 155*

PROVENANCE Marquis de Lassay [as Rembrandt]; Countess de Verrue [as Rembrandt]; sale Blondel de Gagny, Paris, 10 Dec., 1776, no. 69, to Joshua Reynolds [as Rembrandt]; Durney, 1789 [as Rembrandt]; Le Brun, Paris, 1798 [as De Gelder]; Duke of Choiseul [as De Gelder]; Graf Fries, Vienna, 1800 [as Rembrandt]; Baron J. B. Pouthon [as Rembrandt]; Dr. J. Hoser, 1843 [as Rembrandt]; in Prague Museum sometime during second half of 19th century.

EXHIBITIONS Warsaw 1956, no. 44, ill.

SELECTED REFERENCES J. Smith, VII, 1836, no. 189 [as Rembrandt]; W. Bode, 1883, p. 481 [as Rembrandt]; Lilienfeld, pp. 177 f. [as difficult to date; color shows taste of 18th century, especially rich application of blue; Pomona's drapery and flesh colors recall 1685 *Esther and Mordecai*, Budapest; the painting, especially Vertumnus, comes from Rembrandt's ca. 1644 etching of the *Spanish Gipsy* (*Preciosa*) (Münz 1952, I, cat. no. 267, fig. 311)], 180, 197 [color of Pomona's costume is similar to that found in ca. 1700 *Portrait of Peter the Great*, Rijksmuseum, Amsterdam], cat. no. 130, fig. 18; Münz 1952, II, p. 116 [as being in nearly same pose as Rembrandt's etching of *Spanish Gipsy* which was prototype for De Gelder]; Prague, Národní Galerie V Praze, *Catalogue*, 1955, no. 244.

COPIES Nantes Museum, canvas: 90 × 117 cms. (Lilienfeld, pp. 178, 180; with J. Bruinse, Paris, 1926, 86 × 74 cms.; M. Schulthess, Basel, copy of Pomona including background of right side of original

MEZZOTINT Signed bottom-left margin *Peint par Rembrandt* and bottom-right margin *Gravé par Lepicié* (Lilienfeld, p. 178). For a drawn copy after Pomona in the Lepicié print see drawing with V. Spark, N.Y., 1961, as 17th century Dutch School, pen & wash: 180 × 140 mm.

To judge from the photographs, the Prague painting seems to be similar in style to the Chicago *Portrait of a Girl* (cat. no. 68) and especially to the 1685 Budapest *Esther and Mordecai*. Both the Prague and Budapest pictures juxtapose two styles of painting. The costumes of the older figures seem to be broadly and relatively smooth-brushed while the young women wear costumes that are made up of exotic details with thick and heavy Rembrandtesque highlights counter-balanced in part by delicately and thinly painted veils and smooth skirts. This type of detailed brush with thick accents is also evident in the costume of De Gelder's 1685 *Portrait of E. van Beveren*, Rijksmuseum, Amsterdam. Because of these similarities in the application of the paint, a date of ca. 1685 for the Prague painting might be plausible.

## 68  *Portrait of a Girl*

The Art Institute of Chicago, Wirt D. Walker Fund

Canvas 66 × 53 cms. *Ill. p. 154*

PROVENANCE H. Ken-Colville, Jr., Bellport Towers, England; with J. Goudstikker, Amsterdam, 1925; with D. A. Hoogendijk, Amsterdam, 1929; purchased in 1932.

EXHIBITIONS London 1929, no. 288; Chicago, The Art Institute of Chicago, *A Century of Progress. Exhibition of Paintings and Sculpture Lent from American Collections*. 1933, no. 60, ill.; Chicago, The Art Institute of Chicago, *A Century of Progress. Exhibition of Paintings and Sculpture*, 1934, no. 89; Chicago 1935–36, no. 17; Worcester 1936, no. 18 [according to Lilienfeld dates ca. 1690]; Hartford, Conn., Wadsworth Atheneum, *43 Portraits*, 1937, no. 18; Kansas City, Mo., William Rockhill Nelson Gallery of Art, *Seventh Anniversary Exhibition of German, Flemish, and Dutch Painting*, 1940–41, no. 23, pl. XV; New York / Toledo / Toronto 1954–55, no. 25, ill.; Dallas, Texas, Dallas Museum of Fine Arts, *Six Centuries of Headdress*, 1955, no. 11, repr. cover; Winnipeg, Canada, The Winnipeg Art Gallery, *Portraits, Mirror of Man*, 1956, no. 42, ill. p. 9.

SELECTED REFERENCES K. Bauch, "Ausstellung Holländischer Kunst von 1450–1900 in London," *Zeitschrift für Bildende Kunst*, LXIII, 1929–30, p. 20; D.C. Rich, "A Portrait by Arent de Gelder," *Bulletin of The Art Institute of Chicago*, XXVII, no. 2, 1933, pp. 34 ff., ill. [writes that pictorial concept comes from Rembrandt's studio, but De Gelder is less interested in character analysis than Rembrandt and concentrates more on producing greatest possible richness

of effect; suggests that hands, smile and gaze of eyes might show De Gelder unconsciously using engraving after Leonardo's *Mona Lisa*; sees De Gelder as link between 17th and 18th centuries by preserving dignity of old style and combining it with something of richness and profusion of new style]; C. F. Madsen, "Portrait of a Girl by Arent de Gelder," *The Connoisseur*, CX, 1942, p. 96, ill. [as showing little interest in character and mood but with effect of costume which comes from studio resources; style comparable with Rembrandt and from De Gelder's late phase]; Chicago 1961, p. 172; Haak 1969, p. 293, fig. 488 [as ca. 1690; developed his own style in spite of admiration for Rembrandt; De Gelder is lyrical in effect and coloring as seen here].

The placement of a half-length, exotically dressed figure behind a balustrade and looking directly at the spectator is a type used by Rembrandt in his drawings and etchings of the 1630's [cf. the drawn *Portrait of Saskia in a Straw Hat*, Print Room, Berlin, 1633 (Benesch II, cat. no. 427, fig. 483) or the 1636 etched *Studies of the Head of Saskia* (Münz 1952, I, cat. no. 91, fig. 105)]. Although Rembrandt continues to use this straight forward portrait type, with or without the balustrade, throughout the remainder of his career, beginning in the 1640's the exotic costumes are replaced by the sober clothes of daily life [cf. ca. 1644 drawing of a *Portrait of a Man Looking out of a Window*, Petit Palais, Paris (Benesch IV, cat. no. 764, fig. 911) or the 1651 painting of a *Girl Looking out of a Window*, National Museum, Stockholm].

The Chicago painting contains the delicate color harmony and rich texture generally associated with Aert de Gelder's style. The light, coming from above, creates a three dimensional form and causes the figure literally to glow from within (Rich, p. 35). The mixture of techniques, that is brush, palette knife and the sharp wooden handle of the back of the brush, imparts to the surface a decorative and graceful quality very close to that of the 18th century. The variety of surface textures, the decorative accents, and even the awkward fingers are characteristics also present in De Gelder's signed and dated 1684 or 87 *Juda and Thamar*, Mauritshuis, The Hague; the signed and dated 1685 *Esther and Mordecai*, Budapest; and the ca. 1685 *Vertumnus and Pomona*, National Gallery, Prague (cat. no. 67). However, the paint in the Chicago *Portrait of a Girl* seems to be more delicately and thinly laid on than in these paintings. For this reason the Chicago picture might be a few years later, say ca. 1690, as first suggested by Lilienfeld.

**69** *Christ on the Mount of Olives*

Julius H. Weitzner, London

Panel 36 × 41 cms. *Ill. p. 155*

PROVENANCE sale Baron Vivant Denon, Paris, 1826, no. 104; sale Trustees of the Cook Collection, London (Christie's), 25 Nov. 1966, no. 64.

EXHIBITIONS Sheffield, Graves Art Gallery, *Dutch Masterpieces*, 1956, no. 14 [as lent by Sir Francis Cook, Bt.].

SELECTED REFERENCES J. O. Kronig, *A Catalogue of the Paintings at Doughty House Richmond and Elsewhere in the Collection of Sir Frederic Cook Bt.*, London, II, 1914, p. 38, no. 259 [as late work and similar in treatment to Aschaffenburg painting of this subject]; Lilienfeld, pp. 155, 157 f., no. 82 [as probably study for the painting in Aschaffenburg; recalls Rembrandt's engraving of this subject (Münz 1952, II, no. 225) and his drawing in the Kunsthalle, Hamburg (Benesch V, cat. no. 899, fig. 1111)]; Sumowski 1957–58, p. 226, pl. 27 [Rembrandt's drawing of the same subject (Benesch VI, no. 899) being the model for this composition].

Very likely this is the study for the painting of this subject in the Aschaffenburg series of the Passion of Christ. The Weitzner sketch is changed in the final composition where it has become vertical and the sleeping foreground figure is eliminated in favor of shrubbery and a wooden fence. The light is also changed and becomes a shaft moving into the scene from the upper right to the lower left. The figures in the final version are also smaller and set farther back in space. To judge from the photograph, the sketch is very swiftly brushed in and the forms seem evaporated by the light which is so different from De Gelder's usual more precise rendering in the Aschaffenburg series. The Weitzner picture is, however, close in style to the sketchlike painted forms and spotlight effect of the signed Aert de Gelder, *Dream of Jacob*, Dulwich Gallery (Lilienfeld, no. 10).

**70** *Christ Before The Sanhedrim (Caiaphas)*

Rijksmuseum, Amsterdam *Ill. p. 156*

Canvas 73 × 59 cms. signed bottom-left corner *A De Gelder*

PROVENANCE certainly belongs to series of twenty-two paintings representing the *Passion of Christ* and cited in Inventory of Aert de Gelder's effects made in 1727; possibly part of series of twelve pictures of *Passion of Christ* at sale S. J. de Dufresne, Amsterdam, 22 August 1770, no. 270

[each was on canvas: 72 × 57.9 cms.]; Frenkner, Brunswick; bought from the latter in 1908.

EXHIBITIONS London 1953 M.G., no. 37, ill.; Warsaw 1956, no. 43.

SELECTED REFERENCES Houbraken III, p. 163 [the last of his works is the Passion with twenty of twenty-two completed; De Gelder is in good health as I write this in 1715]; C. Hofstede de Groot, *Arnold Houbraken und seine "Groote Schouburgh,"* (*Quellenstudien zur Holländischen Kunstgeschichte*), The Hague, 1893, pp. 66 f. [cites paintings in Aschaffenburg], 125, 466 f. [cites 1770 sale of twelve scenes from *Passion* and closeness of measurements to Aschaffenburg pictures; asks whether there might not be a printer's mistake in Houbraken and instead of twenty-two and twenty, the latter really meant twelve and ten]; Lilienfeld, pp. 59 [cites compositional connection with Rembrandt's 1648 etching of *Medea*], 69, 159 f., no. 85 [style of scene with exaggeratedly elongated figures, with the placement of the main scene and the light source in the middleground are elements that connect this picture with those in Aschaffenburg]; Van Dyke 1923, p. 90 [as hardly characteristic of De Gelder, but remarkable for imagination and novelty of presentation rather than for form and color]; Munich, Bayerische Staatsgemäldesammlungen, *Galerie Aschaffenburg Katalog*, Munich, 1964, p. 79 f. [as part of Passion cycle mentioned in Inventory of Aert de Gelder consisting of twenty-two pictures; two now in Rijksmuseum, Amsterdam and ten in Aschaffenburg; the cycle following Houbraken, dates ca. 1715].

This picture demonstrates De Gelder's continuous debt to his master well into the eighteenth century. As Lilienfeld has pointed out (pp. 59, 159) the high vaulted space and the setting in general is directly dependent upon Rembrandt's 1648 etching of *Medea* [Münz 1952, I, cat. no. 270, pls. 314, 315]. The rich olive-brown tonality and the artificial light effects highlighting the main participants are also strongly reminiscent of Rembrandt [cf. *Christ and the Adulteress*, National Gallery, London, of 1644], but the paint is more thinly and delicately applied, while the light creates an atmospheric effect that dissolves rather than reinforces the forms.

## SAMUEL VAN HOOGSTRATEN
### 1627–1678

Van Hoogstraten was born in Dordrecht on August 2, 1627. From his publication, *Inleyding tot de Hooge Schoole der Schilderkonst*, 1678, p. 257, we learn that he first studied with his father, Dirck van Hoogstraten, and that after the latter's death in December 1640, Samuel went to Amsterdam and became a pupil of Rembrandt. Van Hoogstraten also tells us that Fabritius [certainly Carel] and Abraham Furnerius were in Rembrandt's studio at the same time. Van Hoogstraten was back in Dordrecht by April 1648 where he spread his master's teachings. Three years later, in May 1651, he was working for the Court in Vienna; then in 1652 he was in Rome and probably returned to Vienna in the same year where he seems to have worked until 1653. He probably returned to Dordrecht before November 1654. Two years later, in 1656, he married Sara van Balen, and worked in Dordrecht, as artist and teacher [ca. 1660 Aert de Gelder was his pupil] until shortly before September 1662 when he visited London. From his own writings (1678, p. 266), we know that he witnessed the Great Fire in London of September 1666. Shortly thereafter, he returned to The Netherlands and worked in The Hague where he was enrolled in the painter's guild in January 1668, and was still in The Hague in September 1671. Van Hoogstraten returned to Dordrecht and in 1673 was Provost of the Mint. He remained in Dordrecht where he painted and wrote his *Inleyding tot de Hooge Schoole der Schilderkonst*, which was published in 1678, and died that year on October 19.

We know from the sources, especially Houbraken (II, p. 123), and his extant work, that Van Hoogstraten painted religious themes, portraits, genre works, architectural fantasies, landscapes, seascapes, flowers, and still life. Early in his career he painted portraits in a Rembrandtesque style but soon gave this up in favor of the style of G. Metsu, P. de Hoogh, and Jan Steen.

His most important pupils were A. Houbraken, G. Schalken, and Aert de Gelder. One must also not forget that Van Hoogstraten was a gifted writer of poems and plays.

71 *Portrait of a Young Man*

Sidney van den Bergh, Wassenaar

Canvas 71 × 59.7 cms. *Ill. p. 133*

PROVENANCE Count Lubomirski, Lwòw, before 1790; Count Eduard Raczynski, Castle Rogalin, Poznan; on loan to Mauritshuis, The Hague, 1910; with Duits, London, 1963, as Barent Fabritius; acquired in 1963.

EXHIBITIONS Delft/Antwerp 1964–65, no. 62, fig. 29; Leiden, Lakenhal, *17de eeuwse meesters uit Nederlands particulier bezit*, 1965, no. 27, fig. 6.

SELECTED REFERENCES W. Martin, "Mauritshuis," *Bulletin van den Nederlandschen Oudheidkundigen Bond*, III, 1910, pp. 173 ff., fig. 2 [as not Barent Fabritius but by an unknown Rembrandt pupil, ca. 1650, and directly under influence of Rembrandt's style of ca. 1640–50; compares coat with that worn by *A Seated Man with a Stick*, National Gallery, London (cat. no. 23)]; J. O. Kronig, "Zwei Selbstbildnisse von Samuel van Hoogstraten," *Kunstchronik*, XXV, 1914, p. 58 f., ill. [attributes Van den Bergh *Portrait* to Van Hoogstraten on basis of stylistic affinities to signed and dated 1645 *Self-Portrait*, Liechtenstein Coll., Vaduz]; H. van Hall, *Portretten van Nederlandse Beeldende Kunstenaars*, Amsterdam, 1963, p. 144, no. 4 [as Van Hoogstraten]; A. B. Vries, "Old Masters in the Collection of Mr. & Mrs. Sidney van den Bergh," *Apollo*, LXXX, 1964, p. 357, fig. 10 [as *Self-Portrait of Van Hoogstraten* and ca. 1645; compares jacket with early 16th century Venice—Titian, Giorgione, and says type resembles Rembrandt's 1640 *Self-Portrait*. National Gallery, London]; *Verzameling Sidney J. van den Bergh*, Wassenaar, 1968, no. 72, ill. [states that Van Hoogstraten attribution is not generally accepted and attribution to Barent Fabritius is not plausible, however Drost is a possibility].

The picture has been attributed to Hoogstraten (Kronig, *op. cit.*, p. 587) on the basis of a comparison with the *Self-Portrait* dated 1645 in Vaduz and the 164(?) *Vanitas*, Rotterdam. However, the painting of the costumes in these works is different from the Van den Bergh painting. Perhaps the closest work to the Van den Bergh painting is the *Portrait of the Artist*, Wadsworth Atheneum, Hartford (*Verzameling Sidney J. van den Bergh*, 1968, no. 72) where the treatment of the face and the eyes set in shadow is very similar. It might even be the same sitter. The jacket in the Van den Bergh painting, although it is the same type as in the London *Seated Man with a Stick* (cat. no. 23), seems to be more broadly and freely rendered. If one compares the signed and dated paintings in Vaduz and Rotterdam, there is also a difference in the rendering of the costume. The Vaduz picture is very Rembrandtesque and thick; the other is loose and free, while the faces are alike in the smooth application of the paint. The heads of the Vaduz and Rotterdam paintings, half in and half out of shadow, are similar to the Van den Bergh and Hartford heads and might conceivably be by the same young, experimenting hand.

72 *Resurrection*

The Art Institute of Chicago, Sophia P. Morton Purchase Fund

Canvas 78.7 × 63.2 cms. signed on tomb, bottom right of center *S. v. H. Ill. p. 133*

PROVENANCE sale London (Sotheby's), 13 November 1968, no. 66; with J. H. Weitzner, London; acquired in 1969.

Here Van Hoogstraten appears to combine two very different styles. The lower section contains expressive figures placed in deep shadow but with their gestures and expressions highlighted to give a real sense of emotion. This is found often in Rembrandt's work of the 1630's beginning with the *Raising of Lazarus*, Private Collection, California [Bauch 1966, no. 51]. On the other hand, the upper section contains brightly clothed angels and an idealized and somewhat overly posed figure of Christ. This upper section is highly Italianate, and perhaps if one looked in the direction of the Cavaliere d'Arpino, one might find a source. Because of the close stylistic connections with Rembrandt and Italy, one can suggest that the picture was painted after Van Hoogstraten's trip to Vienna and Rome in 1652–53. It is also possible that it was done during his stay in England around 1662–66, but the provenance of the picture is too uncertain to validate this notion. The figures in the upper zone of the painting are, according to Prof. Haverkamp-Begemann, similar in style to Van Hoogstraten's prints in his *Inleyding tot de Hooge Schoole der Schilderkonst: anders de Zichtbaere Werelt*, Rotterdam, 1678. This is especially evident in *Death Crowning Youth* illustrated between pages 52 and 53.

# PHILIPS KONINCK 1619–1688

Philips Koninck was born in Amsterdam, November 15, 1619, the son of a wealthy goldsmith, Aert de Koninck. Philips went to Rotterdam to study painting with his brother, Jacob, and on January 2, 1640, their father paid Philips' study fee (30 gulden) for a half a year. In 1640 he married Cornelia Furnerius, the sister of the artist Abraham Furnerius. In 1641 the younger Koninck returned to Amsterdam a fully trained painter. Houbraken (II, p. 42) writes that Koninck had been Rembrandt's pupil, but this is not certain; Gerson thinks it highly unlikely. Koninck's wife died in 1642, and nothing is heard about him in the archives for ten years; however, after 1653, he is constantly mentioned as being in Amsterdam. In 1657 he married Margriete van Rijn. He died in Amsterdam, October 6, 1688.

For about a decade after 1645, Koninck seems to have been strongly influenced by Rembrandt and somewhat less by Hercules Seghers' dramatic landscapes. Perhaps Koninck's sensitivity and feeling for panoramic Dutch views was nurtured by his second interest as owner of an inland shipping line between Amsterdam and Rotterdam. He was also well known as a painter of portraits, genre scenes, and historical subjects, and he was a close friend of the famous Dutch poet, Joost van den Vondel, of whom he did several portraits.

**73** *Portrait of Heyman Dullaert*

City Art Museum of Saint Louis

Canvas 63.5 × 55.9 cms. *Ill. p. 135*

PROVENANCE sale Luchtmans, Rotterdam, 20 April 1816, no. 80 [as *Portrait of Willaars*]; with Butterly, London [as Rembrandt]; Neville-Cooper, London; with Ehrich Galleries, N.Y.; acquired in 1923.

EXHIBITIONS New York, Wildenstein & Co., *Fifty Masterworks from the City Art Museum of St. Louis*, 1958, no. 20, ill. p. 38.

SELECTED REFERENCES Houbraken III, p. 61 [cites portrait as memento of friendship and used it later in 1721 publication —Pl. C 8], J. D. Descamps, *La Vie des peintres flamands*, Paris, III, 1753–63, p. 47; J. Kronig, "Een Schildersportret," *Oude Kunst*, II, 1917, p. 99, ill. [as having appeared "several years ago" in winter sale at Christie's under Rembrandt's name; identified sitter and artist from Houbraken's text and illustration]; Van Dyke 1923, pp. 65, 107 [as signed and now (1923) in Ehrich Galleries, N.Y.; says second version, showing a hand, is in Coll. Neville-Cooper, London, and given to Bol]; J. B. M., "A Portrait by Philips Koninck," *Bulletin of the City Art Museum of St. Louis*, X, no. 2, 1925, p. 26, ill. p. 27 [as framed as an oval; earlier given to Bol; romantic sentiment is emphasized by skillful handling of glazed tones characteristic of Rembrandt school]; Gerson 1936, pp. 49 f. [as middle of the 1650's], 123, cat. no. 204, pl. 24 [oval frame covers the left hand].

ENGRAVINGS J. Houbraken, 1719 [for book of poems published that year by Dullaert]; taken over in 1721 in A. Houbraken's *De Groote Schouburgh . . . .* Amsterdam, III, 1721, pl. C 8.

This portrait of the painter and poet, Heyman Dullaert, clearly illustrates Koninck's debt to Rembrandt in the middle fifties. The dark tonality of the drapery, the brightly-lighted face enframed by the curls, and the dark red velvet beret all emerging from an unlit background, bring to mind Rembrandt's portraiture of the 1650's [cf. Bauch 1966, figs. 410–12]—especially the portraits of the young Titus. However, the seriousness of Rembrandt's portraits is replaced in Koninck by a romantic and poetic attitude which must characterize so aptly his sitter.

## 74 *Panoramic Landscape*

Swiss Private Collection

Canvas 138.4 × 167 cms. signed bottom-right corner: *P. Koninck 1665 Ill. p. 136*

PROVENANCE Lord Hillingdon, London [by 1887]; the Hon. Charles Mills, London [at least in 1952–53].

EXHIBITIONS London, Royal Academy, *Winter Exhibition*, 1887, no. 72; London 1952–53, no. 269, ill. [as signed and dated 1665].

SELECTED REFERENCES Gerson 1936, p. 113, no. 97; H. Gerson, "Dutch Landscape," *The Burlington Magazine*, XCV, 1953, p. 48 [as similar to Hunterian picture]; MacLaren 1960, p. 211 [states that *staffage* is most likely by the same artist who painted landscape and not another hand, such as Johannes Lingelbach or Adriaen van de Velde].

This is a type of large, panoramic landscape which Koninck began to paint in the late 1650's. As a composition this is not new for Dutch art but carries on a tradition introduced, as far as we know, into the early seventeenth century by Hendrick Goltzius in his 1603 drawing, now in Museum Boymans-van Beuningen Rotterdam [for details and ill. see Stechow 1966, p. 44 f., fig. 53]. Rembrandt, following the Goltzius-Hercules Seghers line, also executed such panoramic views which combine realistic and fantastic elements into a conceivable landscape view. The most famous was Rembrandt's etching of *The Goldweigher's Field*, 1651 [Münz 1952, I, cat. no. 167, fig. 185] which has a breadth and sense of distance similar to Koninck. Koninck's rich, warm colors and the heroic character of his views show his debt to Rembrandt as well as a connection with Jacob van Ruisdael.

## 75 *View Between Heavy Trees over a Flat Landscape with a River*

Hofje van Aerden, Leerdam, on loan to the Museum Boymans-van Beuningen, Rotterdam

Canvas 65.5 × 80 cms. signed bottom center: *P. Koninck 1668 Ill. p. 136*

PROVENANCE Hofje Mevrouw van Aerden, Leerdam, since before 1761.

SELECTED REFERENCES Gerson 1936, pp. 35 [as a late work introducing a new type to flat landscape, the woods, which takes up a motif from early work], 106, cat. no. 29.

As Gerson (1936, p. 35) points out, Koninck, beginning with this dated work, combines the flat, broad landscape view with the woods which he had used as a single motif in his early works. However, Koninck's wooded landscapes are different from those of Jacob van Ruisdael, where one enters into the forest. In Koninck, one sees the entrance, really a park with beautiful trees and resting shepherds (as in the works of Adriaen van de Velde), but one does not step into the woods. One's eye, instead, passes over the few tall trees into the distance.

## JAN LIEVENS 1607- 1674

Jan Lievens was born in Leiden on October 24, 1607. His father, Lieven Hendricx, was an embroiderer—emigré from Ghent and his mother, Machtelt Jansdr (Hey), a native of Leiden. According to J. Orlers (*Beschrijvinge der Stadt Leyden*, 1641, p. 375 f.), Lievens began studying in Leiden with Joris van Schooten at about the age of eight and around the age of ten went to Amsterdam to study for two years with Pieter Lastman and then returned to Leiden and worked on his own. Schneider (1932, pp. 1–10, for documentation), with reason, suggests that Lievens studied with Lastman from 1619–21. Lievens is mentioned as being in Leiden in 1624, 1626 and 1629. He appears to have worked very closely with Rembrandt in the late 1620's until the latter left for Amsterdam in 1631–32. Orlers (*op. cit.*, p. 377) informs us that Lievens went to England in 1631 where he remained for about three years painting portraits of famous people, including royalty. However, we know from the Leiden archives that Lievens was still there in 1632. This English trip from 1632–1635 is based solely on Orlers' account. We do know, however, that Lievens was in Antwerp by 1635 as he entered the painters' guild in that year. During his Antwerp time which lasted, except for one trip to Leiden in 1639, until 1643, he knew Adriaen Brouwer and Jan Davidsz, de Heem well enough to have them witness a contract for him. Lievens also must have known other members of that group such as Lucas Vosterman, Paulus Pontius and Daniel Seghers. Anthony van Dyck had drawn Lievens' portrait. In 1638 Lievens married Susanna, the daughter of the Antwerp sculptor, Andries Colijn de Nole, and in December 1640, Lievens became a citizen of Antwerp, but by March 1644 he was back in Amsterdam, where records are continuous until 1653. From 1654–58, he lived in The Hague and was a charter member of the painters' confraternity, *Pictura*, which was founded in October 1656. In 1661, he paid dues to *Pictura* although we know that he was in Amsterdam in March 1659 and continued to live there until October 1669. In March 1670 he was back in The Hague living in a rented house where he remained until the middle of 1671 when he is mentioned as being in Leiden in September. In February 1674 he rented a house in Amsterdam where he died in June of that year.

During his Leiden years, Lievens followed a course of development very similar to that of Rembrandt's, and they both strongly influenced each other. However, he changed his style entirely after his move to Antwerp and adopted the elegant seventeenth-century courtly portrait style of Van Dyck and was also affected by the landscape style of Rubens and Brouwer. Lievens painted genre scenes as well as portraits, landscapes and history pictures. He was also an excellent etcher, very close in style to Rembrandt, as well as a woodcut artist following, in the main, the contemporary Flemish style. Upon his return to Holland, he painted stylish portraits and contributed to the decoration of the new Town Hall in Amsterdam; the Huis ten Bosch, near The Hague; the chamber of the provincial assembly of Holland, The Hague; and the Rijnlandhuis, Leiden.

## 76 *Old Woman Reading*

John G. Johnson Collection, Philadelphia

Panel 71.4 × 67.3 cms. signed on book clasp in left background *J. L.* (monogram is questionable) *Ill. p. 115*

PROVENANCE J. G. Deuringer, Augsburg [at least by 1813 where it is catalogued as Lievens]; in Johnson Coll. at least by 1913.

EXHIBITIONS New York 1909, no. 62, ill. [as Nicolaes Maes ca. 1650–55]; Worcester 1936, [as Lievens].

SELECTED REFERENCES M. J. Friedländer, "Die Ausstellung holländischer Bilder im Metropolitan Museum zu New York," *Repertorium für Kunstwissenschaft*, XXXIII, 1940, p. 96 [because signature appears genuine, attributes painting to Lievens]; Hofstede de Groot, VI, 1916, p. 510, no. 120 [catalogued under Maes, but not seen by author; red reminds one strongly of Maes, but character of brushwork seems earlier; signature is very suspicious]; Schneider 1932, p. 176, cat. no. XXXVIII [cannot accept as Lievens without technical examination]; *Catalogue of the John G. Johnson Collection*, Philadelphia, 1941, p. 31, no. 487 [disputed by all scholars; formerly Nicolaes Maes but now called Lievens

as it has been most recently published; could possibly be a late English work]; Bauch 1967, pp. 161 [as part of a group of early paintings by Lievens which are not influenced by Rembrandt but stimulated him; inspired by Haarlem—especially Salomon de Bray or Pieter de Grebber who had strong connections with Utrecht Caravaggisti; probably real source for Lievens and Haarlem are the rare half-length figures of Lastman], 162 [the ermine fur is also found in Lievens and Rembrandt (?), *Esther and Haman*, North Carolina Museum of Art, Raleigh; same type of cartilaginous hands are also present in the Raleigh painting, *Simeon with Christ Child in the Temple*, sale Munich (Helbing), 1908, and *Pilate Washing his Hands*, with E. Speelman, London], 164 [as ca. 1625].

To judge from the reproduction, there is no question that the Johnson picture is not closely related to the early works ascribed by Bauch to Lievens. From reproductions, the Johnson picture seems to be more thickly built up in terms of the paint structure; however, this does not necessarily mean that Lievens was not the artist. All of these paintings, cited by Bauch as early Lievens, seem to be closely connected with Utrecht. *Pilate Washing his Hands* is a close variation on the so-called Terbrugghen in Kassel [for this writer a contemporary copy], while the Johnson picture bears a strong resemblance to the *Old Woman Holding Spectacles*, Painting Gallery, Dresden, which has been ascribed to Terbrugghen, but which Nicolson rightfully attributes to an unknown artist, close to Terbrugghen, who worked in Utrecht, ca. 1625–30. [B. Nicolson, *Hendrick Terbrugghen*, London, 1958, p. 122 f., cat. no. E 103, pl. 109b]. A recent cleaning of the picture reveals that the signature appears to be part of the original paint structure.

## 77 *Portrait of Rembrandt*

Daan Cevat, St. Peter Port

Panel 57 × 44.7 cms. signed bottom left *I. L. Ill. p. 115*

PROVENANCE Earls of Derby, Knowsley Hall, sometime prior to 1736; sale Earl of Derby, London (Christie's), 17 July 1964, no. 48.

EXHIBITIONS Manchester 1857; Delft/Antwerp 1964–65, no. 74; Leiden, Lakenhal-Bolsward, *Rondom Rembrandt—De verzameling Daan Cevat*, 1968, no. 25, ill.

SELECTED REFERENCES Schneider 1932, no. 264b. [as *Portrait of Young Tromp* and hardly by Lievens]; Bauch 1967, p. 263 f., fig. 23 [as ca. 1630 and after cleaning Lievens' monogram appeared and very likely represents an acquaintance of the artist. One can think that the sitter is Rembrandt, but he had brown eyes and not grey-blue. The face is personal, the hair style and costume so Rembrandtesque that the sitter must be traceable to Leiden artistic circles]; Haak 1969, p. 42, fig. 60 [as *Portrait of Rembrandt*, ca. 1628].

The Cevat portrait once again illustrates Lievens' ability to create a highly decorative and beautifully painted picture using the smooth brush and the Caravaggesque lighting characteristic of his Leiden period. Authorities have questioned whether this is a portrait of the young Rembrandt. Bauch, 1967, questioned this identification, because the grey-blue eyes differ from the brown eyes in Rembrandt's 1640 London *Self-Portrait*. However, after Bauch saw the Lievens in Bolsward, he wrote to Cevat stating that the eyes are grey-brown and consequently the Cevat Lievens could represent Rembrandt. Lievens' formal and elegant presentation of the sitter brings to mind Rembrandt's ca. 1629–30 *Self-Portrait*, Mauritshuis, The Hague, where the same type of armored neck piece covered by a collar is present. Here Rembrandt depicts himself as a gentleman in the same spirit as we find in Lievens' portrait. However, the smooth, decorative painting style of Lievens with the decorative light effects produce an effect entirely different from Rembrandt's rougher surface and more powerful contrasts of light and shadow. In spite of these stylistic differences, it is highly possible that the Lievens portrait is the same sitter as the Rembrandt *Self-Portrait* in the Mauritshuis, and that they both date from ca. 1629–30.

## 78 *Eli Instructing Samuel*

H. Shickman Gallery, New York  *Ill. p. 117*

Canvas 106 × 96.5 cms. signed on armrest in center *IL*.

PROVENANCE sale A. Sydervelt, Amsterdam, 23 April 1766, no. 58 [as G. Flinck, 40 florins]; Earl of Craven, Combe Abbey [at least since 1866]; sale Cornelia, Countess of Craven, and J. Taylor, London (Christie's), 13 April 1923, no. 11 [bought in]; sale Cornelia, Countess of Craven, London (Sotheby's), 27 Nov. 1968, no. 88 [as *Jacob Cats instructing the Prince of Orange* and bought by H. Shickman Gallery, N.Y.].

EXHIBITIONS Birmingham, 1833, no. 134; London, British Institution, *Catalogue of Pictures by Italian, Spanish, Flemish, Dutch, French and English Masters*, 1853, no. 47 [as by Flinck and entitled *Samuel and Eli*]; Manchester 1857, no. 922 [as by Rembrandt]; London 1952–53, no. 202 [as *Jacob Cats instructing the Prince of Orange*].

SELECTED REFERENCES Schneider 1932, pp. 32 [as ca. 1628; this type of didactic subject is typical for Leiden; the pure profile is characteristic of Lievens' portrait heads of the early period], 125, cat. no. 135 [entitled *Aristocratic Boy with his Teacher;* the young boy cannot be related to Rembrandt's etched *Portrait of a Boy in Profile* (1641) called William II of Orange by Blanc]; Münz 1952, II, p. 65 f., pl. 71 [for discussion of Rembrandt's 1641 etched *Portrait of a Boy in Profile* and its lack of connection with Lievens]; Van Gelder 1953, p. 37 [as typical of Lievens' work ca. 1628–29 and representing *Eli Instructing Samuel*].

COPIES Leningrad, Hermitage, as Flinck and falsely signed Flinck, canvas: 105 × 88 cms. (A. Somof, *Leningrad Ermitazh Kartiny*, II, 1901, p. 120, no. 842); Coll. Earl of Spencer, Althorp Park, as G. Flinck; sale Hohenzollern, Berlin, 13 May 1890, no. 2, as Eeckhout, canvas: 89 × 72 cms.; sale J. Holländer, Berlin, 9 May 1899, no. 71, as Flinck, canvas: 77 × 60 cms.; sale W. Locket-Agnew & others, London (Christie's), 15 June 1923, no. 105, 106.7 × 86.3 cms.; picture cited in Coll. Prince Frederik of The Netherlands, signed in armrest *IAL*.

ENGRAVING G. Fr. Schmidt, as by Flinck.

As stated by Schneider and Van Gelder, this painting must date from the time of Lievens' Leiden period, ca. 1628–29. The carefully brushed in details and the rich golden color of Samuel's drapery appears to be very similar to the Edinburgh *Portrait of a Young Man* (cat. no. 80) The type of scholarly portrait, with one figure making a point through the gesture of a "speaking hand" in close relation to an open book and the placement of one head in profile and the other full faced, is often found in the group working with Rembrandt in the late 1620's [cf. Rembrandt's 1628 *Two Scholars Disputing*, National Gallery Melbourne; Dou, *Eli Instructing Samuel*, Private Coll., N.Y. (cat. no. 37).

## 79 *Raising of Lazarus*

Brighton Art Gallery, England

Canvas 103 × 112 cms. signed on center of tomb beneath Christ *IL 1631  Ill. p. 114*

PROVENANCE possibly painting cited in Rembrandt's Inventory 25 July 1656, no. 42; possibly painting mentioned in celebrated poem of 1662 by Jan Vos as in Coll. Jan Jacobsz. Hinloopen, Amsterdam; possibly picture listed in estate of Clementia Zeger, widow of Dirk Vennekool, Amsterdam, 14 Feb. 1664; possibly in Coll. Thomas Asselijn, Amsterdam, 1685; possibly at sale Amsterdam, 13 April

1695, no. 8; sale Van Kretschmar, Amsterdam, 29 May 1757, no. 32; sale Amsterdam, 21 June 1774, no. 132; sale J. Knowles, London, 15 April 1842, no. 113; J. Sidney North, 1853; Baroness North, London, 1871; sale London (Christie's), 7 June 1884, no. 98; H. Willet, Brighton; given by latter to Museum in 1903.

EXHIBITIONS London, British Institution, 1852, no. 30; London, British Institution, 1867, no. 123; London, Royal Academy, 1871, no. 17; Brimson Art Loan, 1884; London 1929, no. 170; London 1952-53, no. 76; Leiden 1956, no. 65; London, Royal Academy, 1961, no. 127.

SELECTED REFERENCES F. Saxl, "Rembrandt und Italien," Oud-Holland, XLI 1923-24, pp. 145-148, ill. [states that Rembrandt's first idea in the 1630 red chalk drawing of Raising of Lazarus was made after Lievens' etching and that the composition comes from Italy-Guido Reni]; Schneider 1932, pp. 38 ff., cat. no. 31 [agrees that first idea in Rembrandt's 1630 red chalk drawing of Entombment, London, was made after Lievens' etching and painting by Lievens signifies a high point in his development]; Münz 1952, II, p. 176 f. [says painting in Brighton is model for etching of 1631 and that, although idiom is close to Rembrandt and dependent upon him in Raising, Lievens emerges here as an original artist]; Van Gelder 1953, p. 37 [as still following Rembrandt's development in 1631]; Benesch I, cat. no. 17, fig. 15 [first version of red chalk drawing in British Museum (Entombment), strongly influenced Lievens' 1631 Raising of Lazarus and that Lievens reproduced painting in his etching (ill. in F. W. H. Hollstein, Dutch and Flemish Etchings, Engravings and Woodcuts, Amsterdam, XI, n.d., p. 8, no. 7)]; Sumowski 1957-58, p. 236 f. [as after Rembrandt's 1630 drawing in London]; Begemann 1961, p. 20 [writes that Rembrandt's first version of the 1630 Entombment is a copy of Lievens' etching; if the date of 1631 on the painting in Brighton is right, then Lievens once more repeated the composition of the etching]; Brighton Art Gallery and Museum, Paintings Executed before 1837 in the Permanent Collection, Catalogue, Brighton, 1964, p. 32 f. [states that one of models is recognizeable as Rembrandt's father who died in 1630 and painting was perhaps a memorial to the latter]; Bauch 1967, pp. 166 ff., fig. 9 [sees Rembrandt's 1629-30 Raising of Lazarus, Private Coll., U.S.A. and his 1630 drawing in London as forerunners of Brighton Lievens]; Haak 1969, p. 62 f., fig. 91 [painting must have been inspired by Rembrandt's drawing of 1630 in British Museum, London, but problem is not solved as painting is in reverse of Rembrandt's drawing—must be missing link somewhere].

This is one of the most impressive works executed by Lievens during his Leiden period and illustrates the strong effect Rembrandt and Lievens must have had upon each other. The small figures, the use of chiaroscuro and the careful painting of the surface details are also characteristic of Rembrandt's oeuvre around 1628-29. Lievens' painting is close in concept to Rembrandt's ca. 1628-29 Raising of Lazarus, Private Coll., California, U.S.A., and the 1629 Tribute Money, National Gallery, Ottawa (cat. no. 3). Because Lievens' style is so close to Rembrandt's of two years earlier, it is most likely that Lievens drew his inspiration for the Brighton picture from Rembrandt—not only stylistically but, as a composition. It is also possible that Lievens made a drawing, now lost, for the painting; but it most likely would not have been done before Rembrandt's of 1630.

## 80 Portrait of a Young Man

National Gallery of Scotland, Edinburgh

Canvas 112 × 97 cms. signed with false signature in lower-right corner Rembrandt Ill. p. 116

PROVENANCE Mary, Lady Carberry, Castle Freke, County Cork, Ireland; sale Mary, Lady Carberry, London (Christie's), 4 March 1921, no. 9 [as Portrait of Count Wallenstein by Dou], with H. M. Clark, London [and called Lievens]; with Agnew & Sons, London, 1922 [as Bol]; acquired in 1922.

EXHIBITIONS Leiden 1956, no. 68, ill.

SELECTED REFERENCES Hofstede de Groot, VI, 1916, no. 799a [as ca. 1632 and that original is lost but composition is preserved in 1772 mezzotint by J. R. Smith with inscription calling it Count Wallenstein by Dou; however, following Wurzbach, it seems to be an early Rembrandt; also cites etching of head by C. Hess]; Van Dyke 1923, p. 112, fig. 91 [attributes painting to Salomon Koninck and states that it is similar stylistically to Rembrandt's Portrait of Oriental, Metropolitan Museum of Art, N.Y. and the one in the Petit Palais, Paris]; Schneider 1932, pp. 29 [writes that an increase in the facial expression is sought after by an increase in finery of costume; Lievens' models are dressed as in a masquerade to give greater pleasure to his contemporaries], 158, cat. no. 283; Edinburgh, National Gallery of Scotland, Catalogue of Paintings and Sculptures, 1957, p. 147 f., no. 1564 [as Lievens, and states that Hofstede de Groot, upon seeing the painting gave it to Lievens while

Bredius, on basis of photograph, called it Paulus Bor; catalogued as Ferdinand Bol until 1946 edition].

COPIES Engraved mezzotint: J. R. Smith, 1772, inscribed *Bildnis von Graf Wallenstein von Dou;* Etching of upper-half of body in opposite direction inscribed *Rembr. pinxit Hess fecit aqua fort Graf Wallenstein.*

This portrait illustrates the close proximity in style between Lievens and Rembrandt during the years in Leiden from 1625–31. The major difference between the two young men was very adequately described by their contemporary and patron Constantijn Huygens, who, sometime between May 1629, and April 1631, wrote that Rembrandt was superior to Lievens in judgment and in the representation of lively emotional expression, while Lievens has a grandeur of invention and boldness which Rembrandt does not achieve [see Slive 1953, pp. 9, 15].

The *Portrait of a Young Man* certainly can be characterized as a work of splendor with its stress upon the beautifully highlighted costume and face. Rembrandt also used Caravaggesque lighting for similar subjects, but his light concentrates on the face in an attempt to establish the sitter's mood, and, if it is possible, to achieve an understanding of his inner make-up. This difference is evident if one compares Lievens' *Portrait of a Young Boy* with Rembrandt's *Self-Portrait*, Isabella Stewart Gardner Museum, Boston, where the light increases in intensity from the shoulder to the face, while in the Lievens' the light is of equal intensity whether bringing out a sense of the material of the costume or modeling the face.

The Lievens painting must date from the end of the Leiden period, ca. 1630–31, and the careful treatment of the drapery with the reflected light, appears to be similar to Samuel's in *Eli Instructing Samuel* (cat. no. 78).

## 81 *Christ Washing the Feet of the Disciples*

The Art Institute of Chicago, Robert A. Waller Fund

Canvas, oil on paper made of wood fiber and flax: 48.2 × 60.4 cms. *Ill. p. 118*

PROVENANCE possibly painting cited in Inventory of Abraham Jacobsz Greeven, Amsterdam, 10 March 1660 ["Een schilderijtie daer Christus de voeten wast van Rembrandt."—A small painting where Christ washes the feet by Rembrandt]; possibly cited in Inventory of Harmen Becker, Amsterdam, 19 October 1678 ["een graeutie van Rembrandt daer Christus de voete wast."—A grisaille by Rembrandt where Christ washes the feet]; sale Huybert Kete-

laar, Amsterdam, 19 June 1776, no. 175, purchased by F. Kemper; Count Wilczek, Burg Kreuzenstein, Austria; with E. & A. Silberman, New York, 1934; acquired in 1934.

EXHIBITIONS Chicago 1935–36, no. 2; Worcester 1936, no. 2; Indianapolis, John Herron Art Museum, *Dutch Paintings of the Seventeenth Century*, 1937, no. 60, ill.; Hartford, Wadsworth Atheneum, *Night Scenes*, 1940, no. 30, ill.; New York, Duveen Galleries, *Paintings by the Great Dutch Masters*, 1942, no. 41, ill.

SELECTED REFERENCES Hofstede de Groot, VI, 1916, no. 119 [cites inventories mentioning this subject]; Julius Held, "Seventeenth-Century Dutch Paintings recently added to American Collections," *Art in America,* XXIII, 1934–35, pp. 114, 119, fig. 3 [as Rembrandt of 1630–31 and Apostle is related to some Rembrandt etchings of 1630–31; greatest argument for authenticity is that it seems possible to identify it with painting of this subject described as a grisaille by Rembrandt in the 1678 Inventory of Harmen Becker]; Wilhelm R. Valentiner, "Some early Compositions by Rembrandt," *The Burlington Magazine,* 1936, pp. 80–81, pl. IIIa [as early Amsterdam period; no one but Rembrandt could have invented such a group as the three Apostles with its dramatic counterbalance to the silent Christ; states that composition is very clearly connected with *Doubting Thomas,* Hermitage, *Rest on the Flight into Egypt,* The Hague, and the 1634 chalk drawing of *Christ Among the Disciples,* Teyler Foundation, Haarlem, and therefore, can be dated 1634. Valentiner also states that it is obviously identical with *Washing of Feet* by Rembrandt cited in Inventory of Abraham Jacobsz Greeven, Amsterdam, 10 May 1660; and that it also must be grisaille in Inventory of Coll. Harmen Becker and also picture in Coll. Huybert Ketelaar]; Hans-Martin Rotermund, "Rembrandt und die religiosen Laienbewegungen in den Niederländen seiner Zeit," *Nederlandsch Kunsthistorisch Jaarboek,* IV, 1952–53, p. 164 f. [as by Rembrandt; states that subject was important for the Mennonites and is connected with idea of Communion; possibly Rembrandt had this in mind when painting *Christ Washing Feet of His Disciples*]; Hans-Martin Rotermund, "Wandlungen des Christus-Typus bei Rembrandt," *Wallraf-Richartz-Jahrbuch,* XVIII, 1956, pp. 22 ff., figs. 161, 162; Sumowski 1957–58, pp. 239 [in spite of the distinguished quality, the overall impression makes its attribution to Rembrandt doubtful; the figure types are strange for Rembrandt as are the strong undulating contours], 240 [as by G. van den Eeckhout(?)], 244, fig. 128; Chicago 1961, p. 394 [identity of this artist is not known although Jan Lievens or Benjamin Gerritsz Cuyp have been suggested; neither of these attributions is completely convincing]; Bauch 1967, pp. 168 ff., fig. 12 [as based on Tintoretto's early work of this theme in National Gallery, London; treatment of light and silhouetted figures is not like Rembrandt; however, three Apostles in background related to Lievens' studies of old men in Leipzig and Dresden, Chicago painting is characteristic of Lievens and comes out of paintings like Rembrandt's ca. 1629–30 *Raising of Lazarus*, Private Coll., California (Bauch 1966, no. 51), the 1633 *Daniel and Cyrus* (ibid., no. 11) and the 1634 *Doubting Thomas* (ibid., no. 60); also relates to 1634 Rembrandt drawing of this subject in Haarlem; it must date from after the time Lievens left Rembrandt and Leiden but still shows influence of Rembrandt—ca. 1634].

As has been suggested earlier, the Chicago painting appears to be connected with such paintings as Rembrandt's 1634 *Doubting Thomas*, Hermitage, Leningrad, the 1634 chalk drawing of *Christ Among the Disciples*, Teyler Foundation, Haarlem, the ca. 1629–30 *Raising of Lazarus*, Private Coll., California and a number of etchings from around 1630. However, the painting style is very different from Rembrandt's of these years. Bauch has made a strong case for Lievens, but once again it is difficult to see the similarities he cites between the three speaking Apostles in the background of the Chicago painting and, for example, *The Head of an Old Man*, Museum der bildenden Künste, Leipzig, or *St. Paul*, Coll. Wachtmeister, Wanos. The continuity of the paint structure and the smooth, detailed rendering of the forms are very different from the broken up brush strokes and shapes that seem to be dissolved by the light in the Chicago painting.

## 82  *A Woodland Walk*

National Gallery of Scotland, Edinburgh University Loan, Torrie   Collection

Canvas 52.7 × 70 cms. *Ill. p. 117*

PROVENANCE  possibly painting sold at Amsterdam, 23 May 1764, no. 188 [bought by Koeling]; Sir James Erskine of Torrie [at least by 1880]; presented by latter to College of Edinburgh in 1835.

EXHIBITIONS  Edinburgh, Royal Institution, 1830, no. 120 [as Rembrandt].

SELECTED REFERENCES  G. F. Waagen, *Treasures of Art in Great Britain*, III, London, 1854, p. 272 [as not by Rembrandt]; Hofstede de Groot, VI, 1916, p. 437, no. 958g. [as vigorous in style and according to note by J. van der Marck not by

Rembrandt; sale Amsterdam, 23 May 1764, no. 188, 52 × 69.8 cms]; Schneider 1932, pp. 63 [as somewhat earlier than the 1650's Amsterdam period Berlin landscape (probably late 1640's); the vigorous, almost toxic, green tonality with yellow light between brownish foliage is somewhat strange for Lievens but possible], 162, cat. no. 302; National Gallery of Scotland, *Catalogue of Paintings and Sculpture*, Edinburgh, 1957, p. 147, no. 68 [as ascribed to Jan Lievens and belonging to group of landscapes, some given to Brouwer and others to Lievens; painted at Antwerp about late 1630's].

This landscape is typical of Lievens' ability to create a mood. Lievens was very much affected by the landscapes of Rubens and Brouwer during his stay in Antwerp. However, here, as suggested by Schneider (p. 63), he is a closer observer of nature than we find in his Antwerp landscapes. The darker tonality of the Edinburgh picture is also typical of his post Antwerp days and might show a new interest in Rembrandt's light effects. The placement of the trees in such a way that strong bits of light are seen through the distant woods is a carry over from Antwerp and probably was taken up by other Dutchmen such as Bol (cat. no. 32).

## NICOLAES MAES 1634–1693

Nicolaes Maes was born in Dordrecht in January 1634. According to Houbraken (II, p. 215), Maes learned drawing from an average master and painting from Rembrandt. Maes probably studied with Rembrandt sometime around 1648. He must have returned to Dordrecht sometime before his betrothal there on December 28, 1653. He was married in Dordrecht on January 13, 1654 and remained in that city until 1673 when he moved to Amsterdam. Houbraken (II, p. 216) informs us that Maes made a special trip to Antwerp to study the works of Rubens, Van Dyck, Jordaens and others. It has been suggested that Maes made this voyage sometime between 1660 and 1665. He died and was buried in Amsterdam on December 24, 1693.

Maes' early works still remain highly problematical. A number of religious paintings in a Rembrandtesque style have been called early Maes, but these attributions are very much open to question. We do reach sure ground in a number of genre paintings executed around 1654 to 1659, but they are not Rembrandtesque. These interiors have very much in common with those by Carel Fabritius and Pieter de Hoogh, but the interrelationship between these men is difficult to establish. By 1656 Maes had started to paint portraits in a Rembrandtesque style and from 1660 on he became exclusively a portraitist. After his trip to Antwerp, his portrait style changed. He now combined the elegance of Van Dyck and French court portraiture.

## 83 Portrait of a Man

The Art Institute of Chicago, Gift of Charles L. Hutchinson

Panel 29.8 × 26.7 cms. *Ill. p. 144*

PROVENANCE Gustave Rothan, Paris, before 1873; sale Gustave Rothan, Paris (Galerie Georges Petit), 29–31 May 1893, no. 71; Charles L. Hutchinson [by 1893]; given to Museum in 1925.

EXHIBITIONS Chicago, The Art Institute of Chicago, *Paintings, Sculpture and other objects exhibited at the opening of the new Museum*, 1893, no. 176; Chicago, The Art Institute of Chicago, *Paintings from the Collection of Charles L. Hutchinson*, 1910, no. 12; Chicago, The Art Institute of Chicago, *A Century of Progress, Exhibition of Paintings and Sculpture 1934*, 1934, no. 96.

SELECTED REFERENCES Paul Mantz, "La Galerie de M. Rothan," I, *Gazette des Beaux-Arts*, VII, 1873, p. 282; Hofstede de Groot, VI, 1916, p. 567, no. 389; Valentiner 1924, p. 60, pl. 50 [as painted in middle 1650's in Rembrandt's style]; R.M.F., "The Charles L. Hutchinson Bequest," *Bulletin of the Art Institute of Chicago*, XIX, 1925, p. 103, ill. [as *Portrait of Pierre Corneille*, poet and dramatist]; Chicago 1961, p. 264.

For comments concerning this portrait, see discussion of pendant (cat. no. 84). The identification of the sitter as Pierre Corneille is hardly tenable.

## 84 Portrait of a Lady

The Art Institute of Chicago, Gift of Charles L. Hutchinson

Panel 29.8 × 26.7 cms. *Ill. p. 144*

PROVENANCE Gustave Rothan, Paris, before 1873; sale Gustave Rothan, Paris (Galerie George Petit), 29–31 May 1890, no. 72; Charles L Hutchinson [by 1893]; given to Museum in 1925.

EXHIBITIONS Chicago, The Art Institute of Chicago, *Paintings, Sculpture and other objects exhibited at the Opening of the New Museum*, 1893, no. 176; Chicago, The Art Institute of Chicago, *Paintings from the Collection of Charles L. Hutchinson*, 1910, no. 111; Chicago, The Art Institute of Chicago, *A Century of Progress. Exhibition of Paintings and Sculpture 1934*, 1934, no. 97; Chicago 1935–36, no. 22.

SELECTED REFERENCES Paul Mantz, "La Galerie de M. Rothan. I.," *Gazette des Beaux-Arts*, VII, 1873, p. 282; Hofstede de Groot, VI, 1916, p. 576, no. 440; Valentiner 1924, p. 60, pl. 51 [as painted in middle 1650's in Rembrandt's style]; Chicago 1961, p. 264 [as painted between 1650 and 1660].

The dark tonality and the rough brush indicate that Maes, in this and its pendant (cat. no. 83), was still strongly under the influence of his teacher when he executed these portraits. They are not yet painted in the lighter tonality and thinner, more delicate brush of the 1657 *Portrait of Jacob de Wit, Mayor of Dordrecht*, Dordrecht Museum, which marks the beginning of Maes' more elegant portrait style. The same difference in technique is noticeable in the pair of three-quarter length portraits, Private Coll., London [Valentiner 1924, pl. 52] which represent the same sitters as the Chicago pendants. It is possible that the Chicago portraits were informal studies done in the Rembrandt style and shortly thereafter changed to the more formal and elegant style in the finished portraits. The London portraits might be seen as Maes' earliest attempt at moving away from his master's style, although the tonality is still somewhat Rembrandtesque.

## 85 Portrait of a Young Boy

Cincinnati Art Museum, Gift of Mary Hanna

Canvas 74 × 60.4 cms. *Ill. p. 145*

PROVENANCE Countess W. Sologhoube, Leningrad, at least in 1909; sale Leningrad Castles and Museums, Berlin (Lepke), 6 Nov. 1928, no. 394 [withdrawn before sale]; with Knoedler, London, sometimes before 1948; bought from Knoedler's by Mary Hanna and presented to Museum.

EXHIBITIONS Petrograd, *Exhibition Starye Gody*, 1908–09, no. 398; Minneapolis Institute of Arts, *Great Portraits by Famous Painters*, 1952; American Federation of Arts, *Picture of the Month* [traveling exhibition], 1954–55.

SELECTED REFERENCES N. Wrangel in *Les Anciennes Ecoles de Peinture dans les Palais et Collections Privées Russes representées à l'exposition organisée à St. Petersbourg en 1909 . . .* , Brussels, 1910, p. 84, ill. [mentions a smaller version in Coll. P. P. Séménoff and says that in Sologhoube (Cincinnati) painting Maes is still a humble Rembrandt pupil imitating not only the master's technique but also his compositional arrangement of hands and pose which is close to Rembrandt's *Girl with a Broom*, Hermitage (now National Gallery, Washington) or the Portrait of *Titus*, Lord Kanford,

England (very likely meant to read Lord Crawford which is painting now in Museum Boymans-van Beuningen, Rotterdam)]; Hofstede de Groot, VI, 1916, p. 508, no. 112 [the attribution to Maes might very well be right and it was painted about 1650]; Valentiner 1924, p. 43 f., pl. 11 [conceived as a genre-like portrait very close in spirit to Rembrandt; probably a portrait of Rembrandt's son Titus when he was around nine years old (ca. 1650); stylistically it belongs to paintings such as *The Happy Mother*, Museum of Art, Toledo, Ohio, *Mother with Three Children and a Goat*, formerly Coll. Sir Anthony Rothschild, London, and *The Card Players*, National Gallery, London]; P. Wescher, "Die Auktion von Werken aus den ehem. Privatsammlungen im Besitz des russischen Staates," *Pantheon*, II, 1928, p. 523, ill. [as Rembrandt's son Titus and close to Rembrandt's style]; *Guide to the Collections of the Cincinnati Art Museum*, 1956, p. 49.

This portrait is Rembrandtesque in its dark tonality, in the importance of the chiaroscuro to set the mood and to model the forms and in the presentation of the sitter. This type of figure placed behind a barrier, in this case a railing, in others a balustrade or window, and looking straight out at the viewer is typical of Rembrandt during the first half of the 1650's [cf. the 1655 *Portrait of Titus*, Museum Boymans-van Beuningen, Rotterdam; 1651 *Girl Resting on Balustrade*, National Museum, Stockholm; 1651 *Girl Holding a Broom*, National Gallery, Washington]. It was at this time (ca. 1650–53), when Maes studied with Rembrandt, that this picture was probably painted. However, the attribution to Maes is not documented nor are the other early paintings attributed to him by Valentiner [Valentiner 1924, pls. 1–14]. Of the first fourteen illustrations in Valentiner's book on Maes, the picture that seems closest in style to the Cincinnati portrait, *The Card Players*, National Gallery, London, has been taken away from Maes and called a follower of Rembrandt, ca. 1650. [MacLaren 1960, p. 349 f.].

## 86 *Portrait of a Gentleman*

Miss Monica Hedy Brod, London

Panel 53.3 × 38.1 cms. *Ill. p. 144*

PROVENANCE Herman de Kat van Barendrecht, Dordrecht; sale Herman de Kat van Barendrecht, Paris, 3 May 1866, no. 68 [as Rembrandt]; sale J. Dollfuss, Paris, 20 May 1912, no. 56; Ludwig Mandl, Wiesbaden [at least by 1916]; E. G. Innes, London [at least by 1929]; sale E. G. Innes, London, 13 Dec. 1935, no. 129; D. V. Shaw-Kennedy, London.

EXHIBITIONS The Hague, Kleykamp Galleries, *Oud-Hollandsche en Vlaamsche Meesters*, 1926, no. 30; London 1929, no. 259 [as not yet clear which member of Heinsius family it might be and as an early work strongly influenced by Rembrandt]; Amsterdam, Rijksmuseum, *Drie Eeuwen Portret in Nederland*, 1952, no. 94 [as *Portrait of a Gentleman* and painted around 1655]; London 1952–53, no. 193; Rome, Palazzo delle Esposizioni, *Mostra di Pittura Olandese del Seicento*, 1954, no. 83; Milan 1954, no. 86; Leiden 1956, no. 73, fig. 22.

SELECTED REFERENCES E. W. Moes, *Iconographia Batava*, I, no. 3370, Amsterdam, 1897, no. 33, 70 [as portrait of the Leiden professor and poet Daniel Heinsius (1580–1655) by Rembrandt]; Hofstede de Groot, VI, 1916, p. 525 f., no. 178 [as Dr. Heinsius by Maes; a good portrait influenced by Rembrandt]; R. R. Tatlock, "An Inpublished Nicolaes Maes," *The Burlington Magazine*, XLVIII, 1926, p. 3, ill. [as safe to assume that it was painted during Maes' Amsterdam period, that is not later than about 1665, and that it bears more than just a superficial resemblance to the *Portriat of a Man*, Brussels Gallery, attributed to Vermeer, but it is not by the same hand]; Van Gelder 1953, p. 38, fig. 8 [as no longer thought to represent Dr. Heinsius; attribution to N. Maes is not convincing but Drost is more of a possibility]; E. Plietzsch, "Ausstellung holländischer Gemälde in der Londoner Akademie," *Kunstchronik*, VI, 1953, p. 131 [as ca. 1658 and like *Portrait of a Man*, Brussels, which had been ascribed to early Vermeer].

The directness with which the sitter engages the spectator, the strong use of chiaroscuro placing part of the face in shadow and part in bright light, the playing down of the costume, except for the white collar, which helps to lead the eye to the pensive face, are all elements found in Rembrandt's portraiture of the 1650's [cf. *Portrait of Dr. Arnout Tholinx*, Musée Jacquemart-André, Paris, Bauch 1966, no. 415].

There has been some discussion concerning the attribution of this painting to Nicolaes Maes. The rough application of the paint around the lighted cheek and forehead seems to recall the type of paint surface found in Maes' 1657 *Portrait of Jacob de Witt*, Dordrecht Museum [ill. in Valentiner 1924, p. 53]. This rough and gritty surface is carried even further in the pendants owned by the Art Institute, Chicago (cat. nos. 83 and 84). The notion that the Brod picture might be by Drost seems debatable, given the smoother surfaces and stronger stress upon contours outlining the forms associated with that artist.

The identification of the sitter as Dr. Heinsius must be discarded (as suggested earlier in the literature) as he would have been in his seventies, if not already dead, when the portrait was painted probably ca. 1657.

## 87  *Boys Bathing*

Musée du Louvre, Paris

Canvas 71 × 90 cms.  *Ill. p. 146*

PROVENANCE Schlichting.

SELECTED REFERENCES Hofstede de Groot, VI, 1916, p. 510, no. 97; A Bredius, *Kunstlear-Inventare* V, 1918, p. 619; E. Michel, "La 'Baignade' de la Collection Schlichting Jacob van Loo ou Nicolas Maes?", *Bulletin des Musées de France*, V, 1933, pp. 68–71, ill. [as Jacob van Loo and compares the rendering of the clothes, the light and the landscape with Van Loo's signed and dated 1641 *Garden of Love*, sale Cologne (Lempetz), 8–9 May 1928, no. 26, ill., his signed paintings of *Paris and Oenone*, Dresden, *Mother and Children*, Berlin, the *Factory of Small Glassware*, Copenhagen, Royal Museum and the attributed works representing *Diana and her Nymphs*, Brunswick and the *Allegory of Good Fortune*, Schleissheim].

From the reproductions of Jacob van Loo's paintings, it is difficult to uphold Michel's (pp. 68–71) attribution of the Louvre painting to this master. The *Bathers* presents us with a much more atmospheric type of light which melts the forms rather than helps to reinforce them. Jacob van Loo's figures and objects are strongly outlined, and the stress is on the contour rather than the modeling of form in the broad painterly manner of the Louvre painting. It is also difficult to secure the Louvre picture within the *oeuvre* of Nicolaes Maes. If one compares it with Maes' signed and dated 1656 *Old Man Giving Alms to a Young Beggar* (Valentiner 1924, pl. 41), the styles are also different. The figures in the 1656 painting have streaked highlights which cause strong contrasts and are easily read as brush strokes while in the bathing scene the light and dark areas are broad, more smoothly painted, and blend into each other.

The *Bathers* might be by an unknown Dordrecht artist who had seen the atmospheric Italianate landscapes of the Bamboccianti. Perhaps one should look in the direction of Cornelis Bisschop's signed *Mercury and Argos*, Dordrecht Museum, where a similar use of atmospheric light and shadow is present.

## 88  *Allegory: A Girl Plucking a Duck*

The Philadelphia Museum of Art

Canvas 58 × 66 cms.  *Ill. p. 147*

PROVENANCE sale Count de Turenne, Paris, 17 May 1852, no. 44, bought by Nieuwenhuis for 4860 francs; sale Adrian Hope, 30 June 1894, purchased by Sedelmeyer for 945 pounds; with Sedelmeyer [at least until 1898]; J. Pourgés, Paris; with F. Kleinberger, Paris; sale A. de Ridder, Paris, 2 June 1924, no. 38; with D. A. Hoogendijk, Amsterdam, 1928; with Duveen, N.Y.; given to Museum by Mrs. G. A. Hardwick and Mrs. W. N. Ely in memory of Mr. and Mrs. R. L. Taylor.

SELECTED REFERENCES Hofstede de Groot, VI, 1916, p. 483 f., no. 28 [as reminding one of Maes' *Old Woman Spinning*, Rijksmuseum, Amsterdam]; Valentiner 1924, p. 48 f., pl. 43 [as close in style to 1657 *Eavesdropper*, Coll. Six, Amsterdam, in which the tonality is clearer and the contour is more evident than in his works of 1655–56].

The Philadelphia painting has nothing to do with Rembrandt and illustrates vividly Houbraken's statement that Maes soon stopped painting in Rembrandt's style. This type of domestic interior could very well have been the source for Peiter de Hoogh's paintings executed a few years later. One also wonders what connection, if any, there is between Maes' perspective interior and Carel Fabritius', executed before his death in 1654. We know that the latter's illusionistic perspective paintings gained the attention of his contemporaries, but unfortunately they are all lost. In any case, Maes painted this type of allegorical genre scene from his return to Dordrecht at the end of 1653 until around 1660 when he turned exclusively to portraiture [cf. cat. no. 89].

Although this picture seemingly emphasizes the notion of reality based on daily life, it contains, as is characteristic of Dutch scenes of this type, a second and more important meaning easily recognized by Maes' contemporaries. As E. de Jongh has brilliantly worked out through careful study of sixteenth and seventeenth century texts [E. de Jongh, "Erotica in Vogelperspectief: de dubbelzinnigheid van een reeks 17de eeuwse genrevoorstellingen," *Simiolus*, III, 1968–69, pp. 22–31, 33 ff., 47, 72 ff. and *passim*.], birds and their presence in so-called genre surroundings were closely associated with intercourse. The cat has always been recognized as symbolic of lust or sensual pleasure, and in the early seventeenth century, it represented the female libido. This allusion to seduction and lust is further hinted at by the prominent position given to the hunter's gun. This probably refers to the common practice of the hunter offering his catch, often a bird, to a maiden—a disguised attempt at seduction. The subtle placement of the drinking vessels, such as the crock by the window and the glass and crock enframed by the open door, also must have a specific meaning likewise involved with lust or gluttony but for the moment their presence cannot be explained with certainty. The same can be said for the vessels and fruit in the foreground.

## 89 *Portrait of a Family*

Fogg Art Museum, Harvard University Purchase, Louise E. Bettens and Friends of the Fogg Art Museum Funds

Canvas 109.2 × 108 cms. signed bottom left on base of pier *N. Maes  Ill. p. 147*

PROVENANCE sale Col. Ridgeway, Shipley Court, Devonshire, London (Sotheby's), 19 July 1922, no. 61; with A. M. Bouwens, The Hague, 1926; Städtische Kunstsammlungen, Düsseldorf, during the 1930's; sale London (Christie's), 8 Dec. 1950, no. 94, sold to Hyatt; sale Bowring & others, London (Sotheby's), 23 Feb. 1955, no. 131; with Frost & Reed, London, 1955; purchased from Vose Galleries, Boston, 1957.

EXHIBITIONS San Francisco, Museum of Art, Los Angeles, Museum of Art, San Diego, Fine Arts Gallery, 1938, no. 18; Portland, Portland Art Museum, *Old Master Paintings*, 1940, no. 11; Milwaukee, Art Institute, 1943; Boston, Vose Galleries, *64th Anniversary for Robert Vose*, 1961; Buffalo, Albright-Knox Gallery, *Harvard Club Exhibition*, 1967; New Haven, Yale University Art Gallery, *Exhibition of Paintings, Drawings and Sculpture from the Fogg Art Museum*, 1967.

SELECTED REFERENCES S. Slive, "A Family Portrait by Nicolaes Maes," *The Annual Report of the Fogg Art Museum*, 1957-58, pp. 32-35, 36 [as painted around 1680], pp. 37 ff., ill. The Fogg portrait clearly illustrates Houbraken's statement that "Maes very soon gave up Rembrandt's way of painting, particularly when he saw that he had a real talent for portraiture, and when he discovered that young ladies would rather be painted in white than in brown." [Slive, *op. cit.*, 1957-58, p. 33]. The change-over from Rembrandt's style is striking in this picture which shows Maes' debt to the currently fashionable international style of portraiture. We know that Maes traveled to Antwerp to see the works of Rubens, Van Dyck, and Jordaens. The trip probably reinforced Maes' knowledge of the Flemish style which

was already practiced in Amsterdam in the 1640's and 1650's [cf. Bol, Lievens, Flinck, Van der Helst, etc.].

In this work, Maes' brilliant brush stroke and magnificent command of color is evident in the rendering of the rich and sumptuous drapery. However, in no way do the costumes and trappings detract from the faces which still maintain some of the soft chiaroscuro effects Maes learned from Rembrandt. Certainly pictures like this prompted Houbraken to write that Maes painted better portraits than any artist working before or after him.

## KAREL VAN DER PLUYM 1625(?)-1672

Karel van der Pluym came from an important Leiden family and served that city in a number of official posts, including that of city plumber and member of the Town Council of Forty. His mother was Rembrandt's sister, and in 1662 he included Titus, Rembrandt's only surviving child, in his will. On December 30, 1651, he married and in the following year became the head of the painters' guild (Saint Luke's Guild) in Leiden. He was one of its first members upon its founding in 1648; in 1654 and 1655, he was Dean of the Guild. Because of the style of his painting and his family connections with Rembrandt, it is likely that he studied with the master sometime between 1642 and 1648 when he entered the Guild of St. Luke as an independent master. There are very few paintings extant and this might be explained by his many commitments to the city of Leiden. He is basically known as an allegorical genre painter.

## 90 *The Parable of The Labourers in the Vineyard*

Dr. Willem M. J. Russell, Amsterdam

Panel 43.2 × 54.6 cms. signed bottom right on step *k. v. d. Pluym  Ill. p. 143*

PROVENANCE sale J. Searle, London (Christie's), 7 June 1856, lot 1, as Rembrandt; Sir Herbert Cook, Richmond, as Rembrandt; Sir Frederick Cook Bt., Richmond; Sir Francis Cook Bt.; with Alfred Brod, London.

EXHIBITIONS London 1953 MG, no. 57, ill.; Montreal/Toronto 1969, no. 99, ill.

SELECTED REFERENCES Kronig 1914-15, pp. 172, 177, ill. [states that during restoration Van der Pluym's signature appeared beneath Rembrandt's]; Bredius 1931, pp. 243, 254 f., fig. 1.

Although Rembrandt painted this subject in 1637 [cf. picture in Hermitage, Leningrad] and made several drawings in the late 1640's [Benesch III, cat. nos. 603–605, figs. 734–736], Van der Pluym's composition has no connection with these. His small format of two figures placed in a clearly delineated room with bright light entering from the window on one side and the other side in shadow brings to mind Rembrandt's compositions from around 1645–46 [cf. 1645 *Tobias and his Wife*, Staatl. Museen, Berlin or 1646 *Holy Family*, Painting Gallery, Kassel—Bauch 1966, nos. 26, 77]. Van der Pluym's inclusion of a hanging curtain on a rod giving a "trompe-l'oeil" effect is also present in Rembrandt's 1646 *Holy Family*. This motif appears again in Van der Pluym's signed and dated 1655 *Philosopher*, Lakenhal, Leiden, which also contains a similar looseness in the application of paint, awkwardness in the rendering of the hands, and one side strongly lighted with the other in shadow. Because of these affinities, one can suggest that *The Parable* dates from around the same time as the 1655 *Philosopher*.

## 91  *The Geographer*

Mr. and Mrs. Chester D. Tripp, Chicago  *Ill. p. 143*

Canvas 71.1 × 50.8 cms. signed on book lower right *Karel*

PROVENANCE J. E. Stillwell, New York [at least by 1915]; sale J. E. Stillwell, New York, 1 December 1927, no. 210; sometime between 1927 and 1931 sold to Chester D. Tripp, Chicago, as Rembrandt.

EXHIBITIONS Chicago, The Art Institute of Chicago, *Century of Progress Exhibit*, 1933, no. 72; Chicago 1935–36, no. 25, ill. [as signed *Karel van D*. . . .]; Worcester 1936, no. 23 [as signed *Karel van D*. . . .].

SELECTED REFERENCES Kronig 1914–15, p. 177 [as in Coll. Stillwell, New York]; Bredius 1931, p. 246 f. [as signed *Karel van de* . . . and connected stylistically, especially in the hands, with *Woman with the Bible*, Frick Coll., New York], p. 255 figs. 4–6; Sumowski 1957–58, p. 229 [as imitating Rembrandt's ca. 1645 etching of *Old Man in Meditation* (Münz 1952, I, cat. no. 67, pl. 74].

In this painting, it appears that Van der Pluym built up his forms with heavy layers of impasto to give them a rough quality. His broad brush and light effects are similar to Rembrandt's of the 1650's.

The Chicago *Geographer*(?) seems not far in style from *The Parable of the Labourers in the Vineyard* (cat. no. 90) and the signed and dated 1659 *Allegory of the Goldweigher*, Coll. H. Fraenkel, London.

# JAN VICTORS 1619/20–after 1676

Jan Victors was born in Amsterdam, and when his engagement was announced in 1642 he gave his age as twenty-two. It is likely that he studied with Rembrandt sometime before 1640. From 1642 on he is documented as being in Amsterdam and is last cited in the city records in January, 1676. Sometime in 1676 he set out for the Dutch East Indies and was not heard from again.

Victors painted biblical scenes (cat. no. 92) like those of his teacher but without imagination, and the influence is only external. He was a better portraitist than history painter, but he is best known for his genre paintings which he produced beginning ca. 1650. These genre paintings illustrate subjects that were popular in the circle of Jan Miense Molenaer—that is, scenes from the lives of the people devoid of much action and sometimes containing an amusing failure.

## 92  *The Angel Leaving the Family of Tobit*

Victor Spark, New York

Canvas 103.5 × 141.4 cms. signed on stone balustrade along lower-right margin *Jan Victors Fc 1649  Ill. p. 134*

EXHIBITIONS Raleigh 1956, p. 123, no. 79, ill.; Montreal / Toronto 1969, no. 113, ill.

This subject was treated several times by Rembrandt, and certainly a number of motifs and painterly devices were taken over from the master. The architectural setting with the figures placed before and within it, the opening to one side leading to a clouded landscape, the angel flying up and out of the picture on a diagonal, and the use of light and shadow to create a dramatic effect are all elements present in Rembrandt's rendering of the theme starting with his 1637 painting *Angel Leaving the Family of Tobit*, Louvre. Jan Victors borrows the general format of Rembrandt's work but changes the positions of the figures except for the angel and the general attitude of the young Tobias. Jan Victors' Tobit, as in the original source for Rembrandt, Maarten van Heemskerck's woodcut, rests his chin upon his clasped hands. [A similar motif also occurs later in Rembrandt's ca. 1650 *Study*, Museum of Fine Arts, Budapest (ill. in J. Held, *Rembrandt and the Book of Tobit*, Northampton, 1964, fig. 29) and in the ca. 1652 Rembrandt School drawing, Albertina, Vienna (Benesch VI, cat. no. 1373, fig. 1607)]. Jan Victors also includes a young boy looking out of the window which is a variation of the old servant in a similar position in Rembrandt's 1614 etching of this subject [Münz 1952, I, cat. no. 179, pl. 199].

Jan Victors' use of strong contrasts between the light and dark areas of the picture, the manner of painting with light accents on the costumes and head of the young Tobias, and the careful rendering of surface details are elements very similar to those found in Jan Victors' 1648 *Joseph Explaining Dreams*, Rijksmuseum, Amsterdam. The fine detailing of the brushwork also accompanied by broad areas of color which give a sense of the actual materials is close to the style of another Rembrandt pupil working with the master at roughly the same time, Gerbrand van den Eeckhout (cf. cat. no. 45). Victors repeated this subject with changes but in much the same Rembrandtesque style in his 1651 painting in Munich, inv. 1031.

## 93   *The Fishmonger*

Anonymous, on indefinite loan to Metropolitan Museum of Art, N.Y.

Canvas 49 × 82 cms. signed on boat bottom—left corner *J. Victors f. Ill. p. 134*

PROVENANCE with H. Shickman Gallery, N.Y., 1967.

EXHIBITIONS New York, H. Shickman Gallery, *Exhibition of Dutch Seventeenth-Century Paintings*, 1967, no. 26, ill.; Montreal/Toronto 1969, no. 116, ill.

Jan Victors painted a number of genre paintings like this around the year 1650. In these pictures he obviously has turned away from his teacher Rembrandt and executed more anecdotal outdoor scenes, possibly introduced into Amsterdam in the 1640's by the Haarlem painter, Jan Molenaer. However, in spite of the change in subject matter, the brownish-gray tone reminds one of Rembrandt.

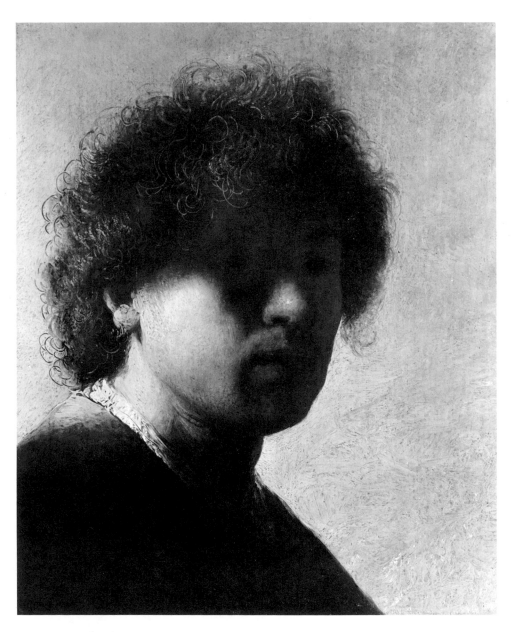

1 *Rembrandt*
*Self-Portrait*
*Daan Cevat*

*2  Rembrandt*
*Artist in His Studio*
*Museum of Fine Arts, Boston*

3  *Rembrandt*
   *The Tribute Money*
   *The National Gallery of Canada, Ottawa*

4  *Rembrandt*
   *Portrait of a Man from the Raman Family, Amsterdam*
   *Los Angeles County Museum of Art*

5   *Rembrandt*
    *Portrait of a Man*
    *Earl C. Townsend, Jr., Indianapolis*

6  *Rembrandt*
   *Self-Portrait*
   *Norton Simon Foundation*
   *Fullerton, California*

7  Rembrandt
   *The Visitation*
   *The Detroit Institute of Arts*

8  Rembrandt
   *Young Girl at an Open Half-Door*
   *The Art Institute of Chicago*

9  Rembrandt
   Winter Landscape
   Staatliche Kunstsammlungen Kassel

11  Rembrandt
   *Christ and the Woman of Samaria*
   *The Metropolitan Museum of Art*

*12 Rembrandt*
*Portrait of a Young Man*
*Wadsworth Atheneum, Hartford*

14  Rembrandt
*Old Man with Mantle and Beret*
*Mr. and Mrs. Nathan R. Allen*
*Greenwich, Conn.*

13  *Rembrandt*
   *Portrait of a Man with Arms Akimbo*
   *Columbia University*

15 *Rembrandt*
*Portrait of Titus*
*The Baltimore Museum of Art*

*16  Rembrandt*
    *Titus (or An Angel)*
    *The Detroit Institute of Arts*

17  Rembrandt
    *Portrait of a Young Man*
    *George Eastman Collection of the University of Rochester*

20 *Rembrandt*
*Saint James*
*Private Collection*

19 Rembrandt
*Old Man Praying*
*The Cleveland Museum of Art*

18  *Rembrandt*
*Christ*
*Collection of Mr. and Mrs. Harry G. John, Milwaukee*

21  *Rembrandt*
   *Lucretia*
   *The Minneapolis Institute of Arts*

22  *Attributed to Rembrandt*
    *Man Reading*
    *Sterling and Francine Clark Art Institute*

*23 Attributed to Rembrandt*
*A Seated Man with a Stick*
*The National Gallery, London*

24  *Attributed to Rembrandt*
*Lamentation*
*John and Mable Ringling Museum of Art*

25 *Attributed to Rembrandt*
 *Tobias and the Angel*
 *Staatliche Museum Berlin,*
 *Gemäldegalerie Dahlem*

28 *Attributed to Rembrandt*
 *Supper at Emmaus*
 *Musée du Louvre, Paris*

27 *Attributed to Rembrandt*
*Apostle Thomas(?)*
*Staatliche Kunstsammlungen Kassel*

26 *Attributed to Rembrandt*
*Fragment of an Annunciation—The Virgin*
*Národní Galerie, Prague*

79  *Jan Lievens*
     *Raising of Lazarus*
     *Brighton Art Gallery, England*

77  *Jan Lievens*
     *Portrait of Rembrandt*
     *Daan Cevat*

76  *Jan Lievens*
     *Old Woman Reading*
     *John G. Johnson Collection*
     *Philadelphia*

*80 Jan Lievens*
*Portrait of a Young Man*
*National Gallery of Scotland, Edinburgh*

78  Jan Lievens
    *Eli Instructing Samuel*
    *H. Shickman Gallery, New York*

82  Jan Lievens
    *A Woodland Walk*
    *National Gallery of Scotland*
    *Edinburgh University Loan*
    *Torrie Collection*

81 *Jan Lievens*
   *Christ Washing the Feet of the Disciples*
   *The Art Institute of Chicago*

37  *Gerard Dou*
*Eli Instructing Samuel*
*Anonymous*

36  Gerard Dou
    *Artist in His Studio*
    *Collection G. Henle, Duisburg*

38  Gerard Dou
    *Vanitas*
    *Museum of Fine Arts, Boston*

29  Jacob Backer
    *Portrait of a Boy*
    *Royal Gallery of Paintings*
    *"Mauritshuis," The Hague*

31  Ferdinand Bol
    Portrait of an Old Woman
    Muzeum Narodowe, Warsaw

30  Ferdinand Bol
    Portrait of Elisabeth Jacobsdr Bas
    Rijksmuseum, Amsterdam

*34 Ferdinand Bol*
*Scene from Ancient History*
*Worcester Art Museum*

*33  Ferdinand Bol*
*Portrait of Saskia*
*M. H. de Young Memorial Museum,*
*San Francisco*

*32  Ferdinand Bol*
*Angel Appearing to Hagar*
*Walker Art Gallery, Liverpool*

35  Ferdinand Bol
    *Portrait of a Young Boy in Polish Costume*
    *Museum Boymans-van Beuningen, Rotterdam*

60   *Govert Flinck*
     *Hermes and Aglauros*
     *Museum of Fine Arts, Boston*

63 Govert Flinck
  Portrait of a Man
  The Minneapolis Institute of Arts

62 Govert Flinck
  Portrait of a Boy
  Barber Institute of Fine Arts,
  University of Birmingham

61 *Govert Flinck*
   *The Return of the Prodigal Son*
   *North Carolina Museum of Art, Raleigh*

45  Gerbrand van den Eeckhout
Isaac Blessing Jacob
The Metropolitan Museum of Art

*46 Gerbrand van den Eeckhout*
*Daniel Proving the Innocence of Susanna*
*Wadsworth Atheneum, Hartford*

48 Gerbrand van den Eeckhout
*Portrait of Jan Pz van den Eeckhout (1584–1652)*
*Musée des Beaux Arts, Grenoble*

49 Gerbrand van den Eeckhout
*Portrait of Cornelia Dedel*
*Dr. Jan B. Hubrecht, Doorn*

Gerbrand van den Eeckhout

47　Gerbrand van den Eeckhout
　　St. Peter Healing the Lame
　　M. H. de Young Memorial Museum,
　　San Francisco

50　Gerbrand van den Eeckhout
　　A Party on a Terrace (Allegory?)
　　Worcester Art Museum

71  Samuel van Hoogstraten
    *Portrait of a Young Man*
    *Sidney van den Bergh, Wassenaar*

72  Samuel van Hoogstraten
    *Resurrection*
    *The Art Institute of Chicago*

Jan Victors

93 Jan Victors
   *The Fishmonger*
   *Anonymous*

92 Jan Victors
   *The Angel Leaving the Family of Tobit*
   *Victor Spark, New York*

73  *Philips Koninck*
    *Portrait of Heyman Dullaert*
    *City Art Museum of Saint Louis*

*Philips Koninck*

75  *Philips Koninck*
    *View Between Heavy Trees over*
    *a Flat Landscape with a River*
    *Hofje van Aerden, Leerdam, on loan to*
    *the Museum Boymans-van Beuningen*

74  *Philips Koninck*
    *Panoramic Landscape*
    *Swiss Private Collection*

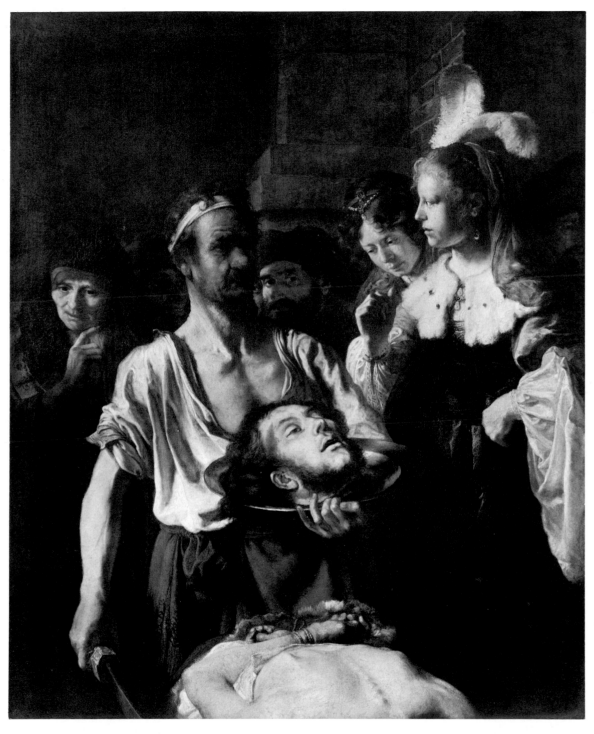

56  Carel Fabritius
    *The Beheading of St. John the Baptist*
    *Rijksmuseum, Amsterdam*

59  Carel Fabritius
    Man with a Helmet
    Groninger Museum voor
    Stad en Lande

58  Carel Fabritius
    Head of an Old Man
    Royal Gallery of Paintings
    "Mauritshuis," The Hague

57  Carel Fabritius
    The Raising of Lazarus
    Muzeum Narodowe, Warsaw

53  *Barent Fabritius*
   *Rebecca Welcomed by Abraham*
   *The Art Institute of Chicago*

51 *Barent Fabritius*
*Self Portrait*
*Museum of Fine Arts, Boston*

52 *Barent Fabritius*
*The Dismissal of Hagar*
*M. H. de Young Memorial Museum,*
*San Francisco*

54  *Barent Fabritius*
    *The Satyr and the Peasant*
    *Wadsworth Atheneum, Hartford*

55  *Barent Fabritius*
    *Allegory: Woman Picking Fleas from a Child's Head*
    *Hessisches Landesmuseum, Darmstadt*

*Karel van der Pluym*

91  *Karel van der Pluym
The Geographer
Mr. and Mrs. Chester D. Tripp,
Chicago*

90  *Karel van der Pluym
The Parable of the
Labourers in the Vineyard
Dr. Willem M. J. Russell,
Amsterdam*

83  Nicolaes Maes
    Portrait of a Man
    The Art Institute of Chicago

84  Nicolaes Maes
    Portrait of a Woman
    The Art Institute of Chicago

86  Nicolaes Maes
    Portrait of a Gentleman
    Miss Monica Hedy Brod, London

85  *Nicolaes Maes*
    *Portrait of a Young Boy*
    *Cincinnati Art Museum*

87  Nicolaes Maes
    Boys Bathing
    Musée du Louvre, Paris

89 Nicolaes Maes
*Portrait of a Family*
*Fogg Art Museum, Harvard University*

88 Nicolaes Maes
*Allegory: A Girl Plucking a Duck*
*The Philadelphia Museum of Art*

39  Willem Drost
*Portrait of a Young Boy*
*Private Collection*

40  Willem Drost
*Self-Portrait (?)*
*The Metropolitan Museum of Art*

41  *Willem Drost*
   *Bathsheba*
   *Musée du Louvre, Paris*

43  *Willem Drost*
   *Noli Me Tangere*
   *Staatliche Kunstsammlungen Kassel*

42  *Willem Drost*
   *Ruth and Naomi*
   *The Ashmolean Museum, Oxford*

44  *Willem Drost*
   *Samuel and Eli*
   *The Art Institute of Chicago*

65  *Aert de Gelder*
    *Esther and Mordecai*
    *Writing Letters to the Jews*
    *Museum of Art,*
    *Rhode Island School of Design*

64  *Aert de Gelder*
    *Forecourt of a Temple,*
    *Figures Before an Imaginary Structure*
    *Royal Gallery of Paintings,*
    *"Mauritshuis," The Hague*

66 *Aert de Gelder*
*Rest on the Flight into Egypt*
*Museum of Fine Arts, Boston*

*68 Aert de Gelder*
   *Portrait of a Girl*
   *The Art Institute of Chicago*

67 *Aert de Gelder*
   *Vertumnus and Pomona*
   *Národní Galerie, Prague*

69 *Aert de Gelder*
   *Christ on the Mount of Olives*
   *Julius H. Weitzner, London*

70  *Aert de Gelder*
    *Christ Before the Sanhedrim (Caiaphas)*
    *Rijksmuseum, Amsterdam*

*Catalogue of Drawings*
*by E. Haverkamp-Begemann*
*and Anne-Marie Logan*

# REMBRANDT

**94** *Old Beggar in a Long Cloak and High Cap*

Rijksprentenkabinet, Amsterdam

Black chalk, 293 × 170 mm. *Ill. p. 203*

INSCRIPTIONS Annotated with brush and black ink at bottom right: *Rem.*

DATE [ca. 1628–1630].

PROVENANCE Jacob de Vos Sen. (sale October 30, 1833, perhaps Pf. L, p. 38, no. 14); J. G. Verstolk van Soelen (sale March 22, 1847); Jacob de Vos Jbzn (L. 1450; sale May 24, 1883, no. 412, together with two other beggars [Henkel 1942, nos. 1 and 3]).

EXHIBITIONS Rotterdam/Amsterdam 1956, no. 8.

BIBLIOGRAPHY HdG 1186 [ca. 1630–35]; Freise and Lilienfeld 30 [1630]; Bauch 1933, p. 187, fig. 30 [ca. 1628]; Benesch 1935, p. 9 [1629]; Henkel 1942, p. 1, no. 4, pl. 3; Benesch I, no. 32, fig. 38; Benesch 1960, p. 13; Bauch 1960, pp. 158–9, fig. 124; Sumowski 1962, p. 275 [ca. 1628]; Sumowski 1964, p. 234.

Throughout his life Rembrandt included the poor in biblical scenes whenever their presence was justified. This interest in the deprived bordered on fascination in his early career in Leiden (ca. 1628–31) when he repeatedly sketched beggars with pen and brush or black chalk, and even lent his own features to a beggar in one of the numerous etchings devoted to this subject (*Beggar Seated on a Bank*, H. 11).

The long tradition of beggars as an artistic subject (Bosch, Bruegel) was revitalized at the beginning of the seventeenth century, particularly by Annibale Carracci and Callot. Rembrandt's beggars are closer to Callot's than to those of any other preceding artist, and his interpretation of the poor probably was stimulated and influenced by his French contemporary. However, in contrast to Callot's more anecdotal and Annibale's rather detached approach, Rembrandt emphasized in his beggars their state of misery and their lack of formal beauty.

Together with other black chalk studies of beggars, this drawing once belonged to a sketchbook that may be dated 1628–30. Rembrandt's treatment of the line, especially the dense vertical parallel hatching, is reminiscent of Callot's prints. As for the black chalk, Rembrandt probably learned to appreciate this medium when he was in Lastman's studio (ca. 1624/25).

**95** *A Team of Horses Resting*

Rijksprentenkabinet, Amsterdam

Black and some red chalk in the head of the front horse, 170 × 272 mm. *Ill. p. 203*

DATE [ca. 1629–32].

PROVENANCE I. de Bruijn, Muri-Bern.

EXHIBITIONS Basel 1948, no. 1; Amsterdam 1961, no. 33.

BIBLIOGRAPHY Henkel 1942, p. 59, under no. 124; Benesch II, no. 461, fig. 518 [ca. 1637]; Van Regteren Altena 1961, p. 85, no. 33, fig. 18, L. C. J. Frerichs, *Openbaar Kunstbezit*, VI, 1962, no. 20.

Rather than a representation of animals *per se*, this is a study of a particular relationship of man and animal, drawn from life. In other instances, Rembrandt sketched dromedaries and elephants with their caretakers. Here, his interpretation of shabby horses is similar to that of the beggars during his last years in Leiden. As Miss Frerichs pointed out, there are also stylistic similarities between the man covering the horses and the *Study of a Man Seen from Behind*, perhaps a wagoner, sketched on the reverse of the *Standing Beggar* of about 1629 (B. 30, fig. 36). The drawing may also date from the same time, and in any event was made not long after Rembrandt moved to Amsterdam. The motif is reminiscent of Jan van Goyen.

**96** *Beggar Woman Leaning on a Stick*

National Gallery of Art, Washington, D. C., Rosenwald Collection *Ill. p. 203*

Brush and brown wash, and in the face and hat a few lines drawn with pen and brown ink, 135 × 120 mm.

DATE [ca. 1629–31]

PROVENANCE J. Richardson Sen. (L. 2183); Th. Hudson (L. 2432); Sir Joshua Reynolds (L. 2364); Lessing J. Rosenwald.

EXHIBITIONS Philadelphia, Art Alliance, 1930; Worcester 1936, no. 62; Raleigh 1956, no. 5; New York/Cambridge, Mass. 1960, no. 1, pl. 1; Washington, National Gallery of Art, 1966; *Ibid.* 1969, no. 26 [illustrated].

BIBLIOGRAPHY Benesch 1947, no. 9; Benesch I, no. 24, fig. 25 [ca. 1628–29]; Bauch 1960, pp. 161–63, fig. 130.

In the emphasis on the light and dark values as well as in subject matter, this drawing is related to the etching of an *Old Beggar Woman with a Gourd* (B. 168, H. 80), according to Hind made in 1631. This is one of the few early studies done almost entirely with the brush, a technique which is also found in Rembrandt's *Self-Portrait* drawing of about

1627–28 (B. 53, fig. 60). Although not as close to some etchings of Callot as the preceding drawings, this one may also reflect the influence of the French artist, particularly of his brush drawings.

## 97 *Seated Old Man*

National Gallery of Art, Washington, D.C., Rosenwald Collection

Red chalk, 157 × 147 mm. *Ill. p. 202*

INSCRIPTIONS Signed in monogram and dated with red chalk at left center: *Rt/1630.*

DATE 1630.

PROVENANCE Narcisse Revil, Paris; Jacob de Vos Jbzn (sale Amsterdam, May 22–24, 1883, no. 410); J. P. Heseltine, London (sale Amsterdam, May 27, 1913, no. 5); H. Eissler, Vienna; Lessing J. Rosenwald.

EXHIBITIONS London 1899, no. 139; Cambridge, Mass. 1948–49, no. 36; Rotterdam/Amsterdam 1956, no. 14, fig. 2; New York/Cambridge, Mass. 1960, no. 2, pl. 2; Washington, National Gallery of Art, 1966; *Ibid.* 1969, no. 24 illustrated.

BIBLIOGRAPHY HdG 997; Lippmann I, no. 187b; C. Vosmaer, *Rembrandt, sa vie et ses oeuvres,* The Hague, 1877, pp. 106–07, 487; E. Michel, *Rembrandt,* II, London, 1894, p. 255. W. von Seidlitz, in *Repertorium für Kunstwissenschaft,* XVII, 1894, p. 120; Heseltine 1907, no. 1; Bauch 1933, p. 201, fig. 93; Benesch 1935, p. 10; Benesch 1947, no. 17; E. Mongan, in A. Mongan, *One Hundred Master Drawings,* Cambridge, Mass., 1949, p. 86; Benesch I, no. 37, fig. 41; Rosenberg D 1956, p. 126, fig. 12; J. Rosenberg, *Great Draughtsmen from Pisanello to Picasso,* Cambridge, Mass., 1959, p. 74, fig. 135; Slive 1965, no. 201.

The old man of this drawing repeatedly served Rembrandt as a model about 1630 and 1631. He appears in eight drawings, all executed in red chalk, a material which the artist favored in these years. In some of these drawings Rembrandt also used black chalk. The wrinkled old face with heavy beard and unkempt hair must have fascinated the artist for various reasons, one being that the features conformed to Rembrandt's conception of venerable scholars or saints. We find this model in paintings as a philosopher, as the Apostle Paul, as St. Peter, and as Jeremiah. He appears also in a number of etchings. Similar types of old men are found in the works of Lievens and Dou.

## 98 *A Negro with a Turban*

Chr. P. van Eeghen, Netherlands

Red and black chalk, 192 × 148 mm. *Ill. p. 204*

DATE [ca. 1630–31].

PROVENANCE Valerius Röver, Delft (bought in or shortly before 1738, Pf. 8, no. 39, as Rembrandt: *Een Persiaan met een tulband, met rood en zwart krijt* [A Persian with a turban, with red and black chalk]); Goll van Franckenstein (1833, Pf. P, no. 9); Van Idsinga (1840, Pf. H, no. 2); De Kat (1867, no. 358, as School of Rembrandt); De Clercq.

EXHIBITIONS Amsterdam, Museum Fodor, *Teekeningen . . . verzameling Mr. Chr. P. van Eeghen,* 1935, no. 76 [illustrated in color; as by Rembrandt]; Rotterdam/Amsterdam 1956, no. 17 [red and black chalk drawing by Rembrandt].

BIBLIOGRAPHY Bauch 1933, p. 221, no. 3 [rather in the manner of Lievens]; Bauch 1939, pp. 250–51, fig. 172 [in color; corrected by Rembrandt; finished red chalk drawing worked over with black chalk]; Benesch II, no. A 4, fig. 593 [hard to place it convincingly among Rembrandt's chalk drawings of 1630–31]; Rosenberg K 1956, pp. 351–52 [doubtful]; Sumowski 1956–57, p. 258 [considers Bauch's opinion correct]; Bauch 1960, p. 208 [red chalk drawing by Lievens gone over and corrected by Rembrandt with black chalk]; Begemann 1961, pp. 89–90 [portrait, probably by Rembrandt about 1630–31, drawn in red and black chalk, "completed" by other hand with black and red chalk].

Later in his life Rembrandt painted Negroes, and occasionally throughout his career he introduced Negroes in religious scenes. This drawing, however, is his only full-size study of a Negro.

The authorship of the drawing has been disputed, and the opinions vary from accepting the drawing in its entirety as a work of Rembrandt to attributing it to Jan Lievens. To the present writer it seems most likely that a more sketchy original version drawn with black and red chalk was reworked in both media by another hand, either in the seventeenth or already in the eighteenth century. Rembrandt made his study probably about 1630–31.

## 99 *The Supper at Emmaus*

Fogg Art Museum, Friends of the Fogg Art Museum Fund, Harvard University, Cambridge, Mass.

Pen and brown ink, 101 × 110 mm. *Ill. p. 204*

DATE [ca. 1630–31].

PROVENANCE Wilhelm von Bode, Berlin.

EXHIBITIONS Cambridge, Mass., Fogg Art Museum, *A Tribute to John Coolidge: Purchases of Two Decades*, 1968.

BIBLIOGRAPHY HdG 189; W. von Bode, in *Leidsch Jaarboekje*, 1906, p. 98 [as first idea, in reverse, for painting in the Musée Jacquemart-André, Paris (Br. 539)]; Stechow 1934, pp. 334–35, fig. 2 [ca. 1633, not study for painting]; Valentiner 1934, no. 525 [ca. 1629]; Benesch 1935, p. 15 [ca. 1632–33]; Van Regteren Altena 1948–49, p. 7, fig. 3; Rotermund 1952, p. 103, pl. 19d; Benesch I, no. 11, fig. 31 [ca. 1629]; Sumowski 1956–57, p. 263, fig. 54 [drawing perhaps in Dirk van Santvoort's possession, because he used it for his painting, in 1942 in Collection Vermunt, Berlin]; Bauch 1960, p. 284 [ca. 1634]; Sumowski 1961, p. 3 [ca. 1634]; Rotermund 1963, p. 266, fig. 243; Gantner 1964, p. 102, note 1 and p. 129; Gerson 1968, p. 28 and under no. 14 [same period as painting].

This drawing is one of the earliest representations of a subject that fascinated Rembrandt throughout his life. The drawing and the painting of the same subject in the Musée Jacquemart-André, Paris (Br. 539) which dates from about 1630 are the earliest instances of Rembrandt's use of rays of light emanating from Christ as an indication of His revelation to man. Rembrandt here represented the moment recounted in Luke 24:31: "And their eyes were opened, and they knew him." The vanishing of Christ immediately following the recognition is represented in the drawing exhibited under no. 122.

Although the drawing may have been made at the same time as the painting, it probably is not a study for it. This supposition is based on the fact that the composition is further removed from Elsheimer's *Jupiter and Mercury Visiting Philemon and Baucis* which served Rembrandt as a point of departure for his painting, and that in the location of both Christ and one disciple on this side of the table, the drawing already includes features of the etching of the same subject of 1634 (B. 88, H. 121). The drawing therefore may have been made shortly after the painting. This date, to some extent, is confirmed by the similarity between the disciple seated at the right and the woman in the lower right corner of the earlier states of the etching *The Raising of Lazarus* of about 1632 (B. 73, H. 96).

Another variation Rembrandt sketched of the subject at the time of the Fogg drawing or slightly later is known only through at least two copies (pen and brown ink, 97 × 113 mm., Chicago Art Institute, Charles Deering

Coll., 27.5195, and HdG 78, Valentiner 1934, 526, Berlin KdZ 5259). In the lost original Rembrandt placed Christ behind the table, as he did again much later.

## 100 *The Last Supper*

The Lehman Collection, New York

Red chalk, 365 × 475 mm. *Ill. p. 205*

Signed with red chalk at bottom right: *Rembrant f.*

DATE [ca. 1635].

PROVENANCE Friedrich August II of Saxony, Dresden.

EXHIBITIONS Paris 1957, no. 122; Washington, D.C. *et al.* 1958–59, no. 60; Cincinnati 1959, no. 268; New York/Cambridge, Mass. 1960, no. 9, pl 9.

BIBLIOGRAPHY Lippmann I, 99; E. Michel, *Rembrandt*, Paris, 1893, opposite p. 406; C. Hofstede de Groot, in *Jahrbuch der preussischen Kunstsammlungen*, XV, 1894, p. 178; HdG 297 [ca. 1635]; R. Graul, *Rembrandt*, Leipzig. 1906, no. 25; Hind 1915, under no. 3; Neumann 1918, pp. 106–08, fig. 34; Neumann 1919, no. 58; Freise and Wichmann 1925, no. 105; W. Weisbach, *Rembrandt*, Berlin, 1926, fig. 46; Kauffmann 1926, p. 177; Hell 1930, p. 111, note 1 [second stage of drawing inconsistent with late style]; Lugt 1931, p. 62, under no. 1369; J. L. A. A. M. van Rijckevorsel, *Rembrandt en de traditie*, Rotterdam, 1932, pp. 236–37, fig. 293; A. M. Hind, *Rembrandt*, Cambridge, Mass., 1932, pl. XXXIX; Valentiner 1934, no. 623 B [ca. 1633]; Benesch 1935, p. 21; J. Poortenaar, *Rembrandt teekeningen*, Naarden, 1943, no. 40; Benesch 1947, no. 43; Van Regteren Altena 1948–49, p. 14; Benesch II, no. 443, fig. 500 [both stages ca. 1635]; Sumowski 1956–57, p. 263; C. White, *The Drawings of Rembrandt*, London, 1962, p. 12; Gantner 1962, pp. 179–84, fig. 4; Scheidig 1962, p. 43 and no. 45, fig. 45; Rotermund 1963, p. 261, fig. 216; Gantner 1964, pp. 27–51, fig. 12; Slive 1965, no. 100; Clark 1968, pp. 53–56, fig. 43; Gerson 1968, p. 86 [illustrated]; C. White, *Rembrandt and His World*, New York, 1968, p. 19 [illustrated].

Rembrandt based his copy after Leonardo's fresco in Santa Maria delle Grazie in Milan on an early sixteenth-century engraving attributed to the Master of the Sforza Book of Hours (cf. A. M. Hind, *Early Italian Engraving in the British Museum*, Pt. II, London, 1948, V, p. 88, no. 9).

The study consists of two superimposed drawings. In the first one, drawn with fairly hard red chalk, Rembrandt followed the engraving rather closely. This under-drawing is best visible in the figure of Christ and the apostles at His left. Later, Rembrandt reworked the drawing with a softer red chalk. While reworking his copy, Rembrandt changed Leonardo's composition, most notably by adding the canopy over Christ and the three apostles at His left, and by changing the position of Christ. The main effect of these changes is the elimination of Leonardo's symmetry.

Valentiner wrongly considered the somewhat timid underdrawing to be by a pupil, which was reworked by Rembrandt himself. The difference between the first and second version rather points to a different time of origin, and it is likely, as Neumann already suggested (1918, p. 107), that the second stage dates from a considerably later period. The first stage probably dates from the mid-thirties, and probably preceded a second copy after Leonardo's *Last Supper*, which Rembrandt drew with the pen and dated 1635 (Berlin, B. 445, fig. 501). In that pen drawing Rembrandt changed the position of the disciples considerably and did not include any architectural background.

Another version in the British Museum (B. 444, fig. 502), also in red chalk, has survived as a fragment only. It represents a further modification of the six figures to the left of Christ and probably was made sometime after the Berlin drawing (B. 445). The second stage of the Lehman drawing may date from the 1650's.

If the reconstruction of this sequence is correct, the second stage of the Lehman drawing is the last of the generally accepted drawings by Rembrandt after Leonardo's *Last Supper*. It seems, however, that the artist made one more version of the final stage of the Lehman drawing, namely in pen and wash on two pieces of Japan paper. The original pen and brush lines of this large drawing (325 × 486 mm.) in Berlin (Bock and Rosenberg 1930, p. 238, Inv. no. 1369, pl. 177) may well be the work of Rembrandt himself, while another artist added accents and retouched large areas. Valentiner rejected the drawing as a copy by a pupil, and Benesch omitted it, while Lugt (1931, under no. 1369) had gone as far as to hesitate whether to attribute the original lines to Rembrandt or not, and Van Regteren Altena had even mentioned it as a work of Rembrandt (1948–49, pp. 14 and 25).

Although in spite of his intensive interest in Leonardo's *Last Supper*, Rembrandt never painted or etched this subject per se, he used Leonardo's composition for various paintings (*Supper at Emmaus*, *Wedding Feast of Samson*, *Conspiracy of Julius Civilis*), and particularly for his etching of *Christ at Emmaus* of 1654 (B. 87, H. 282) where he reintroduced the canopy as well as the attitude of Christ of the second Lehman version.

101   *Sheet of Studies with a Blind Old Woman*

Staatliche Museen Preussischer Kulturbesitz, Kupferstichkabinett, Berlin

Pen and brown ink, corrected with white body color in the figure of the boy, 185 × 170 mm. *Ill. p. 208*

DATE [mid-1630's].

PROVENANCE J. Richardson Sen. (L. 2183); Th. Hudson (L. 2432); Sir Joshua Reynolds (L. 2364); T. Lawrence (L. 2445); W. Esdaile (L. 2617); De Kat; Jacob de Vos Jbzn (L. 1450).

EXHIBITIONS Berlin 1930, no. 242.

BIBLIOGRAPHY HdG 141 [ca. 1635]; Lippmann I, no. 23; Betty Kurth, in Wickhoff, *Seminarstudien, Einige Zeichnungen Rembrandts mit biblischen Vorwürfen*, Innsbruck, 1906, p. 11 ff. [as *Hannah and Samuel*]; Freise and Lilienfeld 131 (132), Bock and Rosenberg 1930, p. 234, no. 3772, pl. 169 [reject identification as *Hannah and Samuel*; ca. 1635]; Benesch 1935, p. 16; Benesch II, no. 223, figs. 242–43 [ca. 1633–34]; Slive 1965, no. 23.

Of the many genre studies of the mid-1630's this is one of the most poignant ones. The briskly drawn lines express convincingly the hesitating movements of the woman walking up some steps and the guidance of the boy who is eager to keep moving.

In this very well preserved drawing, the effect of the pen-lines is enhanced by their contrast with the white paper. Rembrandt repeated the boy in a slightly different position.

102   *Two Studies of a Woman Reading*\*

The Metropolitan Museum of Art, Bequest of Mrs. H. O. Havemeyer, 1929, The H. O. Havemeyer Collection, 1929.

Pen and dark brown ink, 173 × 150 mm. *Ill. p. 206*

DATE [mid-1630's].

PROVENANCE J. Richardson Sen. (L. 2183); W. Mayor; F. Seymour Haden (sale London, Sotheby, June 15, 1891, no. 582); Mr. and Mrs. H. O. Havemeyer.

EXHIBITIONS Rotterdam/Amsterdam 1956, no. 56; New York/Cambridge, Mass. 1960, no. 34, pl. 29.

BIBLIOGRAPHY W. Mayor, *Description of a Collection of Original Drawings*, 1871, no. 356; Lippmann I, 142; W. R. Valentiner, "Aus Rembrandts Häuslichkeit", *Jahrbuch für Kunstwissenschaft*, I, 1923, p. 279, pl. 116; W. R. Valentiner, in *Metropolitan Museum Studies*, III, 1931, p. 139, fig. 6; Benesch 1935, p. 16; W. M. Ivins, *The Unseen Rembrandt*, New York, 1942, pl. 33; *European Drawings from the Collection of the Metropolitan Museum*, II, 1943, no. 9; Benesch 1947, no. 39; Münz 1952, II, under no. 175; Benesch II, no. 249, fig. 272 [ca. 1633–34]; J. Q. van Regteren Altena, in *Oud-Holland*, LXX, 1955, p. 120; Sumowski 1956–57, p. 255; Begemann 1961, p. 24; Slive 1965, no. 147.

This woman is known from several other drawings. In one she is represented seated at the bedside of a woman, perhaps Saskia (B. 426, F. Lugt Collection, Paris), and she may thus have been a member of Rembrandt's household. In this case Rembrandt did not represent the setting except for indicating a dark background by numerous parallel lines adjoining the figure. In manner of execution similar to the preceding *Sheet of Studies with a Blind Old Woman*, this drawing also dates from the mid-thirties.

## 103 *Joseph Interpreting the Prisoners' Dreams*

The Art Institute of Chicago, Clarence Buckingham Collection *Ill. p. 207*

Pen and brown ink and brown wash, 174 × 206 mm.

DATE [ca. 1634–36].

PROVENANCE Baron Grahame (sale March 15, 1878, no. 136); E. J. Poynter (L. 874; sale London, Sotheby, April 24–25, 1918, no. 281); Victor Koch, London; W. H. Schab, New York (1966).

BIBLIOGRAPHY Benesch I, no. 80, fig. 84 [ca. 1632–33]; Sumowski 1956–57, p. 257, fig. 13 [implies Rembrandt's authorship]; Rosenberg *AB* 1956, p. 67; New York/ Cambridge, Mass. 1960, under no. 4; Sumowski 1961, p. 7; [W. H. Schab Gallery], *Great Old Master Prints & Drawings*, XLII, New York, [1966], pp. 144–45, no. 167 [illustrated].

In this and the following drawing, Rembrandt represented two successive episodes from the story of Joseph interpreting the dreams of the Pharaoh's chief butler and chief baker (Genesis 40:1–20). In this drawing, Joseph probably is telling the butler seated at the right that his dream means that he will be set free by the Pharaoh within three days. The baker, in the center of the composition, is listening intently. Rembrandt characterized both imprisoned servants of the Pharaoh as "sad", as they are described in the Bible.

The same episode was once more represented by Rembrandt, many years later, in a drawing in the Rijksprentenkabinet, Amsterdam (Benesch V, no. 912, fig. 1122). The

same "sadness" of the prisoners now is expressed with a minimum of lines and primarily by the attitudes and postures of the figures.

Because of the similarity in the placement of the figures and because of a related architectural background, a painting in 1932 with Douwes in Amsterdam, attributed to Eeckhout (Sumowski 1956–57, fig. 14) and to Flinck (Von Moltke 1965, no. 17) is probably based on this drawing. The composition is taken up once more by Gerbrand van den Eeckhout in 1643 (or 1645) in his painting in the Collection of the Marquess of Zetland (Exhibition London 1952–53, no. 213; Sumowski 1962, p. 11).

See also the following drawing.

## 104 *Joseph Interpreting the Prisoners' Dreams*

Anonymous American Collection *Ill. p. 206*

Pen and brown ink and brown wash, 155 × 180 mm.

DATE [ca. 1634–36].

PROVENANCE Joachim von Bergmann, Störkel-Kauffung, Silesia.

EXHIBITIONS Cambridge, Fogg Art Museum, 1929; Providence, Rhode Island School of Design, 1931; Omaha, Joslyn Art Museum, 1941; Middletown, Wesleyan University, Davison Art Center, 1956 and 1959; New York/ Cambridge, Mass. 1960, no. 4, pl. 4; Cambridge, Fogg Art Museum, 1962.

BIBLIOGRAPHY Valentiner 1925, no. 104 [ca. 1633]; Kauffmann 1926, p. 174 [1633–34]; Benesch 1935, p. 21 [1634–35]; Rosenberg 1948, p. 129, fig. 175 [ca. 1633]; Benesch I, no. 109, fig. 124 [ca. 1635]; Valentiner 1957, p. 56 [ca. 1634–35, example for Bol]; *Harvard Alumni Bulletin*, April 16, 1960; Rotermund 1963, p. 23, fig. 64 [erroneous interpretation of subject]; Sumowski 1964, p. 30, note 4 [lists copy in Brussels]; Rosenberg 1964, p. 208, fig. 174 [ca. 1633].

In this drawing Rembrandt represented the episode of Joseph's story immediately following the one of the preceding drawing. Both were probably executed at approximately the same time.

Upon hearing Joseph's favorable interpretation of the butler's dream, the baker told Joseph his own dream. Joseph, however, had to foretell him that within three days the Pharaoh would hang him on a tree and that the birds would feed on him (Genesis 40:16–19). Rembrandt chose to represent the baker's despair at the prediction of his impending death, and emphasized the dramatic effect by contrasting the figure of the baker with his own dark shadow cast on the wall behind him. A drawing attributed to Rembrandt and, perhaps more likely, to Gerbrand van den Eeckhout, represents the same episode (British Museum, B. 423 verso, fig. 482).

As a draughtsman, Bol learned from Rembrandt's drawings of this type and style, as exemplified by his own interpretation of the same subject (see cat. no. 152).

A rather mediocre copy of this drawing (already mentioned by Sumowski) is in the Royal Library, Brussels (III.58335; pen and brown ink and red chalk, 150 × 170 mm.; architectural background "completed" with the brush).

## 105 Seated Girl in Profile to the Left

Museum Boymans-van Beuningen, Rotterdam *Ill. p. 209*

Black chalk, heightened with white, 199 × 153 mm.

DATE [ca. 1637].

PROVENANCE P. Bureau (sale Paris, May 20, 1927, no. 12); F. Koenigs, Haarlem.

EXHIBITIONS Amsterdam 1929, no. 254; Berlin 1930, no. 323; Stockholm 1956, no. 69; Rotterdam/Amsterdam 1956, no. 69; Vienna 1956, no. 33.

BIBLIOGRAPHY Benesch 1935, p. 28; Benesch 1947, no. 86; Benesch II, no. 376, figs. 424–25 [ca. 1637].

Sketched around 1637, this is one of the few black chalk studies of the nude of the 1630's.

## 106 Odysseus and Nausicaa

Sterling and Francine Clark Art Institute, Williamstown, Massachusetts *Ill. p. 208*

Pen and brown ink and brown wash, 128 × 162 mm.

INSCRIPTIONS Annotated at bottom left: *Remdt*.
DATE [ca. 1637].

PROVENANCE Coll. Reitlinger (?); Hans Schaeffer, New York.

PROVENANCE Coll. Reitlinger (?); Hans Schaeffer, New brandt, ca. 1637].
Odysseus, shipwrecked on Scheria, is found by Nausicaa, the daughter of King Alcinous. While the maids of Nausicaa flee, frightened by the appearance of the naked

Odysseus, the princess stands still and listens to Odysseus' requests to have pity upon him (Odyssey VI: 127–185).

This drawing is similar to drawings by Rembrandt of ca. 1637, particularly the *Sheet of Studies with Two Scenes from the Old Testament* in the Pierpont Morgan Library (B. 145, fig. 160) and *The Daughters of Cecrops Finding Erichthonius* in a private collection in New York (B. 149, fig. 165). It also has features in common with early drawings by Gerbrand van den Eeckhout, to whom Benesch attributed the drawing (in a letter to the Clark Art Institute). It seems more likely that the drawing was made by Rembrandt at the time that Eeckhout was his pupil.

The annotation *Remdt* is written by the same hand as similar, generally shorter annotations on a great number of Rembrandt drawings. The annotator has not been identified.

## 107 Two Studies of Saskia Asleep*

The Pierpont Morgan Library, New York

Pen and brush and brown ink, 130 × 171 mm. *Ill. p. 210*

DATE [ca. 1635–37].

PROVENANCE J. van Rijmsdijk (L. 2167); Tighe; C. Fairfax Murray; J. Pierpont Morgan.

EXHIBITIONS Paris 1908, no. 415; Cambridge, Fogg Art Museum, 1917; New York, Metropolitan Museum of Art, *Handlist of Works by Rembrandt*, 1918, no. 27; New York 1919; San Francisco 1920, no. 367; Cambridge, Fogg Art Museum, 1922; Toronto 1926, no. 41; Buffalo 1935, no. 50; Chicago 1935, no. 31; Worcester 1936, no. 30; Hartford, Wadsworth Atheneum, 1938; New York 1939, no. 86; Toronto, Art Gallery of Toronto, 1951; Rotterdam/ Amsterdam 1956, no. 51; New York/Cambridge, Mass. 1960, no. 24, pl. 20.

BIBLIOGRAPHY Fairfax Murray I, no. 180; Valentiner 690 [ca. 1636]; A. M. Hind, *Rembrandt*, Cambridge, 1932, pp. 49, 125, pl. XXVI; Benesch 1935, p. 22; Tolnay 1943, no. 195; Tietze 1947, no. 65; Benesch II, no. 289, fig. 319 [ca. 1635]; Rosenberg D, 1956, p. 127, fig. 17; J. Rosenberg, *Great Draughtsmen from Pisanello to Picasso*, Cambridge, 1959, p. 75, fig. 139b; [E.H.-B.] 1962, no. 579 [illustrated]; Scheidig 1962, p. 41 and no. 26, fig. 26.

It is very likely that Saskia was the subject of many of the sketches Rembrandt made of a woman sleeping or resting in bed in the second half of the 1630's. Even if the features are not recognizable, the knowledge that she must often have been confined to bed due to illness or childbearing strengthens this hypothesis (her four children were born in 1635, 1638, 1640, and 1641).

The upper study undoubtedly was drawn first. It shows Saskia in deep sleep. In the lower sketch she has moved her right arm slightly toward herself, opened her mouth, and has sunk deeper in her pillow.

The two studies should be dated ca. 1635–37, and thus are among the earliest examples among this considerable group depicting Saskia in bed. Closest in style is the drawing in Groningen, *Saskia Sitting up in Bed* (B. 282, fig. 315).

See also the following drawing.

## 108 *Saskia Lying in Bed*

National Gallery of Art, Washington, D.C., Ailsa Mellon Bruce Fund

Pen and brush and brown ink and brown wash, 125 × 180 mm. *Ill. p. 210*

DATE [ca. 1638].

PROVENANCE Samuel, Graf von Festetits (L. 926); The Prince of Liechtenstein.

EXHIBITIONS Washington 1969, no. 27 [illustrated].

BIBLIOGRAPHY HdG 1508 [ca. 1635]; Schönbrunner and Meder, no. 418 a [illustrated]; Valentiner 1934, no. 689; Benesch 1935, p. 13; Benesch 1947, under no. 98 [study for Rachel in H. 160]; Münz 1952, II, under no. 175 [not study for Rachel in H. 160]; Benesch I, no. 169, fig. 181 [ca. 1638]; Sumowski 1956–57, p. 263 [not study for Rachel in H. 160]; Roger-Marx 1960, p. 152, fig. 39 a; Begemann 1961, p. 23; "Rembrandt Drawing for the National Gallery", *The Connoisseur*, CLXII, July 1966, p. 220 [illustrated].

Rembrandt's studies from nature often contributed to his representation of biblical scenes. This and similar drawings of Saskia in bed (see preceding entry) finally were incorporated in the figure of Rachel in the etching *Joseph Telling His Dreams* of 1638 (B. 37, H. 160; for a preliminary study for this etching see cat. no. 110).

## 109 *Christ as Gardener Appearing to Mary Magdalen*

Rijksprentenkabinet, Amsterdam

Pen and dark brown ink, traced for transfer, 153 × 146 mm. *Ill. p. 211*

DATE [ca. 1637–38].

PROVENANCE C. A. Mariette (1703); Beurnonville (sale Paris, February 16–19, 1885, no. 205); Chausson; I. de Bruijn, Muri-Bern.

EXHIBITIONS Bern 1937, no. 189; Basel 1948, no. 9; Amsterdam 1961, no. 36.

BIBLIOGRAPHY Valentiner 508 [ca. 1638], F. Lugt, in *Old Master Drawings*, IX, 1934/35, pp. 16–17, pl. 17 [ca. 1638; connected with painting of 1638, Br. 559], Henkel 1942, under no. 45 [ca. 1637–38]; Rotermund 1952, p. 103, note 1; Benesch III, no. 538, fig. 668 [ca. 1643]; Rosenberg 1959, pp. 112–13 [sketch for painting of 1638]; Van Regteren Altena 1961, p. 85, no. 36, fig. 21 [one of the sketches for painting of 1638]; Begemann 1961, p. 52 [probably study for painting]; Brussels/Hamburg 1961, under no. 52 [related to painting].

Rembrandt represented the moment after the Resurrection, when Christ disguised as gardener, addressed himself to Mary Magdalen with the words: "Woman, why weepest thou? whom seekest thou?" (John 20:15). In 1638 Rembrandt represented the same subject in the painting now in Buckingham Palace, London. Although the composition of the painting is quite different, it is likely that Rembrandt made the drawing when he was occupied with the painting. Another drawing of the same subject is also in Amsterdam (B. 537), while one representing the moment following that of the present drawing, namely, Mary Magdalen recognizing the gardener as Christ, and which was drawn much later, is in the F. Lugt Collection (Institut Néerlandais, Paris, B. 993).

The main features of the drawing were reproduced in an etching by Mathijs Pool in the beginning of the eighteenth century.

## 110 *Studies of a Woman Reading and an Oriental*

Private Collection, New York

Pen and brown ink and brown wash, corrected with white, 139 × 125 mm. *Ill. p. 212*

DATE [ca. 1637–38].

PROVENANCE T. Dimsdale; Hamian; Rev. Stopford Brooke (sale London, May 28, 1924, no. 75); C. Hofstede de Groot (sale Leipzig, Boerner, November 4, 1931, no. 163).

EXHIBITIONS The Hague 1930, no. 68; Rotterdam/Amsterdam 1956, no. 87; New York/Cambridge, Mass. 1960, no. 29, pl. 24.

BIBLIOGRAPHY Benesch 1947, no. 98; Münz 1952, II, under no. 175; Benesch I, no. 168, fig. 186; Begemann 1961, pp. 51–52 [on sequence of drawings and oil sketch, with erroneous numbering].

Both figures are preliminary studies for the etching *Joseph Telling His Dreams* of 1638 (B. 37, H. 160), where they were incorporated with only slight changes (in reverse). Rembrandt must have thought of introducing the figure of a woman reading only shortly before executing the etching because she is missing in the three other preliminary studies. Rembrandt first drew the one in the Collection Baron Hatvany, London (B. 527, fig. 657), then the one in the Albertina (B. 526, fig. 653) and finally the one in the British Museum (B. 528, fig. 656). These drawings were followed by the grisaille oil sketch in the Rijksmuseum, Amsterdam (Br. 504). Only after the composition had thus been established, did Rembrandt draw this study of a woman reading. He had already the etching in mind, since light and shadow are applied according to the requirements of the etching. The oriental is a further definition of a figure summarily indicated in the oil sketch and not included in the drawings preceding it. This drawing as well as the three other preliminary studies mentioned above many, therefore, be dated 1638 or shortly before.

In a drawing attributed to Jan Victors in Darmstadt (Sumowski 1957–58, p. 229, fig. 48), probably representing the same subject, the reading woman is found seated in front of the bed.

## III *Self-Portrait*

National Gallery of Art, Washington, D.C., Rosenwald Collection *Ill. p. 213*

Red chalk, 129 × 119 mm.

DATE [ca. 1637–38].

PROVENANCE Valerius Röver, Delft, C. F. U. Meek; Lessing J. Rosenwald.

EXHIBITIONS London 1929, no. 574; Philadelphia, Art Alliance, 1930; Worcester 1936, no. 60; Los Angeles 1947, p. 77, no. 1; Rotterdam/Amsterdam 1956, no. 70; New York/Cambridge, Mass. 1960, no. 28, pl. 22; Washington 1969, no. 28 [illustrated].

BIBLIOGRAPHY A. M. Hind, in *Vasari Society*, 2nd Series, I, 1920, no. 8 [ca. 1639]; Valentiner 1934, no. 662 [ca. 1635–37]; Benesch 1935, p. 24; Benesch 1947, no. 81; J. G. van Gelder, in *Burlington Magazine*, XCI, 1949, p. 207 [from Röver Collection]; Slive 1953, p. 175, fig. 41; Benesch II, no. 437, figs. 494–95 [ca. 1637]; Sumowski 1956–57, p. 263; R. Fry, "Rembrandt, an interpretation", *Apollo*, LXXVI, March 1962, pp. 42–55, fig. 5; [E. H. -B.] 1962, no. 571 [illustrated]; A. Livermore, "Rembrandt and Jansen", *Apollo*, LXXXV, April 1967, pp. 240–45, fig. 1; Fritz Erpel, *Die Selbstbildnisse Rembrandts*, Berlin, 1967, p. 167, no. 64, fig. 33 [ca. 1637].

This is Rembrandt's only self-portrait in red chalk. It is closely related to others painted and etched in 1637 and 1638, in particular to the painting of 1637 in the Louvre (Br. 29) and the etching *Rembrandt in Velvet Cap and Plume* (B. 20, H. 156) of 1638. It probably dates from the same time.

The two fragmentary sketches for a *Deposition* or a *Lamentation* on the reverse perhaps were made in connection with Prince Frederik Hendrik's commission of 1633 for a series of *Scenes of the Passion*.

Valerius Röver kept this "portrait of Rembrandt with a bonnet on his head, drawn by himself with red chalk" ('*t portret van Rembrandt met een muts op 't hooft van hem zelfs met root krÿt getekent*), as he described it, unnumbered in portfolio no. 8, immediately following the portrait of Anslo, now in the British Museum.

## 112 *Two Mummers on Horseback* *

The Pierpont Morgan Library, New York

Pen and brown ink and brown wash and yellow and red chalk, and some white gouache, 212 × 153 mm. *Ill. p. 212*

DATE [ca. 1637–38].

PROVENANCE J. Richardson Sen. (L. 2184); Th. Hudson (L. 2432); Earl of Aylesford (L. 58); Sir J. C. Robinson (inscribed by Robinson on the reverse of mount: *J. C. Robinson / July 1/, 1893 / from Lord Aylesford Colln*); C. Newton Robinson; C. Fairfax Murray; J. Pierpont Morgan.

EXHIBITIONS London, 1899, no. 110; Paris 1908, no. 433; Cambridge, Fogg Art Museum, 1922; New York, Metropolitan Museum, 1952; Rotterdam/Amsterdam 1956, no. 74; New York/Cambridge, Mass. 1960, no. 31, pl. 26.

BIBLIOGRAPHY Fairfax Murray I, no. 201; HdG 1109; Valentiner 1934, no. 790 [ca. 1633–35]; Benesch 1935, p. 41; Van Regteren Altena 1952, pp. 59–63; Benesch II, no. 368, fig. 414 [ca. 1637–38]; J. Watrous, *The Craft of Old Master Drawings*, Madison, 1957, pp. 96–97, 106; Scheidig 1962, p. 44 and no. 47, fig. 47.

Particularly in the second half of the thirties Rembrandt showed in his drawings an interest in festivals and theatrical performances. This and three related drawings, one of a horseman (British Museum, B. 367, fig. 415), and two others of Negro drummers and trumpeters (British Museum, B. 365, fig. 412; Mrs. Feilchenfeldt, Zurich, B. 366, fig. 413), were probably sketched at one such occasion, which, as Van Regteren Altena suggested, may have been a pageant staged as part of the festivities in The Hague in honor of the wedding of Wolfert van Brederode with a sister of the Princess of Orange in February, 1638. The costumes, particularly the high hat and ruff of the cavalier on the left, are typical of the first two decades of the seventeenth century.

Technically, the drawing is an example of an unusually complex range of drawing materials used by the artist in one drawing. Watrous analyzed it as follows: "Rembrandt . . . introduced natural red chalk strokes into the plume of a hat and applied moistened red chalk to the boots and along the slits in one of the costumes while the remainder of the drawing was completed with quill pen and bistre ink, bistre washes, yellow ochre fabricated chalk, and semi-opaque whites applied with a brush."

### 113  *Actor in His Dressing Room*

Devonshire Collection, Chatsworth

Pen and brown ink, 183 × 150 mm. *Ill. p. 214*

DATE [ca. 1638].

PROVENANCE N. A. Flinck (L. 959); Duke of Devonshire.

EXHIBITIONS London 1953, no. 316 [illustrated]; Manchester 1961, no. 89; Washington, D.C. et al. 1962/63, no. 88 [illustrated].

BIBLIOGRAPHY HdG 832; Lippmann I, 79; Neumann 1919, no. 50; Benesch 1935, p. 24; Benesch 1947, no. 71; Benesch I, no. 120, fig. 132; H. van de Waal, in *Museum*, LXI 1956, p. 204, note 2; [F. Thompson 1962], no. 1018 [illustrated]; Slive 1965, no. 79; R. H. Fuchs, *Rembrandt en Amsterdam*, Rotterdam, 1968, p. 37, fig. 63.

The bishop's robes hanging on a coat stand at the right have led the seated figure to be interpreted as "St. Gregory" or "St. Augustine in His Study" until Van de Waal identified him as an actor in a dressing room of the Amsterdam "Schouwburg", preparing to play the part of the old Bishop Gozewijn in Joost van den Vondel's *Gysbreght van Aemstel*. As Fuchs observed, a bishop would hardly hang his precious robes so unceremoniously on a stand. This tragedy was performed for the first time on 3 January 1638 at the inauguration of the newly-built theater.

With three others, the drawing belongs to a series representing different actors performing the same play. Rembrandt may have sketched some of these actors at the same occasion (B. 120–23, figs. 132–36), but apparently he also recorded other actors at various visits to different plays (B. 316–21).

### 114  *Two Cottages*

The Lehman Collection, New York

Pen and dark brown ink, corrected with white; in the heavy lines of the roof gallnut ink apparently has been used, 149 × 192 mm. *Ill. p. 215*

DATE [ca. 1640–45].

PROVENANCE Anonymous Collector (sale London, Sotheby, June 30, 1948, no. 147); Colnaghi & Co., London; Hanns Schaeffer, New York.

BIBLIOGRAPHY Benesch II, no. 462 a, fig. 521 [ca. 1632–33].

This drawing is one of the numerous sketches Rembrandt made in the neighborhood of Amsterdam. With three other studies of farm buildings and trees in Vienna, Stockholm and Chatsworth (B. 794, 795 and 796) it probably dates from 1640–1645 because of similarities with etchings of 1641 (B. 114, H. 177, and B. 115, H. 178) and of 1645 (B. 205, H. 212, and B. 242, H. 213). The date ca. 1632–33 suggested by Benesch for the Lehman drawing seems too early, that of ca. 1640–41 for the three comparable studies, too narrow.

### 115  *Satire on Art Criticism*

The Lehman Collection, New York

Pen and brown ink, 156 × 200 mm. *Ill. p. 215*

INSCRIPTIONS Dated at bottom center: *den tyt 1644* and inscribed on the platform on which the "critic" is seated: *dees . . . van d kunst / is .ooting gunst;* on the framed painting: *. . . / . . . and Houdl.os . . . / .indt dat.*; Emmens reads the first inscription: *Dees quack van de kunst / is Jockich gunst.* (for other readings, see New York / Cambridge, Mass. 1960, no. 41). Annotated by a later hand: *Rembrandt*.

DATE *1644*.

PROVENANCE Baron Vivant Denon (perhaps identical with A. N. Pérignon, *Description des objets d'art . . . de feu M. le Baron V. Denon . . . , Tableaux, . . .* , Paris, 1826, p. 166, no. 55 "Un dessin à la plume, représentant un sujet allégorique"); Friedrich August II of Saxony; Mr. and Mrs. Louis H. Silver, Chicago.

EXHIBITIONS New York/Cambridge, Mass. 1960, no. 41, pl. 35.

BIBLIOGRAPHY HdG 303; Freise and Wichmann 1925, no. III [not by Rembrandt]; Valentiner 1934, no. 619 [by Rembrandt]; Benesch IV, no. A 35 a, fig. 1037 [apparently work of a pupil; inscription *den tyt 1644* by Rembrandt]; Rosenberg 1959, p. 116 [could well be by Rembrandt]; J. G. van Gelder, "Dencwerk", *Bundel opstellen in 1959 Prof. Dr. D. T. Enklaar te Utrecht aangeboden*, 1959, p. 308 [mentioned as by Rembrandt]; "Rembrandt Drawings from American Collections", *Arts*, XXXIV, 1960, p. 29 [illustrated]; Van Gelder 1961, p. 150 [probably by Rembrandt]; Begemann 1961, p. 90 [by Rembrandt]; Sumowski 1961, p. 24 [Benesch's doubts justified; perhaps Flinck]; G. F. Koch, *Die Kunstausstellung*, Berlin, 1967, p. 71, fig. 33; J. A. Emmens, *Rembrandt en de regels van de kunst*, Utrecht, 1968, pp. 150-54, 201, fig. 28; C. White, *Rembrandt and His World*, New York, 1968, p. 92 [by Rembrandt; illustrated].

Whatever the exact meaning of the various figures, objects and inscriptions in this drawing may be, it clearly satirizes contemporary art criticism. The critic, seated at the left, is characterized as foolish by the donkey's ears sticking through his hat, and as invidious by a snake around his right arm, while his words are empty and his mind is hollow (as indicated by the pipe and the barrel). He judges a painting lying on the floor, while another one is held in front of him by a man who could be the *bode* or servant of the painter's guild. The man crouching in the foreground at the right expresses his contempt for the "critic" and his pronouncements. In contrast, the onlookers watch the "critic" with awe as they listen to his words.

Emmens recently has ventured the supposition that the critic satirized in this drawing is Franciscus Junius, author of *De Pictura Veterum*, and who for Rembrandt may have personified academic and classical art criticism. Although the head of the "critic" indeed shows a certain resemblance with Junius's portrait by Wenzel Hollar, it remains possible that Rembrandt was directing himself in this drawing against a type of criticism rather than against one author.

Doubts about the attribution of this drawing seem unjustified and may be explained partly by the subject matter, which is unusual for Rembrandt.

## 116 *The Holy Family Asleep*

Lent by the Syndics of the Fitzwilliam Museum, Cambridge

Pen and brown ink, corrected with white body color, 173 × 212 mm. *Ill. p. 216*

DATE [ca. 1645].

PROVENANCE Sir E. J. Poynter (L. 874; sale London, Sotheby, April 25, 1918, lot 268); C. B. O. Clark; Louis C. G. Clarke.

EXHIBITIONS London 1938, no. 553; Cambridge 1966, no. 3.

BIBLIOGRAPHY Benesch 1947, no. 139; Benesch III, no. 569, fig. 699 [ca. 1645]; *Life*, Christmas 1958 [illustrated]; Cambridge 1966, no. 3 [with full discussion]; Gerson 1968, p. 496, illustrated p. 321, fig. 1; White 1969, p. 52, fig. 56.

In front of a fireplace the Holy Family is asleep. Joseph lies in the foreground, while at the left over a table or workbench two *putti* appear, carried by a cloud.

In its subject the drawing is a counterpart to the painting in Leningrad of 1645 (Br. 570-71), and the preparatory drawing for it in Bayonne (B. 567, fig. 698). In both the painting and the Bayonne drawing the scene also takes place in a room, but Joseph is carpentering, and Mary is taking care of the Christ Child.

Rembrandt probably made the drawing in close connection with the painting.

## 117 *Cottage near the Entrance to a Wood*

The Lehman Collection, New York *Ill. p. 216*

Pen and brown ink and brown wash, 298 × 452 mm.

Signed and dated with pen and brown ink: *Rembrandt f. 1644*.

DATE *1644*.

PROVENANCE J. Richardson Sen. (L. 2184); A Pond; J. Barnard; Benjamin West (L. 419); W. Esdaile (L. 2617); Sir Thomas Lawrence; Baron Grahame; J. P. Heseltine (sale Amsterdam, F. Muller, May 27, 1913, no. 24); O. Gutekunst; Jacob Hirsch.

EXHIBITIONS London 1899, no. 160; London 1929, no. 587; London 1938, no. 551; Paris 1957, no. 123; Cincinnati 1959, no. 267 [illustrated]; New York/Cambridge, Mass. 1960, no. 40, pl. 34.

BIBLIOGRAPHY Lippmann I, 186; HdG 1049; Heseltine 1907; Neumann 1919, no. 64; Lugt 1933, pp. 33-34, under no.

245; Benesch 1935, p. 36; Tolnay 1943, no. 197; Benesch 1947, no. 134; Van Regteren Altena 1951, under no. 77; Benesch IV, no. 815, fig. 965; Rosenberg 1959, p. 114; Benesch 1960, no. 45, fig. 45; [E. H.-B.] 1962, no. 585 [illustrated]; Slive 1965, no. 199; Dattenberg 1967, p. 83 [with incorrect B. no.]; Gerson 1968, pp. 96 and 352, llustrated p. 353, fig. a.

In many respects this drawing stands out among the numerous landscapes Rembrandt sketched: it is his largest landscape drawing; it is one of the very few signed and dated drawings; and the subject is to a greater extent than usual defined by broadly applied brush strokes. Lambert Doomer also sketched the same cottage, and the two artists may have done this at the same occasion, as Van Regteren Altena suggested, especially since Doomer's drawing also shows an elderly man in the door opening. Doomer's drawing in the Louvre differs from the Lehman drawing in the foreground and omits the background. Since Rembrandt in his drawings of the Dutch rural scene usually aimed at a rather faithful representation, these differences may be credited to Doomer's imagination. An additional reason for this assumption is that Doomer's drawing in the Louvre, in spite of Dattenberg's opinion to the contrary, may very well be based on an earlier version, while it is known that Doomer was in the habit of introducing variations in subsequent versions.

## 118 *View over the Amstel from the Rampart*

National Gallery of Art, Washington, D.C., Rosenwald Collection *Ill. p. 217*

Pen and brown ink and brown wash, 90 × 186 mm.

DATE [ca. 1645–50].

PROVENANCE Johan van der Marck, Leiden (sale Amsterdam, November 29, 1773); R. P. Roupell; sale Coll. Jhr. A. Boreel and others, Amsterdam, Muller & Co., June 15–18, 1908, no. 487; August Janssen and his heirs, Amsterdam; D. A. Hoogendijk, Amsterdam; Lessing J. Rosenwald.

EXHIBITIONS Delft, *Kunst- en Antiekbeurs*, 1953; Rotterdam/Amsterdam 1956, no. 145, fig. 45; New York/Cambridge, Mass. 1960, no. 45, pl. 39; Washington, National Gallery of Art, 1966; Ibidem 1969, no. 32 [illustrated].

BIBLIOGRAPHY Lugt 1920, p. 86, fig. 47; Henkel 1942, under no. 74; Van Gelder 1961, p. 150; Brussels/Hamburg 1961, under no. 56 [1648–50]; Slive 1965, no. 539.

Rembrandt sketched the view to be seen over the Amstel

River from a bastion situated immediately to the west of the Amsterdam bridge known as the "Blauwbrug". Rembrandt used the piles in the foreground as a *repoussoir* for the lightly sketched middle and background. This drawing is closely related to a view from the "Blauwbrug" now in the F. Lugt Collection (B. A 35$^b$, fig. 1038) which includes at the right the bastion on which Rembrandt stood when he made the Rosenwald drawing. Both drawings were probably made about the same time, probably in the second half of the 1640's.

## 119 *Cottage with a White Paling*

Private Collection

Pen and brown ink and brown wash and touches of white body color and violet wash (on the right hand horizon), 168 × 252 mm. *Ill. p. 217*

INSCRIPTIONS Annotated with pen and brown ink: *Rembrant van Rijn.*

DATE [ca. 1648].

BIBLIOGRAPHY Benesch IV, no. C 41, fig. 1011; C. White, in *Burlington Magazine*, CX, 1968, p. 393, fig. 5 [by Rembrandt; ca. 1648]; White 1969, pp. 207–08, fig. 311.

This drawing is an exception in Rembrandt's *oeuvre* in as much as it is a direct study (in reverse) for the etching of the same subject (B. 232, H. 203). If in general Rembrandt's studies of those landscape motifs which he also etched differ greatly from the prints and should be considered independent rather than preparatory studies, in this case Rembrandt relied heavily on the drawing. The changes consist mainly of a reduction of the large tree, a reformulation of the space in front and to the sides of the cottage, and, above all, of an intensification of the contrasts of the light fence and its darker surroundings, which gave the etching its name.

Christopher White solved the differences of opinion in dating the etching either to 1642 or 1652 by establishing that in fact it was made in 1648. The drawing dates from the same time.

## 120 *Landscape with Farm Buildings and High Embankment*

Museum of Art, Rhode Island School of Design, Jesse Metcalf and Mary B. Jackson Funds, Providence

Pen and brown ink and brown wash; verso: black chalk, 145 × 260 mm. *Ill. p. 218*

DATE [ca. 1645–50].

PROVENANCE Friedrich August II of Saxony (L. 971).

EXHIBITIONS Worcester, Mass., Worcester Art Museum, *The Practice of Drawing*, 1951–52, no. 63; New York/ Cambridge, Mass. 1960, no. 46, pl. 40; Utica/Rochester 1963, no. 24 [illustrated]; New Orleans 1964, no. 17.

BIBLIOGRAPHY HdG 322; W. von Seidlitz, in *Repertorium für Kunstwissenschaft*, XVII, 1894, p. 125 [as by Rembrandt]; Lippmann IV, no. 21; Lugt 1920, pp. 141–42, fig. 89 [probably not by Rembrandt]; Freise and Wichmann, III, no. 130 [ca. 1650–60]; Benesch 1935, p. 41 [ca. 1647–50]; H. Schwarz, "A Drawing by Rembrandt", *Museum Notes . . . Providence*, VII, no. 2, November 1949 [full discussion; ca. 1645–50, closer to 1650]; Benesch IV, no. 831, figs. 982–83 [ca. 1648]; Slive 1965, no. 464 and under no. 117.

The location of the cottages and country house of which a chimney or tower is visible above the trees has not been identified. Frits Lugt thought of one of the farms near the Diemerdijk, Heinrich Schwarz of Huis Kostverloren on the Amstel River. Rembrandt made a second drawing of the same spot from a standpoint a little more to the right and farther back (British Museum; B. 832, fig. 985). In the Providence sketch, he used a broader pen, and the two studies were not necessarily done on the same trip. It is possible that the Providence sketch, the bolder of the two, is to be dated a few years after the more precisely executed British Museum sketch, perhaps at the end of the 1640's.

On the reverse Rembrandt sketched, with black chalk, trees near a fence or bridge.

## 121 *Landscape with a Drawbridge\**

Albertina, Vienna *Ill. p. 218*

Pen and brown ink and brown wash, 156 × 268 mm.

INSCRIPTION Annotated at the bottom: *Rimbrandt 16*.

DATE [ca. 1648–50].

EXHIBITION Vienna 1936, no. 45 [acc. to Benesch by pupil, ca. 1647]; Stockholm 1956, no. 137; Rotterdam/Amsterdam 1956, no. 147; Vienna 1956, no. 81.

BIBLIOGRAPHY Schönbrunner and Meder 688; HdG 1487; Benesch IV, no. 851, fig. 999 [as Rembrandt, ca. 1648–50].

The drawing belongs to a small group of freely invented landscapes probably sketched about 1650, which have characteristics in common both with drawings by Rembrandt of that period and also with drawings of Van

Borssum and Furnerius. This drawing is probably by Rembrandt and represents the style which the other two artists adapted as a point of departure for their own work.

## 122 *The Supper at Emmaus: The Vanishing of Christ*

The Syndics of the Fitzwilliam Museum, Cambridge

Pen and brown ink and brown wash, heightened with white, 198 × 183 mm. *Ill. p. 219*

DATE [ca. 1648–49].

PROVENANCE Frans van de Velde (sale Amsterdam, January 16, 1775); possibly sale Simon Fokke, December 6, 1784; possibly W. P. Kops (sale Haarlem, March 14, 1808); possibly J. Goll van Frankenstein (sale July 1, 1833); J. L. C. van den Berch van Heemstede, Amsterdam (sale Amsterdam, F. Muller, January 19, 1904, lot 291 [illustrated]); possibly Edward Cichorius; (?Eisler, sale London, Christie); Ch. Ricketts and Ch. Shannon.

EXHIBITIONS Leiden 1850; London 1929, no. 589; London 1938, no. 554; Cambridge 1966, no. 4 [see bibliography]; Tokyo/Kyoto 1968, no. 19.

BIBLIOGRAPHY C. Hofstede de Groot, "Arnold Houbraken" . . . , in *Quellenstudien zur holländischen Kunstgeschichte*, I, 1893, p. 193 [on etching in Houbraken and variants]; *Onze Kunst*, 1904, p. 91; Hind 1915, under no. 137; A. M. Hind, in *Vasari Society*, 2nd series, 1920, no. 7; F. Wichmann, in *Festschrift für Adolph Goldschmidt*, 1923, p. 103; Lugt 1927, p. 29, under no. 63 [by Rembrandt]; A. M. Hind, in *Old Master Drawings*, III, 1928, p. 42; Valentiner 1934, no. 528 [ca. 1645]; A. M. Hind, *Rembrandt*, 1932, p. 64, pl. XLIII; Stechow 1934, p. 337, fig. 4 [shortly before 1648; first representation of Christ's disappearance as appearance of light]; Van Regteren Altena 1948–49, p. 10, fig. 9; H.-M. Rotermund, "Begegnungen mit dem Auferstandenen", *Die Neue Schau*, March 1951, p. 62 [illustrated on cover]; Rotermund 1952, p. 103, pl. 19e; Slive 1953, p. 178, note 3, p. 179, note 1, fig. 43; Benesch IV, C 47, fig. 1017 [probably pupil's copy after lost original of ca. 1648–49]; Rosenberg 1959, p. 116 [by Rembrandt]; Van Gelder 1961, p. 150 [not copy]; Rotermund 1963, pp. 266–67, fig. 245; Gantner 1964, pp. 126–29, fig. 34; Cormack 1966, no. 4 [with full discussion].

In this drawing Rembrandt represented the disappearance of Christ which immediately followed His recognition by His disciples: "And their eyes were opened and they recognized him; and he vanished out of their sight." (Luke 24:31). It was the first time in the long history of representations of the *Supper at Emmaus* that the disappearance of Christ was depicted by showing only the light that emanated from Him. This unprecedented interpretation of the scene was copied and reproduced various times, but only once an artist took up the challenge to formulate a similar interpretation of the event. Jan Steen did the latter in his painting in the Rijksmuseum, Amsterdam.

In his compilation of biographies of Dutch artists, *De Grote Schouburgh der Nederlantsche Konstschilders . . .* (Vol. I, opposite p. 258), Arnold Houbraken included an etching after a work of Rembrandt of the same subject and composition. This etching which generally is attributed to Houbraken himself, may be based on this drawing but could also reproduce a painting. In that case the Cambridge drawing should be considered a study for a lost painting.

This interpretation of *The Supper at Emmaus* was very popular in the eighteenth century. The etching in Houbraken's book is one of its very few illustrations other than portraits of artists discussed, and the Fitzwilliam drawing was reproduced twice more: J. Buys made an etching of it in 1765, and a color print appeared in Ploos van Amstel's *Collection d'Imitations de Dessins . . .* (ed. Josi, Vol. I, London, 1821). Except for a drawing in Dresden which probably is a variant of the Cambridge drawing by one of Rembrandt's pupils (Hoogstraten ?; Wichmann, fig. 3), other variants are more likely based on the etching in Houbraken (London; Collection Dutuit, Paris). A third variant is in Edinburgh.

In spite of Benesch's opinion to the contrary, the drawing seems to be a work of Rembrandt, as most Rembrandt scholars think (Lugt, Stechow, Van Regteren Altena, Rosenberg, Van Gelder and others). Around 1645-48, Rembrandt made a number of drawings characterized by a somewhat awkward angularity of line which disturbed Benesch in this *Supper at Emmaus* (B. 599, 600, 630, 753).

## 123 *Tobias and His Wife Sara Praying**

The Metropolitan Museum of Art, Rogers Fund, 1906

Pen and brush and brown ink, corrected with white, 174 × 237 mm. *Ill. p. 220*

DATE [ca. 1648-50].

PROVENANCE Sir Joshua Reynolds (L. 2364); W. Esdaile (L. 2617; annotated on the reverse in Esdaile's hand: *1798 Sr Jos Reynolds colln WE. P 84 Rembrandt*).

EXHIBITIONS New York, Metropolitan Museum, 1918, no. 58; New York/Cambridge, Mass. 1960, no. 44, pl. 38.

BIBLIOGRAPHY "The Collection of Drawings", *Metropolitan Museum Bulletin*, I, 1905-06, p. 160 [illustrated]; G. S. Hellman, in *The Print Collector's Quarterly*, V, 1915, p. 387; W. R. Valentiner, in *Kunst und Künstler*, XXII, 1924, p. 19; Valentiner 1925, no. 242 [ca. 1650]; W. M. Ivins, *The Unseen Rembrandt*, New York 1942, pl. 41; William M. Ivins, in *Metropolitan Museum of Art Bulletin*, XXXVII, no. 1, 1942, p. 14 [illustrated]; *European Drawings from the Collection of the Metropolitan Museum*, I, 1943, no. 12; Benesch III, no. 633, fig. 767 [ca. 1648-50]; Julius S. Held, *Rembrandt and the Book of Tobit* (Gehenna Essays in Art, 2), [Northampton, Mass.], 1964, pp. 13-14, fig. 17; Roger-Marx 1960, p. 196, fig. 60 d; Sumowski 1961, p. 13 [lists copy in Rotterdam]. As Julius Held pointed out, Rembrandt illustrated the Book of Tobit more often than any other biblical text of comparable length. This drawing illustrates the events of the wedding night. Sara's seven previous husbands had died on their wedding nights, but now the demon flies off, expulsed by the burning of the heart and the liver of the fish brought by Tobias. "His departure goes unnoticed by the young couple, who devoutly pray for delivery" (Held, p. 13). Rembrandt stressed in this drawing the delicate relationship between Sara and Tobias in a situation of suspense, and their absolute submission to the will of God in their concerted prayers. Although the episode is not mentioned in the Book of Tobit, the man visible through a door opening at the left might be Sara's father Raguel, concerned about the fate of his new son-in-law.

## 124 *Jael and Sisera*

The Visitors of the Ashmolean Museum, Oxford

Pen and brown ink, border-line by a later hand, 173 × 254 mm. *Ill. p. 222*

DATE [ca. 1650].

PROVENANCE Viscount Fitzharris (sale London, Christie, April 21, 1950, lot 90).

EXHIBITIONS Rotterdam/Amsterdam 1956, no. 139.

BIBLIOGRAPHY [K. T. Parker], *Report of the Visitors of the Ashmolean Museum*, 1950, p. 54, pl. XI; Benesch III, no. 622a, fig. 754 [ca. 1648-49]; Benesch 1960, p. 153, no. 53, fig. 53; A. E. Popham, in *Burlington Magazine*, CIV, 1962, p. 70; Rotermund 1963, p. 91, fig. 77; S. Slive, "Reconsideration of some rejected Rembrandt drawings", *Art Quarterly*, XXVII, 1964, p. 294, fig. 21.

Although according to the story in the Bible (Judges: 4) Jael nailed Sisera to the floor of her tent, Rembrandt placed the scene in the interior of a room with an arched window, and the slain soldier on a bed. The oval object hanging above him is probably his shield which he hung on the wall before falling asleep. Rembrandt "used a whirlwind of furious strokes as he sought for the most effective way to depict the thrashing arms and legs of a man being murdered by a woman powerful enough to drive a nail through his head" (Slive 1964). The figures resemble those of Cain and Abel in the drawing *Abel Slain By Cain* in Copenhagen (B. 860). Both were probably made about 1650.

## 125 The "Diemerdijk" with the Village Houtewael

Museum Boymans-van Beuningen, Rotterdam *Ill. p. 221*

Pen and brown ink and brown and gray wash, 132 × 182 mm.

DATE [ca. 1651].

PROVENANCE J. P. Zoomer (L. 1511); Lady H. F. Wilson; Cte de Robiano (sale Amsterdam, F. Muller & Co., June 15–16, 1926, no. 438); F. Koenigs, Haarlem.

EXHIBITIONS Düsseldorf, Kunstverein, 1929, no. 85; Berlin 1930, no. 339; Amsterdam 1932, no. 303 [ca. 1650]; Rotterdam 1934, no. 96; Rotterdam 1938, no. 321; Brunswick 1948, no. 36; Dijon 1950, no. 84; Rotterdam 1952, no. 44; Rotterdam/Amsterdam 1956, no. 166; Vienna 1956, no. 90.

BIBLIOGRAPHY A. M. H[ind], in *Vasari Society* VII, 1911–12, no. 21; Lugt 1920, pp. 134–36, fig. 83; Benesch 1935, p. 42 [ca. 1648–50]; Benesch VI, no. 1262, fig. 1488 [ca. 1651].

Before Amsterdam expanded in the 1660's, the hamlet Houtewael was situated to the east of it along the dike leading to Diemen. Rembrandt sketched this view standing on the dike, facing east. He included in the distance at the left some ships in the estuary of the river IJ. The gray wash was added later by another hand in an effort to "complete" the drawing.

## 126 The "Rijnpoort" at Rhenen

Devonshire Collection, Chatsworth

Pen and blackish-brown ink and slight brown wash, rubbed with the finger, 120 × 176 mm. *Ill. p. 221*

DATE [ca. 1652–53].

PROVENANCE N. A. Flinck (L. 959).

EXHIBITIONS Stockholm 1956, no. 144; Washington, D.C. *et al.* 1962/63, no. 95 [illustrated].

BIBLIOGRAPHY Lippmann I, 72; HdG 857; Lugt 1920, p. 161. fig. 116 [possibly one trip, taken between 1650 and 1660]; Max Eisler, *Rembrandt als Landschafter*, Munich, 1918, pp. 94, 96; Neumann 1919, p. 9; Hell 1930, pp. 35 and 102 [ca. 1652]; Lugt 1933, under no. 1198; Benesch 1935, p. 41 [ca. 1647, first group of architectural views]; G. Wimmer, *Rembrandts Landschaftszeichnungen*, Frankfurt, 1935, pp. 43, 48; Henkel 1942, p. 39, under no. 77; Benesch 1947, under no. 219; Benesch VI, no. 1301, fig. 1531 [ca. 1652–53, second group of architectural views; cf. also Benesch IV, no. 823 for discussion of whole group]; F. Winzinger, *Rembrandt Landschaftszeichnungen*, Baden-Baden, 1953, under no. 4; Begemann 1961, p. 56; [F. Thompson 1962], no. 1043 [illustrated]; Scheidig 1962, p. 55, fig. 96; Slive 1965, no. 72 [ca. 1648].

In studies of buildings and architecture Rembrandt preferred two distinct categories, namely rural buildings (farms, windmills) and historical structures (churches, city gates, fortifications), while he rarely sketched contemporary buildings. Rembrandt's associations with the architecture of the past probably were closely related to his interpretation of historical scenes.

The several studies of medieval town gates and walls of Rhenen belong to Rembrandt's most impressive architectural drawings. His representations of the "Rijnpoort", seen from within the city, are also of topographical interest because the gate was destroyed by the French shortly after Rembrandt had sketched it (1673).

It is not known whether Rembrandt visited the provinces of Utrecht and Gelderland once or several times, but it seems quite possible that he passed through Rhenen more than once. On stylistic grounds it seems certain that the drawing exhibited here was done during the same visit as another view of the "Rijnpoort" drawn from a standpoint a little closer and a little to the left, in the Louvre (B. 1300, fig. 1530), and the *Town Gate* in the British Museum (B. 1304, fig. 1534). As Lugt pointed out, the shadows indicate that Rembrandt made the Louvre sketch early in the morning and the one here exhibited late in the afternoon. Benesch in 1957 assumed that Rembrandt made two trips, one in 1647–48, the second one in 1652–53, and counted the Chatsworth drawing among those done during the second trip.

## 127 Two Indian Noblemen of the Mughal Court: Abd al-Rahim Khan and a Falconer*

The Pierpont Morgan Library, New York

Pen and brown ink and brown wash with touches of red chalk wash and red and yellow chalk and some white gouache (in turban and skirt of right figure), on oriental paper, 191 × 234 mm. *Ill. p. 222*

DATE [ca. 1650–56].

PROVENANCE J. Richardson, Sen. (L. 2184); Goll van Franckenstein?; Earl of Aylesford (L. 58); C. Fairfax Murray; J. Pierpont Morgan.

EXHIBITIONS Paris 1908, no. 428; New York, Metropolitan Museum, 1918, no. 29; New York/Cambridge, Mass. 1960, no. 62, pl. 55.

BIBLIOGRAPHY Fairfax Murray I, no. 208; HdG 1087; Valentiner 1934, no. 651; Benesch 1935, p. 56; Benesch V, no. 1203, fig. 1429 [ca. 1654–56]; New York/Cambridge, Mass. 1960, under nos. 61 and 63 [for Indian paper]; Richard Ettinghausen, *Paintings of the Sultans and Emperors of India in American Collections*, Lalit Kalā Akademi, India [1961], p. 6 [illustrated]; Theodore Bowie *et al.*, *East-West in Art*, Bloomington/London, 1966, p. 108, fig. 204.

This drawing is one of a series of studies after miniatures made by seventeenth-century Hindustani artists at the court of the Mughal dynasty ruling over India. Such miniatures were well known in Holland at the time and were found in various collections in which they generally were referred to as "drawings from Surat" or "Mogul drawings" ("Suratse" or "Mogolse teeckeningen"). One of these Dutch collections ended up as part of the decorations of the "Millionenzimmer" in Castle Schönbrunn in Vienna. Rembrandt may have owned the miniatures he copied and in that case they perhaps were identical with the book "filled with curious miniature drawings", listed in the inventory of his belongings drawn up in 1656.

For his free copies of Mughal Miniatures, Rembrandt chose what is traditionally known as "Japan paper", i.e., an oriental wove paper which, according to A. Hyatt Mayor, recent Japanese authorities say is actually Indian. This drawing is one of the twenty-five Richardson Sr. had assembled in the eighteenth century, and of which twenty-four are known today. Rembrandt may have copied the two figures from two different miniatures; prototypes for both are found among the mutilated miniatures in Schönbrunn.

Rembrandt made most of these copies at approximately the same time, sometime before 1656, when he etched *Abraham and the Three Angels* (B. 29, H. 286) which compositionally is based on one of the miniatures Rembrandt copied (B. 1187, fig. 1411).

Ettinghausen identified the archer as Abd al-Rahim Khan (1556–1627), a renowned scholar, statesman, and general at the Mughal Court, known under the title Khan-i-Khanan.

## 128 *Detail from Raphael's "The Repulse of Attila"*

Staatliche Museen Preussischer Kulturbesitz, Kupferstichkabinett, Berlin

Red chalk and pen and brown ink and brown wash corrected with white on brown paper, 190 × 317 mm.; top corners arched. *Ill. p. 223*

DATE [ca. 1650–60].

BIBLIOGRAPHY Bock and Rosenberg 1930, p. 243, no. 13733 [style of Rembrandt]; [Oskar Fischel and] A. P. Oppé, "Rembrandt van Rijn, The Repulse of Attila (after Raphael)", *Old Master Drawings*, XIV, 1939–40, p. 59, pl. 52 [as by Rembrandt]; Oskar Fischel, *Raphael*, London, 1948, p. 326, pl. 299; *idem*, *Raphael*, Berlin, 1962, p. 245.

In this drawing Rembrandt copied the central section of Raphael's fresco in the Stanza d'Eliodoro in the Vatican. He eliminated at the left the figure of Pope Leo I riding towards the right to meet the King of the Huns, and also St. Peter and St. Paul appearing above the figures; at the right he omitted a group of riders and warriors. Instead, he concentrated on the figure of Attila frightened by the apparition of St. Peter and St. Paul and on his immediate surroundings.

Sometime before 1930 Oskar Fischel found this drawing in Berlin among the anonymous Italian drawings, and attributed it to Rembrandt. In spite of Fischel's opinion which after his death was published by A. P. Oppé, the drawing was listed by Bock and Rosenberg as "in the style of Rembrandt" and excluded by Benesch from his "Corpus" of Rembrandt drawings. Although few have supported the attribution to Rembrandt (Friedrich Winkler, in conversation), there do not seem to be sufficient reasons to relegate this drawing to the anonymous followers. For the drawing to be evaluated properly, it should be pointed out that another hand added contours and details to figures and horses at the left with a thinner pen and ink over broad brush strokes. Rembrandt himself had first started the drawing with a little red chalk, then carried it out with pen and brown ink, and finally completed it by adding shadows and tone with brush and brown ink.

The character of the pen lines of Rembrandt's copies after other works of art varies according to the example copied and reflects to some degree the characteristics of the proto-type, whether this was by Mantegna, or Polidoro, or a Mughal miniature. Whatever unusual aspects of this drawing may have deterred Rembrandt students from accepting it as a work of the artist, this copy does not differ more substantially from Rembrandt's own compositions than his other copies do. In this case the particular characteristics of the drawing also may have been influenced by the prototype used. That example unfortunately is not known, but it probably was a drawing (a workshop sketch [?] is in the Louvre, a seventeenth-century copy drawn with the brush and heightened with body color is in Oxford [K. T. Parker II, no. 663]; according to Borenius the latter is a copy of an early stage of the fresco).

Another reason to accept the drawing as a work of Rembrandt's was already found by Fischel and published in his posthumous book. Attila's helmet which in the fresco is held by an attendant, and which is difficult to make out, was misinterpreted in the drawing; its visor was transformed into a face and the warrior thus introduced in the drawing (fourth figure from the left) resembles closely Rembrandt's *Man with the Golden Helmet* of ca. 1650 in Berlin. The resemblance may be explained as Rembrandt's reverting to a familiar figure when he had to interpret a difficult passage.

## 129   *The Mocking of Christ**
The Pierpont Morgan Library, New York

Pen and brown ink, rubbed with the finger, 155 × 215 mm. *Ill. p. 225*

DATE [ca. 1652–55].

PROVENANCE Sir John Charles Robinson (L. 1433); C. Fairfax Murray; J. Pierpont Morgan.

EXHIBITIONS London 1899, no. 105; Paris 1908, no. 354; Cambridge, Fogg Museum, 1917; New York, Metropolitan Museum, 1918, no. 55; New York 1919; San Francisco 1920, no. 374; Cambridge, Fogg Museum, 1922; New York, Wildenstein and Co., 1950, no. 36; New York, Metropolitan Museum, 1952; New York, Pierpont Morgan Library, 1957, no. 96; New York, Knoedler and Co., 1959, p. 55, pl. 28; New York/Cambridge, Mass. 1960, no. 59, pl. 52; Minneapolis, Minneapolis Institute of Arts, *Fiftieth Anniversary Exhibition, 1915–1965,* 1965–66.

BIBLIOGRAPHY Fairfax Murray I, no. 189; Valentiner 1934, no. 476 [mid-fifties]; Benesch 1935, p. 51; Tietze 1947, no. 68; Benesch V, no. 920, fig. 1131 [ca. 1652–53]; Begemann 1961, p. 86 [close to B. 1000, fig. 1214]; Malcolm Vaughan,

"Master Drawings: a Royal Occasion", *Connoisseur Year Book,* 1961, p. 29 [illustrated]; Rotermund 1963, pp. 262–63, fig. 227.

Rembrandt essentially followed Matthew 27:27–29: "Then the soldiers of the governor took Jesus into the common hall, and gathered unto him the whole band of soldiers. And they stripped him, and put on him a scarlet robe. And when they had plaited a crown of thorns, they put it upon his head, and a reed in his right hand: and they bowed the knee before him, and mocked him, saying, Hail, King of the Jews!" The main difference between Rembrandt's representation of the event and the biblical text is the fact that Christ's upper body is uncovered. Undoubtedly the artist was influenced by the pictorial tradition of "The Man of Sorrows Seated", a subject especially common in German and Netherlandish art ("Christus op de koude steen"). In another drawing Rembrandt represented Christ draped in "a scarlet robe", and in that case the attitude of Christ resting his head on his hand is also derived from that same tradition (drawing formerly in the Léon Bonnat Collection, sale London, Sotheby, Dec. 10, 1968; B. 1024, fig. 1238).

## 130   *The Prophet Elisha and the Widow with Her Sons*
Private Collection

Pen and brown ink, 172 × 254 mm. *Ill. p. 224*

DATE [ca. 1653–57].

PROVENANCE Artaria: J. C. Klinkosch (sale Vienna, Wawra, April 10, 1889, no. 711); The Prince of Liechtenstein.

BIBLIOGRAPHY HdG 1502; Schönbrunner and Meder 853; Valentiner 1925, no. 188 [important composition; execution somewhat insecure]; E. W. Bredt, *Rembrandt-Bibel,* 1927, I, p. 121; Benesch 1935, p. 62 [late fifties]; Benesch 1947, no. 259; Benesch V, no. 1027, fig. 1240 [ca. 1657]; Sumowski 1957–58, pp. 232 and 237 [drawing by Rembrandt; used for painting attributed to Barent Fabritius]; Sumowski 1961, p. 19 [copy]; Sumowski 1964, p. 33 [lists copy in Düsseldorf]; Sumowski 1964, p. 247 [drawing according to reproduction a copy; painting of 1650's based on it is by anonymous pupil]; White 1969, p. 222 [1657? compares with *St. Francis* etching; Italianate landscape].

The prophet Elisha has listened to the complaints of the widow who has no more left than one pot of oil and whose sons are wanted as bondsmen by her creditor. Replying "What shall I do for thee?" he advises her to return home and fill all the vessels she can borrow with oil which miraculously suffices (II Kings 4:1–3).

As he preferred to do in the 1650's in his etchings as well as in his drawings, Rembrandt placed the figures in front of a mountainous landscape influenced by Venetian examples, particularly of Titian. In this case the setting with trees at the right, hills with buildings in the middle, and a bridge in a valley at the left is particularly reminiscent of the etching *St. Jerome Reading, in an Italian Landscape* (B. 104, H. 267) of about 1653.

For the setting, and also for similar characteristics of lines, this drawing can be compared with the *Rest on the Flight into Egypt*, here also exhibited (no. 132).

Sumowski mentioned a painting by a Rembrandt pupil, according to him Barent Fabritius, which is based on this drawing (sale Brussels, March 15, 1926, no. 37, as Rembrandt), and also a mediocre copy of the drawing in Düsseldorf (F. P. 5109).

## 131 *Christ Finding the Apostles Asleep*

Sterling and Francine Clark Art Institute, Williamstown, Massachusetts

Pen and brown ink and brown and grayish-brown wash, 183 × 280 mm. *Ill. p. 225*

DATE [ca. 1655].

PROVENANCE R. P. Roupell, London (L. 2234); J. P. Heseltine, London (L. 1507); Colnaghi, London (1913).

EXHIBITIONS Paris 1908, no. 353 [dimensions incorrect]; Williamstown, Sterling and Francine Clark Institute, *Dutch and Flemish Masters (Exhibit Twelve)*, 1960, no. 424.

BIBLIOGRAPHY E. Michel, *Rembrandt*, Paris, 1893, p. 584; Lippmann II, 36; HdG 990; Heseltine 1907, no. 79; Kruse 1920, p. 32, under no. II, 10, fig. 37; W. Weisbach, *Rembrandt*, Berlin, 1926, fig. 152; Hell 1930, pp. 100 and 134–35; Bock and Rosenberg 1930, p. 227, under no. 2700; Valentiner 1934, no. 449; Benesch 1935, p. 55; Henkel 1942, p. 35, under no. 69; Benesch 1947, no. 199; Benesch V, no. 941, fig. 1153; Egbert Haverkamp-Begemann, Standish D. Lawder, and Charles W. Talbot, Jr., *Drawings from the Clark Institute*, New Haven and London, 1964, no. 18, pl. 22; A. Werner, "Rembrandt's Bible Drawings", *American Artist*, XXVIII, 1964, p. 57 [illustrated]; Slive 1965, no. 258; White 1969, p. 97, note 37.

At various instances Rembrandt represented successive moments of this subject. In this drawing Christ, returning from His first prayer on the Mount of Olives, finds His disciples asleep and reproaches St. Peter, beginning with

the words, "What, could ye not watch with me one hour?" (Matthew 26:40). While in this drawing St. Peter is not yet responding, in a second version of this subject he is listening intensely to the pleading Christ (Berlin, B. 940, fig. 1152). In a third drawing (Warsaw, B. 613, fig. 745), Christ, after the third prayer, is telling His disciples, "Rise, let us be going: behold, he is at hand that doth betray me" (Matthew 26:46).

Of the two washes on this drawing, the brown one seems to have been applied by Rembrandt, while the grayish-brown one (in the trees, the landscape to the right of Christ, and the left foreground) probably was added later. The drawing should be dated to the mid-fifties.

## 132 *The Rest on the Flight into Egypt*

Norton Simon Foundation, Fullerton, Calif.

Reed-pen and brown ink and some brown wash, 171 × 231 mm. *Ill. p. 226*

DATE [ca. 1655].

PROVENANCE Sir Joshua Reynolds (L. 2364); R. Kann; A. Hamilton Rice; Mr. and Mrs. Louis H. Silver, Chicago.

BIBLIOGRAPHY Valentiner 1925, no. 343 [ca. 1655]; Benesch 1935, p. 55; Benesch V, no. 965, fig. 1179 [ca. 1655]; Clark 1968, p. 113, fig. 102.

Like the preceding drawing, this is one of a group of drawings of the middle 1650's where Rembrandt represented religious scenes in wide, hilly landscape with distant views. In this *Rest on the Flight into Egypt* Rembrandt introduced a city reminiscent of traditional representations of Jerusalem. The landscape itself owes some of its features to Campagnola and through him to Titian.

## 133 *Three Studies for a Deposition from the Cross*

Norton Simon Foundation, Fullerton, Calif.

Pen and brown ink, 180 × 199 mm. *Ill. p. 226*

DATE [ca. 1653–56].

PROVENANCE Earl of Warwick; T. Halstead; A. Hamilton Rice; Mr. and Mrs. Louis H. Silver, Chicago.

EXHIBITIONS New York/Cambridge, Mass. 1960, no. 68, pl. 57.

BIBLIOGRAPHY Valentiner 1934, no. 493 [ca. 1655]; Benesch 1935, p. 55; Benesch V, no. 934, fig. 1145 [ca. 1653–54];

Rosenberg 1959, p. 114 [closer to Bredius 584 than H. 280]; "Rembrandt Drawings from American Collections", *Arts*, XXXIV, 1960, p. 29 [illustrated].

Intermittently Rembrandt represented the *Deposition from the Cross*. First he etched and painted the subject twice in 1633/34, then he made a drawing of it circa 1650 (B. 587, fig. 718) and in 1654 he etched it once more (B. 83, H. 280). The present drawing probably followed the last etching and thus concludes Rembrandt's representations of this subject. His principal aim in these three studies of the two figures is to define the proper relationships of heads and limbs, and to express the compassionate acceptance of the lifeless Christ. In none of the earlier representations had Rembrandt tried to bring the body of the dead Christ in such close proximity to the man lowering him.

## 134 *View of Diemen*

National Gallery of Art, Washington, D.C., Rosenwald Collection *Ill. p. 229*

Pen and brown ink and brown wash, 90 × 225 mm.

DATE [ca. 1653–57].

PROVENANCE A. Firmin-Didot, Paris; Gilhofer & Ranschburg, Vienna; Lessing J. Rosenwald.

EXHIBITIONS Philadelphia, Art Alliance, 1930; Worcester 1936, no. 63; Raleigh 1956, no. 4; New York/Cambridge, Mass. 1960, no. 58, pl. 49; Washington, National Gallery of Art, 1966; Ibidem 1969, no. 34 [illustrated].

BIBLIOGRAPHY Tietze 1947, pl. 43; Benesch VI, no. 1360, fig. 1596 [ca. 1655-56].

This drawing shows Diemen, a village situated to the southwest of Amsterdam and identified by its square church tower. Rembrandt's position in making the sketch was on a road along a canal. To the viewer's right is Diemen; to the left a crowd of people are crossing a bridge and entering the village.

Rembrandt did several drawings of Dieman around 1650 and slightly later (B. 1229-31, 1311). This study has been cut out of a sketchbook, as the rounded bottom corner of the paper shows.

## 135 *Portrait of a Man in a Wide-Brimmed Hat*

Fogg Art Museum, A. S. Coburn and Alpheus Hyatt Funds, Harvard University, Cambridge, Mass.

Reed pen and brush and brown ink, corrected with white; a few black chalk lines added by another hand, 184 × 157 mm. *Ill. p. 227*

DATE [ca. 1655–60].

PROVENANCE F. Koenigs, Haarlem; D. G. van Beuningen, Rotterdam; Lukas H. Peterich, Rotterdam; C. Albert de Burlet, Basel.

EXHIBITIONS New York/Cambridge, Mass. 1960, no. 71, pl. 63.

BIBLIOGRAPHY J. Rosenberg, "A Portrait Drawing by Rembrandt", *Fogg Art Museum*, *Annual Report*, 1952–53 [illustrated; mid-fifties, close to B. 1181 and 1182]; J. Rosenberg, in *Art Quarterly*, XVII, 1954, pp. 80–81; Benesch VI, no. A 80a, fig. 1686 [started by another artist, perhaps finished by Rembrandt]; Rosenberg 1959, p. 117 [by Rembrandt]; Van Gelder 1961, p. 150 [by Rembrandt]; Sumowski 1961, p. 26 [probably Maes]; Slive 1965, under no. 222 [by Rembrandt].

This late portrait drawing is similar to two other half-length portrait drawings of men, both likewise wearing voluminous cloaks, in the Six Collection, Amsterdam, and in the Louvre, Paris (B. 1181, fig. 1407, and B. 1182, fig. 1408). The drawing probably dates from the years 1655–60. Rembrandt repeatedly changed the position of the left arm of the sitter and the cloak covering it. He tried various solutions and corrected with white, which has rubbed off to some extent. He also sketched the hat several times, finally giving it a broad shape corresponding with the wide silhouette of the cloak. The lines to the right of the figure probably indicate a table or similar object.

Benesch's supposition that two artists were responsible for this drawing does not seem to be substantiated by a close inspection. Sumowski's attribution to Maes is understandable in as much as a group of drawings generally attributed to Maes shows similar characteristics of line. Apart from the uncertainty whether Maes actually is the author of that group of drawings (cat. nos. 204 and 205), this similarity rather indicates that the artist, whether Maes or another one, learned from drawings such as the Fogg *Portrait* and related studies.

## 136 *Study of a Female Nude*

The Art Institute of Chicago, Gift of Tiffany and Margaret Blake *Ill. p. 228*

Pen and brown ink and brown wash, 233 × 178 mm.

DATE [ca. 1658–61].

PROVENANCE M (L. 1841; perhaps Bastiaan Molewater, sale Rotterdam, November 14, 1833, or Moelaard, Dordrecht, first half eighteenth century).

EXHIBITIONS Cambridge, Mass. 1948–49, no. 37; Rotterdam/Amsterdam 1956, no. 235, fig. 65; New York/Cambridge, Mass. 1960, no. 72, pl. 64; New York 1963, no. 31, pl. 12.

BIBLIOGRAPHY *The Art Institute of Chicago Bulletin*, XLIII, 1949, p. 12 [illustrated]; H[arold] J[oachim], in A. Mongan, *One Hundred Master Drawings*, Cambridge, Mass. 1949, p. 92 [illustrated]; Benesch V. no. 1127, fig. 1348 [ca. 1654–56]; Van Gelder 1958, pl. 70 [ca. 1658–61]; Rosenberg 1959, p. 115; Claude Roger-Marx, "Les Nus de Rembrandt", *L'Œil*, LXII, 1960, pp. 25–26 [illustrated]; Roger-Marx 1960, p. 294, fig. 121d; Scheidig 1962, p. 59 and no. 137, fig. 137; [E. H.-B.] 1962, no. 597 [illustrated].

Between 1658 and 1661 Rembrandt made six etchings of the female nude, and at the same time a number of sketches with pen and brush. Much earlier in his life, around 1632, he had done some black chalk studies of female nudes (B. 191–193, figs. 205–207), and a number of etchings. Compared with the earlier nudes, the later ones are more painterly and show less attention to detail.

Some of the late studies were done from the same model, and this particular drawing seems to represent the same figure as a study in Amsterdam (B. 1117, fig. 1339). In the pen lines the drawing is similar to *Rebecca Spied upon by Abimelech* (see cat. no. 140). See also the following drawing.

137 *Female Nude Seated on a Stool*

The Art Institute of Chicago, Clarence Buckingham Collection *Ill. p. 229*

Pen and brown ink and brown wash, 211 × 174 mm.

DATE [ca. 1658–61].

PROVENANCE L. Corot, Nîmes (L. 1718); A. Strölin, Paris-Lausanne.

EXHIBITIONS Bern 1937, no. 198; Rotterdam/Amsterdam 1956, no. 237, fig. 64; New York/Cambridge, Mass. 1960, no. 74, pl. 66; New York 1963, no. 32.

BIBLIOGRAPHY *Société de reproduction des dessins de maîtres*, V, Paris, 1913, no. 29 [mark L. 1718 mistaken for that of E. V. Utterson]; Hell 1930, p. 103, note 3; De Bruijn 1932, p. 187 [Dr. Bierens de Haan's theory about Rembrandt

drawing in a hospital]; Benesch 1935, p. 57; A. A. Sidorov *Risunki starykh masterov*, Moscow-Leningrad, 1940, fig. 242; Hanna Prinz, *Das Thema des weiblichen Aktes in Meister- und Schülerzeichnungen aus Rembrandts Spätzeit*, Diss. Marburg, 1945, pp. 100, 126; Rosenberg 1948, I, p. 153, II, fig. 222; H. Joachim, in *The Art Institute of Chicago Quarterly*, XLVIII, 1954, pp. 10–11 [illustrated]; Benesch V, no. 1122, fig. 1344 [ca. 1654–56]; Rosenberg 1959, p. 115; "Rembrandt Drawings from American Collection", *Arts*, XXXIV, 1960, p. 28 [illustrated]; Roger-Marx 1960, p. 293, fig. 121b; [Exhibition Catalogue] Brussels/Hamburg 1961, under no. 59; [E. H.-B.] 1962, no. 599 [illustrated]; A. Frankfurter, "Il 'bon disegno' from Chicago", *Art News*, LXII, 1963, p. 30 [illustrated]; Rosenberg 1964, p. 259, fig. 222.

This drawing belongs to the same group of studies from the nude as the preceding one. The same model is found once more in a drawing where she is seen from the back, slightly turned to the right, sitting on a low stool in front of a stove. Both drawings are related to Rembrandt's etching of a *Woman Sitting Half-Dressed beside a Stove* (H. 296) dated 1658. Since one of the impressions of this etching is inscribed *voor't Chirurgijnsgild* ("for the Surgeon's Guild"), and since in the first state of the etching, the woman seems to show symptoms of a disease diagnosed by Dr. J. C. J. Bierens de Haan, the latter suggested that the woman might have been a patient in a hospital. As many of Rembrandt's friends were doctors, it would not be surprising to find him sketching from life in a hospital ward.

This and the preceding drawing are among the few of the many related studies from the nude which were not retouched by a later hand. Apparently when many of these studies were still part of one collection, they were "completed" by a rather heavy brush with darker brown ink (for instance, B. 1128, fig. 1349; 1143, fig. 1367; 1144, fig. 1368; 1146, fig. 1370; 1147, fig. 1371).

138 *Study of a Franciscan Monk*

Staatliche Museen Preussischer Kulturbesitz, Kupferstichkabinett, Berlin

Pen and brown ink and brown wash corrected with white, touches of red chalk at the bottom, 270 × 191 mm.; top corners arched. *Ill. p. 227*

DATE [ca. 1658–61].

PROVENANCE J. Richardson Sen. (L. 2184); Ch. Rogers (L. 624); Von Rumohr.

EXHIBITIONS Berlin 1968, no. 8 [as Rembrandt].

BIBLIOGRAPHY Charles Rogers, *A Collection of Prints in Imitation of Drawings etc.*, II, London, 1778, 220 [reproduced in etching by W. W. Ryland; as Rembrandt]; R. Weigel, *Die Werke der Maler in ihren Handzeichnungen*, Leipzig, 1865, p. 641, no. 73 [probably Lievens]; Bock and Rosenberg 1930, p. 239, no. 13 785 [probably old copy]; Lugt 1931, p. 62 [good school drawing]; Sumowski 1964, pp. 243–44, fig. 13 [by Rembrandt, ca. 1655].

Although this drawing in the past has been considered as a work of Lievens, as a copy or a school drawing, it seems a characteristic drawing by Rembrandt himself, as was first suggested by Valentiner (note on mount) and subsequently substantiated by Sumowski. There are indeed such close similarities with Rembrandt's studies of nudes of the years 1658–61 that it is difficult to doubt his authorship. To be compared are particularly the studies of seated nudes in Munich (B. 1107), Rotterdam (B. 1121) and Chicago (B. 1122, here exhibited under no. 137), and also the drawing *Woman Looking out of a Window* in the Louvre (B. 1099). In all these drawings the modeling is done in a similar way with few, often angular lines, while shadows and tone are indicated with broadly applied brush strokes.

The drawing seems to date from the same years. It was also at that time that Rembrandt painted monks (*A Franciscan Monk*, London, 1655 or slightly later; *Titus* (?) *in Franciscan Habit*, Amsterdam, 1660; *A Franciscan*, Helsinki, 1661). The barefooted friar of this drawing wears the same hood as the monks of the Amsterdam and Helsinki paintings, and therefore probably also is a Franciscan.

## 139 *Noah's Ark*

The Art Institute of Chicago, Clarence Buckingham Collection *Ill. p. 230*

Reed pen and brown ink and brown wash, 199 × 243 mm.

DATE [ca. 1660].

PROVENANCE Alliance des Arts, Paris; F. van den Zande (?) (sale Paris, April 30, 1855, no. 3042); Marquis de Biron (sale Paris, June 9–11, 1914, no. 50 [illustrated]; P. Mathey, Paris; A. Strölin, Paris-Lausanne.

EXHIBITIONS Bern 1937, no. 204; Rotterdam/Amsterdam 1956, no. 248, pl. 68; New York/Cambridge, Mass. 1960, no. 75, pl. 68; New York 1963, no. 33, pl. 13b; Jerusalem 1965, no. 3 [illustrated].

BIBLIOGRAPHY E. Dutuit, *Tableaux et dessins de Rembrandt . . . Supplément . . .*, 1885, p. 105 ["La Synagogue des Juifs"]; Valentiner 1925, no. 6 [ca. 1660]; Hell 1930, p. 105; Benesch 1935, p. 62 [1656–59]; Rosenberg 1948, I, p. 213, II, fig. 278; H. Joachim, in *The Art Institute of Chicago Quarterly* XLVIII, 1954, pp. 12–13 [illustrated]; Benesch V, no. 1045, fig. 1261 [ca. 1659–60]; Rosenberg 1959, p. 110; [E. H.-B.] 1962, no. 597 [illustrated]; Scheidig 1962, p. 67, no. 170, fig. 170; Rotermund 1963, p. 10, fig. 6; Rosenberg 1964 p. 341, fig. 278.

In contrast to the usual representations of Noah's Ark, Rembrandt did not show the animals embarking, but preferred to stress the human element. Taking as his text Genesis 7:7, he represented the moment in which "Noah went in, and his sons, and his wife, and his sons' wives with him", before the animals entered "two and two". The figures in the foreground at the left are probably two of those whom God destroyed because of their wickedness. Rembrandt imagined them watching Noah and his relatives embark, unaware of their fate and that of all living creatures. The small stooped figure standing at the top of the stairs is probably the six-hundred-year-old Noah.

The very broad pen lines point to the years around 1660.

## 140 *Isaac and Rebecca Spied upon by Abimelech*

Private Collection, New York

Pen and brown ink, corrected with white (partly oxidized), 145 × 185 mm. *Ill. p. 231*

DATE [early 1660's].

PROVENANCE Ludwig Richter; Eduard Cichorius (sale Leipzig, May 5, 1908, no. 581); Oscar Huldschinsky; W. R. Valentiner (sale Amsterdam, October 25, 1932, no. II).

EXHIBITIONS Amsterdam 1936, no. 202; Rotterdam 1938, no. 327; Cambridge, Mass. 1948–49, no. 38; Rotterdam/Amsterdam 1956, no. 210, fig. 63; New York/Cambridge, Mass. 1960, no. 76, pl. 69; Jerusalem 1965, no. 18.

BIBLIOGRAPHY W. R. Valentiner, in *Kunst und Künstler*, XXII, 1924, p. 18 [as Tobias and Sara]; H. Swarzenski and E. Schilling, *Handzeichnunger alter Meister aus deutschem Privatbesitz*, Frankfurt, 1924, no. 47; Valentiner 1925, no. 243 [ca. 1667; Isaac and Rebecca?]; Kauffmann 1926, p. 158 [Isaac and Rebecca]; Hell 1930, pp. 130–31; Benesch 1935, pp. 56, 68 [ca. 1653–55]; Tietze 1947, no. 70, p. 140; Rosenberg 1948, I, pp. 67–68, II, fig. 114 [early fifties, Isaac and Rebecca; couple in painting portrayed as Jacob and Rachel];

J. R[osenberg], in A. Mongan, *One Hundred Master Drawings*, Cambridge, Mass., 1949, p. 88; Benesch V, no. 988, fig. 1202 [ca. 1655–56]; C. Müller Hofstede, in *Kunstchronik*, X, 1957, pp. 147–48; W. R. Valentiner, in *Festschrift Kurt Bauch*, Munich, 1957, p. 228; Sumowski 1957–58, pp. 225–26 [dating in sixties more likely; comparable in pen lines to B. 1057]; Roger-Marx 1960, p. 330, fig. 152a; Begemann 1961, p. 86 [probably after 1660], Rosenberg 1964, p. 128, fig. 114; Clark 1968, pp. 140–41, fig. 133; Gerson 1968, pp. 132, 420, 502, illustrated p. 421, fig. a.

King Abimelech discovers that Rebecca is not Isaac's sister as Isaac had pretended (Genesis 26:8).

Rembrandt drew the head of Isaac twice; he subsequently deleted the first version and also deleted the foliage at the right. Rembrandt used the composition of this drawing for his painting *The Jewish Bride* in which he portrayed a bridal pair in biblical guise, either as Jacob and Rachel or as Tobias and Sara. The drawing is not necessarily made as a study for the painting, but may very well have preceded the painting by a short time only. In that case it would date from the early 1660's.

## 141   *The Meeting of Christ with Martha and Mary after the Death of Lazarus*

The Cleveland Museum of Art. Purchase, Leonard C. Hanna Jr. Bequest

Reed pen and brown ink, corrected with white, 174 × 208 mm. *Ill. p. 231*

DATE [ca. 1662–65].

PROVENANCE E. V. Utterson (L. 909).

BIBLIOGRAPHY O. Benesch, "A Drawing by Rembrandt from His Last Years", *Bulletin of the Cleveland Museum of Art*, L, March, 1963, pp. 42–45 [illustrated]; *idem*, "Ueber den Werdegang einer Komposition Rembrandts", *Bulletin du Musée Hongrois des Beaux-Arts*, XXII, 1963, pp. 86–87, fig. 47; Benesch 1964, pp. 140–41, fig. 37.

Although knowing that Lazarus was ill, Jesus left Bethany to go to Judaea. After his return to Bethany, Mary came to Him and "fell down at his feet, saying unto Him, Lord, if thou hadst been here, my brother had not died" (John 11:33). This is the moment Rembrandt represented in this drawing. Behind Jesus two disciples bow their heads in mourning; Martha kneels before Jesus; at the right Jews accompanying Martha and Mary listen and discuss the tragic events.

This representation of Mary's complaint and sorrow and her trust in Jesus is Rembrandt's last-known formulation of a subject that he had treated in greater detail—although not more eloquently—in *The Hundred Guilder Print*.

Various times Rembrandt changed and corrected the figure of Martha, especially the position of her head and praying hands, and deleted a man standing behind her. The drawing is one of the very few late religious and mythological subjects characterized by broad reed pen lines (*St. Peter at the Deathbed of Tabitha, Diana and Actaeon*, both Dresden). All three date from ca. 1662–1665.

## DRAWINGS BY PUPILS, CORRECTED BY REMBRANDT

### 142   *The Annunciation*

Staatliche Museen Preussischer Kulturbesitz, Kupferstichkabinett, Berlin

Pen and brown ink and red chalk and brown and gray wash corrected with white, 173 × 231 mm. *Ill. p. 233*

PROVENANCE Sir Joshua Reynolds (L. 2364); Th. Hudson (L. 2432); Sir Thomas Lawrence (L. 2445); W. Esdaile (L. 2617); Ch. S. Bale.

EXHIBITIONS Berlin 1930, no. 276.

BIBLIOGRAPHY HdG 47 [pupil corrected by Rembrandt]; Neumann 1918, pp. 115–19, fig. 40 [Rembrandt corrected his own drawing]; Lilienfeld 33 [Maes or Fabritius]; Valentiner 1925, no. 288 [pupil, corrected by Rembrandt]; Falck 1924, pp. 192–93 [illustrated; C. van Renesse, corrected by Rembrandt]; Bock and Rosenberg 1930, p. 224, Inv. no. 2313, pl. 149; A. M. Hind, *Rembrandt*, Norton Lectures, Cambridge, Mass., 1932, pl. XII; Benesch 1935, p. 51; Münz 1935, pp. 213–14, figs. 157, 160–162; Benesch 1947, no. 188; Rosenberg 1948, p. 180; Michael Walichi, in *Biuletyn historii sztuki*, XVI, 1954, p. 244, fig. 8; Benesch VI, no. 1372, fig. 1606 [by Van Renesse, corrected by Rembrandt ca. 1652]; Sumowski 1957–58, p. 234, fig. 65; Sumowski 1964, p. 33, footnote 4 [lists copy in Braunschweig]; Sumowski 1964, p. 244; Benesch 1964, p. 131; Sumowski P 1965, p. 253, fig. 8.

No other drawing by any of Rembrandt's pupils was corrected as drastically and meaningfully as this *Annunciation*. The pupil sketched the angel on the same scale as the Virgin Mary, and tried to express his supernatural character by surrounding him with light and equipping him with large wings. Rembrandt obtained the effect more convincingly by increasing the size of the angel while reducing the wings.

By turning the body of the angel and letting only his head face the Virgin, Rembrandt gave the figure a fleeting instead of a static appearance. Rembrandt also increased the lectern, thus expressing more clearly the concept of the Virgin of Humility, and clearly defined the closed shutters stressing her seclusion from the world.

As most of Rembrandt's corrections of pupils' drawings these date from the early fifties. The similarities with signed drawings (*Daniel in the Lions' Den*, 1652, Rotterdam; *St. Jerome*, 1652, Haarlem) and with others which certainly were made by Van Renesse (*The Judgment of Solomon*, ex-Reitlinger Collection) are such that the *Annunciation* may be considered a work of his.

## 143   *The Departure of Benjamin for Egypt*

Teylers Museum, Haarlem

Pen and brush and brown ink, corrected with white, 190 × 290 mm. *Ill. p. 232*

DATE [ca. 1650].

PROVENANCE Goll van Franckenstein; J. de Vos Sen.; Mendes de Léon; De Kat.

EXHIBITIONS London 1929, no. 633; Haarlem 1951, no. 176.

BIBLIOGRAPHY H. J. Scholten, *Catalogue raisonné des dessins, Musée Teyler à Haarlem*, Haarlem, 1904, p. 105, no. 45; HdG 1317; Lippmann IV, 90; C. Hofstede de Groot, in *Oud-Holland*, XLI, 1923–24, before p. 97; H. Buisman, *Teyler Museum, Handzeichnungen alter Meister der holländischen Schule*, Leipzig, 1924, no. 11; Valentiner 1925, no. 119 [ca. 1656]; W. R. Valentiner, in *Art Bulletin*, XIV, 1932, p. 232, fig. 33 [invention of Rembrandt, open to discussion whether entirely autograph or only touched up by Rembrandt]; Lugt 1933, under no. 1275 [first stage similar to drawings attributed to Barent Fabritius]; Benesch 1935, p. 43 [Barent Fabritius?; end of 1640's]; Henkel 1942, p. 80, under no. 1; Benesch IV, no. 856, fig. 1004 [Barent Fabritius; date of corrections 1648–50]; Sumowski 1957–58, p. 237; Pont 1958, pp. 94 and 129 [first stage of drawing not by Barent Fabritius; attr. painting to Constantijn van Renesse], "Stellingen" VI [considers Nicolaes Maes]; Sumowski 1959, p. 292; Sumowski 1961, p. 15 [attribution of first stage to Fabritius uncertain; second copy at sale Aachen (Lempertz), R. Bonneval, December 18, 1907, no. 183]; Slive 1965, no. 540.

Jacob reluctantly agrees to send the young Benjamin to Egypt and tells his brothers who will accompany him to take fruits and balm and other presents for the King of Egypt (Genesis 43:11–13). While he gives these instructions, a servant carries goods to the standing donkey.

Rembrandt vigorously corrected and strengthened the drawing of a pupil. This pupil may have been Barent Fabritius or Constantijn van Renesse. Rembrandt mainly restructured the architectural background, redefined the figures, and introduced the scene of the loading of the donkey at the right. Rembrandt's corrections were apparently also concerned with a change in format. The direction of the bannister at the side of the steps and the remains of a head and shoulder at the bottom right indicate that originally the drawing extended further downwards. Rembrandt indicated the new ground level by introducing the donkey and its attendants. These corrections probably date from the early 1650's.

A painting corresponding with the left half of the drawing, in the Mauritshuis, The Hague, has been attributed to both Barent Fabritius and Van Renesse. A drawing in Amsterdam is a copy after the corrected drawing.

## 144   *Judas Receiving the Thirty Pieces of Silver*

Devonshire Collection, Chatsworth

Pen and brown ink and brown and gray wash, corrected with pen and brown ink; heads and shoulders of the man at the left blotted out with gray ink; 143 × 220 mm. Top corners arched. *Ill. p. 233*

DATE [ca. 1655].

BIBLIOGRAPHY Münz 1935, pp. 205–06, figs. 150–51 [as Renesse]; Benesch VI, nos. 1378 and ad 1378, fig. 1613 [as Renesse corrected by Rembrandt ca. 1655–56]; Sumowski 1961, p. 22.

PROVENANCE "Cabinet du Mr. Vilenbrock" (according to print by Picart, probably referring to Coll. Gosuinus Uilenbroek, sale Amsterdam, Oct. 23, 1741).

This drawing, attributable to Renesse, was also corrected by Rembrandt. He stressed the structure of the central figures and added the figure to the chair at the very right, balancing the composition and at the same time introducing an element of contrast with the central group.

Two copies of the drawing were made after Rembrandt had corrected it (Stockholm, Kruse 1920, II.25, Benesch ad 1378; Berlin KdZ 1147). The drawing was also reproduced in print by B. Picart (*Impostures Innocentes*, Amsterdam 1734). These copies and the print show that originally the drawing was larger at the left.

**145**  *Lot Defending the Angels from the People of Sodom*

The Pierpont Morgan Library, New York, Gift of Mr. and Mrs. Arnold Whitridge

Pen and gray-black ink and gray and brown wash, with corrections in reed pen and brown ink, also some in white, 197 × 256 mm.  *Ill. p. 235*

INSCRIPTIONS Annotated with pen and brown ink at bottom right: *Rembrandt.*

DATE [ca. 1655–60].

PROVENANCE Charles Rogers (L. 624); Chevalier Ignace-Joseph de Claussin (L. 485); Duke of Somerset at Bulstrode Park (sale London, Christie, June 28, 1890, no. 7); Charles Sedelmeyer, Paris (according to annotation on the reverse); Charles Stewart Smith (1907; according to annotation on the reverse); Mr. and Mrs. Adolph I. Margolis; their son Stephen Margolis.

BIBLIOGRAPHY Van Regteren Altena 1961, p. 87 [re: copy in Amsterdam]; [Felice Stampfle], in *Fifteenth Report to the Fellows of the Pierpont Morgan Library 1967 & 1968*, New York (to be published) [possibly Van Renesse, corrected by Rembrandt].

This subject is taken from Genesis 19:1–11. Before fleeing Sodom, Lot had given shelter to two angels. The drawing represents the moment that the men of the city called on Lot and "said unto him, where are the men which came in to thee this night?" Rembrandt represented a slightly later moment in a drawing which in composition is similar to the one here exhibited; in that drawing (Valentiner 35, as original; B. C 101, as copy; Slive 1965, no. 499, as original) the Sodomites are preparing to force their passage into the house.

In order to correct the work of a pupil who remains anonymous Rembrandt strengthened and tightened the timid outlines of almost all figures, heightened the element of drama by introducing a man talking directly to Lot and an angel behind Lot, and by changing the upper half of the Dutch door from opening outwards to opening inwards. He also added two more figures at the right, reformulated the window and constructed a clearly articulated architectural framework around the door and the figure of Lot.

Rembrandt corrected this drawing in the fifties, probably ca. 1655–60. A mediocre copy after this drawing, including Rembrandt's corrections, is in the Rijksmuseum, Amsterdam.

## UNIDENTIFIED PUPILS OF REMBRANDT

**146**  *The Good Samaritan*

The Art Institute of Chicago, Charles Deering Collection
*Ill. p. 235*

Pen and brown ink, corrected with white, 190 × 230 mm.

PROVENANCE Crozat (?); Charles Deering (L. 516).

BIBLIOGRAPHY Falck 1924–25, p. 83 [painting Louvre attributed to B. Fabritius]; Clotilde Brière-Misme, "Autour de Rembrandt", *Musées de France*, June 1949, pp. 122–28, fig. 6 [pupil, 1644–1650]; Benesch III, under no. 518a [pupil]; Leiden 1956, under no. 17 [direct copy after painting?]; Benesch V, under no. 1018 [after ca. 1656–57]; Sumowski 1957–58, p. 232, fig. 58 [not copy; by pupil; Carel Fabritius?]; Pont 1958, p. 127, no. 4 [mentions Maes as well as Fabritius in connection with Louvre painting, but omits Chicago drawing]; Sumowski 1959, p. 292; Roger-Marx 1960, pp. 262–63, fig. 97f.

Although this drawing is a study for a well-known painting, its author has not been identified. Until Schneider and Falck attributed that painting to Barent Fabritius, it was considered one of the best Rembrandts of the museum (Br. 581) an attribution which probably cannot be upheld. Unfortunately, no other drawings by the artist of the Chicago *Good Samaritan* which could clarify the authorship of the painting have become known.

The anonymous artist evolved his composition from two other drawings of the same subject, in London and Rotterdam (B. 518a and B. 518b; it is not certain whether those two drawings are by Rembrandt). A variation of the composition of this drawing is found in a painting of the same subject and the preparatory drawing for it which both were attributed unconvincingly to Ferdinand Bol by Valentiner. Both may have been made by a pupil who worked in Rembrandt's studio when the Chicago drawing was executed. (Painting in Coll. Captain Palmer, London; drawing formerly with J. Weitzner, New York; Valentiner 1957, figs. 15 and 16).

Although inscriptions by the same hand as the one on this drawing are often found on drawings by Rembrandt and from his school, it is not certain whether indeed Crozat added these as sometimes is supposed (cf. B. 503, 594, 1076 and others).

**147**  *Rembrandt's Studio with Pupils Drawing from the Nude*
Hessisches Landesmuseum, Darmstadt

Black chalk and brown wash, heightened with white, 180 × 266 mm. *Ill. p. 234*

DATE [ca. 1650–60].

EXHIBITIONS Leiden 1956, no. 171, fig. 28; Ingelheim am Rhein 1964, no. 69.

BIBLIOGRAPHY Falck 1924, p. 199, fig. 10 [as Renesse]; *Stift und Feder*, 1928, no. 95 [as Rembrandt pupil]; Lugt 1933, under no. 1327; Lugt 1936, under no. 251; Gerson 1957, p. 149; Scheidig 1962, p. 59 and no. 125A, fig. 125A; Sumowski 1964, p. 239 [as Renesse]; Gerson 1968, p. 62, illustrated p. 64, fig. a.

The master himself and five pupils are sketching a nude model in a room which is furnished only with some boxes that serve as chairs or footrests, a trunk or chestlike structure for the model to lie on, three plaster casts, and curtains.

A second drawing of the same subject is in the Staatliche Kunstsammlungen, Weimar (Hofstede de Groot 1915, fig. 28; Valentiner 1930, fig. 7 [as Hoogstraten]; Bernt 1958, fig. 384 [as Maes]). The main difference with the drawing here exhibited is the absence of the plaster casts, the position of the model that now is standing, and the identity of the master who clearly is Rembrandt himself. As Scheidig already suggested (1962, p. 59), both drawings probably reflect a common prototype. In the drawing here exhibited some details are misinterpreted while these are accurately represented in the Weimar version (the man at the very left carries a dagger instead of the more appropriate writing utensils). The Darmstadt version must remain anonymous because it does not have enough in common with Renesse's ascertained drawings to be attributed to him.

This drawing is remarkably similar in composition to a representation of the "Academy" of the Carracci in Düsseldorf (illustrated in Budde 1930, no. 45 [as Bonzi] and by Pevsner, *Academies of Art . . .* , 1940, fig. 7). Seven artists are also grouped in the center and towards the left sketching from a model that is placed at the very right. Here, too, only one pupil, at the very right, is seated on the ground. The Darmstadt drawing (or rather the lost original that it reflects) may therefore partly conform to a pictorial tradition rather than factually represent a session of drawing from life in Rembrandt's studio.

The drawing nevertheless confirms our knowledge of Rembrandt's way of instructing his pupils. Drawings done in the 1640's by different artists of the same male models from slightly different points of view, prove that sessions as here represented actually took place. We also know from

Sandrart that all kinds of people were to be found in Rembrandt's studio, and older artists or amateurs may very well have been among them. Furthermore, the Weimar drawing identifies the master as Rembrandt.

A drawing in the Lugt Collection (Gerson 1968, p. 471, fig. c) is probably a copy of the Darmstadt version.

## JACOB ADRIAENSZ BACKER

### 148 *Reclining Nude*

Kunsthalle, Hamburg *Ill. p. 237*

Black and white chalk on blue-gray paper, 225 × 271 mm.

PROVENANCE E. Harzen (1863).

EXHIBITIONS Leiden 1956, no. 86, fig. 29.

BIBLIOGRAPHY Bauch 1926, p. 106, no. 49; Pauli 1926, no. 22; Lugt 1929, under no. 272; Gerson 1957, pp. 149, 150.

In the 1650's and 60's both Flinck and Backer made numerous studies of nudes in the Italo-Flemish tradition while Rembrandt at the same time sketched nudes in similar attitudes but in an entirely different style. Despite these differences, this common interest may be the result of an exchange of ideas.

In a drawing in Braunschweig, attributed to Backer and to Van den Eeckhout (Flechsig 1925, no. 87), one of the sleeping companions of Iphigenia is represented in almost the same attitude as the nude of the drawing here exhibited, and it is likely that the other artist studied the same model. The subject of *Cimon Discovering Iphigenia and Her Companions* was also painted by Backer (painting in Braunschweig), and it is possible that a study such as the one here exhibited was made in view of a painting of that subject. Flinck made a similar study, also on blue paper (also in Braunschweig, Von Moltke D. 223) which he used for his drawing of *Cimon and Iphigenia* (Louvre, Lugt 1929, pl. 272).

A modified counterproof is in the Albertina, Vienna, according to Bauch.

### 149 *Self-Portrait**

Albertina, Vienna

Black chalk, 143 × 147 mm. *Ill. p. 237*

INSCRIPTION Signed and dated with pen and brown ink: *Jacob ABacker / fecit 1638. / In Vlissingen.*

DATE *1638.*

PROVENANCE Count Van Neale (sale Amsterdam, March 28, 1774); Nyman; Ploos van Amstel (sale March 3, 1800, no. 17); Van der Schley.

BIBLIOGRAPHY Bauch 1926, no. 59, pl. 1; H. van Hall, *Portretten van Nederlandse beeldende kunstenaars*, Amsterdam, 1963, p. 9, no. 11; Benesch 1964–67, no. 177.

This self-portrait of 1638 is Backer's only drawing which shows a marked influence of Rembrandt's black chalk drawings of the early and mid-thirties. To be compared are, among others, *A Team of Horses Resting* from Amsterdam and *Seated Girl in Profile to the Left* from Rotterdam (here exhibited under nos. 95 and 105). The pose, on the other hand, and even the fashionable hair dress have a sophistication and elegance which is reminiscent of Rubens and Van Dyck rather than Rembrandt.

150 *Portrait of a Man*

Lent by The Metropolitan Museum of Art, Rogers Fund, 1947 *Ill. p. 238*

Black and white chalk and touches of red chalk in the face, on gray paper, 237 × 213 mm.

INSCRIPTIONS Annotated at bottom right: *Bakker.*

PROVENANCE H. L. Larsen (sale New York, Parke-Bernet, November 6, 1947, no. 19).

BIBLIOGRAPHY Louise Burroughs, in *Metropolitan Museum of Art Bulletin*, N. S. VII, 1949, p. 282 [illustrated].

Except for the preceding self-portrait, Backer's drawings show little influence from Rembrandt. His studies of portraits and figures on blue paper are, on the other hand, very similar to Flinck's works in the same medium. Since Backer was seven years older than Flinck, and since both were pupils of Lambert Jacobsz in Leeuwarden before coming to Amsterdam, it is likely that Flinck was influenced by Backer and that both learned some of the common features of their art from their teacher who had absorbed Flemish and Italian elements (Rubens, Feti).

On the reverse of this portrait Backer sketched a landscape with black chalk and with brown (pen) and gray ink (brush); it is the only preserved effort of his in this subject matter.

FERDINAND BOL (?)

151 *The Finding of Moses**

Rijksprentenkabinet, Amsterdam

Pen and brown ink, cut in two vertically and pasted together, 170 × 240 mm. *Ill. p. 247*

PROVENANCE C. Hofstede de Groot.

EXHIBITIONS The Hague 1902–03, no. 34; Leiden 1903, no. 20; London, Whitechapel Art Gallery, 1904, no. 131; Leiden 1906, no. 8; Paris 1908, no. 306; Leiden 1916, no. 28 [ca. 1640]; Amsterdam, Rembrandthuis, 1911, Gids p. 7; Amsterdam 1913, no. 6; Paris 1921, no. 50; The Hague 1930, no. 5; Rome 1951, no. 76 [see Bibliography].

BIBLIOGRAPHY HdG 1251; Lippmann III, 40; H. Teding van Berkhout, *25 Teekeningen door Rembrandt uit de Verzameling Dr. C. Hofstede de Groot*, Amsterdam, 1913, no. 3; Hofstede de Groot 1915, p. 87, pl. 26 [by Rembrandt, used by Bol]; O. Hirschmann, in *Cicerone*, IX, 1917, pp. 13–14, fig. 6 [1638–40]; W. von Seidlitz, in *Zeitschrift für bildende Kunst*, N. F. XXVIII, 1917, p. 252 [ca. 1640]; J. Meder, *Die Handzeichnung*, Vienna, 1923, p. 11, fig. 4; Becker 1923, no. 19 [ca. 1640]; Münz 1924, p. 111, fig. 12 [Bol; after 1660]; Valentiner 1925, no. 123 [Rembrandt; ca. 1635]; Kauffmann 1926, pp. 161, 173 [Rembrandt; 1637–38]; Hell 1930, p. 118, note 1 [Rembrandt]; Henkel 1931, p. 81 [by Bol]; Benesch 1935, p. 29 [pupil, corrected by Rembrandt]; Henkel 1942, no. 49, pl. 34 [by Rembrandt; ca. 1640]; Van Regteren Altena 1951, no. 76 [by Rembrandt, used by Bol]; Benesch II, no. 475, fig. 539 [pupil, corrected by Rembrandt; ca. 1635]; Valentiner, in Raleigh 1956, under no. 11 [by Rembrandt, ca. 1635]; Rosenberg 1956, p. 69 [Rembrandt]; Sumowski 1956–57, p. 264 [Rembrandt; beginning 1640's]; Valentiner 1957, p. 56 [by Rembrandt, ca. 1635, used by Bol]; Begemann 1961, p. 28 [Rembrandt]; Sumowski 1961, p. 7 [Bol; 1640's]; Rotermund 1963, p. 89, fig. 71; Slive 1965, no. 373; Clark 1968, p. 50, fig. 39 [Bol].

Although the drawing shows Rembrandt's style of the mid-1630's, its attribution to the artist himself is complicated by the presence of unusual flourishes and by the existence of a painting of the same subject, based on this drawing. Ferdinand Bol's painting in the Peace Palace in The Hague generally is thought to have been executed ca. 1660. The question whether Bol used a drawing of his own made about 25 years earlier, or one of Rembrandt's has not been solved satisfactorily. There are enough similarities with Rembrandt's drawings of ca. 1635 to attribute it to him, and with Bol's drawings of the same time (*Abraham and the Three Angels*, cat. no. 153; *Joseph Interpreting the Prisoners' Dreams*, cat. no. 152) to justify the supposition that Bol made the sketch, concentrating on contours and omitting details. The flourishes and the shapes of hands seem to be in favor of Bol, and so is the consideration that Bol in executing the painting incorporated one element of the drawing which is difficult to read for anyone else but the artist himself, namely, the nudity of the upper parts of the princesses' bodies.

# FERDINAND BOL

**152** *Joseph Interpreting the Prisoners' Dreams*

Kunsthalle, Hamburg  *Ill. p. 245*

Pen and brown ink and brown wash, 167 × 229 mm.

DATE [ca. 1634–36].

PROVENANCE Sir Joshua Reynolds (L. 2364); E. Harzen (1863).

BIBLIOGRAPHY HdG 343 [Rembrandt]; Hofstede de Groot 1915, p. 87, pl. 25 [Rembrandt drawing, used by Bol for painting in Schwerin]; Kruse 1920, p. 18, under no. I, 16 [probably pupil; same hand as drawing in Bayonne]; F. Saxl, in *Kunstchronik*, LVI, 1921, p. 325 [pupil, corrected by Rembrandt]; Münz 1924, pp. 107–08, fig. 4 [Bol]; Valentiner 1925, p. XXVI, reproduced p. XIV [Bol]; Pauli 1926, no. 18 [as Rembrandt?]; Falck 1927, pp. 178, 180 [by Bol after Rembrandt]; Henkel 1931, p. 81 [as by Bol]; Lugt 1933, under no. 1205 and 1950, under no. 478 [by Bol]; Sumowski 1956–57, p. 256 [Bol]; Valentiner 1957, p. 56, fig. 3 [Bol; ca. 1635]; Sumowski 1957–58, p. 237.

The artist represented here the same subject as Rembrandt in his drawing belonging to an anonymous American collection (cat. no. 104). It is also likely that the pupil gave his version of Joseph foretelling the baker his impending death at the same time that the master designed his. Only by assuming this relationship, the compositional and stylistic similarities can be explained. The differences consist mainly in the pupil's greater use of continuously drawn curving lines, for defining contours and also for patterning a background. Furthermore, the hands in this drawing are more stereotyped than those in Rembrandt's drawings.

It is not known when Bol entered Rembrandt's studio, but it is likely that he did so in 1633 or 1634 as Valentiner supposed; neither is it known how long he stayed with Rembrandt. It may have been as long as 1641 because Bol's first signed painting dates from 1642. Especially in the early part of his apprenticeship Bol's drawings very closely resemble those of Rembrandt's of the same period. Some of these are here exhibited (cat. nos. 153–157); others are listed by Lugt, Valentiner and Sumowski.

Bol used this drawing for a painting which corresponds with it in composition and in its details, but it differs considerably in style. This difference may either imply a later date for the painting or, if he executed both at about the same time, a preference for a different style in painting.

**153** *Abraham Visited by the Three Angels*

Museum Boymans-van Beuningen, Rotterdam.  *Ill. p. 246*

Pen and brown ink and brown wash, 185 × 258 mm.

PROVENANCE F. Koenigs, Haarlem.

EXHIBITIONS Rotterdam 1934, no. 111; Leiden 1956, no. 90.

BIBLIOGRAPHY Valentiner 1925, p. XXVI, illustrated p. XV [as by Bol]; Lugt 1933, under no. 1205 [suggests Bol]; Valentiner 1957, p. 60, fig. 20.

The drawing is a study for the painting formerly in the Lanna Collection. In the painting Bol changed the position of Abraham from sitting to kneeling, and gave wings to the angel seated on this side of the table. The drawing belongs to the same period of Bol's career as *Joseph Interpreting the Prisoners' Dreams* and *The Holy Family* (cat. nos. 152 and 154).

**154** *The Holy Family*

Hessisches Landesmuseum, Darmstadt  *Ill. p. 247*

Pen and brown ink and brown wash, 180 × 272 mm.

DATE [ca. 1634–36].

EXHIBITIONS Ingelheim am Rhein 1964, no. 15; Darmstadt 1964, no. 8.

BIBLIOGRAPHY J. Q. van Regteren Altena, in *Maandblad voor beeldende Kunsten*, II, 1925, p. 371, fig. 1; Valentiner 1925, p. XXVI, reproduced p. XII; *Stift und Feder*, 1930, pl. 215; De Bruijn 1932, p. 77; Münz 1952, II, p. 93; Bernt 1957, no. 88.

The position of the Virgin Mary, the Christ Child and the sewing box next to her is, in reverse, so close to Rembrandt's etching *The Holy Family* (B. 62, H. 95) that De Bruijn suggested that the etching perhaps was made by Bol rather than by Rembrandt. It is more likely that Bol based his drawing on a study Rembrandt made for his etching. The relationship between this drawing and Rembrandt's work would then be similar as in the case of Bol's *Joseph Interpreting the Prisoners' Dreams* and Rembrandt's interpretations of the same subject (see cat. no. 152).

The *Holy Family, Joseph Interpreting the Prisoners' Dreams, St. Jerome* (see cat. no. 155), *The Angel Appearing to Hagar* (Amsterdam), and a few other drawings, probably all were made at approximately the same time (1634–36). The entire group precedes studies for paintings of the early 1640's such as *The Three Marys at the Tomb* in Munich, for the painting of 1644 in Copenhagen.

### 155   *Saint Jerome*

Kunsthalle, Hamburg   *Ill. p. 248*

Pen and brown ink and light brown wash, 174 × 246 mm.

DATE [ca. 1634–36].

PROVENANCE E. Harzen (1863).

BIBLIOGRAPHY Lippmann I, no. 132 [as Rembrandt]; HdG 346; Kruse 1920, fig. 8; Pauli 1926, no. 15 [as Rembrandt]; Lugt 1933, under no. 1205 [suggests Bol]; Rotermund 1952, p. 114, pl. 22e [school of Rembrandt]; Benesch IV, under nos. A 23a and A 56 [as pupil].

As in Rembrandt's drawings, the revelation of God is made visible by means of rays of light. The execution of the drawing, however, is not Rembrandt's. As Benesch pointed out, it is by the same hand as another drawing of the same subject, formerly in the Collection Argoutinsky-Dolgoroukoff (B. A56, fig. 1058). Both are so similar to drawings attributed to Ferdinand Bol, such as *Joseph Interpreting the Prisoners' Dreams* (cat. no. 152) and particularly *Abraham and the Three Angels* (cat. no. 153) that it seems justified to consider this *St. Jerome* also a work of his, made ca. 1634–36.

Another drawing of the same saint made much later by Lievens is exhibited under no. 197.

### 156   *Seated Woman*

Staatliche Museen Preussischer Kulturbesitz, Kupferstichkabinett, Berlin   *Ill. p. 249.*

Pen and brown ink and brown wash, 162 × 128 mm.

DATE [ca. 1635–36].

PROVENANCE C. Hofstede de Groot (sale Leipzig, Boerner, November 4, 1931, no. 179, pl. XII [as Rembrandt, portrait of Saskia; according to Valentiner related to Bol].

EXHIBITIONS Amsterdam 1929, no. 1304 a; The Hague 1930, no. 96.

BIBLIOGRAPHY Lugt 1933, under no. 1300 [suggests Bol];

Sumowski 1957–58, p. 224, fig. 19 [as *Minerva* by Bol, based on Rembrandt].

This drawing is probably a study for a portrait of a young lady, possibly in the role of Minerva, or Esther, or another historical figure, although the headgear may also be part of a fashionable embellishment. For the position of the figure Bol was visibly influenced by works of Rembrandt of the years 1634–35 (*The Great Jewish Bride*, 1635; *Maria Bockenolle*, Boston, 1634; *Saskia* (?) *Seated in an Armchair*, black chalk drawing, Hamburg, Benesch 428, formerly called Bol, ca. 1633). The manner of drawing is reminiscent of Rembrandt's studies of *Saskia in Bed* and related drawings of the mid-thirties.

Bol made a second drawing of the same subject, of somewhat lesser quality and in a wide instead of high format (Berlin KdZ 1102); in that drawing the figure is clearly identified as Minerva by the shield behind her and musical instruments on the table next to her. The figure represented in both drawings, is also known from a painting, now at Wildenstein's, New York (exhibition Montreal-Toronto 1969, no. 23). A similar woman is also found in a drawing by Van den Eeckhout of 1643 in Dublin (Sumowski 1962, fig. 6); she is the mirror image of the figure in the drawing here exhibited.

Also related is the study of a *Woman in an Armchair* in the Hermitage which may be attributed to Bol (Benesch 1964 p. 141, fig. 38 [as Rembrandt]).

### 157   *Woman before a Mirror*

Biblioteca Nacional, Madrid   *Ill. p. 248*

Black chalk, corrected with white, 235 × 177 mm.

DATE [ca. 1649].

PROVENANCE Vicente Izquierdo.

BIBLIOGRAPHY Ángel M. de Barcia, *Catálogo de la colección de Dibujos originales de la Biblioteca Nacional*, Madrid, 1906, pp. 720–21, no. 8712 [as Rembrandt]; E. Lafuente Ferrari, in *Grabados y dibujos de Rembrandt en la Biblioteca Nacional* [*Exhibition Catalogue*], Madrid, 1934, p. 26 [as not by Rembrandt]; Sumowski 1965, p. 123, no. 14 [as Bol; acc. to Lugt study for painting of 1649 in Philips Collection, Eindhoven]; Wegner 1966–67, p. 31, under no. 53 [as Bol].

Frits Lugt was the first to recognize that this drawing is a study by Ferdinand Bol for his painting known as *The Pearl Necklace*, formerly in Lord Northbrook's Collection and since about 1926 in the Philips Collection in Eindhoven. This painting (reproduced by Bernt 1948, I, pl. 101) differs from the drawing mainly in the clothing of the woman, who is more elegantly dressed and who is adjusting a string of pearls. In the painting the man is seated instead of standing near a chair, while the composition extends farther to the right.

The painting is dated 1649 and seems to be a double portrait. It is therefore likely that the drawing was made in connection with a commissioned painting and not a long time in advance. The drawing thus shows that Bol as late as 1649 still based himself on a type of black chalk drawing which was developed by Rembrandt in the early 1640's. Even the paper is similar to that used by Rembrandt for black chalk studies. Bol, therefore, probably remained influenced by Rembrandt after he had left his studio.

Similar to this *Woman before a Mirror* is the *Portrait of a Standing Man* in Berlin (KdZ 5313), also a black chalk study for a painting (Hermitage, Leningrad; ca. 1650).

## ANTHONIE VAN BORSSUM
### 158 *Farm Buildings*
Rijksprentenkabinet, Amsterdam

Pen and brown ink, 99 × 227 mm. *Ill. p. 271*

INSCRIPTIONS Signed [?] in monogram at bottom right: *AVB . . . 66*[?]; and annotated: *Rembrandt*.

PROVENANCE Jacob de Vos Jbzn (L. 1450; sale May 22, 1883, no. 405 [as Rembrandt]).

BIBLIOGRAPHY Henkel 1942, p. 66, no. 2, pl. 97.

Anthonie van Borssum (1629/30–1677) is best known as a spirited draughtsman of landscapes which he often enlivened with watercolors. His paintings, sometimes resembling works of Hobbema, often stand out by their unorthodox compositions and lighting. He probably was in Rembrandt's studio between the years 1645–1650, when he was 25 to 30 years old.

This and similar drawings (Amsterdam, Henkel 1942, nos. 1 and 4; British Museum, Hind 1915, no. 3) were probably made by Van Borssum early in his career since they reflect the style of Rembrandt's landscape drawings and etchings of that time.

Henkel already pointed out the similarity between this drawing and Rembrandt's etching *Cottage with a White Paling* which he then thought to date from 1642. These similarities are confirmed by the preliminary drawing which was unknown to Henkel and by the recently established date of 1648 for the etching (see cat. no. 119).

### 159 *View of Soest*
Amsterdams Historisch Museum (Collection Fodor)

Pen and brown ink and watercolor, 159 × 237 mm. *Ill. p. 271*

PROVENANCE H. van Eyl Sluiter? (inscription on reverse); sale Amsterdam, Coll. F. A. v. S. and others, June 11, 1912, no. 30; C. Hofstede de Groot (L. 561; sale Leipzig, Boerner, November 4, 1931, no. 30); A. W. M. Mensing (sale Amsterdam April 27–29, 1937, no. 76).

EXHIBITIONS Leiden 1916, no. 18; Jerusalem 1960, no. 14; Beograd/Zagreb 1960, no. 14; Brussels/Hamburg 1961, no. 126; Budapest 1962.

BIBLIOGRAPHY O. Hirschmann, in *Cicerone*, IX, 1917, p. 210; Becker 1923, no. 2; *Catalogue Museum Fodor 1863–1938* (Teekeningen keuze uit aanwinsten 1932–1937), no. 38; J. W. Niemeijer, "Varia topografica, II, Antonie van Borssums gezichten te Soest", *Oud-Holland*, LXXVII, 1962, pp. 62–75, fig. 1.

As Niemeijer pointed out, this rather elegant country house with a small tower probably was situated in the village of Soest near Utrecht. Somewhat later Van Borssum made a second drawing of the same motif from a different point of view. He also painted it (Metropolitan Museum of Art, Friedsam Collection, as Paul Potter).

### 160 *Mill and Boat-Lift near a Canal*
Rijksprentenkabinet, Amsterdam *Ill. p. 272*

Pen and brown ink over traces of black chalk and light gray, green, yellow, and red watercolor, 206 × 335 mm.

INSCRIPTIONS Signed at bottom right: *AVBorssom*.

PROVENANCE Abr. van Broyel (sale October 30, 1759, no. 71); C. Ploos van Amstel (L. 2034; sale March 3, 1800, no. 3); Jac. de Vos Sr. (sale October 30, 1833, no. 3); Six van Hillegom (sale July 7, 1845, Pf. A no. 4); J. G. Verstolk van Soelen (sale March 22, 1847, no. 4); G. Leembruggen Jr. (sale March 5, 1866, no. 102); Jacob de Vos Jbzn (L. 1450; sale May 22, 1883, no. 66).

EXHIBITIONS London 1929, no. 667.

BIBLIOGRAPHY E. W. Moes, *Oude teekeningen van de Hol-*

landsche en Vlaamsche school in het Rijksprentenkabinet te Amsterdam, 's-Gravenhage, 1905–06, pl. 16; Henkel 1942, p. 68, no. 10, pl. 102.

The boat-lift, rarely found outside Holland, allows the transfer of a boat from the high-level canal in the foreground to the lower polder beyond the dike. The narrow stretch of water connecting the mill with the canal receives the water from the polder when the mill pumps it out.

In contrast to the preceding drawing, this one shows hardly any relationship with Rembrandt's art. It is a characteristic example of the type of finished, self-contained watercolors as Van Borssum developed it. His drawings of this type were very influential in the eighteenth century and were often imitated, particularly by Erkelens.

## LAMBERT DOOMER

### 161 *The "Hoenderpoort" and the Belvedere in Nijmegen*

Museum Boymans-van Beuningen, Rotterdam.

Pen and brown ink and brown and gray wash, 205 × 317 mm. *Ill. p. 256*

INSCRIPTIONS Inscribed on the reverse: *Belvedere ende hoenderpoort te Niemegen.*

PROVENANCE F. Koenigs, Haarlem.

EXHIBITIONS Paris 1952, no. 55.

BIBLIOGRAPHY Henkel 1942, p. 71, under no. 9; Brussels/ Hamburg 1961, under no. 100.

Lambert Doomer (1622/23–1700) is the only one of Rembrandt's pupils who specialized as a topographer, and who introduced a Rembrandtesque and thereby picturesque element into the tradition of linear precision as developed by Hoefnagel, Merian and Hollar. He made numerous drawings on his travels along the Rhine and in France, and made variations of his drawings after his return to Amsterdam. His paintings which are few in number, show less influence from Rembrandt than his free drawings of which this "Hoenderpoort" is one of the best examples.

The buildings were part of the "Valkhof", the castle built by Charles the Great on the high embankment of the river Waal near Nÿmegen. The tall tower was renamed Belvedere by Alexander Farnese and received the circular balustrade only in 1646–49. Doomer's drawing includes the balustrade, and thus must have been made after 1649. The drawing is particularly sketchy and free, and in that respect displays a greater similarity to Rembrandt's landscapes than most other drawings of Doomer.

The artist represented the same buildings in a less sketchy and more definitive drawing (pen and brown ink, brown and gray and a little blue wash; Amsterdam). A third, finished but less accomplished version is in the Museum in Nijmegen; a fourth view of the Belvedere in the late Clifford Duits Collection, London (Leiden 1956, no. 101).

### 162 *The Well and Fortress at Tal Ehrenbreitstein*

The Pierpont Morgan Library, New York

Pen and brown ink and brown and gray wash, 232 × 362 mm. *Ill. p. 256*

INSCRIPTIONS Inscribed on the reverse: *de tide bron toe Kobelens.*

PROVENANCE Lord Palmerston; C. Fairfax Murray; J. Pierpont Morgan.

EXHIBITIONS New York, The Pierpont Morgan Library, *Landscape Drawings and Watercolors Bruegel to Cézanne*, 1953, no. 76; Raleigh 1956, no. 15.

BIBLIOGRAPHY C. Hofstede de Groot and W. Spies, "Die Rheinlandschaften von Lambert Doomer", *Wallraf-Richartz Jahrbuch*, III–IV, 1926–27, p. 198 [*re* site and Rotterdam version].

As Dattenberg and A. Verbeek established, Lambert Doomer probably traveled from 1658 to 1660 along the Rhine to Switzerland and back to Holland, again along the Rhine. The present drawing represents in the distance Fort Ehrenbreitstein on the Rhine, in the foreground a well, probably a mineral water well still in demand today, in Tal Ehrenbreitstein at the foot of the fortress.

At the sites Doomer often made sketchy drawings with pen and brown wash and sometimes a little color. In many instances he later repeated these drawings, introducing details and figures, and finishing them carefully with pen and brush and gray and brown ink. In the rather freely drawn sketches, Doomer shows his indebtedness to Rembrandt, especially in the pen lines. A second version of the present drawing in the Museum Boymans-van Beuningen, Rotterdam, is probably a later variant.

As a topographer Doomer is part of the long tradition of which Georg Hoefnagel and Wenzel Hollar were outstanding representatives. He modified this tradition by showing a greater interest than his predecessors in single buildings and other structures, and in the purely rural aspect of the places he visited.

## GERARD DOU

**163** *An Elderly Man Sharpening His Pen*

Amsterdams Historisch Museum (Collection Fodor)

Black chalk, 238 × 183 mm. *Ill. p. 236*

INSCRIPTIONS Annotated at bottom right: *G. Dou.*

DATE [ca. 1628–31].

PROVENANCE Sybrand Feitama, Amsterdam (sale October 16, 1758); Goll van Franckenstein (sale July 1, 1833); Ploos van Amstel; Baron J. G. Verstolk van Soelen (sale March 22, 1847); C. J. Fodor, Amsterdam.

EXHIBITIONS Amsterdam, Museum Fodor, *Klassieke Hollandsche teekenaars*, 1932, no. 19; Cologne/Bremen 1955, no. 25; Warsaw 1956, no. 49, pl. 24; Leiden 1956, no. 104, pl. 30; Washington, D.C. et al. 1958–59, no. 76; Jerusalem 1960, no. 22; Beograd/Zagreb 1960, no. 22; Brussels/Hamburg 1961, no. 70; Budapest 1962; Amsterdam 1963, no. 8.

BIBLIOGRAPHY *Beschrijving der Schilderijen, Teekeningen etc. in het Museum Fodor te Amsterdam*, Amsterdam, 1863, p. 28, no. 46; J. H. J. Mellaart, *Dutch Drawings of the Seventeenth Century*, London, 1926, p. 34, no. 57 [illustrated]; Henkel 1931, p. 90; Gerson 1957, p. 122; Wegner 1957, under no. 40 [on similarity with B. 13]; Van Gelder 1958, p. 34, no. 85 [illustrated]; Trautscholdt 1958, p. 367; Trautscholdt 1967, p. 126.

Gerard Dou, who in 1628 came to Rembrandt as a pupil, also painted the same subject of an old man sharpening his pen, although the model is different (two versions, Hannover and formerly Dr. Simon Collection, ca. 1628–31). If the traditional attribution of this drawing is correct, Dou probably made it shortly after he entered Rembrandt's studio in 1628. Around 1635 Rembrandt himself made a drawing of a young man sharpening his pen (B. 263, fig. 288) stressing the contrasts between the light of the candle and the shadows at the side of the table and behind the figure rather than carefully modeling the figure as Dou did in this drawing.

The figure of the old man and his immediate surroundings which are carefully drawn with rather hard black chalk (table top and book, chair, objects above the table to the left) differ so much from the other objects which are broadly and freely drawn (the curtain, side of table and objects in front of it) that these latter parts seem to have been added by another artist. Since these additions are so similar to black chalk drawings of Rembrandt (B. 6ᵛᵒ, 12, 13, 31 and also the other beggars, 38 and others), it seems justified to suggest that Rembrandt added these details.

The drawing is not arched at the top, but instead the corners have been drawn, probably in the eighteenth century.

## GERBRAND VAN DEN EECKHOUT

**164** *Gideon and the Angel*

Herzog-Anton-Ulrich Museum, Braunschweig *Ill. p. 243*

Pen and brown ink and gray wash, 175 × 152 mm.

INSCRIPTIONS Annotated at bottom left: *G. v E.*

DATE [ca. 1642].

EXHIBITIONS Leiden 1956, no. 108, fig. 33; Ingelheim am Rhein 1964, no. 69.

BIBLIOGRAPHY Flechsig 1925, no. 94; Henkel 1931, pp. 83–84; Sumowski 1957–58, p. 237; Sumowski 1962, p. 11, fig. 1.

This is the earliest drawing by Van den Eeckhout which can be dated with certainty. Since it is a study for the painting of the same subject dated 1642 (or 1640?) in the Otto J. H. Campe Collection in Hamburg (ex-Lippmann coll.; *Exhibition Toronto* 1969, no. 44), it must have been made in that year or shortly before. In its composition, in its motifs such as the tower in the distance, and in its mannered lineation, the drawing is greatly dependent on Lastman rather than on Rembrandt. It is the earliest example of Eeckhout's drawings in the Lastman style (see also following drawing). Probably for the same painting the artist made a second drawing, in the same style, and now also in Braunschweig (pen and brown and gray wash, 161 × 179 mm.). Entirely different in style is a finished and colored drawing of the same subject Van den Eeckhout probably made about 1647 in connection with a painting of that year (drawing in London, Hind 1; painting in Brera, Milan). A chalk study for this subject is on the reverse of Van den Eeckhout's *Dismissal of Hagar* in the Teyler Museum, Haarlem.

**165** *Dismissal of Hagar*

Staatliche Museen Preussischer Kulturbesitz, Kupferstichkabinett, Berlin

Pen and brown ink over traces of black chalk, 162 × 186 mm. *Ill. p. 243*

INSCRIPTIONS Signed at bottom right: *Eechout. fᵉ*

DATE [ca. 1642–43].

PROVENANCE H. Oppenheimer (sale London, July 13, 1936, no. 242).

BIBLIOGRAPHY R. Hamann, in *Marburger Jahrbuch für Kunstwissenschaft*, VIII/IX, 1936, p. 487, fig. 23; Bernt 1957, no. 206; Trautscholdt 1958, p. 367; Sumowski 1962, p. 11 [beginning of the 1640's].

This drawing is one of the most accomplished of those Van den Eeckhout made in the Lastman style. It does not have much in common with any of the drawings of the earlier forties that Rembrandt made of this subject; only the architecture at the right is based on a work of Rembrandt's, namely his etching of the same subject of 1637 (H. 149). The figures of Abraham, Hagar, and Ishmael, as well as the bridge, tree and peacock are transformations of similar motifs in Lastman's painting of 1612, which by then had been painted about thirty years ago.

Van den Eeckhout painted the same subject in 1666 (if attribution and date of the painting formerly in the Stroganoff collection are correct) and incorporated features of the drawing in the attitude of the figures and the building at the right. Since Van den Eeckhout seems to have been able to adapt to different styles and to switch from one to the other without any difficulty, it remains to be established, whether the artist reverted in 1666 to a drawing he had made long ago, or whether he applied the Lastman style in a drawing as late as in or about 1666.

## 166  *David's Promise to Bathsheba*

The Metropolitan Museum of Art, Gift of Robert Lehman, 1941

Pen and brown ink and, over it, brown wash and black and red chalk, 188 × 270 mm.  *Ill. p. 242*
DATE [ca. 1646?].

PROVENANCE Valerius Röver (L. 2984c); Goll van Franckenstein (L. 2987); D. Marshag (sale Amsterdam, October 30, 1775, Pf. M, no. 792); Jacob de Vos Jbzn (L. 1450; sale Amsterdam, May 22–24, 1883, no. 169); V. Everit Macy (sale New York, American Art Association, January 6–8, 1938, no. 80 [illustrated]); Robert Lehman, New York.

BIBLIOGRAPHY Sumowski 1962, p. 17, fig. 10 [study for painting in Hannover]; J. Bean, *100 European Drawings in the Metropolitan Museum of Art*, New York [1964], no. 91 [represents I Kings 1:15–20, illustrated].

Probably the moment is represented when King David is saying: "Assuredly Solomon thy son shall reign after me, and he shall sit upon my throne in my stead; even so will I certainly do this day". After finishing his statement, Bathsheba "bowed with her face to the earth and did reverence to the King . . ." (I Kings 1:30–31). The prophet Nathan is standing behind Bathsheba, and King David's young maid Abishag is standing near a column.

The drawing corresponds closely with the painting of 1646 in the Museum in Hannover (on loan from Siecke Collection). Although Sumowski considered the drawing a study for the painting, the degree of finish makes it more likely that Eeckhout designed it as an independent drawing. Another representation of the same episode in Vienna, also by Van den Eeckhout and drawn in the same manner, is probably also a finished, independent drawing (Schönbrunner/Meder no. 783).

## 167  *The Dreamer*

Goldschmidt Collection

Brush and brown ink, 141 × 113 mm.  *Ill. p. 244*
DATE [ca. 1650–60?].

PROVENANCE Jacob de Vos Jbzn (L. 1450; sale Amsterdam, May 22–24, 1883, lot 162); Pieter Langerhuizen Lzn (L. 2095; sale Amsterdam, April 29–May 2, 1919, lot 257, pl. 7).

BIBLIOGRAPHY [*Sale Catalogue Coll. C. R. Rudolf*], Sotheby's, May 21, 1963, under no. 33.

This brush drawing, remarkably similar in technique and mood to works of Fragonard and other eighteenth-century French artists, is one of a group of studies of figures and animals that probably present the most attractive and at the same time most puzzling aspects of Van den Eeckhout's *oeuvre*. Some drawings, especially the *Boy Reading* in the Musée Cognacq-Jay, Paris, until very recently were considered to be by Fragonard. In favor of an attribution to Van den Eeckhout, however, is the tradition that goes back to Ploos van Amstel, who in the second half of the eighteenth century, considered some of them to be by the Dutch artist. No firm connecting link with the artist's established work as yet has been found.

A larger variant of this drawing is in the Walter C. Baker Collection, New York (8 1/16 × 5 3/4 inches; ex-Coll. Mouriau, De Vos, Heseltine, Rudolf). Other drawings of this type are in Amsterdam (*Boy Sleeping on the Ground; Woman Spinning*), Vienna (*Boy Leaning on a Chair*), London (British Museum, *Seated Boy*), Paris (F. Lugt, *Studies of Dogs*), and elsewhere. They probably date from the 1650's.

**168**  *Christ and the Woman Taken in Adultery*

The Art Institute of Chicago, Gift of the Print and Drawing Club  *Ill. p. 244*

Pen and brown ink and brown wash, 145 × 198 mm.

INSCRIPTIONS Inscribed at bottom center: *'t vrouwtie in overspel.*

DATE [ca. 1664].

PROVENANCE Thomas Agnew and Sons, London (1920); C. Hofstede de Groot (L. 561; sale Leipzig, Boerner, November 4, 1931, no. 130, pl. IX [as Philips Koninck]).

EXHIBITIONS The Hague 1930, III, no. 64; Chicago, The Art Institute, *Century of Progress Exhibitions*, 1933, no. 811 [as Philips Koninck]; Chicago 1935–36, no. 55 [as Philips Koninck].

BIBLIOGRAPHY Becker 1923, no. 22, pl. 22 [as Philips Koninck]; Lugt 1933, under no. 1225 [as Van den Eeckhout]; Gerson 1936, no. Z. LXXV [closer to Van den Eeckhout].

The drawing is a study for the painting of 1664 in the Rijksmuseum, Amsterdam. The group of elders with the woman to the right of the composition and the figure of Christ are found again in the painting, but in reverse; the figure at the very right in the drawing has been taken over in the painting in that same place. The only second study for the painting known, in Copenhagen (Sumowski 1962, fig. 38), is farther removed from the painting.

This drawing is one of the most distinguished examples of a group of drawings made by Van den Eeckhout in a very Rembrandtesque style. To this group, already reconstructed by Lugt in 1933, belongs also the series of ten representations of scenes from the life of Joseph. Except for the last drawing of the series (Lugt 1933, no. 1225) these are all retouched with the brush and gray ink, a circumstance which needs to be taken into consideration when this phase of Van den Eeckhout's work is studied. Since another drawing of this group, *Peter and John at the Gate of the Temple*, is a study for the painting of that subject of 1666 (Ex-Lonsdale Coll.; cf. Byam Shaw, *Old Master Drawings*, XIII, 1938/39, pp. 18–20), the artist seems to have favored this style for religious studies for paintings around the years 1664–66. It surprises that the artist worked in a Lastman tradition when in Rembrandt's studio, and in Rembrandt's style long after he had become an independent artist.

## BARENT FABRITIUS (?)

**169**  *The Satyr and the Peasants*

The Art Institute of Chicago, Charles Deering Collection

Pen and brush and brown ink and brown wash, 182 × 165 mm.  *Ill. p. 255*

PROVENANCE Charles, Earl of Shrewsbury; Charles Deering (L. 516).

EXHIBITIONS Chicago 1935/36, no. 28 [as Rembrandt].

BIBLIOGRAPHY D. C. Rich, in *The Art Institute of Chicago Bulletin*, XXIII, no. 4, 1929, pp. 39–40 [as Rembrandt, 1634 or 35 according to Valentiner]; W. R. Valentiner, in *Art Bulletin*, XIV, 1932, p. 239 [as Rembrandt]; Benesch IV, no. A 31, fig. 1031 [as Rembrandt?; if so, ca. 1640–42]; Pont 1958, pp. 79, 81 82, 124, no. 7, fig. 35 [as Fabritius, ca. 1652–62]; Sumowski 1959, pp. 288, 293; Sumowski 1961, p. 24.

The subject of the satyr's surprise about man's blowing hot and cold, taken from Aesop's *Fables*, was often represented by pupils of Rembrandt. Paintings of this subject are attributed to Van den Eeckhout, Barent Fabritius, Constantijn van Renesse, and Salomon Koninck, while Barent Fabritius made at least one drawing of the subject (Rotterdam; Pont fig. 34), Samuel van Hoogstraten and Gerbrand van den Eeckhout each probably one (Rotterdam and Hamburg, Kruse 1920, fig. 52 and Sumowski 1962, fig. 20). For the subject, see the discussion of the painting from Hartford, here exhibited under no. 54.

Although the drawing has some compositional features in common with the drawing in Rotterdam, its attribution to Fabritius proposed by Gudlaugsson and Pont is not easily acceptable. The similarities with his paintings of this subject in Hartford and Bergamo are not compelling, but an attribution to any other pupil of Rembrandt's does not seem justifiable either. The closest parallel in Fabritius' work is *The Adoration of the Shepherds* (cat. no. 170), especially in the pen lines. The drawing has features in common with genre scenes by Rembrandt of the 1640's and even with the later *Garden of an Inn*, dated by Benesch ca. 1654–56 (Rijksprentenkabinet, Amsterdam; B. 1158, fig. 1381). If the drawing is by Barent Fabritius, it is closer to Rembrandt's work than anything else he made.

## BARENT FABRITIUS

**170** *Adoration of the Shepherds*

Museum Boymans-van Beuningen, Rotterdam

Pen and brown ink and brown and blue wash, with touches of red chalk, 244 × 240 mm. *Ill. p. 255*

DATE [ca. 1660–67?].

PROVENANCE F. Koenigs, Haarlem.

EXHIBITIONS Leiden 1956, no. 118.

BIBLIOGRAPHY Valentiner 1932, p. 240, fig. 50; Pont 1958, pp. 90, 91, 123, no. 3, fig. 32; MacLaren 1960, p. 124; Sumowski 1959, pp. 288, 293.

In the figures of Joseph and the Virgin Mary, and in the placement of shepherds in an opening at the right, the drawing is similar to Barent Fabritius's painting of the same subject dated 1667 in the National Gallery, London. This relationship, combined with a similarity in the pen lines existing between this drawing and some certainly by Barent Fabritius (*Judas Returning the Thirty Pieces of Silver*, Louvre), confirm the attribution of the drawing to Barent Fabritius first suggested by Valentiner. The date of 1667 which was only found on the painting in 1959 during a cleaning could indicate that the drawing was made as late as that year.

## GOVERT FLINCK

**171** *Seated Female Nude*

Rijksprentenkabinet, Amsterdam  *Ill. p. 240*

Black chalk heightened with white on blue paper, 315 × 265 mm.

INSCRIPTIONS Signed and dated at bottom right: *G. Flinck f. 1637* [or *1647?*].

DATE 1637(?).

PROVENANCE H. Cremers, The Hague.

EXHIBITIONS Brussels/Hamburg 1961, no. 72 [*1647* more likely than *1637*].

BIBLIOGRAPHY Kleinmann I, no. 44; Henkel 1942, p. 82, no. 1, pl. 137 [dated 1637]; Von Moltke 1965, p. 46 [accepts 1637] and no. D. 203 [1647 more likely].

One of Flinck's most accomplished academic studies of a female model, it is very similar to the work of Jacob Backer as is brought out by a comparison for instance with the *Reclining Nude* from Hamburg (cat. no. 148). Flinck and Backer had both been pupils of Lambert Jacobsz (ca. 1592–1637) in Leeuwarden before coming to Amsterdam. Similar nudes and similar draperies are found in Backer's etchings of ca. 1630 (*The Senses*). There is therefore no reason to interpret the date on this drawing as 1647 instead of 1637, the more since the third digit appears to be a 3. A second study of a nude quite similar to the present one also seems to be dated 1637 (British Museum, Hind 1915, no. 1). Flinck probably painted in 1638 in the Rembrandtesque style of *Isaac Blessing Jacob* while simultaneously with or shortly after having made drawings in the Backer style.

**172** *Study of a Pollard Willow*

Museum Boymans-van Beuningen, Rotterdam

Pen and brown ink, 187 × 193 mm. *Ill. p. 239*

INSCRIPTIONS Signed and dated at bottom right: *G. flinck.f 1642.*

DATE *1642*

PROVENANCE Pitcairn Knowles (sale Amsterdam, June 25–26, 1895, no. 233).

EXHIBITIONS Dijon 1950, no. 57; Leiden 1956, no. 121; Cleves 1965, no. 72.

BIBLIOGRAPHY Jaarverslag Museum Boymans, 1932, p. 5 [illustrated]; Lugt 1933, under no. 1340; Henkel 1942, p. 82, under no. 2; Von Moltke 1965, no. D 226 [illustrated].

Only three landscape drawings by Flinck are known, and all three of them were made in 1642. Although the pen lines show a certain similarity with Rembrandt's drawings, they are more directly molded on the work of an earlier generation (Jan Pynas, Cornelis Vroom). The willow itself with its somewhat anthropomorphic deformations is reminiscent of similar studies of Jacques de Gheyn. Since Flinck signed all three drawings, he must have considered them as finished works of art.

Flinck, who painted landscapes only as backgrounds to portraits and settings for historical scenes, included trees with similar foliage and branches in his *Portrait of a Boy* of 1640 (see cat. no. 62) and the double portrait of *Dirck Graswinckel and Geertruyt van Loon* of 1646 (Rotterdam).

**173** *Young Boy Asleep*

Coll. F. Lugt, Institut Néerlandais, Paris  *Ill. p. 239*

Pen and brown ink and brown wash, 163 × 147 mm.

INSCRIPTIONS Signed and dated at bottom left:[ ƒ ] linck ƒ 1643: ; annotated with pencil on the reverse: flinck.

DATE 1643.

PROVENANCE Probably D. de Jong Azn. (sale Rotterdam, March 26, 1810, Pf. K, no. 25); probably Gerrit Muller (sale Amsterdam, April 2, 1827, Pf. C, no. 51); Obach & Co., London (1908); C. Hofstede de Groot (L. 561; sale Leipzig, Boerner, November 4, 1931, no. 91); H. Tietje, Amsterdam; P. Cassirer, Amsterdam; B. Houthakker, Amsterdam.

EXHIBITIONS Leiden 1916, no. 50; The Hague 1930, no. 50; Amsterdam 1936, no. 175; Amsterdam, B. Houthakker, *Dessins*, 1959, no. 15 [illustrated]; Cleves 1965, no. 70.

BIBLIOGRAPHY A. M. Hind, in *Vasari Society*, 1st Series, Part V, 1909–10, no. 25; C. Hofstede de Groot, in U. Thieme and F. Becker, *Allgemeines Lexikon der Bildenden Künstler*, XII, 1916, p. 100; O. Hirschmann, in *Cicerone*, IX, 1917, p. 205, fig. 6; Becker 1923, no. 12; Henkel 1931, p. 80; J. Byam Shaw, in *Old Master Drawings*, VIII, 1933, p. 44; Henkel 1942, p. 9, under no. 22; Gerson 1957, p. 123; Trautscholdt 1958, p. 368; Von Moltke 1965, p. 52 and no. D. 84, pl. 65 [probably identical with Von Moltke D. 85 and D. 86]; Gerson 1968, p. 471 [illustrated].

This is the only signed drawing by Govert Flinck in a Rembrandtesque style. In the pen lines and also, although to a lesser extent, in the brushstrokes, it is modeled upon the example of Rembrandt's figure studies from nature from the second half of the thirties. There is an affinity to Rembrandt's *Study of a Sleeping Child* (Amsterdam, B. 379, Henkel 22) which is more than similarity of motif. The Flinck drawing differs from Rembrandt's studies in a greater looseness of form and a preference for flowing lines and little curlicues. Since it is signed and dated, it should serve as a point of reference for further attributions which, however, have not been made.

## 174 *Portrait of a Young Man Standing*

Bernard Houthakker, Amsterdam

Black chalk heightened with white on blue paper, 390 × 240 mm. *Ill. p. 240*

DATE [ca. 1646].

EXHIBITIONS Amsterdam, B. Houthakker, 1956, no. 38 [as Backer]; Amsterdam, Rijksprentenkabinet, *De Verzameling van Bernard Houthakker*, 1964, no. 31, fig. 14 [as Flinck]; Cleves 1965, no. 64 [illustrated].

BIBLIOGRAPHY Von Moltke 1965, no. D. 153, pl. 63; Jan Lauts, *Staatliche Kunsthalle Karlsruhe, Katalog alte Meister*, Karlsruhe 1966, under no. 2479.

This drawing is one of the few that can be recognized as a study for a portrait signed and dated by Flinck and thus is a welcome point of reference for distinguishing between Backer's and Flinck's drawings of this type. The painting for which Flinck made this study is a *Portrait of a Couple*, dated 1646, in the museum in Karlsruhe.

## GOVERT FLINCK (?)

### 175 *Isaac Blessing Jacob*

Museum Boymans-van Beuningen, Rotterdam

Red over black chalk, and gray-brown wash, 192 × 182 mm. *Ill. p. 241*

PROVENANCE C. Fairfax Murray (sale London, January 30, 1920, no. 98); Parsons & Sons, London (Cat. 38, 1921, no. 131); F. Koenigs, Haarlem.

EXHIBITIONS London 1929, no. 652; Brussels 1937/38, no. 98; Rotterdam 1938, no. 266; Braunschweig 1948, no. 8; Leiden 1956, no. 119; Brussels/Hamburg 1961, no. 71; Cleves 1965, no. 48.

BIBLIOGRAPHY Hofstede de Groot 1929, p. 144 [probably copy after painting]; Henkel 1931, pp. 80, 126, pl. LXII [probably study for painting]; Lugt 1933, under no. 1314 [study for painting; best available document for early Flinck drawings]; Bernt 1957, no. 231; Trautscholdt 1958, p. 367 [generally considered as by Flinck]; Von Moltke 1965, pp. 17, 18, 170, no. D 4 [questions Flinck's authorship]; Sumowski 1967, p. 339, fig. 1 [as by Flinck].

The drawing corresponds in its composition and in its details with the painting of the same subject in the Rijksmuseum, Amsterdam, which on the basis of a former signature and date always is considered as Govert Flinck's earliest painting, made in 1638 under direct influence of Rembrandt. In contrast to the painting, the drawing shows hardly any similarity with Rembrandt's drawings. Since it is also without parallel in Flinck's *oeuvre*, its authorship needs to be reviewed. Although in certain details, particularly the draperies on the bed, the drawing seems to be a study for the painting, it perhaps is a copy after it, as Hofstede de Groot thought in 1929.

In technique and style the Rotterdam drawing has much in common with *Granida and Daiphilo* in Braunschweig (Flechsig 1925, no. 95). That drawing, also sketched with red over black chalk and washed with brown ink, is signed or annotated *G.v. Eekhout* and may very well be by him. If so, it probably dates from the 1650's (Sumowski 1962, p. 18). The Rotterdam drawing could date from the same period and may even have been made by the same artist— Gerbrand van den Eeckhout.

## ABRAHAM FURNERIUS (?)

### 176 *Tower of the Westerkerk in Amsterdam*

Amsterdams Historisch Museum (Collection Fodor) *Ill. p. 267*

Pen and brown ink and brown wash, 189 × 147 mm.

INSCRIPTIONS Annotated in the seventeenth century at bottom left: *Westerkerks Tooren / a Amsterdam;* and in the eighteenth century: *Rembrand.*

DATE [ca. 1650–60?].

PROVENANCE J. de Groot (sale December 10, 1804); W. Baartz, Rotterdam (sale Rotterdam, June 6–8, 1860, no. 96); C. J. Fodor, Amsterdam.

EXHIBITIONS Amsterdam, Oude Mannenhuis, *Historische tentoonstelling van Amsterdam 1876*, 1876, no. 1294; Amsterdam, *Historische tentoonstelling*, 1925, no. 617; Amsterdam, Rijksprentenkabinet, 1930; Amsterdam 1932, no. 288 [ca. 1646]; Haarlem 1951, no. 168; Utrecht, Centraal Museum Utrecht, *Nederlandse architectuur schilders 1600–1900*, 1953, no. 131; Cologne/Bremen 1955, no. 68 [illustrated on cover]; Warsaw 1956, no. 32 pl. 16; Rotterdam/Amsterdam 1956, no. 143; Jerusalem 1960; Beograd/Zagreb 1960, no. 61; Budapest 1962; Amsterdam 1963, no. 30; Ingelheim am Rhein 1964, no. 65, pl. XII.

BIBLIOGRAPHY *Beschrijving der schilderijen, teekeningen, etc. in het Museum Fodor te Amsterdam*, Amsterdam, 1863, no. 172; Lippmann III, 86; Kleinmann III, 4; HdG 1230; Lugt 1920, pp. 11–12, fig. 5 [identifies point of view; by Rembrandt, ca. 1640–50]; J. Q. van Regteren Altena, in *Maanblad voor beeldende Kunsten*, II, 1925, pp. 170–73 [illustrated; questions Rembrandt's authorship; Abraham Furnerius?]; J. Poortenaar, *Rembrandt teekeningen*, Naarden, 1943, no. 67; Benesch VI, no. A 62, fig. 1642 [pupil; 1650's]; Rosenberg 1959, p. 117 [Rembrandt; early 1650's]; Van Gelder 1961, p. 150 [drawing judged too harshly by Benesch]; Slive 1965, no. 423 [Rembrandt; ca. 1650–52]; Rosenberg 1968, p. 342, fig. 281 [Rembrandt; early fifties]; Gerson 1968, pp. 136, 487, note 16 [probably pupil].

The "Westerkerk" is seen from the Leliebrug, a bridge

over the Prinsengracht. It is the church where Rembrandt was buried in 1669.

The authorship of Rembrandt was first doubted by Van Regteren Altena in 1925. Benesch followed him and pointed out that the manner of drawing reflects that of Rembrandt of ca. 1650–60 without showing the characteristics of his own work of that time.

Altena's suggestion that the drawing may be by Furnerius probably should be accepted. The structure of the pen lines and washes has much in common with those of his views of farms under trees (see the two following drawings).

## ABRAHAM FURNERIUS

### 177 *Wooded Landscape**

Rijksprentenkabinet, Amsterdam

Pen and brown ink and brown and gray wash, over black chalk, 162 × 225 mm. *Ill. p. 268*

INSCRIPTIONS Annotated at top right: *Rembrandt.*

DATE [ca. 1660–70?].

PROVENANCE Hauth; Solms-Braunfels, Amsterdam (sale Amsterdam, R. W. P. de Vries, January 24, 1922, no. 195); C. Otto (L. 611c; sale Leipzig, November 7, 1929, no. 59).

BIBLIOGRAPHY G. Swarzenski and E. Schilling, *Handzeichnungen alter Meister aus deutschem Privatbesitz*, Frankfurt-Berlin, 1924, pl. 54; Henkel 1942, p. 83, no. 1, pl. 139; Cormack 1966, under no. 31; Van Hasselt 1968–69, under nos. 57 and 58 [for Furnerius' *oeuvre*].

Little is known about this artist who apparently specialized in landscape drawings to the exclusion of other subjects and media. Born between 1620 and 1628, Furnerius generally is assumed to have worked in Rembrandt's studio between 1640 and 1645.

The present drawing and the one exhibited under the following number belong to a group of views of woods with winding roads, drawn with a broad pen and slashing, expressive lines and washes. There is no doubt that these views, some of the most impressive landscape drawings by Dutch artists of the seventeenth century, are by one and the same artist, and it is very likely that this was Furnerius since they are similar in the design of leaves and of occasional figures to drawings of a second group (see cat. nos. 179–180) which is related to a landscape in Dresden, annotated probably still in the seventeenth century *abrah. farnerius* (Henkel 1931, pl. 68).

Only to a limited extent are these drawings similar to the late landscape drawings of Rembrandt of the 1650's. They have more in common with the work of Philips and Jacob Koninck. It is known that Philips Koninck married a sister of Furnerius in 1640, and it is very well possible that the artist was more impressed by the work of his brother-in-law than that of Rembrandt.

The attribution of a third group of drawings to the artist on the basis of an annotated drawing in Brussels (see Van Hasselt 1968/69) needs to be verified.

See also comments to the following drawing.

## 178  *Wooded Landscape*

Central College, Pella, Iowa, The Brower Collection

Pen and brown ink and gray and brown wash, 168 × 202 mm.; top corners arched. *Ill. p. 270*

DATE [ca. 1660–70?].

PROVENANCE H. Oppenheimer (sale London, Christie, July 13, 1936, no. 245); H. L. Larsen, Amsterdam-New York; Frank E. Brower, Pella, Iowa.

EXHIBITIONS London 1929, no. 664.

BIBLIOGRAPHY G. Falck, in *Old Master Drawings*, III, 1928–29, pp. 47–48, pl. 41; Henkel 1931, p. 86; Henkel 1942, p. 83, under no. 1; Van Hasselt 1968–69, under no. 58.

This drawing is another example of Furnerius' woody landscapes (see notes to the preceding drawing). This one is particularly similar to one in the Van Eeghen Collection, Amsterdam (Van Gelder 1958, pl. 94). By virtue of these views of woods, Furnerius is one of the most original and independent Dutch landscape draughtsmen of the seventeenth century. Apart from the two drawings here exhibited, and the Van Eeghen drawing just mentioned, four more belong to the same group (British Museum, Hind nos. 163, 165, 166; Coll. Lugt, Van Hasselt 1968–69, no. 58).

## 179  *Cottage under Trees*

Mr. and Mrs. Winslow Ames, Saunderstown, R.I. *Ill. p. 269*

Pen and brown ink and brown wash, 178 × 254 mm.

DATE [ca. 1660–70].

PROVENANCE E. Parsons & Sons, London; C. Hofstede de

Groot (sale Leipzig, Boerner, November 4, 1931, no. 129 [as Philips Koninck]).

EXHIBITIONS The Hague 1930, no. 66, Washington, D.C. et al. 1966–67, no. 17 [illustrated].

BIBLIOGRAPHY Gerson 1936, no. Z. XXXVII [probably by Furnerius].

This and the following drawing are two of a group of landscapes which are certainly by one artist and which have many characteristics in common with works of Philips and Jacob Koninck. Since in the outline of trees and broad treatment of the foreground these landscapes are similar to one drawing in Dresden annotated *farnerius* (see note to no. 177), the authorship of Furnerius rests on rather safe grounds. As often Furnerius includes in this drawing a few schematically outlined figures which give the impression of posing for the artist.

See also notes to the two preceding drawings and to the following one.

## 180  *Farm Buildings under Trees*

Kunsthalle, Hamburg

Pen and brown ink and brown wash over black chalk, 150 × 271 mm.; top corners arched. *Ill. p. 269*

PROVENANCE WB (L. 2603a, unidentified); E. Harzen (1863).

BIBLIOGRAPHY HdG 355 [as Rembrandt]; Kruse 1920, p. 99, under VII, 4, fig. 117 [as Furnerius]; Pauli 1924, no. 21; Henkel 1931, p. 86; Bernt 1957, no. 239.

The drawing is similar in subject matter and execution to the preceding one.

## AERT DE GELDER

## 181  *Group of Figures in Oriental Costumes*

Miss Annette Ruth Brod, London

Pen and brown ink, 152 × 200 mm. *Ill. p. 266*

DATE [ca. 1679].

PROVENANCE Parsons, London (1923, no. 190 [as Rembrandt]); Ch. de Burlet, Basel (1951); Herbert List, Munich.

BIBLIOGRAPHY Valentiner 1934, p. XXXIV, fig. 34 [as study for painting of 1679 in The Hague]; *Musée Royal de tableaux Mauritshuis à La Haye, Catalogue raisonné des tableaux et sculptures*, The Hague, 1935, p. 100, under no. 737.

This study for a group of figures in Aert de Gelder's painting here exhibited under no. 64 is the only drawing which is documented as by the artist. The painting is dated 1679, and the drawing probably preceded it shortly, unless Aert de Gelder reverted to a study he had made earlier. While basing himself in this study on Rembrandt's drawings of the 1650's, Aert de Gelder indicates contours with broken and sometimes multiple lines instead of defining them with single strokes, corrects emphatically without using white body color or chalk to mask the mistakes, and indicates eyes with dots. The drawing conveys something of the colorful, shimmering appearance of the figures in the painting.

**182** *Jacob Being Shown Joseph's Coat*

The Art Institute of Chicago, Charles Deering Collection

Pen and brown ink and brown wash and some white body color, 120 × 180 mm. *Ill. p. 266*

PROVENANCE Unidentified collector (L. 2844a); Ph. Moore (L. 2844; sale 1856); Charles, Earl of Shrewsbury; Charles Deering (L. 516).

EXHIBITIONS Chicago, The Art Institute, *Century of Progress*, 1933, no. 813 [as Rembrandt]; Chicago 1935–36, no. 50 [as Aert de Gelder].

BIBLIOGRAPHY D. C. Rich, in *The Art Institute of Chicago Bulletin*, XXIII, no. 4, 1929, pp. 40–41 [as Rembrandt]; Valentiner 1934, p. XXXV, fig. 35 [as Aert de Gelder]; Benesch VI, no. A 83, fig. 1689 [close to drawings of about 1655–56].

This drawing is so similar to the preceding one in the character of the pen lines that there can hardly be any doubt that it is also by Aert de Gelder. In subject matter and to some extent in the composition and manner of drawing it shows features of Rembrandt's study of the same subject in Rotterdam (B. 991; it seems to combine two different ideas for the subject).

The preceding drawing and this one may be considered a basis for attributing further pen drawings to the artist. Since it is likely that Aert de Gelder, as other pupils of Rembrandt, expressed themselves in a variety of media and "styles" it is hoped that other drawings linked with his paintings will be found and thus will provide further nuclei for the reconstruction of his *oeuvre*.

SAMUEL VAN HOOGSTRATEN

**183** *Adoration of the Shepherds*

Kunsthalle, Hamburg

Pen and brown ink and brown wash over sketch in pencil, 155 × 204 mm. *Ill. p. 254*

INSCRIPTIONS Signed at bottom right: *S v Hoogstraten.*

PROVENANCE W. Esdaile (L. 2617); E. Harzen (1863).

BIBLIOGRAPHY Bernt 1957, no. 309.

Hoogstraten was a pupil of Rembrandt's in the 1640's, perhaps simultaneously with or shortly before Constantijn van Renesse and Barent Fabritius were in Rembrandt's studio.

In contrast to all other pupils of Rembrandt, Hoogstraten used to sign his drawings either in full or with his initials, and invariably in a neat classical handwriting befitting a poet and art theoretician. Sometimes his initials are accompanied by a two digit number which indicates a large series of drawings (not the date of origin, as usually is supposed, cf. *Finding of Moses*, Coll. Dutuit, numbered 53).

The present drawing is perhaps not one of the most attractive ones that Hoogstraten signed, but since it is one of the few that is not colored it is a useful point of reference for attributing pen or pen and wash drawings to the artist.

It also demonstrates a certain dependence upon Elsheimer, which is characteristic for many of Hoogstraten's drawings, and to which Sumowski has drawn attention.

PHILIPS KONINCK (?)

**184** *Christ among His Disciples*

Ecole Nationale Supérieure des Beaux-Arts, Paris *Ill. p. 262*

Pen and black ink and light brown wash, 198 × 260 mm.

PROVENANCE Sylvestre (sale Paris, Dec. 4–6, 1861, no. 156); Jules Boilly (sale Paris, March 19, 1869, no. 29); A. Armand and P. Valton.

EXHIBITIONS Paris 1879, no. 359; Paris 1908, no. 489.

BIBLIOGRAPHY Ph. de Chennevières, in *Gazette des Beaux-Arts*, 1880, p. 64; Valentiner 362 [copy, probably by Ph. Koninck after Rembrandt]; Kauffmann 1926, p. 175 [Rembrandt, 1635 or 36]; Falck 1927, p. 178 [copy by Koninck after Rembrandt]; M. Delacre and P. Lavallée, *Dessins de maîtres anciens*, Paris/Brussels, 1927, pl. 23 [as Rembrandt];

Lugt 1933, under no. 1132 and no. 1263 [neither by Rembrandt nor Ph. Koninck]; Gerson 1936, no. Z 150, pl. 54 [as Ph. Koninck]; Lugt 1950, no. 479 [neither Rembrandt nor Ph. Koninck; gray ink added]; Benesch III, no. 495, fig. 619 [Rembrandt ca. 1640–42; figure at left and two at bottom right added by Ph. Koninck].

Since only ten disciples are present, the drawing probably represents Christ's appearance to his disciples after the Resurrection.

The attribution of this drawing is problematical. It seems to be by the same artist as *The Death of Jacob*, formerly in the Museum at Montreal (B. 493), *Christ's Body Carried to the Tomb* in Rotterdam (B. 484) and *The Entombment of Christ* in Berlin (B. 485), all three considered by Benesch to be works of Rembrandt. The man at the very left in the drawing here exhibited is very similar to figures in early drawings of Philips Koninck (cf. *Simeon*, Coll. T. Christ, Gerson 1936, no. Z. 142; *Dismissal of Hagar*, Coll. Friedrich August, Gerson 1936, no. Z. 117) and was accordingly by Benesch attributed to Philips Koninck as an addition to a drawing by Rembrandt. Since the whole drawing, however, seems to be by one hand (except touches of gray ink), Philips Koninck is a very strong candidate. If he made the drawing, it is one of his most Rembrandtesque works.

## PHILIPS KONINCK

### 185 *Elijah and the Prophets of Baal*

Mr. and Mrs. Seymour Slive, Cambridge, Mass.

Pen and brown ink and some gray wash over traces of pencil, 206 × 324 mm. *Ill. p. 263*

PROVENANCE W. Esdaile (L. 2617; perhaps identical with Sale London, W. Esdaile, Part III, June 18, 1840, no. 946 [as Ph. Koninck]); Defer-Dumesnil; Marsden J. Perry, Providence; Joseph E. Widener, Elkins Park; W. R. Valentiner, Berlin/Raleigh. (According to other information the drawing was also in the collections of Berlant, Gersaint, John Barnard, James Butler, W. Young Ottley, Horace Walpole, and Captain Donnadieu).

BIBLIOGRAPHY [*Rembrandt Drawings in the Collection of Joseph E. Widener, Volume of Photographs*, ca. 1921], pl. 32 [acc. to Valentiner by Ph. Koninck]; Gerson 1936, no. Z 129 [probably copy].

The drawing represents King Ahab (standing, in the center) and the prophets of Baal witnessing the burning of the offerings on the altar built by Elijah. The King and the prophets had been summoned by Elijah (kneeling) to a contest between Baal and Jehovah on Mount Carmel. While the day-long prayers of the prophets failed to ignite their offerings, Elijah's few calm words immediately had the desired effect and demonstrated the victory of the true over the false religion (I Kings 18:17–38).

While Rembrandt treated the subject entirely differently (Konstanz, B. 593), Samuel van Hoogstraten represented it in 1646 with a similar composition (British Museum, H. 1). Since it is not very likely that the Koninck drawing dates from the same time, it probably is either based on the one by Hoogstraten or on a common model available to both artists (Hoogstraten made a study for his drawing, Berlin KdZ 5664; cf. Sumowski 1966, p. 303). There certainly is no reason to consider the drawing a copy as Gerson suggested (cf. also F. Lugt in a manuscript note in the Institute in The Hague: "P. Koninck").

The drawing is in the same style derived from Rembrandt as the following *Visitation*.

### 186 *The Visitation*

The Pierpont Morgan Library, New York

Pen and brown ink and some gray-brown wash, 267 × 205 mm. *Ill. p. 263*

INSCRIPTIONS Annotated with pen and brown ink at bottom left: *Rembrant*.

DATE [ca. 1655–60].

PROVENANCE C. Fairfax Murray; J. Pierpont Morgan.

BIBLIOGRAPHY Gerson 1936, no. Z 140, pl. 56 [mid-forties].

The Visitation takes place near the entrance to a dwelling. Zacharias is standing in the entrance.

The drawing is a characteristic work of Philips Koninck. Only the date presents problems: although Gerson suggested the mid-forties, the composition seems to have originated in connection with Rembrandt's own representations of the subject, namely two drawings which are dated by Benesch ca. 1656–57 (Louvre, Paris; B. 1019). Possibly Koninck used the style of this drawing longer, and in that case it could be considered as a work of the second half of the 1650's.

### 187 *Distant View from the Dunes*

Groninger Museum voor Stad en Lande, Groningen *Ill. p. 265*

Pen and brown ink and brown wash, 140 × 220 mm.

DATE [ca. 1650–55].

PROVENANCE T. Dimsdale, London; T. Humphrey Ward, London (1906); C. Hofstede de Groot.

EXHIBITIONS The Hague 1902, no. 45; Leiden 1903, no. 12; Paris 1908, no. 475; Leiden 1916, no. 61; The Hague 1930, no. 65; Groningen 1931, no. 71; Groningen 1948, no. 96; Groningen 1952, no. 53; The Hague 1955, no. 31; Leiden 1956, no. 144; Vancouver 1958, no. 42; Padua/Florence/Venice, *Disegni Olandesi del Seicento*, 1968, no. 49, fig. 38.

BIBLIOGRAPHY O. Hirschmann, in *Cicerone*, IX, 1917, p. 202; Becker 1923, no. 23; Gerson 1936, no. Z 30, pl. 30; Van Gelder 1958, no. 97a; L. C. J. Frerichs, *Openbaar Kunstbezit*, 1959, no. 33; Bolten 1967, no. 41 [illustrated].

Although it is fairly certain that here represented is a stretch of the dunes, as long as the country house or castle at the left remains unknown a more precise identification of the site cannot be given. Koninck who generally preferred a high viewpoint must have been sketching from a rooftop or a tower, as Miss Frerichs pointed out. The arrangement of spaces, the blank areas of paper, and the fine, rather delicate pen lines are reminiscent of drawings and etchings by Rembrandt of ca. 1650, particularly the etching *The Goldweigher's Field* (H. 249) of 1651 and the drawing closely connected with it, *Open Landscape with Haarlem in the Distance* (B. 1259, Rotterdam), as well as the *Landscape with the 'Huys met het Toorentje'* (H. 244).

## 188 *River Landscape with High Embankment*

Musées royaux des Beaux-Arts de Belgique, Bruxelles

Pen and brown ink and brown wash and watercolor, 129 × 188 mm. *Ill. p. 265*

DATE [ca. 1663].

PROVENANCE J. Gildemeester (sale Amsterdam, November 24, 1800, Pf. U, no. 8); Goll van Franckenstein (sale Amsterdam, July 1, 1833, Pf. F, no. 14); H. v. Cranenburg (sale Amsterdam, October 26, 1858, no. 6, Pf. A); Jacob de Vos Jbzn (L. 1450; sale Amsterdam, May 22, 1883, no. 217); De Grez.

BIBLIOGRAPHY Gerson 1936, no. Z 23, pl. 31.

The artist may have found this site in the southern part of the present Netherlands (Limburg) or in what is now West Germany, but it has not been identified. He probably made the drawing around 1663, as Gerson suggested.

## 189 *River Scene*

Bowdoin College Museum of Art, Brunswick, Maine

Pen and brush and brown ink, heightened with white, 199 × 317 mm. *Ill. p. 264*

DATE [ca. 1663].

PROVENANCE James Bowdoin III (1811).

BIBLIOGRAPHY [Henry Johnson, comp.], *Catalogue of the Bowdoin College Art Collections*, Part I, *The Bowdoin Drawings*, Brunswick, Maine, 1885, no. 50 [as Rembrandt]; Rev. Fred. H. Allen, *The Bowdoin Collection*, Part I, Brunswick, Maine, 1886, no. 1 [as Rembrandt]; Frank Jewett Mather, "Drawings by Old Masters at Bowdoin College Ascribed to Northern Schools: II", *Art in America*, II, 1914, p. 111, no. 250, fig. 4 [as Ph. Koninck]; Gerson 1936, no. Z 20, pl. 38.

This study of a bend in a river is related in execution to other drawings by Koninck of about 1663, for example the *Farm*, signed and dated *1663* in Berlin (Gerson 1936, no. Z 12), and according to Gerson may date from the same time. This and similar drawings presuppose Rembrandt's landscape sketches of the late forties and early fifties (e.g. B. 1227, 1234). The fence in the foreground probably has been reenforced by another hand.

Since this sketch was already in this country by 1811 it is one of the earliest, if not the earliest, drawing from Rembrandt's school to enter an American collection.

## JOHANNES LEUPENIUS

## 190 *View of Trees and Houses Across a Stream**

Albertina, Vienna

Pen and brush and brown ink, 193 × 313 mm. *Ill. p. 273*

INSCRIPTION Signed and dated at bottom right: *JLeupeni[us] 1665;* and inscribed: *N° 6.*

DATE *1665.*

BIBLIOGRAPHY Bernt 1958, no. 358; Benesch 1964–67, no. 183; Van Hasselt 1968–69, under no. 92.

Johannes Leupenius, son of a minister who had come to the Netherlands from England, was trained as a surveyor and was qualified as such in 1669. Active also as a mathematician and mapmaker, he combined his scientific interests in geography with an artistic approach to his surroundings, and sketched mainly country houses on the rivers Amstel and Vecht. Apparently he deployed his great artistic gift as a landscape draughtsman mainly or even exclusively in the years 1665 and 1666, when he was about eighteen or nineteen years old. About 1668–1671 he also made a series of etchings of country houses which are less accomplished as an artistic performance.

Like the following drawing this one probably represents a country house surrounded by trees situated along the Vecht between Utrecht and Amsterdam, or on the Amstel near Amsterdam. Both are among the best he made, and show the proximity of his work to that of Jan Lievens from which he may have learned. If ever he was a pupil of Rembrandt, he probably was in his studio about 1660.

## I9I  *Castle Nijenrode*

Rijksprentenkabinet, Amsterdam

Pen and brown ink and brown wash and traces of black chalk, 171 × 281 mm.  *Ill. p. 273*

INSCRIPTIONS  Signed at bottom right: *J Leupenius;* annotated on the reverse: *D'Riddermatige Hofstad Neyenrode van Agteren in 't Stigt 1665 J. Leupenius fect. No. 6.*

DATE  *1665*

PROVENANCE  C. Ploos van Amstel (sale March 3, 1800, no. 20); probably J. H. Molkenboer (sale October 17, 1825, no. 32); Jacob de Vos Jbzn (L. 1450; sale May 22, 1883, no. 292).

BIBLIOGRAPHY  Henkel 1931, p. 86, pl. LXIX; Henkel 1942, p. 99, no. 3, pl. 152; Bernt 1958, no. 357; Van Hasselt 1968–69, under no. 92.

Leupenius sketched this view of *Castle Nijenrode* in the same year as the preceding drawing. In 1666 he made a second view of the same country house, this time in winter and from a different point of view (Van Eeghen Collection). One of his etchings (Hollstein 1) represents also the same subject.

See also note to the preceding drawing.

## JAN LIEVENS

## I92  *Evangelist Mark**

Albertina, Vienna

Black chalk, 278 × 211 mm.  *Ill. p. 250*

PROVENANCE  Sale Amsterdam, S. Fokke, December 6, 1784, no. 802; sale Amsterdam, Ploos van Amstel, March 3, 1800, Pf. C, no. 17.

BIBLIOGRAPHY  Schneider 1932, no. Z 21, fig. 40.

In the type of head of this old scholar and also in the manner of drawing, Lievens approximates Van Dyck closer than in almost any other of his drawings.

Lievens intended some of his black chalk portraits to be finished works of art by themselves, but made others as studies for his own etchings (*Portrait of Caspar Streso*, Lugt Collection, 1654–58? for etching Rovinski 76; *Man with a Skull*, Amsterdam, for Rovinski 31), or as preparatory drawings for woodcuts.

The present drawing probably was made as an independent study and was later reproduced in an etching. In the etching which is one of a series of four evangelists the figure is identified as St. Mark by the addition of a lion. Although the etching which is considerably smaller than the drawing usually is attributed to Jan Lievens, it is probably made by another artist, perhaps Laurent de la Hire to whom two other prints of the series have been attributed.

See also note to the following drawing.

## I93  *Portrait of a Scholar*

Museum Boymans-van Beuningen, Rotterdam.

Black chalk, traced for transfer, 255 × 189 mm.  *Ill. p. 253*

PROVENANCE  F. J. O. Boymans, Rotterdam.

EXHIBITIONS  Oberlin, Allen Memorial Art Museum, *Seventeenth-Century One-Block Woodcuts*, 1962.

BIBLIOGRAPHY  A. M. Hind, "The Woodcut Portraits of Jan Lievens and Dirk de Bray", in *The Imprint*, I, 1913, pp. 233 ff.; Schneider 1932, no. Z 42.

When he was in Rembrandt's studio, Lievens must have become acquainted with the portraits and studies of figures Rembrandt made with black chalk, but the style of almost all drawings in this medium owes much to Van Dyck. An exception is the *Portrait of Petrus Scriverius* of 1631 (or 1637?, British Museum, London) which combines Rembrandtesque and Van Dyck-like elements.

The central part of this drawing without the background was reproduced in a woodcut signed *IL*. Because of the cape-like upper part of the costume which was introduced in the print but which is not present in the drawing, Bartsch and later writers called it *Portrait of a Venetian Nobleman*. In the drawing the books, the papers and what looks like a globe on the large table in front of the sitter, and the inkpot on the small table behind him characterize him as a scholar. The differences between this drawing and the print support the supposition made by Hind that another artist (François Dusart?) cut Lievens' woodcuts.

See also note to the following drawing.

**194** *Entrance Gate to a Garden*

Amsterdams Historisch Museum (Collection Fodor)

Reed pen and brown ink on Japan paper, 222 × 371 mm.
PROVENANCE W. Baartz (sale Rotterdam, June 6, 1860, Pf. P, no. 341); C. J. Fodor. *Ill. p. 251*

EXHIBITIONS Amsterdam, Museum Fodor, *Klassieke Hollandsche teekenaars*, 1932, no. 34; Paris 1950, no. 138; Cologne/Bremen 1955, no. 47; Vancouver 1958, no. 49; Jerusalem 1960, no. 42; Beograd/Zagreb 1960, no. 40; Brussels/Hamburg 1961, no. 69, pl. XXXVII and detail on cover; Budapest 1962.

BIBLIOGRAPHY *Beschrijving der schilderijen, teekeningen, etc. in het Museum Fodor te Amsterdam*, Amsterdam, 1863, no. 96; Schneider 1932, Z 391.

This *Entrance Gate to a Garden* stands out among the best landscape drawings of Lievens by virtue of the subject matter. Although Lievens often included figures in his drawings, these generally are either farmers, shepherds, travelers or occasionally a painter, and they invariably are subordinated to the landscape. Here, however, he introduced a well-dressed lady with a child in a park or garden near a pond in the very center of the composition. The gate enframing them stresses their importance. A similar element of country elegance is more generally found in Flemish art, and Rubens' *La Promenade* comes easily to mind. As many of Lievens' drawings, this one shows in the pen lines an affinity to Campagnola and Titian.

**195** *Wooded Landscape*

The Pierpont Morgan Library, New York

Pen and brown ink, 222 × 375 mm. *Ill. p. 252*

PROVENANCE C. Fairfax Murray; J. Pierpont Morgan.

EXHIBITIONS Raleigh 1956, no. 69.

BIBLIOGRAPHY Fairfax Murray I, no. 183; Schneider 1932, no. Z 309.

These oak trees standing on a hill and similar wooded scenes were developed by Jan Lievens after he had come in contact with landscapes painted by Adriaen Brouwer and Rubens. Heavy foliage and light coming from the distance

between the heavy trunks are common features of these drawings and of some of the artist's paintings (Rotterdam, and elsewhere).

**196** *Trees*

Staatliche Museen Preussischer Kulturbesitz, Kupferstichkabinett, Berlin *Ill. p. 253*

Pen and brown ink on Japan paper, 378 × 232 mm.

INSCRIPTIONS Annotated in monogram at bottom left: *J.L.;* annotated on the reverse by Ploos van Amstel: *Landschap Jan Lievens f. de Staffage Ad. van de Velde f. Hoog 14 3/9 d br 9 d.*

PROVENANCE Sale Amsterdam, November 23, 1767, Pf. F, no. 487; sale Amsterdam, December 12, 1768, Pf. A, no. 45; J. van der Marck (sale Amsterdam, November 29, 1773, no. 254); C. Ploos van Amstel; J. C. van Hall (sale Amsterdam, February 21, 1814, Pf. D, no. 14); Six van Hillegom (sale Amsterdam, July 7, 1845, Pf. A, no. 11); L. Dupper Wzn (sale Dordrecht, July 28, 1870, no. 221); B. Suermondt.

BIBLIOGRAPHY C. Josi, in *Collection d'imitations de dessins d'après les principaux maîtres hollandais, commencé par C. Ploos van Amstel, continué par C. Josi*, London, 1821 [as scene of the "Haagsche Bosch" in the collection of the banker Müller]; Bock and Rosenberg 1930, p. 178, no. 2622; Schneider 1932, Z 303.

This is one of a small number of large drawings by Jan Lievens representing one or a few trees showing their age in the twisted forms of their trunks and branches (similar examples are in Rotterdam and Dresden). Lievens sketched these trees on Japan paper in the same style as his woody landscapes and views of farms.

The tradition going back as far as the eighteenth century that Lievens would have sketched these oak trees and beaches in the woods near The Hague is attractive but cannot be substantiated. The "staffage" is by Lievens himself in spite of Ploos van Amstel's opinion to the contrary.

**197** *St. Jerome*

Kunstmuseum der Stadt Düsseldorf

Pen and brown ink, 217 × 318 mm. *Ill. p. 251*

INSCRIPTIONS Signed in monogram and dated at bottom left: *I L 1665.* Annotated: *23.*

DATE *1665*.

PROVENANCE Lambert Krahe; Kunstakademie, Düsseldorf (L. 2309).

EXHIBITIONS Düsseldorf 1968, no. 62.

BIBLIOGRAPHY Budde 1930, no. 894, pl. 197; Schneider 1932, no. Z 12; Eckhard Schaar, in [Düsseldorf] 1968, no. 62.

As Rembrandt did in his etching *St. Jerome in an Italian Landscape* and in accordance with a long pictorial tradition, Jan Lievens represented the saint near a large tree. The drawing is one of the very few that Lievens dated and shows that as late as 1665 Lievens included stylistic elements of Rembrandt of the 1630's and 1640's, combining these with impressions from Rubens's work. There is also similarity with the drawing of the same subject by Ferdinand Bol, here exhibited under no. 155.

## NICOLAES MAES

### 198   *Christ Blessing the Children*

Rijksprentenkabinet, Amsterdam

Pen and brush and brown ink; the kneeling woman in the foreground drawn first with red chalk; corrected with white, 223 × 193 mm. *Ill. p. 257*

DATE [ca. 1652–53].

PROVENANCE Matthys Balen, Dordrecht (1766).

EXHIBITIONS Brussels/Hamburg 1961, no. 138, pl. 28.

BIBLIOGRAPHY Wegner 1966–67, under no. 101.

The subject, "Suffer little children to come unto me" was also represented by Rembrandt as part of his illustration of the entire chapter 19 of the Gospel according to Matthew (the so-called *Hundred Guilder Print*).

The drawing is a study for the painting of the same subject in the National Gallery, London and preceded a second drawing (British Museum) which is closer to the painting. Both drawings document the gradual transformation of a motif inspired by *The Hundred Guilder Print* into a virtually independent painting. In the drawing here exhibited the figure of Christ standing, and both the kneeling woman and the one standing next to her are reminiscent of the corresponding figures in the print. In the second drawing Christ is seated as he is in the painting, and a child is standing between him and the kneeling woman. In the painting Maes retained the child, but eliminated the kneeling woman altogether. The composition of the second

drawing, as that of the painting, is closed at the left by a standing woman with a child in her arms.

Already in 1923 Hind (1915, pp. 50–51, no. 144) attributed the drawing in London to Maes because of a similarity with three drawings (*Milk Maid* at Dresden and two others in Cambridge), and he concluded that the painting in the National Gallery also should be considered a work of the artist. Since then both attributions have been confirmed (*pace* Hofstede de Groot 1929, p. 144; see Maclaren 1960, pp. 229–31, and Pont 1958, pp. 155–6). The painting is the most significant early work of Nicolaes Maes, painted perhaps still in Amsterdam before he returned to Dordrecht at the end of 1653.

### 199   *Woman Scraping a Parsnip*

Coll. F. Lugt, Institut Néerlandais, Paris   *Ill. p. 258*

Brush and brown ink; verso: red chalk, 123 × 84 mm.

DATE [ca. 1655].

PROVENANCE Unidentified collector (L. 1460d); Earl of Dalhousie (L. 717a).

EXHIBITIONS Dordrecht 1934, no. 31.

BIBLIOGRAPHY Valentiner 1923, p. 21, pl. I b; Valentiner 1924, p. 50, fig. 43–44; Maclaren 1960, p. 228.

One of the few drawings from a scrapbook which until 1922 was in the collection of the Earl of Dalhousie; it is a study for a painting by Nicolaes Maes of the same subject, dated 1655, in the National Gallery, London. A second drawing for the same painting in the same album is a little further removed from the painting (Valentiner 1924, fig. 42). Since most of the drawings in the volume were by one artist, these and similar drawings identified Nicolaes Maes as their author. The volume apparently contained mainly early drawings by the artist.

Rembrandt's use of the brush in the 1650's apparently impressed his pupils: both Van den Eeckhout and Maes gladly took it over.

On the reverse is a summary sketch of a woman eavesdropping closely related to the painting of 1656 in the Wallace Collection, London.

### 200   *Old Woman with a Yarn Winder and a Spool*

Staatliche Museen Preussischer Kulturbesitz, Kupferstichkabinett, Berlin *Ill. p. 258*

Red chalk and brush and brown ink, 222 × 174 mm.

DATE [ca. 1654–60].

PROVENANCE Baron J. G. Verstolk van Soelen; A. H. E. van Pallandt; B. Suermondt.

BIBLIOGRAPHY Lippmann and Grote 1st ed., no. 69 (2nd ed., no. 291); Bode and Valentiner 1907, pl. 18; Valentiner 1924, pp. 45–46, 50, fig. 28; Hofstede de Groot 1929, p. 145 [by Maes]; Bock and Rosenberg 1930, p. 183, no. 2611, pl. 125; Benesch 1948, p. 289, fig. 2; Bernt 1957, no. 383.

The numerous paintings Nicolaes Maes devoted to the subject of the old woman seated and absorbed by her work or by her prayers have contributed much to the artist's fame. Only three drawings of these subjects are known, and of these three this is the most accomplished and impressive one. The woman apparently is fastening the end of the thread that she has wound unto the spool from the yarn winder. The drawing is closely related to two paintings of similar subjects in Amsterdam (Valentiner figs. 32 and 30)

## 201  *The Young Mother*

The Metropolitan Museum of Art, Rogers Fund, 1947
*Ill. p. 259*

Pen and brown ink and brown wash, 35 × 180 mm.

DATE [ca. 1655–56].

PROVENANCE Private Collection, Berlin (1924); W. R. Valentiner, Detroit (sale Amsterdam, Mensing, October 25, 1932, no. XXVI); H. L. Larsen, Amsterdam-New York (sale New York, Parke-Bernet, November 6, 1947, no. 16).

BIBLIOGRAPHY Valentiner 1924, p. 51, fig. 55; Louise Burroughs, in *Metropolitan Museum of Art Bulletin*, N.S. VII, 1949, p. 282; Bernt 1958, no. 381.

Similar domestic scenes were frequently painted by the artist in 1655 and 1666, and this drawing probably dates from that time. It is the most finished version of this subject among Maes' drawings.

## 202  *Young Man Descending a Staircase*

Museum Boymans-van Beuningen, Rotterdam  *Ill. p. 259*

Pen and brown ink, corrected with white, 174 × 175 mm.

DATE [ca. 1655–60?].

PROVENANCE Earl of Dalhousie (L. 717a); F. Koenigs, Haarlem.

EXHIBITIONS London 1929, no. 669; Dordrecht 1934, no. 22; Dijon 1950, no. 71; Leiden 1956, no. 165.

BIBLIOGRAPHY Valentiner 1924, p. 50, fig. 47; Hofstede de Groot 1929, p. 144 [questions attribution to Maes; copy after painting?].

One frequently recurring subject in Maes's paintings is an interior with one or two young couples embracing in the background, while a maid servant, her hand against her lips, enjoins silence. Sometimes it is a young man instead of a maid, but they always are placed prominently in the foreground, and they invariably smile. Rather than eavesdropping or trying to prevent others from disturbing the lovers, these central personages are amused by the couples that trust that they are not observed. As in this drawing these paintings often include a view into a farther room beyond a staircase in the center of the space (Apsley House, Wallace Collection, Buckingham Palace, Six Collection).

The lines of this drawing are simplified variations of Rembrandt's pen lines, and are found in a large number of early drawings by Nicolaes Maes. On the reverse of the paper the artist made a sketch of a man seated.

## 203  *A Scholar in His Study*

Wadsworth Atheneum, Hartford

Pen and brown ink and brown wash, 184 × 184 mm.; top corners canted.  *Ill. p. 261*

DATE [ca. 1655–60?].

PROVENANCE Earl of Dalhousie (L. 717a).

EXHIBITIONS Detroit, The Detroit Institute of Arts, *Sixty Drawings from the Wadsworth Atheneum*, Hartford, 1948; Montreal, The Monteal Museum of Fine Arts, *Five Centuries of Drawings*, 1953, no. 127 [illustrated]; Middletown 1959.

BIBLIOGRAPHY Valentiner 1924, pp. 56–57, fig. 69; *Wadsworth Atheneum* [Handbook], Hartford, 1958, p. 74 [illustrated].

The subject of the scholar in his study has occupied Rembrandt and many of his pupils for long periods of time (Bol, Van der Pluym, Koninck, and others). Maes made two drawings of the subject, the one here exhibited and a second one formerly also in the Dalhousie Collection. In both, Maes payed more attention to accessories such as books and clocks, than Rembrandt, who tended to focus the attention on the figure.

## 204 *Man Standing*

Museum Boymans-van Beuningen, Rotterdam *Ill. p. 260*

Pen and brown ink and brown wash, 162 × 52 mm.

PROVENANCE Earl of Dalhousie; F. Koenigs, Haarlem.

EXHIBITIONS Dordrecht 1934, no. 26; Rotterdam 1934, no. 117; Dijon 1950, no. 73; Leiden 1956, no. 163.

See note to the following drawing.

## 205 *Man Standing, Leaning against a Doorpost*

Museum Boymans-van Beuningen, Rotterdam

Pen and brown ink, 162 × 67 mm. *Ill. p. 260*

PROVENANCE Earl of Dalhousie; F. Koenigs, Haarlem.

EXHIBITIONS Dordrecht 1934, no. 27; Rotterdam 1934, no. 118; Dijon 1950, no. 72; Leiden 1956, no. 164.

BIBLIOGRAPHY Sumowski 1961, p. 26 under no. A 80ᵃ.

This and the preceding drawing are not directly connected with any paintings by Nicolaes Maes or with any of the drawings that are certainly by him. Because of their provenance from the Dalhousie album and a general resemblance with other drawings by the artist they are also considered to be his work.

97　*Rembrandt*
　*Seated Old Man*
　*National Gallery of Art, Washington, D.C.*
　*Rosenwald Collection*

94 *Rembrandt*
*Old Beggar in a Long Cloak and High Cap*
*Rijksprentenkabinet, Amsterdam*

96 *Rembrandt*
*Beggar Woman Leaning on a Stick*
*National Gallery of Art, Washington, D.C.*
*Rosenwald Collection*

95 *Rembrandt*
*A Team of Horses Resting*
*Rijksprentenkabinet, Amsterdam*

98  Rembrandt
    *A Negro with a Turban*
    Chr. P. van Eeghen

99  Rembrandt
    *The Supper at Emmaus*
    Fogg Art Museum,
    Harvard University

100 *Rembrandt*
   *The Last Supper*
   *The Lehman Collection*

103  *Rembrandt*
    *Joseph Interpreting the Prisoners' Dreams*
    *The Art Institute of Chicago*

101 Rembrandt
*Sheet of Studies with a Blind Old Woman*
*Staatliche Museen Preussischer Kulturbesitz,*
*Kupferstichkabinett, Berlin*

106 Rembrandt
*Odysseus and Nausicaa*
*Sterling and Francine Clark Art Institute*

105 *Rembrandt*
*Seated Girl in Profile to the Left*
*Museum Boymans-van Beuningen*

107 Rembrandt
Two Studies of Saskia Asleep
The Pierpont Morgan Library

108 Rembrandt
Saskia Lying in Bed
National Gallery of Art
Washington, D.C.

109  *Rembrandt*
*Christ as Gardener Appearing to Mary Magdalen*
*Rijksprentenkabinet, Amsterdam*

112  *Rembrandt*
     *Two Mummers on Horseback*
     *The Pierpont Morgan Library*

110  *Rembrandt*
     *Studies of a Woman Reading and an Oriental*
     *Private Collection*

111 *Rembrandt*
*Self-Portrait*
*National Gallery of Art, Washington, D.C.*
*Rosenwald Collection*

113  *Rembrandt*
     *Actor in His Dressing Room*
     *Devonshire Collection*
     *Chatsworth*

114 Rembrandt
   *Two Cottages*
   *The Lehman Collection*

115 Rembrandt
   *Satire on Art Criticism*
   *The Lehman Collection*

116 Rembrandt
   *The Holy Family Asleep*
   *Syndics of the Fitzwilliam Museum*

117 Rembrandt
   *Cottage near the Entrance to a Wood*
   *The Lehman Collection*

119 *Rembrandt*
*Cottage with a White Paling*
*Private Collection*

118 *Rembrandt*
*View over the Amstel from the Rampart*
*National Gallery of Art, Washington, D.C.*
*Rosenwald Collection*

121  Rembrandt
     *Landscape with a Drawbridge*
     *The Albertina*

120  Rembrandt
     *Landscape with Farm Buildings and High Embankment*
     *Museum of Art, Rhode Island School of Design*

122   *Rembrandt*
   *The Supper at Emmaus: The Vanishing of Christ*
   *The Syndics of the Fitzwilliam Museum*

123  *Rembrandt*
    *Tobias and His Wife Sara Praying*
    *The Metropolitan Museum of Art*

126  *Rembrandt*
    *The "Rijnpoort" at Rhenen*
    *Devonshire Collection, Chatsworth*

125  *Rembrandt*
    *The "Diemerdijk" with the Village Houtewael*
    *Museum Boymans-van Beuningen*

128 Rembrandt
*Detail from Raphael's "The Repulse of Attila"*
*Staatliche Museen Preussischer Kulturbesitz,*
*Kupferstichkabinett, Berlin*

124 Rembrandt
*Jael and Sisera*
*The Visitors of the Ashmolean Museum*

127 Rembrandt
*Two Indian Noblemen of the Mughal Court:*
    *Abd al-Rahim Khan and a Falconer*
*The Pierpont Morgan Library*

130 Rembrandt
*The Prophet Elisha and the Widow with Her Sons*
*Private Collection*

129 Rembrandt
*The Mocking of Christ*
*The Pierpont Morgan Library*

131 Rembrandt
*Christ Finding the Apostles Asleep*
*Sterling and Francine Clark Art Institute*

133 *Rembrandt*
*Three Studies for a Deposition*
*from the Cross*
*Norton Simon Foundation*

132 *Rembrandt*
*The Rest on the Flight into Egypt*
*Norton Simon Foundation*

135 *Rembrandt*
*Portrait of a Man in a Wide-Brimmed Hat*
*Fogg Art Museum, Harvard University*

138 *Rembrandt*
*Study of a Franciscan Monk*
*Staatliche Museen Preussischer Kulturbesitz,*
*Kupferstichkabinett, Berlin*

136 *Rembrandt*
*Study of a Female Nude*
*The Art Institute of Chicago*

134 *Rembrandt*
*View of Diemen*
*National Gallery of Art, Washington, D.C.*
*Rosenwald Collection*

137 *Rembrandt*
*Female Nude Seated on a Stool*
*The Art Institute of Chicago*

*139 Rembrandt*
*Noah's Ark*
*The Art Institute of Chicago*

*140 Rembrandt*
*Isaac and Rebecca Spied upon by Abimelech*
*Private Collection*

*141 Rembrandt*
*The Meeting of Christ with Martha and Mary*
*after the Death of Lazarus*
*The Cleveland Museum of Art*

*143  Pupil, corrected by Rembrandt*
    *The Departure of Benjamin for Egypt*
    *Teylers Museum, Haarlem*

*142  C. van Renesse, corrected by Rembrandt*
    *The Annunciation*
    *Staatliche Museen Preussischer Kulturbesitz,*
    *Kupferstichkabinett, Berlin*

*144  C. van Renessee, corrected by Rembrandt*
    *Judas Receiving the Thirty Pieces of Silver*
    *Devonshire Collection, Chatsworth*

147 *Unidentified Pupil*
*Rembrandt's Studio with Pupils Drawing from the Nude*
*Hessisches Landesmuseum, Darmstadt*

145 *Pupil, corrected by Rembrandt*
*Lot Defending the Angels from the People of Sodom*
*The Pierpont Morgan Library*

146 *Unidentified Pupil*
*The Good Samaritan*
*The Art Institute of Chicago*

Le Samaritain conduit a l'hostellerie son malade.                    167

163  Gerard Dou
*An Elderly Man Sharpening His Pen*
*Amsterdams Historisch Museum*
*(Collection Fodor)*

148  *Jacob Adriaensz Backer*
     *Reclining Nude*
     *Kunsthalle, Hamburg*

149  *Jacob Adriaensz Backer*
     *Self-Portrait*
     *The Albertina*

150  *Jacob Adriaensz Backer*
*Portrait of a Man*
*The Metropolitan Museum of Art*

172 *Govert Flinck*
   *Study of a Pollard Willow*
   *Museum Boymans-van Beuningen*

173 *Govert Flinck*
   *Young Boy Asleep*
   *Coll. F. Lugt, Institut Néerlandais, Paris*

*171   Govert Flinck*
*Seated Female Nude*
*Rijksprentenkabinet, Amsterdam*

*174   Govert Flinck*
*Portrait of a Young Man Standing*
*Bernard Houthakker, Amsterdam*

175  *Govert Flinck?*
*Isaac Blessing Jacob*
*Museum Boymans–van Beuningen*

166  Gerbrand van den Eeckhout
David's Promise to Bathsheba
The Metropolitan Museum of Art

165 Gerbrand van den Eeckhout
The Dismissal of Hagar
Staatliche Museen Preussischer Kulturbesitz,
Kupferstichkabinett, Berlin

164 Gerbrand van den Eeckhout
Gideon and the Angel
Herzog-Anton-Ulrich Museum, Braunschweig

*Gerbrand van den Eeckhout*

167  *Gerbrand van den Eeckhout*
     *The Dreamer*
     *Goldschmidt Collection*

168  *Gerbrand van den Eeckhout*
     *Christ and the Woman Taken in Adultery*
     *The Art Institute of Chicago*

152 *Ferdinand Bol*
*Joseph Interpreting the Prisoners' Dreams*
*Kunsthalle, Hamburg*

153  Ferdinand Bol
     *Abraham Visited by the Three Angels*
     *Museum Boymans-van Beuningen*

151  Ferdinand Bol?
     *The Finding of Moses*
     *Rijksprentenkabinet, Amsterdam*

154  Ferdinand Bol
     *The Holy Family*
     *Hessisches Landesmuseum, Darmstadt*

247

155 *Ferdinand Bol*
*St. Jerome*
*Kunsthalle, Hamburg*

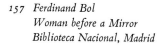

157 *Ferdinand Bol*
*Woman before a Mirror*
*Biblioteca Nacional, Madrid*

156  Ferdinand Bol
Seated Woman
Staatliche Museen Preussischer Kulturbesitz,
Kupferstichkabinett, Berlin

192  *Jan Lievens*
     *Evangelist Mark*
     *The Albertina*

197  *Jan Lievens*
     *St. Jerome*
     *Kunstmuseum der Stadt Düsseldorf*

194  *Jan Lievens*
     *Entrance Gate to a Garden*
     *Amsterdams Historisch Museum*
     *(Collection Fodor)*

195  *Jan Lievens*
     *Wooded Landscape*
     *The Pierpont Morgan Library*

193  *Jan Lievens*
*Portrait of a Scholar*
*Museum Boymans-van Beuningen*

196  Jan Lievens
*Trees*
*Staatliche Museen Preussischer Kulturbesitz,*
*Kupferstichkabinett, Berlin*

183  *Samuel van Hoogstraten*
    *Adoration of the Shepherds*
    *Kunsthalle, Hamburg*

170  Barent Fabritius
     *Adoration of the Shepherds*
     *Museum Boymans-van Beuningen*

169  Barent Fabritius?
     *The Satyr and the Peasants*
     *The Art Institute of Chicago*

162  *Lambert Doomer*
     *The Well and Fortress at*
     *Tal Ehrenbreitstein*
     *The Pierpont Morgan Library*

161  *Lambert Doomer*
     *The "Hoenderpoort" and the*
     *Belvedere in Nijmegen*
     *Museum Boymans-van Beuningen*

198  Nicolaes Maes
*Christ Blessing the Children*
*Rijksprentenkabinet, Amsterdam*

199 *Nicolaes Maes*
*Woman Scraping a Parsnip*
*Coll. F. Lugt,*
*Institut Néerlandais, Paris*

200 *Nicolaes Maes*
*Old Woman with a Yarn Winder and a Spool*
*Staatliche Museen Preussischer Kulturbesitz,*
*Kupferstichkabinett, Berlin*

201 Nicolaes Maes
   The Young Mother
   The Metropolitan Museum of Art

202 Nicolaes Maes
   Young Man Descending a Staircase
   Museum Boymans-van Beuningen

259

204  Nicolaes Maes
     *Man Standing*
     *Museum Boymans-van Beuningen*

205  Nicolaes Maes
     *Man Standing, Leaning against a Doorpost*
     *Museum Boymans-van Beuningen*

*203 Nicolaes Maes*
*A Scholar in His Study*
*Wadsworth Atheneum*

184 *Philips Koninck?*
*Christ among His Disciples*
*Ecole Nationale Supérieure des Beaux-Arts, Paris*

185  Philips Koninck
     *Elijah and the Prophets of Baal*
     Mr. and Mrs. Seymour Slive

186  Philips Koninck
     *The Visitation*
     The Pierpont Morgan Library

189   *Philips Koninck*
     *River Scene*
     *Bowdoin College Museum of Art*

187   *Philips Koninck*
     *Distant View from the Dunes*
     *Groninger Museum voor Stad en Lande*

188   *Philips Koninck*
     *River Landscape with High Embankment*
     *Musées royaux des Beaux-Arts de Belgique*

Aert de Gelder

266

*176  Abraham Furnerius?*
*Tower of the Westerkerk in Amsterdam*
*Amsterdams Historisch Museum*
*(Collection Fodor)*

*182  Aert de Gelder*
*Jacob Being Shown Joseph's Coat*
*The Art Institute of Chicago*

*181  Aert de Gelder*
*Group of Figures in Oriental Costume*
*Miss Annette Ruth Brod*

177  *Abraham Furnerius*
    *Wooded Landscape*
    *Rijksprentenkabinet, Amsterdam*

179  *Abraham Furnerius*
    *Cottage under Trees*
    *Mr. and Mrs. Winslow Ames*

180  *Abraham Furnerius*
    *Farm Buildings under Trees*
    *Kunsthalle, Hamburg*

178  *Abraham Furnerius*
     *Wooded Landscape*
     *The Brower Collection*
     *Central College, Pella, Iowa*

158  *Anthonie van Borssum*
     *Farm Buildings*
     *Rijksprentenkabinet, Amsterdam*

159  *Anthonie van Borssum*
     *View of Soest*
     *Amsterdams Historisch Museum*
     *(Collection Fodor)*

160   *Anthonie van Borssum*
      *Mill and Boat-Lift near a Canal*
      *Rijksprentenkabinet, Amsterdam*

190   *Johannes Leupenius*
      *View of Trees and Houses across a Stream*
      *The Albertina*

191   *Johannes Leupenius*
      *Castle Nijenrode*
      *Rijksprentenkabinet, Amsterdam*

# References

## ABBREVIATIONS OF WORKS
## MOST FREQUENTLY CITED

B.        Adam Bartsch, *Catalogue Raisonné de toutes les Estampes qui forment l'Oeuvre de Rembrandt, et ceux de ses principaux Imitateurs*, I–II, Vienna, 1797.

BAUCH 1926        Kurt Bauch, *Jakob Adriaensz Backer*, Berlin, 1926.

BAUCH 1933        ———, *Die Kunst des jungen Rembrandt*, Heidelberg, 1933.

BAUCH 1939        , "Rembrandt und Lievens", *Wallraf Richartz Jahrbuch*, XI, 1939, pp. 239–68.

BAUCH 1960        ———, *Der frühe Rembrandt und seine Zeit*, Berlin, 1960.

BAUCH 1966        ———, *Rembrandt Gemälde*, Berlin, 1966.

BAUCH 1967        ———, "Zum Werk des Jan Lievens," *Pantheon*, XXV, 1967, pp. 160–70; 259–69.

BECKER 1923        Felix Becker, *Handzeichnungen holländischer Meister aus der Sammlung Dr. C. Hofstede de Groot im Haag*, N. F., Leipzig, 1923.

BEGEMANN 1961        Egbert Haverkamp-Begemann, review of "Otto Benesch, The Drawings of Rembrandt," *Kunstchronik*, XIV, 1961, pp. 10–28; 50–57; 85–91.

[E. H.-B.] 1962        ———, in *Great Drawings of All Time*, II, New York, 1962.

BENESCH 1935        Otto Benesch, *Rembrandt, Werk und Forschung*, Vienna, 1935.

BENESCH 1947        ———, *Rembrandt, Selected Drawings*, London/New York, 1947.

BENESCH 1948        ———, "Rembrandt's Artistic Heritage I, From Rembrandt to Goya," *Gazette des Beaux-Arts*, série 6, XXXIII, 1948, pp. 280–300.

BENESCH I–VI        ———, *The Drawings of Rembrandt*, I–VI, London, 1954–57.

BENESCH 1960        ———, *Rembrandt as a Draughtsman*, New York, 1960.

BENESCH 1964        ———, "Neuentdeckte Zeichnungen von Rembrandt," *Jahrbuch der Berliner Museen*, VI, 1964, pp. 105–50.

BENESCH 1964–67        ———, *Master Drawings in the Albertina*, Greenwich, Conn., 1967.

BERNT 1948 I–II        Walther Bernt, *Die niederländischen Maler des 17. Jahrhunderts*, Munich, 1948.

BERNT 1957, 1958        ———, *Die niederländischen Zeichner des 17. Jahrhunderts*, I and II, Munich, 1957 and 1958.

BOCK AND ROSENBERG 1930        Elfried Bock and Jakob Rosenberg, *Staatliche Museen zu Berlin, Die niederländischen Meister*, Berlin, 1930.

BODE AND VALENTINER 1907        W. von Bode and W. R. Valentiner, *Handzeichnungen alt-holländischer Genremaler*, Berlin, 1907.

BOLTEN 1967        , J. Bolten, *Dutch drawings from the collection of Dr. C. Hofstede de Groot*, Utrecht, 1967.

BREDIUS I–VII        A. Bredius, *Künstler-inventare*, I–VII, The Hague, 1915–22.

BREDIUS 1931        ———, "Karel van der Pluym, neef en leerling van Rembrandt," *Oud-Holland*, XLVIII, 1931, pp. 241–64.

BR.        ———, *The Paintings of Rembrandt*, London/New York, [1935].

BREDIUS (GERSON) 1969        ———, *Rembrandt*, revised by Horst Gerson, London, 1969.

DE BRUIJN 1932        I. de Bruijn, *Catalogus van de verzameling etsen in het bezit van I. de Bruijn. . . .*, 's-Gravenhage, 1932.

BUDDE 1930        Illa Budde, *Beschreibender Katalog der Handzeichnungen in der Staatlichen Kunstakademie Düsseldorf*, Düsseldorf, 1930.

CHICAGO 1961        *Paintings in The Art Institute of Chicago, A Catalogue of the Picture Collection*, Chicago, 1961.

CLARK 1968        Kenneth Clark, *Rembrandt and the Italian Renaissance*, New York, 1968.

CORMACK 1966        Malcolm Cormack, *Drawings by Rembrandt and his Circle* [Exhibition Catalogue], Cambridge (Fitzwilliam Museum), 1966.

DATTENBERG 1967        , H. Dattenberg, *Niederrheinansichten holländischer Künstler des 17. Jahrhunderts*, Düsseldorf, 1967.

VAN DYKE 1923        John C. van Dyke, *Rembrandt and his School*, New York, 1923.

FAIRFAX MURRAY        C. Fairfax Murray, *J. Pierpont Morgan Collection of Drawings by the Old Masters Formed by C. Fairfax Murray*, London, 1905–12.

FALCK 1924        Gustav Falck, "Ueber einige von Rembrandt übergangene Schülerzeichnungen," *Jahrbuch der preussischen Kunstsammlungen*, XLV, 1924, pp. 191–200.

FALCK 1924–35        ———, "Noble Arbejder of Barent Fabritius," *Tidskrift för Konstvetenskap*, 1924–25, pp. 74 ff.

FALCK 1927        ———, "Einige Bemerkungen über Ph. Konincks Tätigkeit als Zeichner," *Festschrift für Max J. Friedländer*, Leipzig, 1927, pp. 168–90.

FLECHSIG 1925        Eduard Flechsig, *Zeichnungen alter Meister im Landesmuseum zu Braunschweig, Niederländer des 17. Jahrhunderts (IX. Veröffentlichungen der Prestel-Gesellschaft)*, Frankfurt, 1925.

FREISE AND LILIENFELD        K. Freise and K. Lilienfeld, *Rembrandts Handzeichnungen*, I, Parchim, 1921.

FREISE AND WICHMANN 1925        ——— and H. Wichmann, *Rembrandts Handzeichnungen*, III, Parchim, 1925.

GANTNER 1962        Joseph Gantner, "Rembrandt und das Abendmahl des Leonardo," *Variae Formae veritas una, Kunsthistorische Studien, Festschrift Friedrich Gerke*, Baden-Baden, 1962, pp. 179–84.

GANTNER 1964 ———, *Rembrandt und die Verwandlung klassischer Formen*, Bern [1964].

VAN GELDER 1953 J. G. van Gelder, "Rembrandt and his Circle," *The Burlington Magazine*, XCV, 1953, pp. 34–39.

VAN GELDER 1958 ———, *Prenten en tekeningen*, Amsterdam, 1958.

VAN GELDER 1961 ———, "The Drawings of Rembrandt," *The Burlington Magazine*, CIII, 1961, pp. 149–51.

GERSON 1936 Horst Gerson, *Philips Koninck*, Berlin, 1936.

GERSON 1957 ———, "Probleme der Rembrandt-Schule," *Kunstchronik*, X, 1957, pp. 121–23.

GERSON 1957 ———, "Aktdarstellungen bei Rembrandt und seinen Schülern," *Kunstchronik*, X, 1957, pp. 148–50.

GERSON 1968 ———, *Rembrandt Paintings*, Amsterdam, 1968.

HAAK 1969 Bob Haak, *Rembrandt, His Life, His Work, His Time*, New York, 1969.

VAN HASSELT 1968–69 Carlos van Hasselt, *Dessins de paysagistes hollandais du XVIIe siècle de la collection particulière conservée à l'Institut Néerlandais de Paris* [Exhibition Catalogue], Brussels / Rotterdam / Paris / Berne, 1968–69.

HELL 1930 H. Hell, "Die späten Handzeichnungen Rembrandts," *Repertorium für Kunstwissenschaft*, LI, 1930, pp. 4–43; 92–136.

HENKEL 1931 Max D. Henkel, *Le Dessin hollandais des origines au XVIIe siècle*, Paris, 1931.

HENKEL 1942 ———, *Catalogus van de Nederlandsche Teekeningen in het Rijksmuseum te Amsterdam, I. Teekeningen van Rembrandt en zijn School*, 's-Gravenhage, 1942.

HESELTINE 1907 *Original Drawings by Rembrandt in the Collection of J. P. H. [eseltine]*, London, 1907.

H. Arthur M. Hind, *A Catalogue of Rembrandt's Etchings*, I–II, London, 1912.

HIND 1915 ———, *Catalogue of Drawings by Dutch and Flemish Artists preserved in the Department of Prints and Drawings in the British Museum, I. Drawings by Rembrandt and his School*, London, 1915.

HdG Cornelis Hofstede de Groot, *Die Handzeichnungen Rembrandts*, Haarlem, 1906.

HOFSTEDE DE GROOT 1915 ———, "Rembrandts onderwijs aan zijne leerlingen," *Feest-bundel Dr. Abraham Bredius*, 1915, pp. 79–94.

HOFSTEDE DE GROOT, VI, 1916 ———, *A Catalogue Raisonné of the works of the Most Eminent Dutch Painters of the Seventeenth Century*, VI, London, 1916.

HOFSTEDE DE GROOT 1929 ———, "Einige Betrachtungen über die Ausstellung holländischer Kunst in London," *Repertorium für Kunstwissenschaft*, L, 1929, pp. 134–46.

HOLLSTEIN , F. W. H. Hollstein, *Dutch and Flemish Etchings Engravings and Woodcuts*, X, Amsterdam.

HOUBRAKEN I–III Arnold Houbraken, *De Groote Schouburgh der Nederlantsche Konstschilders en Schilderessen*, I–III, edited by P. T. A. Swillens, Maastricht, 1943–53.

KAUFFMANN 1926 Hans Kauffmann, "Zur Kritik der Rembrandtzeichnungen," *Repertorium für Kunstwissenschaft*, XLVII, 1926, pp. 157–78.

KLEINMANN H. Kleinmann, *Handzeichnungen alter Meister der holländischen Schule*, Haarlem, 1894–99.

KRONIG 1914–15 J. O. Kronig, "Carel van der Pluym," *The Burlington Magazine*, XXVI, 1914–15, pp. 172–77.

KRUSE 1920 John Kruse and Carl Neumann, *Die Zeichnungen Rembrandts und seiner Schule im National-Museum zu Stockholm*, The Hague, 1920.

LILIENFELD Karl Lilienfeld, *Arent de Gelder*, The Hague, 1914.

LIPPMANN I–IV F. Lippmann, continued by C. Hofstede de Groot, *Original Drawings by Rembrandt*, Berlin, 1888–92, The Hague, 1898–1911.

L. Frits Lugt, *Les Marques de collections de dessins & d'estampes*, Amsterdam, 1921; *Supplément*, The Hague, 1956.

LUGT 1920 ———, *Mit Rembrandt in Amsterdam*, Berlin, 1920.

LUGT 1927 ———, *Palais des Beaux-Arts (Petit Palais), Inventaire général des dessins dans les collections publiques de France, Les Dessins des écoles du Nord de la Collection Dutuit*, Paris, 1927.

LUGT 1929 ———, *Musée du Louvre, Inventaire général des dessins des écoles du Nord, Ecole hollandaise*, I, Paris, 1929.

LUGT 1931 ———, "Beiträge zu dem Katalog der Niederländischen Handzeichnungen in Berlin," *Jahrbuch der preussischen Kunstsammlungen*, LII, 1931, pp. 36–80.

LUGT 1933 ———, *Musée du Louvre, Inventaire général des dessins des écoles du Nord, Ecole hollandaise, III, Rembrandt*, Paris, 1933.

LUGT 1936 ———, *Bibliothéque Nationale, Inventaire géneral des dessins des écoles du Nord*, Paris, 1936.

LUGT 1950 ———, *Ecole Nationale Supérieure des Beaux-Arts, Inventaire général des dessins des écoles du Nord*, I, Paris, 1950.

MacLAREN 1960 Neil MacLaren, *National Gallery Catalogues, The Dutch School*, London, 1960.

MARTIN II, 1936 W. Martin, *De Hollandsche Schilderkunst in de zeventiende Eeuw, II, Rembrandt en zijn tijd*, Amsterdam, 1936.

MICHALKOWA J. Michalkowa, "Lekcja Rembrandta O Lejdelskiej Wystawie *Rembrandt als Leermeester*," *Biuletyn Historii Sztuki*, XIX, 1957, pp. 261–68.

VON MOLTKE 1965 J. W. von Moltke, *Govaert Flinck 1615–1660*, Amsterdam, 1965.

MÜNZ 1924 Ludwig Münz, "Federzeichnungen von Rembrandt und Bol," *Belvedere*, VI, 1924, pp. 106–12.

MÜNZ 1935 ———, "Rembrandts Altersstil und die Barockklassik," *Jahrbuch der kunsthistorischen Sammlungen in Wien*, N. F. IX, 1935, pp. 183–222.

MÜNZ 1952, I–II ——, *Rembrandt's Etchings*, I–II, London, 1952.

NEUMANN 1918 Carl Neumann, *Aus der Werkstatt Rembrandts*, Heidelberg, 1918.

NEUMANN 1919 ——, *Rembrandt Handzeichnungen*, Munich, 1919.

PAULI 1924 Gustav Pauli, *Zeichnungen alter Meister in der Kunsthalle zu Hamburg, Niederländer (VIII. Veröffentlichungen der Prestel-Gesellschaft)*, Frankfurt, 1924.

PAULI 1926 ——, *Zeichnungen alter Meister in der Kunsthalle zu Hamburg, Niederländer (XII. Veröffentlichungen der Prestel-Gesellschaft)*, N. F., Frankfurt, 1926.

PONT 1958 D. Pont, *Barent Fabritius 1624–1673*, 's-Gravenhage, 1958.

PONT 1960 ——, "De composities 'Ruth en Naomi' te Bremen en te Oxford. Toeschrijving aan Willem Drost," *Oud-Holland*, LXXV, 1960, pp. 205–21.

VAN REGTEREN ALTENA 1948–49 J. Q. van Regteren Altena, "Rembrandt's Way to Emmaus," *Kunstmuseets Årsskrift*, 1948–49, pp. 1–25.

VAN REGTEREN ALTENA 1951 ——, *Mostra di incisioni e disegni di Rembrandt* [Exhibition Catalogue], Rome/Florence, 1951.

VAN REGTEREN ALTENA 1952 ——, "Retouches aan ons Rembrandt-beeld, II, 'De Eendracht van het land'," *Oud-Holland*, LXVII, 1952, pp. 59–67.

VAN REGTEREN ALTENA 1961 ——, "[Schenking De Bruijn-van der Leeuw], De tekeningen," *Bulletin van het Rijksmuseum*, IX, 1961, pp. 68–89.

ROGER-MARX 1960 Claude Roger-Marx, *Rembrandt*, New York, 1960.

ROSENBERG 1948 Jakob Rosenberg, *Rembrandt*, Cambridge, Mass., 1948.

ROSENBERG K 1956 ——, "Die Rembrandt-Ausstellungen in Holland," *Kunstchronik*, IX, 1956, pp. 345–54.

ROSENBERG D 1956 ——, *Rembrandt the Draughtsman with Consideration of the Problem of Authenticity*, Fogg Museum of Art, Harvard University, 1956 (reprinted from *Daedalus*, LXXXVI, September 1956).

ROSENBERG AB 1956, 1959 ——, review of "Otto Benesch, The Drawings of Rembrandt," *Art Bulletin*, XXXVIII, 1956, pp. 63–70, and XLI, 1959, pp. 108–19.

ROSENBERG 1964 ——, *Rembrandt Life & Work*, 2nd edition, London/New York, 1964.

ROSENBERG, SLIVE, TER KUILE 1966 Jakob Rosenberg, Seymour Slive, E. H. ter Kuile, *Dutch Art and Architecture, 1600–1800*, London, 1966.

ROTERMUND 1952 Hans-Martin Rotermund, "The Motif of Radiance in Rembrandt's Biblical Drawings," *Journal of the Warburg and Courtauld Institutes*, XV, 1952, pp. 101–21.

ROTERMUND 1963 ——, *Rembrandts Handzeichnungen und Radierungen zur Bibel*, Stuttgart, 1963.

ROVINSKI , D. Rovinski, *L'Oeuvre gravé des élèves de Rembrandt*, I, St. Petersburg, 1894.

SCHEIDIG 1962 Walther Scheidig, *Rembrandt als Zeichner*, Leipzig, 1962.

SCHNEIDER 1932 H. Schneider, *Jan Lievens*, Haarlem, 1932.

SCHÖNBRUNNER AND MEDER J. Schönbrunner and J. Meder, *Handzeichnungen alter Meister aus der Albertina*, Vienna, 1896–1908.

SCHUURMAN 1947 K. E. Schuurman, *Carel Fabritius*, Amsterdam, 1947.

SLIVE 1953 Seymour Slive, *Rembrandt and his Critics*, The Hague, 1953.

SLIVE 1965 ——, *Drawings of Rembrandt, with a Selection of Drawings by His Pupils and Followers based on the Facsimile Series Edited by F. Lippmann, C. Hofstede de Groot, and Others*, New York, 1965.

J. SMITH, VII, 1836 John Smith, *A Catalogue Raisonné of the Works of the Most Eminent Dutch, Flemish and French Painters*, London, 1829–42. VII: *Rembrandt*, 1836.

J. SMITH, IX, SUPPLEMENT, 1842 ——, *A Catalogue Raisonné of the Works of the Most Eminent Dutch, Flemish and French Painters*, London, 1829–42. IX: *Supplement*, 1842.

STARING 1948 A. Staring, "Portretten door Gerbrand van den Eeckhout," *Oud-Holland*, LXIII, 1948, pp. 180–88.

STARZYŃSKI 1935–36 J. Starzyński, "Doniosłe odkrycie obrazu szkoły Rembrandta w Warszawie," *Biuletyn Historii Sztuki*, IV, 1935–36, pp. 93–113.

STARZYŃSKI 1956 ——, "Fabritius-uczeń Rembrandta," *Biuletyn Historii Sztuki*, XVIII, 1956, pp. 402–18.

STECHOW 1934 Wolfgang Stechow, "Rembrandts Darstellungen des Emmausmahles," *Zeitschrift für Kunstgeschichte*, III, 1934, pp. 329–41.

STECHOW 1966 ——, *Dutch Landscape Painting of the Seventeenth Century*, London, 1966.

SUMOWSKI 1956–57 Werner Sumowski, "Bemerkungen zu Otto Beneschs Corpus der Rembrandt-Zeichnungen," I, *Wissenschaftliche Zeitschrift der Humboldt-Universität zu Berlin*, VI, 1956–57, pp. 255–81.

SUMOWSKI 1957–58 ——, "Nachträge zum Rembrandtjahr 1956," *Wissenschaftliche Zeitschrift der Humboldt-Universität zu Berlin*, VII, 1957–58, pp. 223–78.

W. Sumowski "Daniel Pont: Barent Fabritius 1624–1673, (Utrecht 1958)." *Kunstchronik*, XII, 1959, pp. 287–94.

SUMOWSKI 1961 ——, *Bemerkungen zu Otto Beneschs Corpus der Rembrandtzeichnungen*, II, Bad Pymont, 1961.

SUMOWSKI 1962 ——, "Unbekannte Rembrandtzeichnungen," *Kunstchronik*, XV, 1962, pp. 274–76.

SUMOWSKI 1962 ——, "Gerbrand van den Eeckhout als Zeichner," *Oud-Holland*, LXXVII, 1962, pp. 11–39.

SUMOWSKI 1964 ——, "Zwei Rembrandt-Originale," *Pantheon*, XXII, 1964, pp. 29–34; "Rembrandtzeichnungen," *Ibid.*, pp. 233–48.

SUMOWSKI P 1965 ——, "Eine Renesse-Zeichnung mit Rembrandt-Korrekturen," *Pantheon*, XXIII, 1965, pp. 246–56.

SUMOWSKI *FT* 1965 ———, "Notizen zu Zeichnungen von F. Bol," *Festschrift Dr. h. c. Eduard Trautscholdt . . .*, Hamburg, 1965.

SUMOWSKI 1966 ———, "Hoogstraten und Elsheimer," *Kunstchronik*, XIX, 1966, pp. 302–03.

SUMOWSKI 1967 ———, "Eine frühe Federzeichnung von Govaert Flinck," *Pantheon*, XXV, 1967, pp. 336–40.

[F. THOMPSON] 1962 [F. Thompson], *The Devonshire Collection, Old Master Drawings at Chatsworth, . . . Drawings by Rembrandt . . .*, Derby, England [1963].

TIETZE 1947 Hans Tietze, *European Master Drawings in the United States*, New York, 1947.

TOLNAY 1943 Charles de Tolnay, *History and Technique of Old Master Drawings*, New York, 1943.

TRAUTSCHOLDT 1958 Eduard Trautscholdt, review of "Walther Bernt, Die niederländischen Zeichner des 17. Jahrhunderts," *Kunstchronik*, XI, 1958, pp. 361–71.

TRAUTSCHOLDT 1967 ———, "Rembrandt und sein Kreis," *Kunstchronik*, XX, 1967, pp. 124–31.

VALENTINER 1908 Wilhelm R. Valentiner, *Rembrandt des Meisters Gemälde (Klassiker der Kunst)*, Stuttgart/Leipzig, 1908.

VALENTINER 1921 ———, *Rembrandt Wiedergefundene Gemälde (Klassiker der Kunst)*, Stuttgart/Berlin, 1921.

VALENTINER 1923 ———, "Early Drawings by Nicolaes Maes," *Burlington Magazine*, XLIII, 1923, pp. 16–22.

VALENTINER 1924 ———, *Nicolaes Maes*, Berlin/Leipzig, 1924.

VALENTINER 1925, 1934 ———, *Rembrandt, Des Meisters Handzeichnungen*, I and II, Stuttgart/Berlin, 1925 and 1934.

VALENTINER 1930 ———, "Rembrandt and Samuel van Hoogstraten," *Art in America*, XVIII, 1930, pp. 123–43.

VALENTINER 1932 ———, "Carel and Barent Fabritius," *The Art Bulletin*, XIV, 1932, pp. 197–240.

VALENTINER 1939 ———, "Willem Drost Pupil of Rembrandt," *Art Quarterly*, II, 1939, pp. 295–325.

VALENTINER 1957 ———, "Drawings by Bol," *Art Quarterly*, XX, 1957, pp. 49–68.

VOGEL 1958 H. Vogel, *Katalog der Staatlichen Gemäldegalerie zu Kassel*, Kassel, 1958.

WEGNER 1957 Wolfgang Wegner, *Rembrandt-Zeichnungen* [Exhibition Catalogue], Munich (Staatliche Graphische Sammlung), 1957.

WEGNER 1966–67 ———, *Rembrandt und sein Kreis* [Exhibition Catalogue], Munich, (Staatliche Graphische Sammlung), 1966–67.

WHITE 1969 Christopher White, *Rembrandt as an Etcher, A Study of the Artist at Work*, London, 1969.

WIJNMAN 1931 H. F. Wijnman, "De Schilder Carel Fabritius (1622–1654)," *Oud-Holland*, XLVIII, 1931, pp. 100–41.

WOERMANN Karl Woermann, *Handzeichnungen alter Meister im königlichen Kupferstichkabinett zu Dresden*, Munich, 1896 ff.

WURZBACH I–III A. von Wurzbach, *Niederländisches Künstler-lexicon*, Wien/Leipzig, 1906–11.

## ABBREVIATIONS OF EXHIBITIONS MOST FREQUENTLY CITED

AMSTERDAM 1929 Amsterdam, Rijksmuseum, *Oude Kunst*, 1929.

AMSTERDAM 1932 Amsterdam, Rijksmuseum, *Rembrandt*, 1932.

AMSTERDAM 1935 Amsterdam, Rijksmuseum, *Rembrandt Tentoonstelling*, 1935.

AMSTERDAM 1936 Amsterdam, Rijksmuseum, *Oude Kunst uit het bezit van den internationalen handel*, 1936.

AMSTERDAM 1961 Amsterdam, Rijksmuseum, *De schenking De Bruijn-Van der Leeuw aan het Rijksmuseum*, 1961.

AMSTERDAM 1963 Amsterdam, Museum Fodor, *Fodor 100 jaar*, 1963.

BASEL 1948 Basel, Galerie Katz, *Rembrandt*, 1948.

BEOGRAD/ZAGREB 1960 Beograd/Zagreb, Moderna Galerija, *Crtezi nizozemskik majstora iz kolekcije Fodor u Amsterdam*, 1960.

BERLIN 1930 Berlin, Preussische Akademie der Bildenden Künste, *Rembrandt*, 1930.

BERLIN 1968 Berlin, Gemäldegalerie Berlin-Dahlem, *Rembrandt zeichnet*, 1968.

BERN 1937 Bern, Kunstmuseum, *Rembrandt*, 1937.

BRAUNSCHWEIG 1948 Braunschweig, Herzog Anton-Ulrich-Museum, *Holländische Zeichenkunst des 17 Jahrhunderts*, 1948.

BRUSSELS 1937–38 Brussels, Palais des Beaux-Arts, *Dessins hollandais de Jérôme Bosch à Rembrandt*, 1937–38.

BRUSSELS/HAMBURG 1961 Brussels, Albert I-Bibliotheek, Hamburg, Kunsthalle, *Hollandse Tekeningen uit de gouden eeuw/Holländische Zeichnungen der Rembrandt-Zeit*, 1961.

BUDAPEST 1962 Budapest, Szépművészeti Múzeum, *One Hundred Drawings from the Fodor Collection*, 1962.

BUFFALO 1935 Buffalo, Albright Knox Art Gallery, *Master Drawings*, 1935.

CAMBRIDGE, MASS. 1948 Cambridge, Mass., Fogg Art Museum, *Rembrandt Paintings and Etchings*, 1948.

CAMBRIDGE, MASS. 1948–49 Cambridge, Mass., Fogg Art Museum, *Seventy Master Drawings*, 1948–49.

CAMBRIDGE, 1966 Cambridge, Fitzwilliam Museum, *Drawings by Rembrandt and his Circle*, 1966.

CHICAGO 1935 Chicago, The Art Institute of, *Rembrandt and his Circle*, 1935.

CHICAGO 1935–36 Chicago, The Art Institute of, *Loan Exhibition of Paintings, Drawings, and Etchings by Rembrandt*, 1935–36.

CHICAGO 1942    Chicago, The Art Institute of, *Paintings by the Great Dutch Masters of the Seventeenth Century*, 1942.

CINCINNATI 1959    The Cincinnati Art Museum, *The Lehman Collection of New York*, 1959.

CLEVES 1965    Cleves, Städtisches Museum Haus Koekkoek, *Govert Flinck der Kleefsche Apelles 1616–1660*, 1965.

COLOGNE/BREMEN 1955    Cologne, Wallraf-Richartz-Museum, and Bremen, Kunsthalle, *Rembrandt und seine Zeitgenossen*, 1955.

DARMSTADT 1964    Darmstadt, *Zeichnungen alter und neuer Meister*, 1964.

DELFT/ANTWERP 1964–65    Delft, Het Prinsenhof, and Antwerp, Koninklijk Museum voor Schone Kunsten, *De Schilder in zijn Wereld*, 1964–65.

DETROIT 1930    The Detroit Institute of Arts, *Paintings by Rembrandt*, 1930.

DIJON 1950    Dijon, Musée, *Jérôme Bosch à Rembrandt, peintures et dessins du Musée Boymans de Rotterdam*, 1950.

DORDRECHT 1934    Dordrecht, Museum, *Nicolaes Maes*, 1934.

DÜSSELDORF 1968    Düsseldorf, *Niederländische Handzeichnungen 1500–1800*, 1968.

GRONINGEN 1931    Groningen, Groningsch Museum, *Verzameling Dr. C. Hofstede de Groot*, 1931.

GRONINGEN 1948    Groningen, Museum van Oudhede voor de Provincie en Stad Groningen, *Oude Meesters*, 1948.

GRONINGEN 1952    Groningen, Groningsch Museum, *Honderd Tekeningen*, 1952.

HAARLEM 1951    Haarlem, Vleeschal, *Rembrandt*, 1951.

THE HAGUE 1902–03    The Hague, Haagsche Kunstkring, *Teekeningen van Oude Hollandsche Meesters uit de Verzameling van Dr. C. Hofstede de Groot*, 1902–03.

THE HAGUE 1930    The Hague, Gemeente Museum, *Verzameling Dr. C. Hofstede de Groot*, 1930.

THE HAGUE 1955    The Hague, Rijksbureau voor Kunsthistorische Documentatie, *Keuze van Schilderijen en Tekeningen uit de Verzameling C. Hofstede de Groot*, 1955.

INDIANAPOLIS/SAN DIEGO 1958    Indianapolis, John Herron Art Museum; San Diego, The Fine Arts Gallery, *The Young Rembrandt and His Times*, 1958.

INGELHEIM AM RHEIN 1964    Ingelheim am Rhein, *Holländische Zeichnungen des 17. Jahrhunderts*, 1964.

JERUSALEM 1960    Jerusalem, *Master Drawings from the Fodor Collection*, 1960.

JERUSALEM 1965    Jerusalem, The Israel Museum, *Rembrandt*, 1965.

LEIDEN 1903    Leiden, Vereeniging "Die Laecken-Halle," *Teekeningen van Oud-Nederlandsche Meesters*, 1903.

LEIDEN 1916    Leiden, Stedelijk Museum "De Lakenhal," *Teekeningen van Hollandsche Meesters uit de Verzameling Dr. C. Hofstede de Groot*, 1916.

LEIDEN 1956    Leiden, Stedelijk Museum "De Lakenhal," *Rembrandt als Leermeester*, 1956.

LONDON 1899    London, Royal Academy of Arts, *Rembrandt*, 1899.

LONDON 1929    London, Royal Academy of Arts, Burlington House, *Dutch Art 1450–1900*, 1929.

LONDON 1938    London, Royal Academy of Arts, *17th Century Art in Europe*, 1929.

LONDON 1952–53    London, Royal Academy of Arts, *Dutch Pictures 1450–1750*, 1952–53.

LONDON 1953    London, Royal Academy of Arts, *Drawings from Old Masters*, 1953.

LONDON 1953 MG    London, The Matthiesen Gallery, *Rembrandt's Influence in the 17th Century*, 1953.

LOS ANGELES 1947    Los Angeles County Museum, *Frans Hals-Rembrandt*, 1947.

MANCHESTER 1857    Manchester, *Art Treasures of the United Kingdom. Collected at Manchester*, 1857.

MANCHESTER 1961    Manchester, City Art Gallery, *Drawings from Chatsworth*, 1961.

MIDDLETOWN 1959    Middletown, Conn., Wesleyan University, Davison Art Center, *Rembrandt and His School*, 1959.

MILAN 1954    Milan, Palazzo Reale, *Mostra di Pittura Olandese del Seicento*, 1954.

MONTREAL/TORONTO 1969    Montreal, The Montreal Museum of Fine Arts; Toronto, Art Gallery of Toronto, *Rembrandt and His Pupils*, 1969.

NEW ORLEANS 1964    New Orleans, Tulane University, Newcomb College, *Dutch and Flemish Paintings, Prints and Drawings of the 17th Century*, 1964.

NEW YORK 1909    New York, The Metropolitan Museum of Art, *The Hudson–Fulton Celebration. Loan Exhibition of Paintings by Old Dutch Masters*, 1909.

NEW YORK 1919    New York Public Library, *Drawings from the J. Pierpont Collection*, 1919.

NEW YORK 1925    New York, M. Knoedler & Co., *Dutch Masters of the Seventeenth Century*, 1925.

NEW YORK 1939    New York, The Pierpont Morgan Library, *An Exhibition Held on the Occasion of the New York World's Fair*, 1939.

NEW YORK 1940    New York World's Fair, *Masterpieces of Art, Catalogue of European and American Paintings 1500–1900*, 1940.

NEW YORK/CAMBRIDGE, MASS. 1960    New York, The Pierpont Morgan Library; Cambridge, Mass., Fogg Art Museum, *Rembrandt Drawings from American Collections*, 1960.

NEW YORK/TOLEDO/TORONTO 1954–55    New York, The Metropolitan Museum of Art; Toledo, Museum of Art; Toronto, Art Gallery, *Dutch Paintings, The Golden Age*, 1954–55.

NEW YORK 1963    New York, Wildenstein & Co., *Master Drawings from The Art Institute of Chicago*, 1963.

PARIS 1908    Paris, Bibliothèque Nationale, *Exposition d'Oeuvres de Rembrandt*, 1908.

PARIS 1950    Paris, L'Orangerie, *Le Paysage hollandais au XVIIe siècle*, 1950.

PARIS 1952    Paris, Bibliothèque Nationale, *Musée Boymans, dessins du XVe au XIXe siècle*, 1952.

PARIS 1957    Paris, L'Orangerie, *Collection Lehman de New York*, 1957.

RALEIGH 1956    Raleigh, North Carolina Museum of Art, *Rembrandt and His Pupils*, 1956.

ROTTERDAM 1934    Rotterdam, Museum Boymans, *Nederlandsche teekeningen uit de 15e–17e eeuw, Verzameling Koenigs*, 1934.

ROTTERDAM 1938    Rotterdam, Museum Boymans, *Meesterwerken uit vier eeuwen 1400–1800*, 1938.

ROTTERDAM/AMSTERDAM 1956    Rotterdam, Museum Boymans, and Amsterdam, Rijksmuseum, *Rembrandt*, 1956.

SAN FRANCISCO 1920    San Francisco Art Association, *Drawings and Etchings from the J. Pierpont Collection*, 1920.

SAN FRANCISCO/TOLDEO/BOSTON 1966–67    San Francisco, California Palace of the Legion of Honor; Toledo, Museum of Art; Boston, Museum of Fine Arts, *The Age of Rembrandt*, 1966–67.

STOCKHOLM 1956    Stockholm, Nationalmuseum, *Rembrandt*, 1956.

TOKYO/KYOTO 1968    The Tokyo National Museum, and The Kyoto National Museum, *Masterpieces of Rembrandt*, 1968.

TORONTO 1926    Art Gallery of Toronto, *Inaugural Exhibition*, 1926.

UTICA/ROCHESTER 1963    Utica, Museum of Art, Munson-Williams-Proctor Institute, and The Rochester Memorial Art Gallery of the University of Rochester, *Masters of Landscape: East and West*, 1963.

VANCOUVER 1958    Vancouver, The Fine Arts Gallery, *The Changing Landscape of Holland*, 1958.

VIENNA 1936    Vienna, Albertina, *Die holländische Landschaft im Zeitalter Rembrandts*, 1936.

VIENNA 1956    Vienna, Albertina, *Rembrandt*, 1956.

WASHINGTON, D.C. *et al.* 1962–63    Washington, D.C. *et al.*, *Old Master Drawings from Chatsworth* (A Loan Exhibition from the Devonshire Collection, circulated by the Smithsonian Institution), 1962–63.

WASHINGTON, D.C. *et al.* 1966–67    Washington, D.C. *et al.*, *17th and 18th Century European Drawings* (Exhibition organized and circulated by The American Federation of Arts, New York), 1966–67.

WASHINGTON, D.C. 1969    Washington, D.C., The National Gallery of Art, *Rembrandt*, 1969.

WORCESTER 1936    Worcester, Mass., Worcester Art Museum, *Rembrandt and His Circle*, 1936.

Composition by The University of Chicago Printing Department
Printing and binding by Meriden Gravure Company
Design by Everett McNear